The Social Dynamics of Roman Ir

C000192927

Images relating to imperial power were produced all over the Roman Empire at every social level, and even images created at the centre were constantly remade as they were reproduced, reappropriated, and reinterpreted across the empire. This book employs the language of social dynamics, drawn from economics, sociology, and psychology, to investigate how imperial imagery was embedded in local contexts. Patrons and artists often made use of the universal visual language of empire to navigate their own local hierarchies and relationships, rather than as part of direct communication with the central authorities, and these local interactions were vital in reinforcing this language. The material examined ranges from large-scale monuments adorned with sculpture and epigraphy to quotidian oil lamps and lead tokens and covers the entire empire from Hispania to Egypt, and from Augustus to the third century CE.

AMY RUSSELL is an Assistant Professor of Classics at Brown University. Her research interests include the political history and topography of the Republic and early empire. Her first book, *The Politics of Public Space in Republican Rome* (Cambridge University Press, 2015), winner of the 2017 C. J. Goodwin Award of Merit, investigates the concept of public space and the construction and operation of the public/private divide in the Republican city of Rome. Other research projects tackle the building activity of the imperial Senate and the contributions of multiple groups to the creation of imperial imagery and ideology. She also works on Republican political history, with ongoing interests in the tribunate of the plebs and the role of the *populus* and the interactions between scholarship written in German and the Anglophone world. In 2018 she was awarded a Philip Leverhulme Prize.

MONICA HELLSTRÖM is a Leverhulme Early Career Fellow in the Department of Classics and Ancient History at Durham University. She works on society and culture in the high and late Roman imperial periods, with a particular interest in visual culture. She has held the Fondazione Famiglia Rausing fellowship at the Swedish Institute in Rome. Her publications range from studies on historiography to church architecture, with current research topics including the communications and monumental output of the imperial government, inscriptions in North Africa, and the arts, social dynamics, and architecture of the city of Rome.

The Social Dynamics of Roman Imperial Imagery

Edited by

AMY RUSSELL
Brown University, Rhode Island

MONICA HELLSTRÖM
Durham University

CAMBRIDGE
UNIVERSITY PRESS

University Printing House, Cambridge CB2 8BS, United Kingdom

One Liberty Plaza, 20th Floor, New York, NY 10006, USA

477 Williamstown Road, Port Melbourne, VIC 3207, Australia

314-321, 3rd Floor, Plot 3, Splendor Forum, Jasola District Centre, New Delhi - 110025, India

103 Penang Road, #05-06/07, Visioncrest Commercial, Singapore 238467

Cambridge University Press is part of the University of Cambridge.

It furthers the University's mission by disseminating knowledge in the pursuit of education, learning and research at the highest international levels of excellence.

www.cambridge.org
Information on this title: www.cambridge.org/9781108799720
DOI: 10.1017/9781108891714

© Cambridge University Press 2020

First published 2020
First paperback edition 2022

A catalogue record for this publication is available from the British Library

ISBN 978-1-108-83512-1 Hardback
ISBN 978-1-108-79972-0 Paperback

Contents

Figures

Contributors

Caillan Davenport is Senior Lecturer in Roman History at Macquarie University, Sydney.

Megan Goldman-Petri is a Lecturer at NYU Gallatin.

Olivier Hekster is Professor of Ancient History at the Radboud Institute for Culture and History (RICH), Nijmegen.

Monica Hellström is Leverhulme Early Career Fellow in the Department of Classics and Ancient History and Fellow of University College at Durham University.

Benjamin Kelly is Associate Professor in the Department of History at York University, Toronto.

Nandini B. Pandey is Associate Professor of Classics at the University of Wisconsin–Madison.

Clare Rowan is Associate Professor in the Department of Classics and Ancient History at Warwick University.

Amy Russell is Assistant Professor of Classics in the Department of Classics at Brown University.

Nicolas Tran is Professor of Roman History at the University of Poitiers.

Julia Wilker is Associate Professor of Classical Studies at the University of Pennsylvania.

Acknowledgements

This book would not have seen the light of day without the generous support of several bodies. Amy Russell's participation and the workshops that brought us together were funded by a Leadership Fellowship from the Arts and Humanities Research Council; Monica Hellström's time on the project was funded by Durham's Institute for Advanced Studies and the European Research Council COFUND Junior Research Fellowship, followed by a Leverhulme Early Career Fellowship. We thank each of these funding bodies. The IAS and the Department of Classics and Ancient History at Durham University provided the venues for the three workshops that resulted in the present volume.

Not only the authors represented in this volume, but all participants in the workshops have contributed significantly to the themes here explored. We owe a special debt of gratitude to Gregory Rowe, whose enthusiasm and keen observations kept the rest of us on point, and whose presentations and written materials have impacted all our chapters. Thanks are due also, in alphabetical order, to Arkadiy Avdokhin, Sarah Beckmann, Panayiotis Christoforou, James Corke-Webster, Peter Heslin, Mark Humphries, Ted Kaizer, Michael Koortbojian, Katja Kröss, Fabio Luci, Christian Rollinger, Paula Rondon-Burgos, Michele Salzman, Christian Seebacher, Edmund Thomas, Andrew Wallace-Hadrill, and Bobby Xinyue.

The editors would like to thank Cambridge University Press, its staff, and the anonymous readers whose comments have improved this volume. We are particularly grateful to Natasha Burton, Hal Churchman, Sarah Lambert, and Michael Sharp. Jane Burkowski's copy-editing was exemplary. We also thank Nosheena Jabeen for compiling the index.

Abbreviations

Where not stated, translations are the author's own and dates are CE. For journal titles, we have used the abbreviations in *L'Année philologique*; for ancient texts and authors, the abbreviations in the *Oxford Classical Dictionary* (3rd ed. revised).

AE	*L'Année épigraphique: Revue des publications épigraphiques relatives à l'antiquité romaine.* 1888– (Paris).
ANRW	*Aufstieg und Niedergang der römischen Welt.* 1972– (Berlin).
BCTH	*Bulletin archéologique du Comité des traveaux historiques et archeologiques.*
BMC	*British Museum Catalogues of Coins.* 1863– (London).
BMCRLT	Thornton, M. K. *Catalogue of Roman Lead Tesserae in the British Museum.* Unpublished manuscript.
CIL	*Corpus inscriptionum Latinarum.* 1863– (Berlin).
CILA	*Corpus de inscripciones latinas de Andalucía*, 1989–2002 (Seville).
CIRB	Struve, V. 1965. *Corpus inscriptionum Regni Bosporani* (Moscow).
CNNM	Mazard, J. 1955–8. *Corpus nummorum Numidiae Mauretaniaeque* (Paris).
CSIR	*Corpus signorum Imperii Romani.* 1963–.
DFH	Khanoussi, M. and L. Maurin (eds.) 2000. *Dougga, fragments d'histoire: Choix d'inscriptions latines éditées, traduites et commentées* (Bordeaux).
FIRA	Riccobono, S. *et al.* (eds.) 1968. *Fontes Iuris Romani Anteiustiniani* (Florence). 2nd ed.
IG	*Inscriptiones Graecae.* 1903– (Berlin).
IGRR	Cagnat, R. *et al.* (eds.) 1901–27. *Inscriptiones Graecae ad res Romanas pertinentes* (Paris).
ILAfr.	Cagnat, R., A. Merlin, and L. Chatelain (eds.) 1923. *Inscriptions latines d'Afrique* (Paris).
ILAlg.	Gsell, S. 1922. *Inscriptions latines de l'Algerie* (Paris).

ILLRP	Degrassi, A. 1957–63. *Inscriptiones Latinae liberae rei publicae* (Florence).
ILPB	Ben Abdallah, Z. 1986. *Catalogue des inscriptions latines païennes du Musée du Bardo* (Rome).
ILS	Dessau, H. (ed.) 1892–1912. *Inscriptiones Latinae selectae* (Berlin).
ILTun.	Merlin, A. (ed.) 1944. *Inscriptions latines de la Tunisie* (Paris).
KAI	Donner, H. and W. Röllig (eds.) 1962–. *Kanaanäische und Aramäische Inschriften* (Wiesbaden).
LIMC	*Lexicon iconographicum mythologiae classicae.* 1981–99. (Zurich; Munich).
LSJ	Liddell, H. G., R. Scott, and H. S. Jones (eds.) 1996. *A Greek–English Lexicon* (Oxford). 9th ed., with revised supplement.
LTUR	M. Steinby (ed.) 1993–2000. *Lexicon topographicum urbis Romae*, 6 vols. (Rome).
MAA	*Monumenta Avarorum archaeologica.* 1995– (Budapest).
RIB	*The Roman Inscriptions of Britain.* 1965– (Oxford).
RIC	*Roman Imperial Coinage.* 1923– (London).
RIL	Chabot, J.-B. 1940–1. *Recueil des inscriptions libyques* (Paris).
RPC	Burnett, A., M. Amandry, and P. P. Ripollès 1992–. *Roman Provincial Coinage* (London; Paris).
RRC	Crawford, M. H. 1974. *Roman Republican Coinage* (London).
SEG	*Supplementum epigraphicum Graecum.* 1923– (Leiden).
TAM	*Tituli Asiae Minoris.* 1901– (Vienna).
TURS	Rostovtzeff, M. 1903. *Tesserarum urbis Romae et suburbi plumbearum sylloge* (St Petersburg).

1 | Introduction

Imperial Imagery and the Role of Social Dynamics

MONICA HELLSTRÖM AND AMY RUSSELL

The two concepts that provide the framework for the present volume –
'imperial imagery' and 'social dynamics' – emerged from a series of workshops held at Durham University between 2014 and 2017. The workshops
aimed to establish new methods for exploring how images relating to the
Roman emperors were used, produced, and received, at all social levels.[1]
We deliberately sought to identify categories of material created or used in
social contexts beyond the immediate sphere of the imperial family itself, in
order to establish whether, how, and why the roles played by imperial
imagery were consistent or changed in different situations. From the very
start, we worked from the premise that no universal model can adequately
encompass all such images, or explain how they all communicated. For
instance, imperial imagery could be dangerous or entirely uncontroversial,
depending on the materials, people, and locations involved. Local agents,
histories, hierarchies, and image systems made for different attitudes to
imperial images, and even images that look the same to our eyes may have
meant very different things to different contemporary viewers. People
related to these images in individual ways; even more importantly for us,
they used these images to relate to each other.

'Imperial Imagery' and 'Social Dynamics'

The visual world of the Roman Empire was huge and diverse. From
Romano-British sculpture on Hadrian's Wall to the mummy portraits of
Egypt, images drew on local styles, materials, and content.[2] Yet there were

---

[1] In this volume, following convention and for the sake of smooth English, we have freely used the
words 'emperor' and 'empire' alongside 'imperial'. The various labels for emperorhood (such as
princeps, imperator, or αὐτοκράτωρ) are not sequential but simultaneous; all three occur already
in the *Res gestae*.

[2] For Romano-British sculpture, Henig, 1995 provides an overview; Webster, 2001 is an important
'bottom-up' interpretation. On mummy portraits and their contexts in Egyptian funerary art, see
Riggs, 2002.

some images that were so widespread that they deserve the label 'imperial'. One way to define 'Roman imperial imagery', then, would be imagery that is characteristic of the Roman Empire. We have chosen a definition that is more specific, yet allows for considerable diversity: imagery that makes reference to imperial power. Most obviously, portraits of the emperors spread across the empire and beyond, appearing on the coins used in everyday transactions, statues or busts used for imperial cult, and even silverware or cameos commissioned and displayed privately. A suite of other images connected to imperial power, from oak crowns to legionary eagles, also recurs across geographical boundaries. These all belong in our category, but so might, for example, images of provincial elites holding imperial priesthoods or freedmen *vicomagistri* sacrificing to the Lares Augusti: both groups used self-representation to reflect on their relationship to central power.

Images vested with imperial authority travelled well beyond the emperors' own sphere. They form an imperial *koine*, a shared visual language of power largely developed under Augustus but modified during the centuries by new elements and juxtapositions. Innovations were often introduced without the emperors' control or even knowledge. None of the patrons or artists examined in this volume were emperors, and few were imperial officials: some did not even dwell within the empire. Yet all contributed to the evolving Roman imperial image-world. In new contexts, an image's power to denote a relation between ruler and ruled could be exploited in new ways. Our approach has allowed us to explore the functions imperial imagery performed for those who sought to harness its power, and how the aggregate of imperial imagery was enlarged and modified as a result.

Imperial images were remarkably elastic. They found uses in all manner of negotiations, whether vertical or horizontal, elite or sub-elite. We could read them as propaganda and vectors of Romanisation, as victims and weapons of aggression, as benefactions and bids for benefactions, as tokens of loyalty, genuine enthusiasm, or subversion, or simply as tokens, to be exchanged for things desired but beyond our reach. They could be exclusive, unique, and significant, or they could take the form of routinely reproduced ornamentation. Their imperial connotations could be inescapably emphatic, or activated only on certain occasions, or powerful precisely because of their banal omnipresence.[3] Their use could be tightly controlled by central or local authorities, or could be completely unmonitored.

---

[3] On the power of repetition, see Noreña, 2011, esp. 197–8, 304–6; Rowan in this volume.

Rather than seeking simple answers to the question of what imperial images were and were meant to do, therefore, we have sought to find tools that enable us to talk about imperial imagery with enough precision to allow for comparisons, over time, space, and social context. For this volume, we have adopted a lens we find particularly helpful in interpreting how imperial images developed and were understood: that of social dynamics. These images, vested with their own power, were always intimately entangled with the relationships that patrons and viewers had with others around them – and not just their ultimate rulers, but those immediately above and below them on the social scale. In some ways, our volume resonates with a recent monograph by Emma Dench on Romanisation, in which she highlights the importance of understanding this development from the local perspective.[4] Yet 'Romanisation' is not one of our keywords. Rather than tracing how Roman power and culture as such were received, embraced, or opposed, we are exploring how a semantic system of power could be adopted and adapted to fit local aims. For the questions this volume pursues, 'social dynamics' are at least as important as 'imperial imagery'.

In economics, sociology, and psychology, 'social dynamics' refers to a way of studying the relationship between individuals and groups. Large-scale, group behaviour is seen as the sum of thousands and millions of small-scale interactions between individuals.[5] In using the language of social dynamics, we propose an interpretative model in which both the remarkably stable library of imperial imagery and its variation over time and space are the product of the way these images were used in local contexts, and in particular of their place within specific social relationships. Those making, viewing, and interpreting imperial images drew on and reacted to the attitudes and ideas of those immediately around them, geographically and socially. They used images associated with imperial power to map out the hierarchies they encountered in daily life, advance their own social position, or triangulate their relationships with local and central authorities. At the same time, they brought their own ideas about power and its expression to the imperial imagery. More simply, then, to

---

[4] Dench, 2018.

[5] The term 'social dynamics' goes back at least as far as John Stuart Mill, who used it to describe how societies change over time. For most current scholarship, including in social archaeology, the 'dynamics' element refers less to large-scale change over time and more to the dynamic state of societies constantly in flux. Economists like Durlauf and Young, 2001 tend to use it to emphasise how individuals' decisions are affected by those around them. In psychology, see e.g. Brown, 2000, who writes that 'dynamics *within* groups and dynamics *between* groups are closely related' (xvii; his italics).

adapt a phrase of Lieve Van Hoof, social dynamics refers to the dynamic relationship between imperial images and their social context.[6]

Defining imperial imagery as imagery referring to central power already suggests questions about social dynamics: senators and subsistence farmers had different relationships with the emperor and the apparatus of imperial power, and these, in turn, were conditioned by social structures closer at hand. Our definition is less straightforward than one based on the frequency or geographical spread of any given image, because it relies ultimately on the images' meaning, whether in the eyes of patrons or audiences. But it is precisely the creation, interpretation, and reinterpretation of these images in local contexts that makes them so fascinating, and that the chapters in this volume explore. Yet how do we (and how did they) know when an image referenced imperial power? Did the Victory on a lamp read 'emperor is victorious' to its viewer, or simply 'appropriate ornament for lamp'? Did the colour purple always imply 'imperial', and if not, when and where did it cease to do so? Here, too, social dynamics can help. We cannot tell what individuals thought about the images and objects they made and saw, but we can study the role the images played in human interactions.

In a monograph which has served as a key inspiration for this project, Olivier Hekster noted the existence of multiple, locally defined practices and iconographies related to imperial imagery which were parallel to, not in communication with, central ones.[7] Sometimes, our sources show us, the emperor's image could be understood as a direct symbol of central authority, as in the episode of Jesus and the coin (Mark 12:14–17). As a token of the emperors' numinous presence it could be the focus of symbolic acts of submission to Roman power, or a target of formal abuse or even vandalism (Fig. 1.1).[8] But imperial imagery was also used to chart relationships other than that between subject and ruler – even when drawing on that very relation for its power. It is with these situations that this volume is concerned.

[6] Van Hoof, 2010: 1.

[7] Hekster, 2015: 30, 37, 268–73, developed further in his contribution to this volume. The most flagrant example is how emperors are represented in Egypt.

[8] We argue below that using imperial images was not necessarily a declaration of loyalty. But when loyalty declarations were required, images were often involved: consider Pliny's use of an image of Trajan as a test for suspected Christians (*Ep.* 10.96), or Corbulo forcing Tiridates to lay his diadem at the feet of a portrait of Nero (Tac. *Ann.* 15.28). On attacks on imperial images and *damnatio memoriae*, see Stewart, 2003: 267–99; Varner, 2004; Flower, 2006. Even *damnatio* was embedded in social dynamics: for example, Dickenson, 2017: 137 suggests that three statues of Nero at Messene escaped damage because of the continuing prominence of the local patrons who had set them up.

Figure 1.1 Fragment of a head of Geta showing signs of deliberate damage, *c.*198–204 CE. Rome, Musei Capitolini 2519. Image: FittCap70-97-03 (H. Fittschen Badura), arachne.dainst.org/entity/3444056.

We examine the status and actions of those who made, used, or saw imperial imagery, and how drawing on a link to imperial power played into their social relationships. Images establish connections, in the first place between authors and audiences (including, but not limited to, emperors, peers, subordinates, enemies, and god(s)) but also between individuals depicted, designers, manufacturers, purveyors, transporters, donators, owners, dedicators, decision-making bodies, viewers, and connoisseurs. All the individual interactions that formed this web had an impact on imperial images. Examining the social dynamics of imperial images can help us understand not only why they permeated the Roman world so thoroughly, but also how they could mean such different things in different contexts. It also means that in situations where the images themselves are lost we can still analyse the networks of which they were part, and that they helped create.

Top-Down or Bottom-Up? Approaching Imperial Imagery

Interpretative models for the spread and meaning of imperial imagery have shifted in recent decades: rather than viewing imagery as emanating from the centre and spreading to the periphery, more attention is paid to the creation of individual objects at the other end of the scale.[9] This shift from a top-down to a bottom-up model is analogous to the change in how scholars conceive imperial power: from active to passive governance.[10] To speak of imperial monuments as conscious statements of Roman hegemony over conquered territories (or to use the word propaganda) has become unfashionable (although these terms still remain current for the later empire).[11] The bottom-up approach, by contrast, reflects the fact that very few surviving monuments were created by the emperor himself or at his direct order, as noted by Jane Fejfer in her study on Roman portraiture.[12] Newer models, therefore, afford more agency to the monuments' actual creators and patrons. For example, we could interpret imperial arches and statues as unintentional monuments (using the terminology of Aloïs Riegl[13]) to Roman power, through the voluntary adoption of Roman symbols by self-Romanising local elites.[14] Meanwhile, art historians have found new interest in 'bad' or divergent portraits, or imperial imagery rendered in local styles (Fig. 1.2).[15] Methodologies applied to imperial images have shifted accordingly, away from treating them as evidence of a top-down monologue and towards reflecting a more reciprocal relation, such as the 'panegyric milieu' coined by Emanuel Mayer to describe how locals and emperors both contributed to shaping imperial imagery and ideology, or the two-way dialogue between benefactions and honours examined by Zanker.[16] Most insistent on a from-below perspective are approaches that position honours as didactic, providing clues to how the authors of images, monuments, and panegyrics would like the emperor to behave.[17]

Even these studies still tend to position the emperor at the centre of the story, if now more often in the role of audience than agent.[18] In the wake of the demise of the propaganda model, imperial images are often viewed as responses to imperial benefactions (and attempts at angling for them), or as expressions of loyalty to the emperor, variously styled as voluntary or obliged.

[9] This introduction is not intended as a bibliographic conspectus: it would be impossible to do justice to the vast scholarship on imperial imagery. For an overview of the development of theoretical perspectives on imperial imagery (including a bibliography), see Hekster in this volume. Dally, 2007 explores how and why scholars once fixated on a top-down model and have now shifted their emphasis.

[10] This shift is usually attributed to Fergus Millar's enormously influential book (2001) pointing out how unlikely it is that emperors actively devised all policies attributed to them.

[11] See for instance the articles by both editors in Boschung and Eck, 2006.

[12] Fejfer, 2008: 421–5, 428.   [13] Riegl, 1982 [1903]: 23.   [14] So e.g. Woolf, 1998.

[15] Zanker, 1983; good discussion in Smith, 1996 and Mayer, 2010: 114–19.

[16] Mayer, 2002; Zanker, 2002: 9–37, esp. 10–14.

[17] E.g. Marlowe, 2006 on the Arch of Constantine.

[18] A consequence best outlined by Levick, 1982, on coins.

Figure 1.2 Titus Caesar offers gifts to the god Khnum. Detail of a relief in the temple at Deir el-Haggar, Dahkleh, Egypt, first century CE. Photograph: M. Hellström.

Yet, it is not obvious how an image, as such, would have guaranteed loyal behaviour.[19] None of the examples we examine include any explicit statement of allegiance or submission, forced or freely given. And how would the

[19] The predicament we face as modern scholars mirrors that an emperor might have faced had he tried to use imagery as an index of loyalty: though the ritual performance of loyalty was always important, we can never know whether an image expressed any sincere sentiments (and we have, for the most part, left that question aside). Treating statues of emperors as an index of enthusiasm: e.g. Polley, 2004/5 [2007]: 147–8; as responses to benefactions: Papi, 2004; as attempts to curry favour: Patterson, 2003. On dedications to emperors as demonstrations of loyalty, obliged but not by default unwilling: Moralee, 2004.

Figure 1.3 Atypical colossal head of Hadrian from Egypt, second century CE. Alexandria, Musée Gréco-Romain 20885. Image: FA-Oe292 (H. Oehler), arachne.dainst.org/entity/1060558.

emperor be expected to know about (and duly reward) some individual's use of an imperial image on a cup, or a bust in a professional association's meeting place, or even a statue in the forum of a provincial town?

One famous example of a locally produced image that did apparently reach the emperor's ears, if not his eyes, is the statue of Hadrian at Trapezus in Cappadocia mentioned by Arrian (*Peripl. M. Eux.* 1.3–4). Arrian, then governor of the province, writes that the statue is poorly made and not a good likeness: perhaps something like the portrait from Athribis (Fig. 1.3). He asks that Hadrian send a better version, since the spot on which the statue stands facing the sea is extremely appropriate for an eternal monument. This passage has been used to support both top-down and bottom-up models of the dissemination of imperial portraiture: the poor quality of the portrait argues for local agency, while the fact that Arrian asks for a substitute direct from the centre suggests that a top-down process for disseminating imagery existed at least in theory.[20] Which is Arrian's own

---

[20] Discussion in Zanker, 1983: 7–8; Ando, 2000: 229–30; Mayer, 2010: 118–19.

position? His plans to 'correct' the statue suggest that his ideal would be perfect fidelity to a central model. Yet his purpose in writing the letter is surely to flatter Hadrian with his attention to the emperor's image, and by letting him know that his provincial subjects have chosen to honour him independently of any central encouragement.[21] And what did the people of Trapezus, or perhaps the individual *euergete* among them, have in mind when they put up the statue? Arrian records that Hadrian has visited this very spot himself in person: did the Trapezians imagine that he might return to see his statue? Or that a visiting governor would happen to report it to him? Both hypotheses seem inherently unlikely. But one function the statue did serve in practice was to impress not the emperor, but the governor: a much more likely visitor. The emperor was neither author nor primary audience, but a means of triangulating a relationship between the city and Arrian himself.

Arrian specifically mentions one potential function of the statue: as an eternal monument. It served this purpose for its patron or patrons too, memorialising their generosity to future generations of Trapezians and travellers as well as beautifying (depending on your level of connoisseurship!) a prominent spot on the coastline. If put up by one rich patron, it demonstrated his local pre-eminence; if by the town, it participated in Trapezus' own competition with other nearby communities. For some of these purposes, any monument would do. But they chose a statue of the emperor for good reason. It doubtless memorialised Hadrian's earlier visit, a distinction few polities could claim even for this most well-travelled emperor. The visit and the statue allowed a tiny portion of imperial glamour to rub off onto the Trapezians. Rather than signalling their loyalty to the emperor, they were signalling their imperial connection to their peers and neighbours.

The most relevant point about the Trapezus statue, however, is that it is exceptional. It was only by chance that Arrian saw it and reported it to the emperor. Perhaps, indeed, he only mentioned it because it was so interestingly ugly: its success comes from its failure. The vast majority of such statues never made it into a literary geography. Some other images, especially those set up in public by civic communities, might be reported to the emperor via official letters from the cities themselves, or proleptically by petitions asking for permission to use the imperial image. Some were

---

[21] Section 5 of the *Periplus* makes this point clearly: Arrian emphasises that the Trapezians offered prayers on Hadrian's behalf, even though they had less to thank him for than Arrian himself did. As Ando, 2000: 229 points out, the situation is made more complex by the fact that this was not a real imperial communiqué, but a literary exercise written for a wide audience: the governor's official correspondence with Hadrian would have been in Latin.

placed where he might actually see them. But the majority of objects discussed in this volume were both produced and received in social contexts that the emperors would scarcely have been aware of, or have been likely to receive (or wish to receive) reports about.

We have not sought to place imperial imagery in a linear model that connects central power with the empire's subjects, whether top-down, bottom-up, or reciprocal. Regardless of directionality, such models are ultimately too simplistic to cover the amorphous world of imperial imagery. For the same reasons, many theories from modern media studies that we surveyed proved inadequate, working as they often do from a basic proposition of sender and receiver.[22] For us, there is no easily defined group of 'receivers': ordinary Romans might have been the audience for centrally produced objects such as coins, but also created, commissioned, or purchased images themselves. We treat them as agents, whose aims were not obviously defined by central authorities. Our social dynamics approach allows us to situate imperial imagery within a web of social relationships, without assuming that a given image was intended to achieve (or actually achieved) any kind of direct communication with the emperor. Rather than a top-down or bottom-up approach, we privilege the horizontal and near-horizontal: the full range of social interactions that took place within an image's immediate context.

Social Dynamics in Practice: Hierarchy and Agency

The images we discuss were created and received by groups ranging from senators and client kings with personal relationships with the emperor to provincials for whom imperial power was distant and abstract (though no less real). No Roman emperor, however autocratic, had the power (or the time) to create or approve every new contribution to imperial imagery, and even images that were indeed created at the centre were constantly remade as they were reproduced, reappropriated, and reinterpreted by multiple audiences. Equally, imperial imagery was not a free-for-all; real power differentials on large and small scales could shape how these images were used, or bring danger for those who overstepped the mark. Our approach has allowed us to explore how imperial imagery was interwoven with social hierarchy and how its use gave scope for individual agency at multiple social levels.

---

[22] Hekster's chapter in this volume puts our approach in the context of a related set of debates surrounding imperial imagery, propaganda, and mediation.

Imperial images accompanied, and helped create, social structure. We find them acting as the trump card in any situation that involves hierarchy, from gaming pieces with imperial images to ranked metals on client kings' coinage (Wilker).[23] They assisted in both the creation and performance of status, marking the stages of advancement (Tran, Hellström) along similar patterns in municipal assemblies as well as associations. Dedication ceremonies for new statues or altars made for pageants that displayed and reinforced the local powers that be. Imperial images help remind us of the verticality and strict ordering of Roman society, even in contexts that to an outsider may have looked homogeneous. Even a slave *familia* was deeply stratified, and even slaves set up imperial images, with all the expected pomp.

Imperial insignia were not only used to express vertical social structure: horizontal divisions also sported them. The *curiae* in African municipalities almost always carried the names of emperors, with no relation to their moment of creation – they were the finest labels around, perhaps comparable to how some names have become appropriate for fine hotels.[24] Just as there is a Grand, a Plaza, and an Excelsior in most major cities around the globe, so ancient cities had their Flavian, their Trajanic, and Antonine institutions. To name a *curia* in a hick town 'the Nervan' may have seemed to the metropolitan viewer like calling a corner store the 'Excelsior', but it served its local purposes. Pre-existing social divisions assumed a new, imperial layer, which allowed for comparison and participation. New opportunities were opened up, for example for elite women who could take empresses as their model for public benefaction.[25] This would have been particularly important in a society with so many parallel social hierarchies, between which questions of primacy would always arise.

On a symbolic level, too, imperial imagery could empower its users, granting them a scope for self-expression that would otherwise have been denied them. The omnipresence of imperial imagery was part of its ideological power, but it also placed agency in the hands of the viewer. The

[23] In a set of gaming pieces retrieved from a tomb in Panticapaeum (modern Kerch) on the Black Sea, the highest-ranking piece sported an image of Augustus; see Rostovtseff, 1905, Alföldi-Rosenbaum, 1980, and Clare Rowan in this volume. The set is unique, but stray finds from across the empire testify to widespread popularity of the (unknown) game.

[24] On the *curiae*: Dawson, 2016: 98–130, on names esp. 126–7. For example, Lepcis Magna had *curiae* named *Augusta*, *Ulpia*, and *Pia*, Thamugadi a *Commodiana*, and Lambaesis a *Traiana*, *Sabina*, *Aurelia*, and an *Antoniniana*. Small-town *curiae* bring to mind a (now closed) deli in New York's 2nd Ave called 'Diana-Dodi Corp.'.

[25] See further e.g. Hemelrijk, 2015 on women in the west; Severy, 2003: 167–9 on Eumachia at Pompeii; Boatwright, 1991 on Plancia Magna at Perge.

handler of an image had the power to reframe it by altering it, recontextualising it, or translating it into other media. Imperial symbols provided a space within which to assert one's own place in relation to other groups and individuals, and even occasionally the emperors. When expressed in imperial terms, self-aggrandisement was allowable, even at the extreme level of Herod's monumental projects at Sebaste. Without their imperial name tags, these would have spelt power, not submission; but under a universal and quasi-divine emperor, it was possible to wield power without humiliation, and to display considerable ostentation. This is no less true at the other end of the social spectrum. Adding an imperial flavour to their ceremonials and ranks lent respectability to *vici* and *collegia* (Russell, Tran), or even to individuals like Hedulus at Carthage (Goldman-Petri), and afforded them a legitimate public role. Within the system of imperial images and symbols, volatile situations could be defused and disparate groups could be integrated. In this manner, their inherent power could be put to constructive use; meanwhile, each transaction reproduced, enhanced, but also had the potential to gradually alter that power.

Towards a Taxonomy of Imperial Imagery: Context

The different chapters in this volume home in on specific social contexts, and examine the uses of imperial images within them. We asked contributors to start with the images themselves (including those which are now lost, or which were always fictional) and to consider the people who made and used them. Each resulting case study discusses a category of materials belonging to a particular place in the social matrix of the empire. The materials treated range from large-scale monuments adorned with sculpture and epigraphy to quotidian oil lamps and lead tokens; chronologically and geographically, they stretch across the entire empire from Hispania to Egypt, and from Augustus to the third century CE. We have not aimed to group images or objects by medium or style, nor have we emphasised the development of iconography over time either by reign or by art-historical period. Instead, our primary tool for classification has been the history and evolution of the practices associated with imperial imagery.

The first three chapters (Russell, Wilker, Pandey) concern the Augustan period, but our aim has not been to follow a chronological outline; rather, they demonstrate the remarkably broad social and geographic range throughout which imperial imagery was used for multiple purposes from the very beginning. The following three (Davenport, Kelly, Hellström) discuss how imperial imagery became part of the self-representation of local elites, including the elites of Rome itself, while the last group (Goldman-Petri, Tran, Rowan) concerns its incorporation in more quotidian, commercial, or private contexts – though such distinctions are inevitably arbitrary and break down under close analysis. Hekster's contribution, finally, places our discussions in a wider theoretical framework.

Each author has contributed their own models and methods, but we have shared terminologies, materials, and thoughts throughout the process. The images discussed in this volume can be analysed through a number of complementary lenses: parameters that affect the function, meaning, and use of each example. In this section, we discuss some of the ways in which we have aimed to categorise and locate imperial images in terms of social dynamics, and the new conclusions these lenses can offer.

Time

More often than not, our investigation of the practices and relationships in which imperial images are embedded has found continuity rather than change over time. As a result, we have not set out to write a history of imperial imagery. The images themselves do have a history: the shared visual language of imperial power drew on older visual elements (many of Hellenistic origin) and also conveyed them to later eras. During our period, however, they show a remarkable persistence. It is astonishing how quickly an iconographic system was assembled that was recognisable as 'imperial', and not only by imperial diktat. Institutional vectors no doubt played a part, but rather than the (presumed) active central will to disseminate imperial imagery, a social dynamics approach emphasises the new sociopolitical structures in which the use of imperial images was quickly embedded. This iconographic system almost immediately superseded previous meanings attached to its various components; already in Augustus' reign, there was a visual shorthand for 'imperial'.

Although several chapters treat early imperial material, this is not a volume on the 'Augustan moment', nor on how imperial imagery differs from earlier iconographies of power. Our aim is not to describe how this visual shorthand came to be, other than in the sense that it was continuously recreated and reproduced.[26] The activities described by Russell are

---

[26] For the Augustan moment itself, Zanker, 1988 remains fundamental, especially 265–95 on the use of new imperial imagery in the private sphere. See further Zanker, 2002: 9–37 and 79–91, for additional nuances to his approach to the agency of patrons across social levels – but always positioning the need to communicate loyalty to the emperor as a central mechanism in the spread of the new imagery.

not, in essence, different from later ones within comparable social spheres, as we see in the material showcased by Tran. The processes which affected the content and use of the images remained the same, even when other factors changed. Image-makers would continue to juxtapose visual elements that registered as 'imperial' in ways that suited their aims and audiences, as on the Arch of the Argentarii in Rome, or on the frescoes of the synagogue in Dura-Europos.[27] The use Wilker finds Augustan-era client kings making of images of obscure imperial family members mirrors the priesthoods of a long range of *divi* in the grandest cities of the empire, such as Carthage. The sentiments expressed by Ovid (Pandey) would have been as relevant for an author writing about the Severan family, and the admonitions that Cassius Dio, in his fictive speeches, offers to Augustus about the correct (moderate) attitude towards honorifics are strongly suggestive of critique of contemporary rulers.[28] If any period merits singling out it is the Severan era, emerging as a time when emperors sought to meddle with their images, with varying success. It is perhaps no coincidence that the explosive spread of imperial images at the turn of the third century coincided with drastic changes to the empire's sociopolitical fabric through the globalisation of citizenship, which gave each inhabitant a nominal claim to the emperor's person.

Only in late antiquity does, arguably, an image system arise that could compete with imperial images for authority: images of Christ, saints, and bishops, as well as symbols such as the cross.[29] It could be argued that emperors seeking to exploit Christianity to bolster their power did themselves a disservice, vesting so much power into Christian symbols that their own authority was undercut (and eventually overcome). At least for images, it was not so simple. Figurations of Christ (or bishops) triumphant only appear at the turn of the fifth century, and the deep suspicion against images within the (in theory aniconic) Christian faith delayed their spread.[30] This resistance made for fewer imperial images as well, but one must note that although Christianity had a role to play in the decline of

---

[27] Arch of the Argentarii: Elsner, 2005, esp. 85–6. Dura-Europos: Elsner, 2001, with references.

[28] Cass. Dio 52.30.3; 52.35.3–5, discussed by Hellström in this volume.

[29] On early Christian art: Elsner, 1998a, 1998b, 2003. For a different explanation of its late development: Finney, 1997. On Christian art borrowing imperial imagery, Grabar, 1980; for a counterargument, Mathews, 2003, who posits a showdown between an old pagan and a radically new, anti-imperial Christian art. Although refreshing, his proposition has many problems and has not been widely accepted; see further below, n. 42.

[30] Tertullian, *De spectaculis* warns against images (of all kinds) as evoking emotion and devotion and therefore favourite haunts of demons pining for human attention. His position may be extreme, but the view that images were related to (pagan) religious practices was widespread. Imperial images counted as *sacra*, which made them particularly tainted.

imperial images, it was not by replacing them with Christian ones. Even in the medieval period we do not see (as far as we know) weights guaranteed with saints, or game tokens with the Holy Family. Although now with crosses on their globes, coins still sported kings, not Christ. As a shorthand for 'power' and a way to map and understand local relationships, it seems that the world of Heaven was not as useful as the emperor (and far more sensitive to misuse).

Audiences

One of our primary ways of categorising imagery is by dividing up not the images themselves, but the audiences who saw them (including the primary audiences: the patrons). Local audiences understood imperial images within existing interpretative frameworks, many of which predated the empire. Egyptian patrons portrayed emperors according to Pharaonic image systems, with attributes and features that would not have been recognisable outside Egypt (or even, most likely, to the emperor himself) but carried messages to locals that were laden with long traditions (Fig. 1.2).[31] Similarly, image configurations current in the Greek east (Davenport) drew on iconographic cues which held meaning – indeed, were only decodable – in the local context. This does not preclude that they also communicated to foreign viewers, but the messages would not have been the same. Such layered interpretations could be intentional. Client kings' coins (Wilker) used a visual language that could offer different messages to different audiences: Roman soldiers would see the emperor's portrait as a guarantee that the coin was valid (and would remain so when they were deployed elsewhere) and be reassured by the ranked metals as to who was actually in charge, while the kings' own subjects would see him in his royal diadem and view his juxtaposition with the emperor's image as yet another testimony to his power.

Other elements of the coin images were only legible to a more informed, exclusive audience; the choice to depict lesser-known members of the imperial family surely resonated most with other client kings, who sought to impress each other with their privileged positions of intimacy at court. Similarly, the reliefs showing praetorians (Kelly) bore nuanced political meaning for courtiers, but could be read simply as 'soldiers' by a wider audience. Assessing the level of specificity in imperial imagery has turned out to be useful when distinguishing between audiences and messages. The

---

[31] On the idiosyncrasies of Egyptian imperial imagery, Hekster, 2015: 268–73.

images of violence that adorned the Sebasteion at Aphrodisias (Davenport) function both as reminders of particular conquests, potentially discomfiting to those conquered, and as allusions to Rome's military supremacy in general, and in extension, to the security and felicity of the realm. The Victories with shields that appeared everywhere from altars to lamps (Russell) are sometimes highly specific, referring directly to the Victory placed by Augustus in the Curia after Actium, and sometimes so generic that they are purely ornamental, suitable for New Year's gifts.[32] Here, too, pre-existing interpretative frameworks matter: the motif of Victory and shield had existed before Augustus, and passed back into the general visual repertoire for success and prosperity – but with a new imperial colouring.

Purpose

Closely tied to interpretative framework is the question of purpose, which affects how we judge the success of an image. We can assess the vitality of images by their geographical spread, their longevity, or how often they were translated into other media. By any of these measures, the Victory with shield (Russell) was a successful image, and the gradual spread of violent iconography to 'official' monuments (Davenport) is testimony to the resonance these images found with a wide audience. Yet the apparent popularity of an image can also be deceptive; for instance, if a particular image configuration on a token (Rowan), which only carried its specific message for one day, failed to be reproduced elsewhere, then that is not evidence of its failure. The purpose of an image determines what elements carried the most meaning: if the reason for setting up an imperial statue was to display to peers that the donor was wealthy, its likeness or attributes were less important than the fact that it was made of gold (and pursuing too fine an analysis of the former would be misleading). The Trapezians were apparently not concerned with capturing the features of the emperor correctly; the point was that he had been there. In this respect, the image did not 'fail' at all. It is when remediated through the words of Arrian for different purposes and then reinterpreted by modern scholars that it 'fails': indeed, even for Arrian it succeeded in providing an opportunity for him to flatter Hadrian.

The same considerations apply to images that are usually interpreted as imitating a metropolitan or higher-status model. As we look at the remixed Augustan imagery on Hedulus' altar (Goldman-Petri), we should not

---

[32] Compare Laird, 2015 on the generic force of the oak wreath on funerary monuments.

automatically assume that the patron got his iconography wrong. Perhaps it was entirely right for its main purpose, which lay closer to home. Yet there must have been real examples of mistakes and misunderstandings too. The very adaptability of imperial imagery made it susceptible to change: as it moved across time, space, media, and class it risked losing its original meaning or value, and there is plenty of room for misinterpretation. Without access to the patrons' or audiences' thought processes, mistakes are hard to pin down, and we must be careful. The clearest examples come from Ovid's heavily ironised 'misreadings' of the images before him (Pandey), demonstrating how an apparent mistake could in fact be a deliberate and creative act. Should we see the absurd panegyric imagery of the *corporati* (Tran) as a sign that the patrons lacked the information or means to get things right, or take it alongside Ovid's poetry and the dog-headed Aeneas of Stabiae as a deliberate (if less subversive) reappropriation of a well-known theme?[33]

Official–Unofficial

One traditional way of distinguishing imperial images has been to separate 'official' or 'state' art from 'unofficial' or 'vernacular' production. We have not entirely abandoned the distinction, though it must be seen as a scale along which to locate an image rather than a pair of unproblematic absolutes. Kelly's relief sculptures are for the most part commissioned and paid for by public authorities, while some of Rowan's tokens were issued by private individuals – though drawing on an image repertoire from the 'official' coinage. Russell's altars had the sanction of Augustus himself, but were under no form of central control. Social dynamics can help us to see that the 'officialness' of an image is often a function of the local context rather than an empire-wide absolute, and could be manipulated. Hellström's statues had an important civic role in their communities, but stood outside the purview of the provincial governor, let alone the emperor himself. The *corporati* studied by Tran used imperial imagery as a talisman of 'officialness', to bolster their claim to a respectable public role. Meanwhile, the inhabitants of Rome's *vici* experienced their local altars as no less official and authoritative as sources of imagery than monuments set up by senatorial decree.

Keeping a critical eye on the official–unofficial scale can help break down some persistent assumptions that have been imported from older,

---

[33] On the painting of a dog-headed Aeneas found at Gragnano near Stabiae and now in the Museo Archeologico Nazionale di Napoli, Gabinetto Segreto, Inv. 9089, see e.g. Zanker, 1988: 202.

top-down models. Images created outside the centre of power have often been labelled imitations of official prototypes, like Roman copies of Greek sculpture that were once valued primarily as clues pointing us to a lost original. In this volume, Goldman-Petri warns us that reliefs from Carthage must be treated in their own context: their motifs belong to the wider *koine*, and are not necessarily direct imitations of 'official' state reliefs in Rome which few of their viewers had ever seen. Similarly, Davenport finds Greek communities attributing violent titles and attitudes to emperors not found in imagery created at the centre. Creativity at all social levels contributed to, rather than merely deriving from, the stock of imperial imagery, and it was often low-ranking officials or even just local audiences who determined to what extent individual images were treated as 'official' or canonical.

Distance and Control

There is little evidence of pressure to use imperial images. Their distribution was too slow and uneven to be an uncomplicated response to central stimuli (such as the accession of a new emperor).[34] Evidence for central dissemination is slight, and ambiguous.[35] If we consider the realities of materials and production, it also seems likely that most imperial statues, at least, were locally made: Italian marble rarely left the peninsula.[36] Instead, the decision to use an imperial image was the product of local agency.

Even in cases where the use of imperial images was regulated by a legal framework, it was always conditioned by social dynamics. The *koina* of Asia Minor fought bitterly over a handful of *neokoria*, while plenty of tiny communities (and even large farms) in the same area displayed multiple imperial *sacella* and statues.[37] On a macro level, the pattern is clear: the level of control exercised over the use of imperial symbols is proportionate to the social significance of the users, and their relative role in the political

---

[34] Fejfer, 2008: 411–16, who tones down the link between image prototypes and imperial celebrations, and Højte, 2005: 145–6. The exception is Nerva, who was honoured widely immediately upon accession. Though short, his reign may have represented more of a sea change than previously imagined in terms of the relation between emperors and subject communities.

[35] An inscription from Termessos (*IGRR* 3.481) that celebrates the arrival of an imperial image (likely of the prince Valerian II) has been used as evidence for images being sent out on imperial command (see Højte, 2005: 146). This may well be the case, but the text says nothing about the circumstances.

[36] Meanwhile, the spread of consumer goods carrying imperial imagery followed economic rather than ideological logic: see further Woolf, 1998.

[37] *Neokoroi*: Burrell, 2004.

matrix of the empire. The higher the status of the patron or the place, the more restrictions tended to apply.

High-status patrons may have been the most powerful, but they also had the most to lose. If they made a mistake or used the 'wrong' imperial image, they were more likely to be noticed. For Kelly's courtiers, the limits of allowable imagery could be very narrow. But even using the 'right' imperial image could be dangerous, as it potentially empowered the user. Any honour for the emperor ran the risk of offending him by placing him in the giver's debt.[38] It is therefore no coincidence that precisely those from whom the emperors might have wished to see some token of loyalty – the highest social echelons – have been the most difficult to identify among users of imperial images. We do not see provincial governors dedicating statues of emperors before late antiquity, nor individual senators in Rome. Instead, some of the most prolific and innovative creators of imperial images were at the periphery, where there was less oversight, more room for creativity, and less danger.

Distance can be both spatial and social, and the two do not always go hand in hand. Some of the most creative images we discuss come from Rome itself, but from contexts at a remove from power in social terms (Russell's *vici* and Tran's *corpora*): here, no less than in villages thousands of miles away, imperial images were used in remarkably inventive ways.[39] Other patrons claimed metaphorical closeness to the emperor even though they were geographically distant, and found their own means of innovation. The client kings (Wilker), outside the boundaries of the empire proper, employed imperial images precisely in order to play on the ambiguous hierarchy between the one honouring and the one being honoured. Meanwhile, the veiled threat posed by Ovid from far-off Tomis shows that his ownership of Augustus' image could be perceived to put the emperor at risk, making him vulnerable to manipulations (Pandey). It hints at the power that might become available when imperial imagery came into consumers' hands in material form, revealing both why control over it was a thing desired, and why it was so difficult to achieve.[40]

---

[38] On the perils of placing the emperor in gift-debt, see Lendon, 1997: 56–67; Roller, 2001: 193–210.

[39] The same is the case for legends, as seen in North African dedications styling emperors as *deus*, e.g. Augustus at Thinissut, *ILAfr.* 306, Septimius Severus at Musti, *AE* 1999.1844, even Constantine or one of his sons at Henchir Damous, *BCTH* 1928/29.669. It was not part of their official titles but should be put down to local creativity. Similarly, a *sacellum* to the *Gens Valeria* of Diocletian at Thibaris, *AE* 2003.2010, is entirely unique. It may not be a coincidence that these come from small towns, not cities such as Carthage or Cirta.

[40] At the extreme, it could be vandalised or destroyed. In Durham in 2017, Greg Rowe pointed out that Cassius Dio (58.27, 58.11) writes that the mobs who defaced statues of Sejanus were acting out their desire to hurt the man himself, while Pliny (*Pan.* 52) says that although Domitian was

Conclusion: Where Is the Emperor?

The danger in Ovid's poem relates to the notion that an image not only referenced but could actually be the emperor, embodying his spirit and linking the viewer to him. This potential was certainly mobilised on occasion, and could engender violence both to, and through, imperial images. Yet often we have found that this direct bond between emperor and image was likely dormant: for example, few abuses of imperial imagery were actually punished.[41]

The images we discuss transmitted a range of messages to the emperor, by way of the emperor, in opposition to the emperor, and often with little relation to the emperor at all. But even in cases where imperial imagery was produced with minimal direct reference to the emperor himself, the agency it allowed to its patrons and viewers still ultimately depended on the remarkable accumulation of power in his hands. In a controversial study on early figurations of Christ, Thomas Mathews argued that the grassroots of Rome rejected the emperor's image as their iconographic template, in marked resistance to prevailing political structures. He blamed earlier art historians for conforming to traditional elitist perspectives, adhering to an 'emperor mystique' inspired by the overbearing majesty of their contemporary kaisers and czars.[42] However, judging by the several contributions in this volume that deal with grassroots of different kinds, it would appear that people across the social spectrum had at least as much use for the imperial images as elite groups did: such images appear everywhere where authority serves a purpose. At times, our scope becomes almost infinite: images are powerful because they are imperial, but also imperial because they are powerful.

Without the emperor as its referent, this vast, dynamic network would (and did) crumble. He was the ultimate source of the authority of his imagery, and all its users were connected to him, if not in the ways we often imagine.

---

already dead when his statues were toppled, the blows were inflicted as if to cause pain: less a dignified posthumous *damnatio memoriae*, and more an execution in effigy. These (elite) accounts use popular violence in a symbolic sense and are perhaps exaggerated (or even fictive), but no less interesting as such.

[41] It would in any case have been impossible to respond in decisive fashion to all abuses. To insist on an active bond (as, for instance, in attempting to apply centralised *damnatio memoriae* to coin images) and fail would only expose the imperial government as weak.

[42] Mathews, 2003; see above, n. 29. *Contra* Grabar, 1980, who saw it as springing from Roman artistic traditions, Mathews styled Christian art – its content, iconography, and aim – as fundamentally new. More: it was key to the victory of Christianity, with Darwininan assuredness sweeping out the weak, empty art of the classical world. He placed it in strong opposition to central power, even when the emperor was himself Christian.

Rather than kowtowing to his majesty, they sought to share in his authority by adopting his symbols. It is this remote yet personal quality which allowed the *vicomagistri* to claim a special connection to the emperor (Russell), or Ovid, exceptionally, to turn the images against themselves (Pandey).

At one of the Durham workshops, Greg Rowe proposed the term 'loyalism' as a label suited to many of the practices studied in this volume. Loyalism does not imply that an image was meant to declare loyalty to the emperor in any real sense, but that it formed part of a wider culture of according imperial images pride of place in visual systems. This culture encompassed all social groups, all regions, and governed relations both vertical and horizontal, most of which the emperor had little or nothing to do with. In our interpretation, the element that remained stable through numerous remediations and that all the users bought into was power. Imperial imagery formed a semantic system that was both ubiquitous and exclusive, that allowed for multiple uses, was recognised by all, and was crucially linked to tangible, overwhelmingly real imperial authority. Save perhaps Ovid, we have not found any consistent attempts at subverting this authority, no moustaches painted on to undercut it.[43] Everyone had a vested interest in upholding the schematic hierarchy that the imperial image-world made visible: as they used it to negotiate their own local relationships and hierarchies, they performed a loyalism that did, in the end, perpetuate real imperial power.

Bibliography

Alföldi-Rosenbaum, E. 1980. 'Ruler portraits on Roman game counters from Alexandria (Studies on Roman game counters III)', in Stucky, R. A. and I. Jucker (eds.), *Eikones: Studien zum griechischen und römischen Bildnis* (Bern: Francke Verlag), 29–39.

Ando, C. 2000. *Imperial Ideology and Provincial Loyalty in the Roman Empire* (Berkeley: University of California Press).

Boatwright, M. 1991. 'Plancia Magna of Perge: women's roles and status in Roman Asia Minor', in Pomeroy, S. B. (ed.), *Women's History and Ancient History* (Chapel Hill: University of North Carolina Press), 249–72.

Boschung, D. and W. Eck 2006. *Die Tetrarchie: Ein neues Regierungssystem und seine mediale Präsentation* (Wiesbaden: Reichert).

---

[43] Those looking for subversion might consider Paul's use of imperial imagery: Maier, 2013 offers the most visual interpretation. But even the most 'resistant' readings, such as Horsley, 2004, show Paul co-opting the power of imperial imagery, rather than undercutting it.

Brown, R. 2000. *Group Processes: Dynamics Within and Between Groups*, 2nd ed. (Malden, MA: Blackwell).

Burrell, B. 2004. *Neokoroi: Greek Cities and Roman Emperors* (Leiden; Boston: Brill).

Dally, O. 2007. 'Das Bild des Kaisers in der klassischen Archäologie – oder: gab es einen Paradigmenwechsel nach 1968?', *JDAI* 122: 223–57.

Dawson, C. D. 2016. Intimate Communities: Honorific Statues and the Political Culture of the Cities of Africa Proconsularis in the First Three Centuries CE. Diss., York University (Toronto).

Dench, E. 2018. *Empire and Political Cultures in the Roman World* (Cambridge: Cambridge University Press).

Dickenson, C. 2017. 'Public statues as a strategy of remembering in early imperial Messene', in Dijkstra, T. M., I. N. I. Kuin, M. Moser, and D. Weidgenannt (eds.), *Strategies of Remembering in Greece under Rome (100 BC–100 AD)* (Leiden: Netherlands Institute at Athens), 126–42.

Durlauf, S. N. and H. P. Young (eds.) 2001. *Social Dynamics* (Cambridge, MA: MIT Press).

Elsner, J. 1998a. *Imperial Rome and Christian Triumph: The Art of the Roman Empire, A.D. 100–450* (Oxford; New York: Oxford University Press).

1998b. 'Art and architecture', in Cameron, A. and P. Garnsey (eds.), *The Cambridge Ancient History*, 2nd ed., Vol. 13: *The Late Empire, AD 337–425* (Cambridge: Cambridge University Press), 736–61.

2001. 'Cultural resistance and the visual image: the case of Dura Europos', *CPh* 96: 269–304.

2003. 'Inventing Christian Rome: the role of early Christian art', in Edwards, C. and G. Woolf (eds.), *Rome the Cosmopolis* (Cambridge, Cambridge University Press), 71–99.

2005. 'Sacrifice and narrative on the Arch of the Argentarii at Rome', *JRA* 18: 83–98.

Fejfer, J. 2008. *Roman Portraits in Context* (Berlin; Boston: De Gruyter).

Finney, P. C. 1997. *The Invisible God: The Earliest Christians on Art* (Oxford: Oxford University Press).

Flower, H. 2006. *The Art of Forgetting: Disgrace and Oblivion in Roman Political Culture* (Chapel Hill: University of North Carolina Press).

Grabar, A. 1980. *Christian Iconography; A Study of its Origins: The A. W. Mellon Lectures in the Fine Arts, 1961, The National Gallery of Art, Washington, D.C.*, 2nd ed. (Princeton, NJ, Princeton University Press).

Hekster, O. 2015. *Emperors and Ancestors: Roman Rulers and the Constraints of Tradition* (Oxford: Oxford University Press).

Hemelrijk, E. A. 2015. *Hidden Lives – Public Personae: Women and Civic Life in the Roman West* (New York; Oxford: Oxford University Press).

Henig, M. 1995. *The Art of Roman Britain* (London: Batsford).

Højte, J. M. 2005. *Roman Imperial Statue Bases: From Augustus to Commodus* (Aarhus: Aarhus University Press).

Horsley, R. A. 2004. *Paul and the Roman Imperial Order* (New York: Trinity).

Laird, M. 2015. *Civic Monuments and the Augustales in Roman Italy* (New York: Cambridge University Press).

Lendon, J. E. 1997. *Empire of Honour: The Art of Government in the Roman World* (Oxford: Oxford University Press).

Levick, B. 1982. 'Propaganda and the imperial coinage', *Antichthon* 16: 104–16.

Maier, H. O. 2013. *Picturing Paul in Empire: Imperial Image, Text, and Persuasion in Colossians, Ephesians, and the Pastoral Epistles* (London: Bloomsbury).

Marlowe, E. 2006. 'Framing the sun: the Arch of Constantine and the Roman cityscape', *Art Bulletin* 88: 223–42.

Mathews, T. 2003. *The Clash of Gods: A Reinterpretation of Early Christian Art* (Princeton, NJ: Princeton University Press).

Mayer, E. 2002. *Rom ist dort, wo der Kaiser ist: Untersuchungen zu den Staatsdenkmälern des dezentralisierten Reiches von Diocletian bis zu Theodosius II* (Mainz: Verlag des Römisch-Germanischen Zentralmuseums; Bonn: Rudolf Habelt).

2010. 'Propaganda, staged applause, or local politics? Public monuments from Augustus to Septimius Severus', in Ewald, B. and C. Noreña (eds.), *The Emperor and Rome* (New Haven: Yale University Press), 119–27.

Millar, F. 2001. *The Emperor in the Roman World: 31 BC–AD 337*, 3rd ed. (London: Duckworth).

Moralee, J. 2004. *For Salvation's Sake: Provincial Loyalty, Personal Religion, and Epigraphic Production in the Roman and Late Antique Near East* (New York; London: Routledge).

Noreña, C. 2011. *Imperial Ideals in the Roman West: Representation, Circulation, Power* (Cambridge: Cambridge University Press).

Papi, E. 2004. 'A new Golden Age? The northern *praefectum urbi* from the Severans to Diocletian', in Swain, S. and M. Edwards (eds.), *Approaching Late Antiquity* (Oxford: Oxford University Press), 53–81.

Patterson, J. R. 2003. 'The emperor and the cities of Italy', in Lomas, K. and T. Cornell (eds.), *Bread and Circuses* (London; New York: Routledge), 89–104.

Polley, A. R. 2004/5 [2007]. 'Usurpations in Africa: ruler and ruled in the Third Century Crisis', *AJAH* n.s. 3/4: 143–70.

Riegl, A. 1982 [1903]. 'The modern cult of monuments: its character and its origin'. *Oppositions* 25 (Fall 1982): 21–51.

Riggs, C. 2002. 'Facing the dead: recent research on the funerary art of Ptolemaic and Roman Egypt', *AJA* 106: 85–101.

Roller, M. B. 2001. *Constructing Autocracy: Aristocrats and Emperors in Julio-Claudian Rome* (Princeton, NJ: Princeton University Press).

Rostovtzeff, M. 1905. 'Interprétation des tessères en os avec figures, chiffres et légendes', *Revue Archéologique* 5: 110–24.

Roueché, C. 1989. '*Floreat Perge*', in Mackenzie, M. M. and C. Roueché (eds.), *Images of Authority: Papers Presented to Joyce Reynolds on the Occasion of her Seventieth Birthday* (Cambridge: Cambridge Philological Society): 206–22.

Severy, B. 2003. *Augustus and the Family at the Birth of the Roman Empire* (New York: Routledge).

Smith, R. R. R. 1996. 'Typology and diversity in the portraits of Augustus', *JRA* 9: 30–47.

Stewart, P. 2003. *Statues in Roman Society: Representation and Response* (Oxford: Oxford University Press).

Van Hoof, L. 2010. *Plutarch's Practical Ethics: The Social Dynamics of Philosophy* (Cambridge: Cambridge University Press).

Varner, E. 2004. *Mutilation and Transformation:* Damnatio memoriae *and Roman Imperial Portraiture* (Leiden; Boston: Brill).

Webster, J. 2001. 'Creolizing the Roman provinces', *AJA* 105: 209–25.

Woolf, G. 1998. *Becoming Roman: The Origins of Provincial Civilization in Gaul* (Cambridge; New York; Melbourne: Cambridge University Press).

Zanker, P. 1983. *Provinzielle Kaiserporträts: zur Rezeption der Selbstdarstellung des Princeps* (Munich: Bayerische Akademie der Wissenschaften).

1988. *The Power of Images in the Age of Augustus* (Ann Arbor: University of Michigan Press).

2002. *Un'arte per l'impero: funzione e intenzione delle immagini nel mondo romano* (Milan: Electa).

2 | The Altars of the Lares Augusti

A View from the Streets of Augustan Iconography

AMY RUSSELL

The development of imperial iconography, particularly in its early stages during the Augustan period, tends to be analysed either implicitly or explicitly using a 'trickle-down' model. New imagery, it is claimed, found its debut in major state monuments, which were then copied by patrons lower down the social scale. There is undoubtedly some truth in this reconstruction, but it fails to capture both the experiences and the creativity of Rome's non-elites. They too were both audiences and creators of imagery, and many more factors than just 'official' media affected how they understood and used images.

We have little direct evidence for the inspirations or intentions of the ordinary Romans who created or commissioned art. In this chapter, however, I propose that we can benefit from taking the view from the streets, exploring some of the possible contexts in which new imagery might have been produced without assuming that it originated in an 'official' or higher-status prototype. I examine some early imperial images created without direct central oversight, arguing that they fit better into a less hierarchical model. Imagery trickled, flowed, and flooded sideways and even upwards, as patrons from across the social scale came up with new ways to express their new relationships with imperial power.

The trickle-down model can be complex and nuanced: Paul Zanker's seminal study of Augustan imagery includes a chapter on imagery in the private sphere which examines interplays between the desire to use imperial images as a symbol of loyalty, the dictates of fashion, and the need to convey personal messages in the style of the times.[1] For Zanker, the result is somewhat bleak: Augustan imagery and style dominated to the extent that they eclipsed all else. As he puts it, 'owing to the dominance of official imagery, it became impossible to find a means of individual expression. Sculptors and patrons had to try to formulate personal sentiments, if that was the goal at all, using the language of imperial politics.'[2] More recently,

---

[1] Zanker, 1988b: 265–95; cf. 1988a; 2002: 9–37.   [2] Zanker, 1988b: 278.

in an analysis of the same altars I treat here, Kathleen Lamp has challenged what she sees as a lack of agency for individual artists and patrons in Zanker's model; though 'state art served to limit the inventional means available to the people of Rome', they had the power to be selective in what they imitated, and the vernacular pastiches of state iconography they produced are thus still the result of choice and agency.[3] Lamp's reading, however, still assumes that state art was the ultimate source of inspiration and meaning for patrons and audiences, and thus of interpretative guidelines for scholars.

Although many of the images from antiquity which are most iconic today were centrally produced by the emperor himself or some other high-ranking authority, such items were only a small part of the visual and material world of Rome. An ordinary Roman could marvel at the Ara Pacis or the statues in the Forum of Augustus, but over the course of a day he or she also saw hundreds of other images, including many which made implicit or explicit reference to the *princeps* and his power.[4] This kaleido-scope of images, and not merely a few centrally produced examples, formed the context in which Romans interpreted any given monument, painting, or sculpture. Similarly, anyone commissioning or creating a new object could draw visual inspiration from any of these sources, from centrally minted coins to scenes from daily life. What is more, when the new object was produced it too joined the Romans' shared visual world, and had the potential to influence how other imagery was seen and understood.[5] If we focus on identifying the 'official' prototype of any given image, we lose much of this vitality and diversity. More fundamentally, not all the imperial imagery that circulated had a single central prototype at all. As Megan Goldman-Petri demonstrates elsewhere in this volume, the imagery used on 'official' artworks itself derived from a pre-existing visual landscape, and it is impossible to know whether other artists or patrons who used similar motifs were directly copying a single model or merely shared the same sources of inspiration. Meanwhile, it is possible and even likely that some artists and patrons at all social levels created imagery that was entirely new. The particular images and objects with which I am concerned in this chapter were 'imperial' in the sense laid out in the Introduction: they

---

[3] Lamp, 2013: 109–30; quotation 111. At times, Lamp overstates Zanker's argument: he does not deny ordinary patrons any creative power at all, but shows how they gradually came to use their agency within a framework dominated by Augustan style and iconography.

[4] Even now, the majority of surviving images come from the minor arts: everything from tiny votive figurines to humble terracotta lamps: D'Ambra and Métraux, 2006: xi.

[5] Consider, for example, the tokens treated by Clare Rowan in this volume: they circulated alongside 'official' coins, and each would have informed viewers' interpretation of the other.

were (explicitly) intended to express a relationship between their patrons, audiences, and users on the one hand and imperial power on the other. That relationship was new and developing: it is only natural that in order to express it the artists reached for new imagery.

The objects that will be my main concern are a group of small altars to the Lares Augusti, set up by the freedman and slave *vicomagistri* and *ministri* of Rome's urban neighbourhoods. These altars have been treated by a number of previous scholars as emblematic of the way Augustan imagery permeated society, and they continue to fascinate.[6] Yet when we contrast them with the finely sculpted images of the Ara Pacis or the Forum of Augustus, it is easy to dismiss them as clumsy – or, alternatively, fetishise them as authentic glimpses of lower-class taste while cordoning them off from the wider image-world. For their patrons and users, however, even though they could hardly be more socially distant from the *princeps'* own political and artistic networks, the Lares altars were public, official, and important examples of imperial imagery and statements of imperial ideology.

The *vici* and their Cult

These small altars were part of a cult which helped Augustus' name permeate the city, and fitted perfectly into his programme of religious renewal and the redrawing of social hierarchies. At the same time, for the community of each *vicus* the cult also served important local functions, offering groups including slaves and freedmen a prestigious and highly visible way to mark their place in a society from which they might otherwise have been alienated.[7] The *vici* were a long-standing aspect of Rome's urban organisation.[8] Cult sites, often known as *compita* from their usual

---

[6] The altars have been collected by Hano, 1986. With particular relevance to the question of the dissemination of Augustan imagery, see Hölscher, 1994: 161–5; Zanker, 2002: 16–17; Lamp, 2013: 109–30. Other important studies include Zanker, 1970–1; Alföldi, 1973: 18–35; Hölscher, 1988; Dräger, 1994: 67–8; Rowe, 2002: 91–101; Lott, 2004; Flower, 2017.

[7] For full discussions of the history and functions of Rome's *vici* and compital cults, see Fraschetti, 1990; Tarpin, 2002; Lott, 2004, with evidence and references to earlier scholarship; Wallace-Hadrill, 2008: 266–87; Flower, 2017, esp. 116–36, 192–254.

[8] The argument of Fraschetti, 1990 that more or less the entire system of *vici* was an Augustan creation has not won wide approval. It has been suggested that even the name Lares Augusti predates Augustus: *CIL* 5.4087=*ILLRP* 200, from 59 BCE, has been restored as a dedication to [*a*]*ug*(*ustis*) *laribus*: so e.g. Gradel, 2002: 113–14. But Gregori, 2009 has proposed an alternative restoration [*m*]*ag*(*istrateis*) for the first word, making the inscription a dedication set up by the local magistrates to Lares without an adjective.

position at major crossroads, served as religious foci for surrounding *vici*. At each *compitum*, representatives of the *vicus*'s residents presided as *vicomagistri* and *ministri* over the worship of the Lares Compitales, local spirits of place.

In 7 BCE Augustus reorganised the *compita* and the associated cults of the local Lares, as part of a more general reform of Rome's urban geography.[9] The *princeps* himself donated new cult images of the Lares to each *vicus*.[10] From now on, the Lares Compitales were known as the Lares Augusti.[11] The new name was taken up immediately and simultaneously across the capital, providing good evidence that the change was instigated centrally. But other aspects of the reform show wide variation.[12] Just as had always been the case for the workshop of the Lares Compitales and the household Lares, individual *vici* seem to have been free to go their own way.[13] The internal organisation of *vici* differed from place to place, as did the construction and decoration of their cult sites.[14] Whoever might have been in charge of regulating them clearly felt no urge to standardise.

This 'light touch' supervision presumably allowed the *magistri* to feel more invested in their office – often quite literally, as they paid for the

[9] For full discussion, see Tarpin, 2002: 137–64; Lott, 2004; Wallace-Hadrill, 2008: 266–87; and especially Flower, 2017: 255–347, esp. 336–45, arguing persuasively that the date of 7 BCE was chosen as a vicennalia. Scheid, 2001 and Gradel, 2002: 116–28 treat the reforms from a religious perspective.

[10] Ov. *Fast.* 5.145–6: *mille lares geniumque ducis, qui tradidit illos | urbs habet, et vici numina trina colunt*. The Fasti Magistrorum Vici inscription of 2 or 1 BCE begins *Imp(erator) Caesar August[us pontif(ex) maxim(us)] co(n)s(ul) XI tribun(icia) potes[tate X] VII | Lares Aug(ustos) mag(istris) vici dedit*. The Belvedere altar has a scene showing Augustus handing statuettes of Lares to three (not four) hard-to-identify recipients.

[11] These are not the Lares of Augustus' own house: discussion in Lott, 2004: 106–10; Flower, 2017: 288–91; *contra* Galinsky, 1996: 301. 'Augusti' is an adjective in the nominative plural, not the genitive singular form of Augustus' name: 'Augustan Lares', not 'Lares of Augustus'.

[12] Taylor, 1931: 184–93, followed by most other commentators, including Gradel, 2002: 116–28 and Pollini, 2012: 328–9, claims that at the same time as he reorganised the cult of the Lares, Augustus introduced the worship of his own Genius as a regular and central feature of the compital cults. Lott, 2004: 110–14, however, has pointed out that this is an assumption relying on very little evidence, and Flower, 2017: 299–310 denies it entirely. If individual *vici* venerated a Genius of any kind, it was a local innovation and not widely taken up. See esp. Flower, 2017: 304–6 on the altar of the Sale delle Muse.

[13] For religious innovation in the *vici*, see esp. Gradel, 2002: 116–28, esp. 128; Flower, 2017: 329–35. Lott, 2004 *passim* demonstrates the wide diversity of practices of all kinds; and cf. Nock, 1972 for a similar pattern of freedom for the Augustales.

[14] Augustus' New Year's gifts to the *vici* embraced their diversity: unlike the Lares statuettes, these gifts were made individually, to different *vici* in different years, and consisted of statues of a wide variety of gods likely chosen for their local importance, such as the Apollo Sandaliarius he gave presumably to the Vicus Sandaliarius (Suet. *Aug.* 57). For more evidence and discussion of these gifts, bought with the New Year's donations the people themselves gave to the *princeps*, see Rowe, 2002: 94–5; Lott, 2004: 73–80; Flower, 2017: 263–9.

decoration of their shrines, including the altars I consider, out of their own pockets. It also gave the *princeps* a chance to distance himself from an institution which, if centrally controlled, might seem overly close to an official imperial cult. But even if Augustus and his proxies had ulterior motives for granting the *magistri* so much latitude, the result was a cult enmeshed in local concerns and contexts. Significant elements of what we see as the Augustan urban reform were determined not by the *princeps* himself, but by the local communities' reactions to the changes he made; that is, by social dynamics, as individual colleges of *vicomagistri* made decisions in the context of their own social relationships. Many (though not all) groups of *vicomagistri* responded to Augustus' generosity by starting a new era in their records; they usually identify themselves as the *vicomagistri* of year *x*, with 7 BCE as year 1.[15] Some also commissioned new architecture and decoration for their cult sites, including altars. It is these altars that concern me here. Their position between central impetus and the free reign given to individual patrons and artisans makes them valuable for the study of image-making in the early empire.[16]

The Altars

In 2 CE, the *magistri* of the Vicus Aesculeti set up a new altar in their shrine (Fig. 2.1).[17] Its short inscription identifies it as an altar to the Lares Augusti, set up by the *magistri* of year 9. Their names were included, but are now mostly unreadable. The small square altar is decorated on all four sides, though the back is now very fragmentary. The names of the four

[15] Examples collected by Lott, 2004: 181–209. Exceptions include *CIL* 6.30975 (*ILS* 3090, Lott, 2004: 198–9), an altar dedication from a *vicus* whose era begins in 8 BCE; *CIL* 6.449 (*ILS* 3617, Lott, 2004: 206), an inscription recording the restoration of the *aedicula* of the Vicus Honoris et Virtutis, whose era begins in 9 BCE; and *CIL* 6.452 (Lott, 2004: 207), a similar restoration inscription from the Vicus Iovis Fagutalis, with an era beginning in 12 BCE. Because of the importance she attaches to 7 BCE, Flower, 2017: 344 suggests that these could be simple errors by the later counters or stonemasons. To me, it seems equally likely that there was a large-scale central reform in 7 BCE, but that it did not involve forcing the *vici* to adopt a new era; some – perhaps especially those who had only recently started one – kept a different era that recalled some other date, probably of more local importance.

[16] Noted by e.g. Zanker, 1970–1; Hölscher, 1994: 163; Mayer, 2010: 123–4.

[17] Rome, Musei Capitolini 855. For further discussion of this example see the works cited in n. 6, above; Ryberg, 1955: 59; Alföldi, 1973: 33; Hano, 1986: 2339–40; Hölscher, 1988: 390–1; Clarke, 2003: 81–5; Lott, 2004: 142–4, Hackworth Petersen, 2015: 439–43; Flower, 2017: 312–16. The altar was found *in situ* near the Via Arenula, surrounded by a mosaic pavement bearing the words [*ma*]*g*[*i*]*stri vici Aescleti anni VIIII*. For the excavation, see Pisani Sartorio, 1993 with references; for the inscription, *CIL* 6.30957 = *ILS* 3615, Panciera, 1987: 68–70.

Figure 2.1 Altar of the Vicus Aesculeti, Rome, 2 CE. Musei Capitolini 855. Photographs: D-DAI-ROM-2001.2178 (K. Anger); D-DAI-ROM-6274A (C. Faraglia); D-DAI-ROM-2001.2175 (K. Anger), arachne.dainst.org/entity/1076071.

vicomagistri are inscribed on the four sides. The main image on the front of the altar (Fig. 2.1, left) is the four *vicomagistri* sacrificing. They are accompanied by a musician, a lictor, and two attendants, who lead forward a bull and a pig for sacrifice. The two short sides (Fig. 2.1, right) are identical; they show the two Lares, one on each side, characterised as Lares Augusti by the laurel branches which they carry. They stand on small podia, identifying the images as depictions of statuettes rather than direct representations of the Lares themselves. On the damaged back face of the altar (Fig. 2.1, centre) it is possible to discern the remains of an oak wreath.

Hano has identified eighteen altars as pertaining to the Lares Augusti, based on epigraphic evidence in some cases but in others by iconography alone. Across his sample, he finds eight sacrifice scenes, seven images of the Lares, and nine oak wreaths.[18] Nevertheless, repeated images are not enough to characterise the altars as a coherent group. All of these features occur frequently on other surviving decorated altars from Rome and beyond. At least one known altar to the Lares Augusti lacks images of sacrifices, Lares, or oak wreaths: placed outside the building usually identified as the temple of Romulus in the Forum Romanum, this altar of unknown date identifies itself in a large inscription on its front face as *laribus* | *Aug(ustis)* | *sacrum* ('sacred to the Lares Augusti'), but is otherwise

---

[18] Hano, 1986, table between pages 2352 and 2353. In this chapter I have confined my analysis to the most secure examples. Wreaths are particularly characteristic of altars dedicated by the *ministri vici*, which usually lack any other decoration and therefore form only a minor part of my analysis.

decorated only with an *urceus* and *patera* on its short side.[19] Meanwhile, sacrifices and oak wreaths are found on altars of all kinds and beyond. The Lares images Hano frequently finds on these altars designate the gods to whom the altar is dedicated, but some lack laurels and could be equally suited to an altar for the Lares Familiares.[20] We also find a huge variety of other imagery, often unparalleled, from an enigmatic seated woman (Fig. 2.7, top left) to a scene of augury (Fig. 2.5, centre).[21] There was no single iconographic feature by which these altars' original audiences and users would have identified them as pertaining to the Lares Augusti. Instead, they recognised them by their location in a compital shrine, the rest of the shrine's decoration, and the religious practices that took place there. Just as in other aspects of the cult, then, the wide range of imagery used on these altars strongly suggests that the individual patrons who commissioned them made their own decisions about their decoration, without central guidance or a single prototype.[22]

Ideology, Intention, and Reception

Produced at low social levels but crammed with ideologically laden Augustan imagery, the altars of the Lares Augusti provide a counterpoint to the prestige monuments we know so well. At the same time, they submit to analysis more easily than the many lamps, tables, or wall-paintings whose messages may have been entirely private. We will never know whether the patron who commissioned a sphinx table for his own home, say, meant his choice as a statement of loyalty to the regime or was simply following fashion. In aggregate, however, patterns might emerge. Zanker proposes a picture highly dependent on the trickle-down model, in which early adopters (usually among the elite) consciously choose motifs linked to Augustan ideology. Their choices set the fashion; in a second stage, a wider group of artists and patrons copy them, reusing the same motifs without necessarily intending to send an ideological message. The overall result,

---

[19] *CIL* 6.30954; Hano, 1986: 2343–4.

[20] E.g. the Lares on the short sides of the Vicus Sandaliarius altar, Fig. 2.5, left; and see below, pp. 44–5 for the spread of laurels into domestic lararia.

[21] Each of these examples is discussed below, pp. 40–3

[22] Contrast the cult statuettes of the Lares, presumably mass-produced to be given to each of the *vici* by Augustus; as a result, the iconography of the Lares themselves on the altars is consistent. Zanker, 2002: 16 suggests that Augustus' own shrine of the Lares Publici could have served as a model, but if so, the altars' own diversity shows that it was only in the broadest of terms.

however, is that both imagery and ideology are assimilated and internalised.[23]

When we see them from street level, the altars of the Lares Augusti are different. They declare (one of) their intentions explicitly: they honour Augustus by incorporating his name into an important local cult.[24] Rather than copying fashionable Augustan imagery as it trickled down from above, and thereby taking in Augustan ideology along with it, the *vicomagistri* were deliberately adopting elements of the Augustan ideological programme. As scholars, we are faced with almost a mirror image of the trickle-down model in which 'fashionable' images can serve as a vehicle for the almost subconscious propagation of ideological messages. The ideological aspects of the altars' message – at least those parts with direct relevance to imperial power – were relatively straightforward and lucid. It is the imagery that is difficult to parse, both for us and for the altars' patrons and artists. They knew what they wanted to say, but not all the visual vocabulary they needed yet existed.

Without, it seems, any guidance about what iconography to use, the altars' creators had to look around them for inspiration. In the creative ferment of Augustan Rome, they had a vast buffet of objects and artworks to choose from. Some, though not all of these, were commissioned by the *princeps* and issued in his name. I do not deny that a large proportion of imagery started at the top and trickled its way down, as a range of motifs that first appear in more prestigious media found their way onto these altars. There are multiple elements of the Altar of the Vicus Aesculeti's iconography that refer directly to the wider visual rhetoric of Augustus' power as seen in the objects he himself commissioned or used. The Lares depicted on the side of the altar carry laurels (Fig. 2.1, right). Laurels appear in all periods with generic connotations of victory, but it is hard to escape the similarity to Augustus' own imagery. We do not know if the *vicomagistri* and their artists understood the laurels as directly quoting the twin laurels outside the *princeps*' house or intended a more generic Augustan

---

[23] Zanker, 1988b: 265–74. Compare Hölscher, 1994, esp. 160–9, whose treatment does not make strict distinctions between the transmission of imagery and ideology; in the examples he chooses (including these altars), the two are close to inseparable. 'L'imperatore aveva permeato a tal punto la società con le sue concezioni ideologiche, che la necessaria unitarietà delle manifestazioni si verificava senza particolari disposizioni' (163).

[24] In line with the themes of this volume, we should not assume that they intended to communicate anything directly *to* Augustus, who was unlikely to have set eyes on any given altar. This is loyalism, in the sense laid out in the Introduction, rather than a proclamation of loyalty.

reference.[25] But we do know that Romans would have seen twin laurels associated with the *princeps* in a range of media all around them, including on coins. The oak crown and acorns in the altar's moulding recall Augustus' *corona civica*. This crown, traditionally given for saving the life of a citizen and now with expanded resonances of Augustus' role as saviour of the entire *res publica*, had also been one of Augustus' key visual signifiers since it and the laurels had both formed part of the honours of 27 BCE.[26] It too was frequently depicted on coins, and portrait statues of Augustus such as the Bevilacqua bust wear it.[27] One way to read the altars, therefore, is as documents of reception.[28]

The altars preserve for us a trace of how their patrons understood the images they saw around them. One of the patrons' aims was to (be seen to) honour Augustus; they signalled their aim by borrowing motifs they understood as appropriately Augustan. In the case of the laurels and oak wreaths it is possible that 'official' imagery from coins and honorific statues played a significant role. But even in these cases we should not focus too tightly on potential artistic prototypes. These patrons and artists lived in the capital: they would have had the chance to set eyes on the *princeps* himself, perhaps wearing an oak wreath or attended by lictors with laurel-wreathed *fasces*.

Artistic Practices and Artistic Innovation

Reading the altars as documents of reception fits well into a standard trickle-down model. New imagery (or old imagery revitalised and imbued with new meaning) is created at the top, displayed in prestigious monuments, circulated widely through coinage, and then taken up by private patrons. But to treat the altars purely as imitating 'official' or 'central' imagery ignores the completely new situation in which their patrons found themselves, and downplays the more unusual elements of the altars' iconography.

On a very basic level, these altars are more or less contemporary with the more prestigious monuments we might be tempted to see them as imitating. The artistic genre of decorated altar was itself a newcomer: Republican

---

[25] On the generic force of laurels, see Alföldi, 1973; and discussion below, p. 45.

[26] In general on the oak wreath see now Bergmann, 2010: 135–83; Zanker, 1988b sees it as a 'dynastic symbol' (216) and 'approaching the status of an insigne of empire' (276).

[27] For discussion of the Bevilacqua bust's crown and further examples from sculpture and coinage, see Bergmann, 2010, esp. 283.

[28] An approach deployed sensitively by Hölscher, 1994: 'I motivi iconographici . . . manifestavano il loro nuovo carattere non tanto nella propagazione, quanto nella recezione' (161).

altars tend to be plain, and the Ara Pacis itself was only completed in 9 BCE, just two years before the reorganisation of the *vici*. The altars I treat in this chapter turn up at the beginning of the sequences of small dedicated altars in our handbooks.[29] They were part of a new phenomenon, meaning their artists had few models to work with.

Zanker has looked closely at the workshops producing these altars and their methods. An example once held in the Chigi collection at Soriano and a very similar fragment now in the Musei Capitolini, he demonstrates, were made in the same workshop from the same pattern-book – or, rather, from a series of models of generic sacrificial scenes joined haphazardly together.[30] The main sacrificial image of the Soriano altar (Fig. 2.2) differs from that of the Vicus Aesculeti altar (Fig. 2.1, left). In the first example, four men were shown sacrificing as a group, appropriately for a cult presided over by four *vicomagistri*. Here, there is only a single officiant. Zanker attributes the difference to the Soriano sculptor's artistic limitations. He did not have a model available for a scene of four men sacrificing, and did not even have the limited creative ability of the sculptor responsible for the Vicus Aesculeti altar, who squeezes the four celebrants together somewhat inelegantly, or the imagination of the sculptor of the altar now in the Sale delle Muse (Fig. 2.6, right), who includes all four *magistri* by depicting them in two pairs on the sides of the altar.[31] Consequently, the *magistri* of the Soriano altar and its twin had to accept an image in which one man stood for all four. What is more, he is depicted with a round altar, whereas all known altars to the Lares Augusti are square. The bull, sacrificial attendants, and musician all follow standard iconography, but are all shown at different scales, this time (Zanker claims) without the artistic rationale which seems clear on the Vicus Aesculati example.

Zanker concludes that the Soriano altar and the Musei Capitolini fragment were made by a workshop which relied entirely on pattern-books, but which did not have a pattern available for this particular scene, showing a novel kind of sacrifice by four *magistri*. Instead, a reasonably apt image was created by mixing together various pre-existing patterns, without

[29] My thanks to Megan Goldman-Petri for this point. The so-called Altar of Domitius Ahenobarbus is surely a statue base; on the sequence of altars with relief sculpture, see further Dräger, 1994; Hölscher, 1988.

[30] Zanker, 1970–1. Soriano: Rome, Musei Capitolini no. 3352; Ryberg, 1955: 61; Hano, 1986: 2346; Hölscher, 1988: 391–2; Lott, 2004: 214. Musei Capitolini (this altar is often referred to as the altar from the Palazzo dei Conservatori from its previous display location, but is now at Centrale Montemartini): Rome, Musei Capitolini no. 1276; Hano, 1986: 2347; Lott, 2004: 214–15.

[31] Vatican, Museo Pio Clementino 311; Ryberg, 1955: 58–9; Hano, 1986: 2338; Lott, 2004: 184–5; Flower, 2017: 304–6; further discussion below, p. 42.

Figure 2.2 Altar of the Lares Augusti once held in the Chigi collection at Soriano. Rome(?), *c.*7 BCE. Musei Capitolini 3352. Photograph: D-DAI-ROM-2001.2174 (K. Anger), arachne.dainst.org/entity/1125145.

much care for composition. Other workshops faced the same problems, but reached different solutions. Zanker's analysis of the way the different artists approached the problem allows us to deduce not only that these workshops were not well integrated into the networks of sculptors producing the high-quality reliefs of the Ara Pacis and other large-scale works of art, but also that they were not well connected with each other.

For my approach, however, the most important point to take away from Zanker's convincing analysis is that these artists were working in entirely new territory, without any standard iconography to draw upon. Their choices were conditioned by local concerns, and designed to be legible to local audiences. If the patrons of this altar only wanted to honour the *princeps* or send him a message about their loyalty, they could have done so in any number of different ways. Instead, they chose a visual scheme which placed emphasis not only on the Augustan-ness of their cult but also the prominence of their own role. The idea that new Augustan institutions and objects served local purposes is not a new one. These *vicomagistri* simultaneously honoured Augustus and raised their own local status, just like every patron of an imperial statue or temple did across the empire.[32] The complex relationship between central and local is a major theme of this volume. On these altars, the local takes pride of place, and the result is not only reinterpretation of existing imagery but innovation. To achieve their goals, they commissioned sacrifice scenes that required their artists to move beyond their existing stock images, whether by combining old motifs in new ways (as in the Soriano example) or by creating entirely new visual schemes (as on the Vicus Aesculeti altar).

The sacrifice scenes on these altars have been recognised as anomalous in various ways. Scholars note that the sacrificiants, attendants, and animals tend to be shown at different scales: is this because the sculptors lacked the technical skills to make their composition fit the field while preserving realistic proportions, or is it a deliberate decision suited to the altar's local context, using an existing artistic convention and chosen to emphasise the ritual role of the *vicomagistri* above all else?[33] Any final analyses of quality must be left to art historians, but from a social dynamics perspective it is clear that the prominence of the *vicomagistri* must be an important part of the altar's message.

Another altar (Fig. 2.3), recently re-analysed by Harriet Flower and Megan Diluzio, shows a similar pattern of iconographic innovation.[34] On each short side, we see a woman libating at a round altar. These images have generated plenty of discussion concerning women's role in the cult of the Lares, and Flower and Diluzio convincingly argue that they should represent brides, who according to Varro gave an offering to the local Lares on their wedding day.[35] For my purposes, the key point is that there are vanishingly

---

[32] Compare, in particular, the chapters in this volume by Wilker, Tran, and Hellström.

[33] Compare, for example, the negative assessment of Clarke, 2003: 83–5 with Hackworth Petersen, 2015: 442–3. The classic discussion of variation in scale in 'plebeian' art, Bianchi Bandinelli, 1969, mentions the Vicus Aesculeti altar at 81–4.

[34] Flower and Diluzio, 2019. The altar is now in the Museo Nazionale Romano alle Terme, MNR 49481. Previous discussions include Candida, 1979: 95–8; Hölscher, 1984; Hano, 1986: 2348–9; Hölscher, 1988: 392; Hölscher, 1994: 164; Lott, 2004: 218. Hano does not see the figures as female, while Lott is not convinced that this altar should belong to the Lares Augusti. Flower and Diluzio have full discussion of the various controversies.

[35] Varro *ap.* Nonius 852L; see further Flower, 2017: 78–85.

Figure 2.3 Lares altar with depiction of women sacrificing, Rome, *c.*7 BCE. Museo Nazionale Romano alle Terme, MNR 49481. Photographs: H. Flower. Su concessione del Ministero per i beni e le attività culturali e per il turismo – Museo Nazionale Romano.

few Roman images in any medium of women sacrificing, and there does not seem to have been any consistent iconography for brides at all.[36] The patron of this altar also required her(?) artist to come up with new iconography.

The choice of a sacrifice or libation scene in the first place is something of an anomaly in itself. Richard Gordon has shown that the iconography of sacrifice becomes closely related to the *princeps* himself very early in the principate.[37] Images of Augustus and his successors sacrificing are frequent; images of other living humans sacrificing are incredibly rare. The one exception is the *vicomagistri*, who as in this example are usually shown sacrificing on their own altars. Gordon explains away the exception by calling the *vicomagistri* 'freedmen aping their social superiors' (205): in essence, they got it wrong because they didn't know any better. Lamp and Flower offer more positive readings, in which they assume that the *vicomagistri* were not ignorant, but consciously or at least unconsciously aware of Augustus' own domination of sacrificial imagery. For them, the

---

[36] Flower and Diluzio, 2019: 216 and an appendix list and count sacrifice scenes with women; 229–30 discusses bridal iconography.

[37] Gordon, 1990; discussion of the *vicomagistri* at 205.

vicomagistri are deliberately imitating the way Augustus himself is depicted, demonstrating their adherence to his policy of exemplary piety.[38]

Such interpretations, whether positive or negative, take the 'official' sacrifice scenes as their starting point, and in doing so imply that the altars' creators did the same; the interest comes in the ways in which they deviate from the assumed prototype. But why should we assume that these patrons and artists looked directly and solely to Augustan state art for their inspiration? For the specific iconography and style of the sacrifice scenes, the altars' artists and patrons had access to multiple sources. Augustus' own sacrificial iconography developed from Republican scenes of priests and magistrates sacrificing; these would have continued to be available as models.[39] For the composition of the Soriano altar (Fig. 2.2), which with its single officiant looks closest to a hypothetical model depicting the *princeps* in sacrificial pose, the closest parallel is in fact a coin of 16 BCE which Gordon does not treat (Fig. 2.4, left): with the legend PRO VALETVDINE CAESARIS SPQR, it seems unlikely that the sacrificing figure in this case is the Caesar for whose health he is praying. For the Augustan period, the coin is an outlier; the theme of vows would not become popular until the second century CE, at which point the sacrificiant should be identified as the emperor.[40] But it has a non-Augustan visual precedent in a Republican coin of 97 BCE showing Numa sacrificing a goat (Fig. 2.4, right).[41] The coins, of course, are still official products; but rather than assuming that our artist copied a single coin, we should conclude that the coin and the altar both draw on compositions which had circulated for centuries in multiple media. These altars and their artists independently appropriated them to express their own relationship with imperial power, in their own terms.

If the *vicomagistri* were aware of the close connection between the sacrificial iconography they chose and the developing iconography of the *princeps* himself, it was surely a bonus rather than an error. But their choice of sacrifice imagery would also have been conditioned by their regular experience of sacrificing at the altar: rather than departing, deliberately or by mistake, from their imperial prototype, they chose to depict themselves

---

[38] Lamp, 2013: 126–7; Flower, 2017: 316–18, esp. n. 25 with citation of Gordon, 1990. We might add euergetism; Gordon's main argument is that the sacrificing emperor is a symbol of benefaction as much as of *pietas*, and the *vicomagistri* were indeed involved in financing projects within their *vici*.

[39] Discussion and examples in Ryberg, 1955: 20–37.   [40] See further Ryberg, 1955: 178.

[41] *RRC* 334/1. This coin's closeness to the Soriano altar is noted by Ryberg, 1955: 37 n. 77; cf. also *RRC* 372/1, of 81 BCE, which shows a cow being sacrificed to Diana in a similar composition, but without the attendant guiding the animal.

Figure 2.4 (left) Aureus of C. Antistius Vetus, Rome, 16 BCE. *RIC* I² Augustus 369. Photograph © The Trustees of the British Museum. (right) Denarius of L. Pomponius Molo, Rome, 97 BCE. *RRC* 334/1. Photograph: www.cngcoins.com.

in this way because this is what they did.[42] The innovative composition of the Vicus Aesculeti scene confirms it: the artist made a deliberate decision to cram all four *magistri* into the scene despite limitations of space, because in reality all four were indeed involved. The same goes for the scenes of brides libating: it is perhaps a surprise that no other visual depictions of the ritual survive, but if brides did visit their local compital altar on their wedding day it would have been a frequent but visually interesting element of Roman street life. These objects do not show us copies of more prestigious images, but scenes from daily life.[43] Artistically, they deserve to be considered as examples of innovation as well as reception.

The Unique Scenes

Perhaps the sacrifice scenes could be squeezed into Lamp's category of pastiche: elements of the 'official' iconography combined in new ways, thus providing a space for creativity and agency even within a world of Augustan images. I have contended that we should see more innovation in the sacrifices than Lamp allows. What is more, the meanings that patrons and audiences attributed to all their scenes must be interpreted in their local contexts as well as in the context of the Augustan iconography from which they sometimes borrowed individual elements. But even more

---

[42] Flower, 2017: 317 suggests that the bull sacrifice, often taken as confirmation that the *vici* worshipped the emperor's Genius, may represent annual lustration of the area performed by the *vicomagistri*.

[43] Lamp, 2013: 126 cites Bodnar, 1992: 13–14 for a theory that vernacular art typically draws from first-hand experience.

Figure 2.5 Altar of the Vicus Sandaliarius. Rome, 2 BCE. Florence, Uffizi 972. Photographs: D-DAI-ROM-2007.0678 (H. Behrens); D-DAI-ROM-75.291 (C. Rossa); D-DAI-ROM-2007.0682 (H. Behrens), arachne.dainst.org/entity/1066186. Su concessione del Ministero per i beni e le attività culturali e per il turismo.

problematic for a trickle-down model are the altars' other scenes. Beside the relatively standard laurels, oak wreaths, and sacrifices already discussed, many of the altars are decorated with other images which are unusual or even unique.

The Altar of the Vicus Sandaliarius (Fig. 2.5) of 2 BCE has proven the most controversial of all the surviving *vicus* altars.[44] The rear panel shows the standard oak wreath, laurels, and sacrificial implements. One of the side panels, too, follows an expected pattern, with two Lares. The other short side has an image of a Victory bringing a trophy to adorn a shield, which I discuss below. The controversial panel is the front (Fig. 2.5, centre). Here a togate man carrying a *lituus* is depicted alongside a pecking bird; he is flanked by a woman in sacrificial pose wearing a diadem and torque, and a second male figure.

The central figure of this composition, all agree, should be Augustus. This is not the iconography of a Genius, who would presumably hold a cornucopia; instead, he is shown as augur. The bird at his feet represents the *tripudium*, an augural practice involving watching the feeding patterns of chickens. But who are the other figures? Various scholars have argued that the man 'must be' Gaius, or Lucius; and that the woman 'must be' Livia, or Julia, or Livilla, perhaps depicted in the guise of a priestess or with some of the attributes of Venus Genetrix.[45] These identifications are based not on the figures' iconography, but on the altar's date and the messages that various

[44] Florence, Uffizi 972. Ryberg, 1955: 60–1; Hano, 1986: 2338–9; Lott, 2004: 192–3.
[45] Discussions include Zanker, 1970–1: 151–2; Hölscher, 1994: 162–3; Galinsky, 1996: 304–6; Rowe, 2002: 95–6; Koortbojian, 2013: 73–7; Marcattili, 2015; Flower, 2017: 291–8.

commentators feel ought to be expressed on such a monument. Prime candidates include the taking of the auspices before Gaius' departure for the east, or the entry of Lucius into the augurate; the identity of the female figure is usually decided based on whether the scholar feels that Livia or Julia is more prominent in the dynastic propaganda of the period. In the end, the altar gives us few clues about the identity of the figures depicted.

Brian Rose has made a convincing argument that the female figure should not be seen as a member of the imperial family at all.[46] Depictions of imperial women in large-scale state art are relatively rare, and depictions of imperial women sacrificing are unknown until Julia Domna. The torque she wears would be very out of place on Livia or Julia: Roman men might wear torques as military decorations, but Roman women rarely did. And the diadem poses a problem, too.[47] Rose points out that all of these elements can be reconciled if we see in this figure a priestess of the Magna Mater: such priestesses did indeed wear torques and diadems. For Rose, it makes sense that a priestess of the Magna Mater might have been involved in the ceremonies surrounding Gaius Caesar's departure for the east in 2 BCE.[48]

Rose's identification of the figure as a priestess of the Magna Mater is persuasive, explaining as it does all her attributes in a way no other solution has managed. But the choice to include her in the ensemble (and, indeed, the identification of the second male figure) must depend on local needs. The *vicomagistri* who commissioned this altar were able to create new iconographic schemes by picking and choosing from an existing visual repertoire. It is possible but not necessary that a specific occasion took place which involved Augustus as augur, a priestess of the Magna Mater, and another male, and which caught the imagination of these patrons or artists. Even if they did have a specific occasion in mind, its memory would have faded fast. Can we even be confident that the altar's original audience was sufficiently au fait with the iconography of the imperial family to distinguish one prince from another in these small and sketchy depictions? But

---

[46] Rose, 1997: 18 and 104–6.

[47] Though there are parallels for imperial women wearing diadems when depicted in the guise of goddesses, there is not much precedent for combining mythical/divine and historical representation in relief. It would be odd in this period to show living members of the imperial family both with and without divine attributes in the same composition.

[48] The arguments for this particular date are circumstantial, however; Koortbojian, 2013: 150–1 demonstrates that the impact of the Augustus-as-augur figure across a wide range of examples is not necessarily to call to mind any specific occasion but to highlight the importance of augury as a whole and the role of Augustus as sole bearer of the auspices.

Figure 2.6 Altar of the Sale delle Muse, Rome, 7 BCE. Vatican, Museo Pio Clementino 311. Photographs: D-DAI-ROM-34.73; D-DAI-ROM-34.74; D-DAI-ROM-34.75 (C. Faraglia), arachne.dainst.org/entity/1086098. Per concessione dei Musei Vaticani.

this composition does not need a specific model.[49] Perhaps the Magna Mater had a following amongst the inhabitants of this *vicus*, or a long-standing shrine nearby. Whatever the answer, the appearance of these figures was the choice of the local patrons, and their meaning must lie in local rather than imperial concerns.

The same arguments apply to the similarly enigmatic togate figure on the front of the Altar of the Sale delle Muse (Fig. 2.6, right);[50] he is often assumed to be a Genius given the traditional (and probably mistaken) assumption that the Genius Augusti was worshipped at these shrines and a single letter that may or may not be a G in the altar's inscription, but there is no positive evidence for this identification. He is in fact completely unidentifiable to us – though presumably highly meaningful to the altar's original audience.[51] A final case is the 'Altar of Manlius' (Fig. 2.7), which

---

[49] In an ingenious solution, Zanker, 1970–1: 151 observes that the *tabula ansata* at the bottom of the composition, on which the names of the *vicomagistri* are inscribed, serves double duty. Taking the image as a whole, it looks more like a plinth on which the three figures stand. The model for this composition, he proposes, was a statue group. Yet even if this does give us an 'official' prototype, the choice to remediate it as a relief would itself be innovative, and probably the product of local concerns: a statue that the *vicus*'s inhabitants would have passed by regularly, perhaps.

[50] For scholarship, see n. 31, above.

[51] Flower, 2017: 304–6 has a clear and comprehensive treatment of the evidence, which I shall not repeat here.

Figure 2.7 'Altar of Manlius', Rome, *c*.7 BCE. Vatican, Museo Gregoriano Profano 9964. Photographs: D-DAI-ROM-7509; D-DAI-ROM-7525; D-DAI-ROM-81.2875 (H. Schwanke), arachne.dainst.org/entity/1215881. Per concessione dei Musei Vaticani.

appears to be a compital altar to the Lares Augusti which was later repurposed by Manlius' clients to honour their patron.[52] It is decorated with the traditional Lares on each side and a sacrifice scene on the front which, like the others I have analysed, is traditional in theme but innovative in composition, this time showing all four *magistri* and four *ministri*. Its rear panel shows an unparalleled scene with a seated female figure (a goddess?) who, like the Magna Mater priestess on the Vicus Sandaliarius altar, must have had local resonances.

We cannot ignore these one-off scenes in analysing the Lares altars. Nor should we assume that they each refer to some now-lost prototype. Even though we have no clear way of interpreting their meaning, they provide evidence that the patrons and artists who created them were not merely interested in copying or even reconfiguring the motifs found in higher-status artworks. They chose iconography that made sense for their local context; and if that iconography could not be found, they invented it.

The Altars as Sources of Imagery

I have argued that the creators of these altars, as well as taking in influences from all around them, were innovators in their own right. But the story does not stop there: the altars themselves were sources of imagery for others. Seen from the street, the category of 'state' or 'official' art breaks down. To passers-by and *vicus* inhabitants, these altars were at least as official or important as any other imagery related to the Augustan programme. The new images they created had the potential to spread further, making them prototypes in their own right.

It is hard to track the exact process by which any given image moved across time, space, and media. Many of the motifs that are frequently used on Lares altars appear in a variety of contexts. The oak wreath, for example, has sometimes been identified as an emblem of the Augustales, and thus connected to emperor worship; but Margaret Laird has recently shown that the Augustales were not primarily concerned with ruler cult, and we know that the oak wreath was used in funerary and religious contexts by patrons of all

---

[52] Vatican, Museo Gregoriano Profano 9964. Hano, 1986: 2345–6; Fless *et al.*, 2018: 129–36. Ryberg, 1955: 84–8 correctly notes that the main problem presented by this enigmatic altar is that the inscription and iconography do not match. The suggestion hinted at by both Hano and Alföldi, 1973: 34–5 that it is a reused Lares altar fits the evidence far better than the complex explanations of scholars including Taylor, 1921; Ryberg, 1955: 84–8; Torelli, 1982: 16–20; Gradel, 2002: 251–60.

kinds without any obvious connection to the *princeps* beyond a general sense of prestige.[53] The trickle-down model, with a first wave of high-status conscious adopters followed by ever-largening circles of imitators, is a sufficient (though not necessary) explanation for these phenomena.

The fact that some images trickled downwards, however, does not mean that they all did. In a few cases, we can see tantalising hints that the Lares altars themselves may have been points of transmission. The laurels associated with the Lares Augusti were a standard imperial motif, transmitted on coins and in any number of other media and appearing quickly across Italy and beyond. In a notable development, however, in Pompeii laurels appear on private *lararia* inside houses.[54] Though we cannot trace exact paths of transmission, the combination of laurels and Lares may well have been influenced by the compital altars. This newly combined motif did not trickle down to our altars and then further outwards to Pompeian householders; so far as we can see, it originated in the compital cult. If anything, it trickled up, as the decisions made by a group of freedman *vicomagistri* attached a new set of meanings to parts of the existing imperial image portfolio. Laurels alone meant Augustus and victory; the combination of laurels and Lares had its own ideological message, to which we have imperfect access but which the inhabitants of Pompeii found suitable for their homes.

Even where there is some plausible prototype at the start of a pattern of dissemination, concentrating too much on the way an image might have flowed outwards and downwards from that single point can obscure other elements of its transmission and development. The figure of Victory attaching a shield to a trophy on the short side of the Vicus Sandaliarius altar (Fig. 2.5, right) is in some ways an example of very standard Augustan iconography. To modern eyes, it irresistibly recalls the statue of Victory set up by Augustus in the Curia and the original *clipeus virtutis* which was displayed alongside it. In the Curia, the sculpture was a monument to victory at Actium, and the shield to Augustus' actions as victor. The entire assemblage carried a clear and specific message to its senatorial audience: Augustus had defeated his and Rome's enemies, brought the civil war to an end, and saved the *res publica*, for which he was justly rewarded. Recently, however, Bridget Buxton has pointed out that not all Augustan-period images of Victory with a shield should be understood so specifically as a reference to one single prototype.[55] At one end of the

[53] Laird, 2015, esp. 204 for the wreath. Zanker, 1988a: 6–7, Zanker, 1988b: 276, and Hölscher, 1994: 157 also discuss how the wreath lost its specificity.

[54] Examples throughout Frölich, 1991; discussions in Alföldi, 1973: 55–6; Frölich, 1991: 127; Gradel, 2002: 122–3.

[55] Buxton, 2014: 97–100.

Figure 2.8 (left) Aureus of Q. Rustius Fortunatus, Rome, 19 BCE. *RIC* I² Augustus 321. Photograph © The Trustees of the British Museum. (right) Belvedere Altar, Rome, between 12 BCE and 2 CE. Vatican, Museo Gregoriano Profano 1115. Photograph: FA2322-04, arachne.dainst.org/entity/1081150. Per concessione dei Musei Vaticani.

spectrum, we find images like a coin of 19 BCE (Fig. 2.8, left) with a Victory in flight holding a shield inscribed SC; the shield is supported by a pillar. The Victory panel of the Belvedere altar is similar (Fig. 2.8, right); the shield and Victory are again supported by a pillar, and the shield is inscribed

> SENATVS POPVLVSQ
>
> ROMANVS
>
> IMP CAESARI DIVI F AVGVSTO
>
> PONTIF MAXVM
>
> IMP (*vacat*) COS (*vacat*) TRIB
>
> POTEST (*vacat*).[56]

In both images, the pillars show that a sculptural group is depicted, which makes a reference to the statue in the Curia seem likely. If the shield on the Belvedere altar is indeed intended to represent the *clipeus virtutis* of 27 BCE, however, it is odd that Augustus is named as Pontifex Maximus, a title he did not take up until 12 BCE. Buxton suggests that it could represent some other shield given to Augustus at a later date.

---

[56] The Belvedere altar itself has been identified as an altar of the Lares Augusti by Zanker, 1969, followed by scholars including Hano, 1986: 2344; Beard, North, and Price, 1998: 185–6; Holliday, 2015: 202–3; Flower, 2017: 275–83. I do not consider it part of the group, with Hölscher, 1988: 394–6; Buxton, 2014: 93. It shares many themes with the altars under discussion, but it has no inscription identifying it as an altar to the Lares Augusti, nor are there any Lares shown in its pictorial panels.

Figure 2.9 Drawing of a discus from a mould-made lamp showing Victory with shield flanked by two Lares, Italy, 1–50 CE. British Museum 1756,0101.618.a. Image: H. B. Waters, *Catalogue of the Greek and Roman Lamps in the British Museum* (London: Trustees of the British Museum): 206, no. 1372.

On the Vicus Sandalarius altar, the iconography of Victory and shield has been repurposed more fundamentally. There is no inscription referencing the *clipeus virtutis*, and the pillar which indicated that the Belvedere image showed a statue group is also gone; instead, this is a generic scene of a winged Victory decorating a military trophy.[57] To what extent does it make sense to call this a copy or imitation of the Curia group?

Like the *corona civica*, the image of Victory with shield was widely disseminated through Italy and beyond. Tonio Hölscher collected examples of lamps showing the scene, and a quick look through any major museum catalogue reveals dozens more.[58] Some of them label the shield as the *clipeus virtutis* by connecting it with the *corona civica* given to Augustus at the same time *ob cives servatos*; others do not. On some, the shield has been entirely repurposed and is used to hold a New Year's greeting. But the example which is of most interest is Fig. 2.9: it shows a winged Victory holding a shield (uninscribed), a legionary standard, and a cornucopia. On either side are two Lares. This lamp testifies not only to the omnipresence of Augustan iconographic elements in Roman culture, or even to the ways in which their symbolism is diluted over time; it also shows how the way such imagery is transmitted – here, I propose, via a compital altar – affects the way we as scholars should approach it. This Victory has travelled far from any original connection to

---

[57] Full discussion in Hölscher, 1994: 160–1; see further Hölscher, 1967: 102–12.
[58] Hölscher, 1967: 108–12, with plate 13; see also Zanker, 1988b: 274–5.

a specific statue in the Curia, through multiple media and iconographic shifts. In the process, it has probably lost much of its original specificity of meaning, but has acquired other resonances: in this case, to the cult of the Lares Augusti and the variety of iconography connected to their altars.[59]

Conclusion

The unusual iconography of these altars makes them harder for us to interpret, especially if I am right that they primarily reflected local conditions of which we know little or nothing. But it does not make them artistic failures, and it does not mean that they should be written off. They often reuse highly specific Augustan motifs in ways which to us look like a trickle-down phenomenon, complete with the attendant generalisation and loss of meaning.[60] But this is partly because we do not know enough about the new contexts these motifs acquired as they were reused. If we see centrally produced, 'official' imagery as ideologically potent and tell the story of its diffusion as a downwards process, it becomes easy to assume that motifs inevitably lose power over time. At some point, on this reading, 'fashion' takes over from messages of loyalty, and new users adopt the motifs as empty forms. But the images in this chapter, I propose, do not necessarily derive their power from a central prototype or original. They gain new meanings and new power in each moment of transmission. The remediation and recombination of existing motifs could potentially form extremely sophisticated ideological messages for their local viewers.

More pointedly, it is not necessarily the case that these altars followed where Augustus led. Much of their imagery was drawn from a common visual world that predated Augustus, while other elements, from content to composition, were entirely new. These altars' motifs were available to be taken up by other artists and other media. The laurels which become a standard part of Pompeian *lararia* are potential examples, as is the lamp which links Victory and the Lares. It is not necessary to posit a direct line of inspiration from these specific altars; rather, the comparison should prompt us to consider the altars in the category of sources, as well as recipients, of imagery. John Clarke has written that 'if the

---

[59] This example is also discussed by Hölscher, 1967: 109–10 and 1994: 164, who thinks the legionary standard must mark this as an Augustan Victory, and thus the shield as the *clipeus virtutis*; nevertheless, he tracks this example of the Victory-with-shield motif directly from the Lares altars of the *vici* to household *lararia* to the lamp.

[60] Lamp, 2013: 113–23 assumes that the 'official' Augustan ideological meanings in symbols like the oak wreath were carried over wholesale, and that the patrons who chose it were expressing support for Augustus' claim to be a saviour of the *res publica*.

altar of the magistri of the Vicus Aesculeti, despite its modest execution, seemed familiar to the ancient viewer, it is because it imitated the elite monuments of the state religion'.[61] His assessment makes sense for the modern viewer. For the inhabitants of the *vicus*, however, it was partly through these altars that images of laurels and Lares, sacrificial motifs, and oak crowns became recognisable and legible as symbols of imperial power.

Bibliography

Alföldi, A. 1973. *Die zwei Lorbeerbäume des Augustus* (Bonn: R. Habelt).

Beard, M., J. North, and S. Price 1998. *Religions of Rome* (Cambridge: Cambridge University Press).

Bergmann, B. 2010. *Der Kranz des Kaisers: Genese und Bedeutung einer römischen Insignie* (Berlin; New York: De Gruyter).

Bianchi Bandinelli, R. 1969. *Roma: L'arte nel centro di potere, dalle origini al II secolo d.C.* (Milan: Rizzoli).

Bodnar, J. 1992. *Remaking America: Public Memory, Commemoration and Patriotism in the Twentieth Century* (Princeton: Princeton University Press).

Buxton, B. A. 2014. 'A new reading of the Belvedere Altar', *AJA* 118: 91–111.

Candida, B. 1979. *Altari e cippi nel Museo Nazionale Romano* (Rome: Bretschneider).

Clarke, J. R. 2003. *Art in the Lives of Ordinary Romans: Visual Representation and Non-Elite Viewers in Italy, 100 B.C.–A.D. 315* (Berkeley: University of California Press).

D'Ambra, E. and G. Métraux 2006. *The Art of Citizens, Soldiers, and Freedmen in the Roman World* (Oxford: British Archaeological Reports).

Dräger, O. 1994. *Religionem significare: Studien zu reich verzierten römischen Altären und Basen aus Marmor* (Mainz: Philipp von Zabern).

Fless, F., S. Langer, P. Liverani, and M. Pfanner 2018. *Vatikanische Museen: Museo Gregoriano Profano ex Lateranense. Katalog der Skulpturen IV: Historische Reliefs*. Monumenta Artis Romanae 40 (Wiesbaden: Reichert Verlag).

Flower, H. I. 2017. *The Dancing Lares and the Serpent in the Garden: Religion at the Roman Street Corner* (Princeton: Princeton University Press).

Flower, H. I. and M. J. Diluzio 2019. 'The women and the Lares: a reconsideration of an Augustan altar from the Capitoline in Rome', *AJA* 123: 213–36.

Fraschetti, A. 1990. *Roma e il principe* (Rome; Bari: Laterza).

Fröhlich, T. 1991. *Lararien und Fassadenbilder in den Vesuvstädten* (Mainz: Philipp von Zabern).

Galinsky, K. 1996. *Augustan Culture: An Interpretative Introduction* (Princeton: Princeton University Press).

---

[61] Clarke, 2003: 85.

Gordon, R. 1990. 'The veil of power: emperors, sacrificers and benefactors', in Beard, M. and J. North (eds.), *Pagan Priests: Religion and Power in the Ancient World* (Ithaca: Cornell University Press), 199–231.

Gradel, I. 2002. *Emperor Worship and Roman Religion* (Oxford: Clarendon Press).

Gregori, G. L. 2009. 'Il culto delle divinità Auguste in Italia: un'indagine preliminare', in Bodel, J. and M. Kajava (eds.), *Dediche sacre nel mondo greco-romano: Diffusione, funzioni, tipologie / Religious Dedications in the Greco-Roman World: Distribution, Typology, Use* (Rome: Institutum Romanum Finlandiae), 307–30.

Hackworth Petersen, L. 2015. 'Non-elite patronage', in Friedland, E., M. G. Sobocinski and E. K. Gazda (eds.), *The Oxford Handbook of Roman Sculpture* (New York: Oxford University Press), 436–50.

Hano, M. 1986. 'À l'origine du culte impérial: les autels des Lares Augusti. Recherches sur les thèmes iconographiques et leur signification', in *ANRW*, II.16.3: 2333–81.

Holliday, P. J. 2015. 'Roman art and the state', in Borg, B. E. (ed.), *A Companion to Roman Art* (Chichester: Wiley-Blackwell), 195–213.

Hölscher, T. 1967. *Victoria Romana* (Mainz: Philipp von Zabern).

1984. 'Beobachtungen zu römischen historischen Denkmälern II', *AA*: 283–94.

1988. 'Historische Reliefs', in *Kaiser Augustus und die verlorene Republik: eine Ausstellung im Martin-Gropius-Bau, Berlin, 7. Juni–14. August 1988* (Mainz: Philipp von Zabern), 351–400.

1994. *Monumenti statali e pubblico* (Rome: 'L'Erma' di Bretschneider).

Koortbojian, M. 2013. *The Divinization of Caesar and Augustus: Precedents, Consequences, Implications* (Cambridge: Cambridge University Press).

Laird, M. 2015. *Civic Monuments and the Augustales in Roman Italy* (New York: Cambridge University Press).

Lamp, K. S. 2013. *A City of Marble: The Rhetoric of Augustan Rome* (Columbia: University of South Carolina Press).

Lott, J. B. 2004. *The Neighborhoods of Augustan Rome* (Cambridge: Cambridge University Press).

Marcattili, F. 2015. 'L'altare del *vicus Sandaliarius* agli Uffizi', *BABesch* 90: 127–37.

Mayer, E. 2010. 'Propaganda, staged applause, or local politics? Public monuments from Augustus to Septimius Severus', in Ewald, B. and C. Norena (eds.), *The Emperor and Rome* (New Haven: Yale University Press), 119–27.

Nock, A. D. 1972. 'Seviri and Augustales', in Steward, Z. (ed.), *A. D. Nock: Essays on Religion and the Ancient World* (Cambridge, MA: Harvard University Press), 348–56.

Panciera, S. 1987. 'Ancora tra epigrafia e topografia', in *L'Urbs: Espace urbain et histoire* (Rome: École française de Rome), 61–86.

Pisani Sartorio, G. 1993. '*Compitum vici Aesc(u)leti*', in *LTUR* 1: 316.

Pollini, J. 2012. *From Republic to Empire: Rhetoric, Religion, and Power in the Visual Culture of Ancient Rome* (Norman: University of Oklahoma Press).

Rose, C. B. 1997. *Dynastic Commemoration and Imperial Portraiture in the Julio-Claudian Period* (Cambridge: Cambridge University Press).

Rowe, G. 2002. *Princes and Political Cultures: The New Tiberian Senatorial Decrees* (Ann Arbor: University of Michigan Press).

Ryberg, I. S. 1955. *Rites of the State Religion in Roman Art*. Memoirs of the American Academy in Rome 22 (Rome: American Academy in Rome).

Scheid, J. 2001. 'Honorer le prince et vénérer les dieux: culte public, cultes des quartiers et culte impérial dans la Rome augustéenne', in Belayche, N. (ed.), *Rome, les Césars et la Ville aux deux premiers siècles de notre ère* (Rennes: Presses universitaires de Rennes), 85–105.

Tarpin, M. 2002. *Vici et pagi dans l'Occident romain* (Rome: École française de Rome).

Taylor, L. R. 1921. 'The Altar of Manlius in the Lateran', *AJA* 25: 387–95.

1931. *The Divinity of the Roman Emperor* (Middletown: American Philological Association).

Torelli, M. 1982. *Typology and Structure of Roman Historical Reliefs* (Ann Arbor: University of Michigan Press).

Wallace-Hadrill, A. 2008. *Rome's Cultural Revolution* (Cambridge: Cambridge University Press).

Zanker, P. 1969. 'Der Larenaltar im Belvedere des Vatikans', *MDAI(R)* 76: 205–18.

1970–1. 'Über die Werkstätten augusteischer Larenaltäre und damit zusammenhängende Probleme der Interpretation', *BCAR* 82: 147–55.

1988a. 'Bilderzwang: Augustan political symbolism in the private sphere', in Huskinson, J., M. Beard, and J. Reynolds (eds.), *Image and Mystery in the Roman World: Papers Given in Memory of Jocelyn Toynbee* (Gloucester: Sutton), 1–13.

1988b. *The Power of Images in the Age of Augustus* (Ann Arbor: University of Michigan Press).

2002. *Un'arte per l'impero: Funzione e intenzione delle immagini nel mondo romano* (Milan: Electa).

3 | Modelling the Emperor

Representations of Power, Empire, and Dynasty among Eastern
Client Kings

JULIA WILKER

The creation, development, dissemination, and establishment of the image
of the *imperium Romanum*, the *princeps*, and his power was an intricate
process that happened simultaneously across the empire. It drew on different traditions and needed to be adjusted depending on local circumstances, expectations, and modes of interpretation. This chapter deals with
a small yet crucial group that wielded significant influence during the early
principate until roughly the end of the first century CE but has often been
overlooked in modern scholarship: the eastern client kings.[1] From the time
of Augustus on, client kingdoms were perceived not only as areas under
Roman control but as integral parts of the *imperium Romanum*, even
though they were not under direct Roman provincial administration.[2]
For the contexts explored in this volume, three aspects of the client kings'
role in shaping the emperor's image are of importance: first, client kings by
definition depended on good relations with the emperor and constantly
had to confirm their loyalty in order to keep their position and status.[3]
Most dependent dynasties maintained and cultivated close relationships
with the *princeps* and his family. These political and often also personal
friendships were in many cases already established during their youth, as it
was customary for the male offspring of client rulers to be raised in Rome
together with the sons of the Julio-Claudian family and the highest circles
of the imperial elite.[4] This personal closeness to the centre of the empire
helped to bridge the large geographical distance, as the vast majority of
client kingdoms were situated on the fringes of the empire. Secondly,

---

[1] Although the institution of client kingship did, of course, also exist in the north and the west of
the Roman Empire, the political and cultural traditions and circumstances differed significantly
from those in the east. This chapter will thus only include examples from the kingdoms in the
east, the Bosporan–Thracian region, and Mauretania that shared many of the features
commonly associated with the eastern realms.

[2] Most prominently expressed in Suet. *Aug.* 48; see also Strabo 17.3.24–5; Tac. *Ann.* 4.5.

[3] As became most obvious at the beginning of Octavian's reign when the new ruler had to
determine whether to keep or depose dynasts in the east, most of whom had sided with Antony
in the civil war; cf. Bowersock, 1965: 42–61.

[4] Cf. Braund, 1984: 9–21; Wilker, 2008: esp. 166–8, 176–81.

although they were appointed (and deposed) by the Roman emperor, client kings also had to establish, maintain, and communicate a legitimacy of their own, expressed through a distinctively royal representation that was commonly based on local and dynastic traditions. These local traditions differed significantly among the various realms. Yet client rulers faced similar challenges: while the intricate political status required them to carefully navigate the political interests of the empire and their own, it was an equally delicate task to find a mode of representation that reflected both authorities appropriately and without either impeding the other. Finally, although their respective realms were spread across the east of the empire and the Mediterranean, the dependent dynasties formed a distinctive social group. Most dynasties in the east were connected with each other through kinship, marital relations, and personal friendship, forming a network that Augustus himself explicitly supported and sought to foster.[5] These peer networks turned the dependent dynasties into a group of considerable political influence, yet the client rulers also competed among each other for status and reputation.

The evidence discussed in this chapter shows that client kings played a significant, even leading role in disseminating the images associated with the *princeps* and the *imperium Romanum* at the outskirts of the empire.[6] Yet their specific political and cultural circumstances also led them to develop equally specific modes of representation. A closer look at the self-presentation of Roman client kings reveals that from the beginning of the reign of Augustus on, dependent rulers adopted and adapted these examples for their own purposes, turning the imperial model into a shared language of power. Whereas these processes were similar to the ways other social groups appealed to imperial imagery in local contexts,[7] the client kings faced a special challenge: to pay homage to the emperor as the superior authority while at the same time maintaining their own royal prestige and local legitimacy, a phenomenon that Fergus Millar has aptly called a two-level sovereignty.[8]

This chapter examines in particular how the emperor was presented in client kingdoms and then, in turn, how this model informed and

[5] Cf. Suet. *Aug.* 48.
[6] Client kings also helped to spread the image of the emperor, and especially the imperial cult, outside their kingdoms, most prominently in the joint undertaking of several dynasts to finish the building of the Olympieion in Athens and dedicate it to Augustus, Suet. *Aug.* 60. However, this chapter focuses on representations in their own realms. For the role of client kings in shaping the emperor's image in the rest of the *imperium Romanum*, see Wilker, 2015.
[7] Cf., for instance, the chapters by Hellström, Russell, and Tran in this volume.
[8] Millar, 1996.

influenced the self-representation of dependent rulers. The aim is not to present a single model but to illustrate some general ideas concerning the mutual influence of visual representation and languages of power. Client kingdoms were vastly heterogeneous in character, and this heterogeneity was also reflected in the representation their rulers employed. There is no indication that the imperial centre ever directly intervened or issued orders concerning how the empire and/or the emperor should be represented, honoured, or revered in any of the eastern realms. Instead, these forms of representation were up to the discretion of the respective rulers and informed by local dynastic traditions as well as, we may assume, the personal preferences of each dynast. That many of them nevertheless adopted similar means and modes of representing the emperor and participated in a shared idiom of power makes the topic an even more intriguing subject of research.

The Image of the Emperor in the Client Kingdoms

Presence of the Emperor in Client Kingdoms: Coinage

The majority of dependent rulers actively promoted the emperor's image and their own loyalty to the empire in a way that left no doubt about their position in the new Roman world. This becomes evident in the coinage minted by client kings. The first to depict Octavian/Augustus on his coins was Zenodorus, ruler of Iturean Chalcis, but his peers followed suit very quickly after 27 BCE.[9] From the beginning of Augustus' rule on, the portrait of the present emperor became a common feature on the coinage of most client kings in the east and North Africa. These representations emulated those on imperial and provincial types and were thus closely in line with the presentation of the emperor in areas under direct Roman administration. In some instances, such emulation of Roman imperial or provincial types can also be seen on the reverses. For instance, coins of Rhoemetalces I of Thrace and Juba II of Mauretania showed the capricorn, imitating Augustan coins and alluding to the emperor's zodiacal sign (Fig. 3.1).[10] Agrippa II, the last king of the Herodian dynasty, followed the Roman models so closely that not a single coin is known to have featured his own portrait; instead, they usually

---

[9] *RPC* I.584. Kropp, 2013a: 5, 79; Wright, 2013: 68.

[10] Rhoemetalces I: *RPC* I.1704, 1705, 1707. Juba II: Alexandropoulos, 2000, Revers S; Coltelloni-Trannoy, 1997: 166–7. Dahmen, 2010: 101; Suspène, 2015: 197. The capricorn is also shown after the death of Augustus on some coins of Antiochus IV of Commagene, who ruled from 38 to 72 CE (*RPC* I.3855, 3861, 3862, 3866).

Figure 3.1 Silver coin of Juba II. British Museum 1844,0425.2332 (Alexandropoulos, 2000: 185). Obverse: Diademed head of Juba, right; border of dots. Inscription: REX IVBA. Reverse: Capricorn, right; between legs, a globe; to left, a cornucopia; below, a rudder; border of dots. Inscription: RXXXXV. Photographs © The Trustees of the British Museum.

show the portrait of the present emperor and most of them also emulate Roman designs on the reverse.[11] In cases like these, only the inscription, or even only the monogram of the respective client king, indicated that the coin was not, in fact, the product of a mint under direct Roman control.

The large variety of choices in motifs and styles that can be found in client king coinage demonstrates that these images and references to the *princeps*, the imperial family, and the empire at large were deliberate, and the respective iconography was consciously chosen and adapted to the preference of each ruler and the specific circumstances of his kingdom. All these types firmly communicated the superiority of the *imperium* and its emperor. Yet there is no reason to assume that the kings were ordered, compelled, or even formally encouraged to follow the Roman numismatic lead.[12] The vast majority of client rulers issued primarily bronze coinage meant for local markets and targeting the immediate subjects of the respective dynast. One may argue that the dependent status of the rulers was well known to all of their subjects anyway,[13] so ignoring and hiding the hierarchic relationship was not an option. However, the dynamics at play appear to be more intricate: in fact, they worked to the advantage of the client kings as well.

[11] *RPC* II.2242–99.

[12] Nor should we assume that the Roman emperors cared significantly about coinage used almost exclusively in client kingdoms; *contra*, for instance, Meshorer, 2001: 63.

[13] The famous story in the Gospels culminating in the logion τὰ Καίσαρος ἀπόδοτε Καίσαρι καὶ τὰ τοῦ θεοῦ τῷ θεῷ (Mark 12:13–17, quote 12:17, cf. Matthew 22:15–22; Luke 20:20–6) refers to provincial coinage, but its reading of a coin's imagery can be also applied to a client king coin featuring the emperor's effigy.

The prominence given to Rome in general and the Roman emperor in particular was perceived as a feature enhancing the client king rather than undermining him. This dynamic highlights two interconnected phenomena: by putting the emperor's portrait on their coins, client kings expressed their loyalty while also capitalising on the *princeps'* authority to support and enhance their own status. This hierarchy was openly expressed through the emperor's portrait and other symbols connected to the empire, yet it required that the local subjects immediately distinguished between the local king and the emperor and did not interpret the two levels as rivals, or understand the superiority of the emperor as undercutting the local king's status. Imagery already found on imperial and provincial coinage thus acquired an additional meaning in the context of client kingdoms.

Coins of client kings were primarily minted for the local market and, therefore, a local audience. However, the almost simultaneous adoption of imperial types and symbols and the similarities in the coinage of several client kings indicate that these issues were also recognised outside of the respective realms. This should not lead us to assume a centralised policy or imperial demand; instead, it demonstrates a process of mutual influence and peer competition among the various client kings. The more the emperor's portrait was featured on client rulers' coins, the more it was considered expected, if not normative. The coins of client kings continued to be an important medium, even if limited in terms of geographical range and prominence, for client kings to spread their own rendition of the emperor's image. Yet similar dynamics can be shown in two other related areas of activity that demonstrate the special relationship between dependent rulers and the *princeps* in more monumental ways.

Putting the Emperor on the Map: City Foundations

More monumental, indeed, were the numerous cities founded or re-founded in client kingdoms that bore the name of the emperor or other members of his family. This became such a common pattern already during the time of Augustus that Suetonius states that 'his [Augustus'] friends and allies among the kings each in his own realm founded a city called Caesarea'.[14] Suetonius exaggerates, but the general observation is correct: the number of newly founded cities or settlements renamed as Caesarea, Sebaste, Juliopolis, Autocratoris, etc. in the eastern client kingdoms in only the first decades of

---

[14] *Reges amici atque socii et singuli in suo quisque regno Caesareas urbes condiderunt*, Suet. *Aug.* 60.1.

Roman imperial rule is stunning. Beyond the person of the emperor, his relatives and successors were given the same honours, so that cities named Tiberias, Livias, Julias, Agrippeia/Agrippion, Germanicopolis, Claudiopolis, Neronias, or Neroneia ensured the strong ideological presence of the imperial family in the eastern realms.[15] Cities named in honour of the emperor and his relatives were not a feature limited to client kingdoms; yet, again, the specific political circumstances added a new layer to what otherwise was a rather simple gesture of allegiance.

The foundation of cities was one of the outstanding features of the Hellenistic royal tradition, and the client kings kept this tradition alive.[16] However, naming significant buildings or cities not only after themselves or members of their family – a tradition that was continued[17] – but also, and even more often, after the emperor or members of his family put the new political realities literally on the map of the Roman Near East. Furthermore, most of these new cities reaffirmed the Roman character implied by their name in their general layout. Juba II thus not only renamed Iol as Caesarea but also carried out an extensive building programme that gave the city a distinctively Roman identity.[18] One of the most impressive examples of such city foundations, and the best attested one, is Caesarea Maritima in Judaea, founded by Herod the Great at the site of the Hellenistic city Straton's Tower. The lengthy description of the city's layout and character that Flavius Josephus gives in the *Bellum Judaicum* and the *Antiquitates Judaicae*, together with extensive archaeological excavations, prove that the city was appropriately named after the emperor.[19] With its rectangular street grid, its public buildings, temples, and venues for mass entertainment (including a Roman-style theatre), Caesarea was firmly Roman in character. Caesarea Maritima was the largest city in Judaea, but it gained even

---

[15] For an extensive (although far from complete) list of examples see Braund, 1984: 107–9.

[16] Kropp (2009: 104) rightly points out that Josephus' description of Herod's motivation for founding Sebaste closely emulates Hellenistic models: τὸ δ' εὐπρεπὲς ὡς ἂν ἐκ τοῦ φιλοκαλεῖν καὶ μνημεῖα φιλανθρωπίας ἀπολιπεῖν ἐν ὑστέρῳ (Joseph. *AJ* 15.298). Braund (1984: 109) firmly ascribes this phenomenon to the Hellenistic tradition.

[17] For instance, Herod named a fortress after his mother Cypros (Joseph. *BJ* 1.417; *AJ* 16.143), one of his main palaces outside of Jerusalem Herodeion (Joseph. *BJ* 1.419–21; *AJ* 15.323–5), the cities Antipatris and Phasaelis after his father and brother (Joseph. *BJ* 1.417–18; *AJ* 16.142–5), and three towers in Jerusalem after his wife (Mariamme), brother (Phasael), and friend (Hippicus) (Joseph. *BJ* 5.161–72 with the most detailed description); his son and successor Archelaus founded the city Archelaïs (Joseph. *AJ* 17.341); Archelaus of Cappadocia founded a city of the same name in his own realm (Plin. *HN* 6.8).

[18] Strabo 17.3.12. Coltelloni-Trannoy, 1997; Roller, 2003: 119–31.

[19] Joseph. *BJ* 1.408–15; *AJ* 15.331–41.

more importance through its seaport. Lacking a natural harbour, Judaea was in desperate need of a way to connect the kingdom more firmly and conveniently with the rest of the Mediterranean, and the foundation of a new, strategically located port city fulfilled a pragmatic, political need. However, the port also demonstrated that Herod had much more in mind. The king did not settle for less than the largest, most elaborate, and most technically challenging harbour facilities of his time. The creation of an enormous artificial outer mole using hydraulic concrete, despite the local sandy ground and a strong current, was a project unprecedented in scope and difficulty, and it has been rightly assumed that Herod hired Roman specialists to carry out his plans.[20]

The exceptionality of this project was further emphasised by the fact that the harbour itself was given the name Sebastos. The Greek parallel with Caesarea was fitting, but it also made clear that the harbour as such was too important and too impressive to be just a part of the city.[21] For visitors coming from the sea, there was no doubt to whom this city (and, consequently, the kingdom) belonged. Josephus describes how ships entering the outer harbour had to sail through a passage between two sets of statues, three on each side, most probably depicting Augustus and Livia, accompanied by Tiberius and the elder Drusus respectively.[22] Another structure on the outer mole, which may have served as a lighthouse, was named the Druseion, presumably in honour of Drusus after his death in 9 BCE.[23] The first building in sight of visitors coming from the sea would then have been the Temple to Augustus and Roma, built on an elevated platform and overlooking the harbour.[24] That this effect was deliberate is indicated by the fact that the temple diverted from the general orientation of the street grid in order to face the entry from the sea.[25]

The scale of Herod's building programme, in Caesarea and elsewhere, exceeded those of his peers, but it offers some general insights into the phenomenon. The foundation of cities was a central feature of Hellenistic kingship, yet naming the city after a superior ruler at first glance appears counter-intuitive, even contradicting the main purpose. More than just

[20] The archaeological and scientific analysis of the harbour's remains has shown that pozzolana from the Bay of Naples and timber from Seleucia Pieria together with local materials were used for the breakwaters. Cf. Hohlfelder, 2000; Hohlfelder, Brandon, and Oleson, 2007; Votruba, 2007; Burrell, 2009.

[21] Cf. the coins struck by Herod's grandson Agrippa I with the inscription ΚΑΙΣΑΡΙΑ Η ΠΡΟΣ ΤΩ ΣΕΒΑΣΤΩ ΛΙΜΕΝΙ, RPC I.4984–5. Hohlfelder, 2003: 22–4; Holum, 2004: 190.

[22] Joseph. BJ 1.413. Cf. Hohlfelder, 2003: 29.   [23] Joseph. BJ 1.412; AJ 15.336. Cf. Vann, 1991.

[24] Joseph. BJ 1.414; AJ 15.339. Cf. Holum, 2015: 51*, 60*.   [25] Kropp, 2009: 109; Holum, 2015.

promoting the emperor, it literally designated the country as ultimately his and sent a strong message to the client ruler's subjects, a message that was comparable with that of the coins discussed above, although on a much larger scale, more permanent, more monumental, and requiring more resources. Yet the foundation of cities honouring the emperor and/ or his dynasty also emphasised another aspect that was vital to the legitimacy of every client king. Whereas none of the rulers were ordered to found a city named Caesarea, they presumably needed the emperor's approval to do so.[26] The city thus served as testimony to a king's loyalty, but at the same time it also monumentalised his close relationship with the emperor, who granted the local ruler the right to use his name. These city foundations thus fulfilled a multidimensional purpose: to honour the emperor and give testimony to the benevolence and power of their founder, the client king. Again, the inherent hierarchy was neither meant nor, apparently, understood as diminishing the client king's status. Connecting these new urban centres to the designating ruler and to the emperor, and through him to the empire at large, employed a familiar symbolic language while boasting a powerful and empowering relation-ship with a ranking authority. The vast display of the wealth and resources of the ruler were thus amplified.[27] In the eyes of the client kings them-selves and their local subjects, the two levels of power did not compete but rather embellished each other.

In contrast to the coinage that circulated predominantly locally, grand projects such as city foundations also addressed a larger audience outside of the respective realm. For the imperial *oikoumene*, the new cities offered monumental proof that they were integral parts of the new, wider, and up-to-date Roman world, and attaching the emperor's name to them emphasised this integration even further. Whereas the local coinage presumably did not catch most emperors' interest, city foundations expressed one's loyalty in a more spectacular way. In turn, we may assume that, at least for a major project like Herod's Caesarea, the close connec-tion with the emperor ensured that the enterprise would not be inter-preted in the wrong way. Caesarea Maritima not only changed Judaea but also the eastern Mediterranean at large by providing a major new centre for trade, traffic, and potentially even military purposes. With his new city, Herod claimed to be part of the new world order Augustus was about to create. The king was particularly close with the emperor and Agrippa, but such a claim could nevertheless be easily interpreted as preposterous.

---

[26] Cf. Hohlfelder, 2003: 21.   [27] Cf. the interpretation of Gruen, 2009: 18.

Making such a claim under the name of Augustus lent it imperial legitimacy and made royal ostentation compatible with imperial interests.[28]

The generalising statement by Suetonius quoted above implies that all client rulers founded cities bearing the emperor's name and highlights the striking simultaneity of these processes. Whereas it is impossible to reconstruct a relative (not to mention an absolute) chronology of the many Caesareae founded under Augustus alone, the larger imperial visibility of such city foundations may explain the rapid pace at which they spread across the client kingdoms. Herod's political and financial commitment may have been singular, but once city foundations had become a common, even customary act among dependent rulers, every dynast presumably thought twice as to whether he wanted to remain the only one among his peers who did not devote a city to the honour of the emperor. The process was then further accelerated as client rulers found themselves in competition with their peers for who founded the most impressive city, built the biggest harbour, or paid the greatest honour to the emperor and his family. The devotion shown to the *princeps* elevated the peer competition even further and turned every dedication into an expression of 'agonistic loyalism'[29] in the contest for the recognition and benevolence of the emperor.

As in the case of the emperor's portrait on coins, the city foundations named after the emperor required from any audience an immediate distinction between the two levels of authority and their respective mode of representation. The potential for confusion became evident in the 60s of the first century CE, when civic unrest broke out in Caesarea Maritima, now the provincial capital of Judaea. In this conflict between Greeks and Jews, both factions appealed to the governor by referring to the beginnings of Caesarea. Whereas the Greeks explicitly referred to the Roman features of the city (including its temples and hence also the imperial cult) to underline its pagan character, the Jews insisted that it had, after all, been founded by a Jewish king.[30] In most cases, however, the concept of dual representation proved successful. How this clear distinction was achieved and communicated can be seen in another main feature that ensured the continuous presence of the emperor in client kingdoms: the imperial cult.

---

[28] Agrippa visited Herod's kingdom in 15 BCE and arrived in Judaea, of course, via the harbour Sebastos and Caesarea Maritima, Joseph. *BJ* 1.396–7; *AJ* 15.217. For the political implications and Herod's purpose in founding Caesarea and, in particular, the major labour involved, see Hohlfelder, 2000: esp. 243; Hohlfelder, 2003: esp. 19–30; Votruba, 2007.

[29] This apt term was coined by Greg Rowe at one of the workshop meetings at Durham.

[30] Joseph. *BJ* 2.266; cf. *AJ* 20.173.

Elevation and Distance: The Imperial Cult

As mentioned above, a temple dedicated to Roma and Augustus towered over the harbour of Herod's Caesarea Maritima.[31] Although only the foundations and a few additional remains are left, excavations have confirmed Josephus' general description as well as the general architectural design. The institution of a festival, following imperial fashion, was presumably also tied to the imperial cult.[32] Caesarea was not the only location in which Herod established the imperial cult. Fittingly, another temple dedicated to the emperor was the central sanctuary in the new city of Sebaste,[33] and Paneas to the north of the Sea of Galilee also housed a shrine dedicated to Augustus.[34] The establishment of an imperial cult was, of course, impossible in those parts of Herod's kingdom where the population was predominantly Jewish; yet, daily offerings for the well-being of the emperor in the Jewish Temple in Jerusalem nonetheless communicated and emphasised the relationships between the kingdom, the empire, and the emperor in an appropriate and, for most people, acceptable way.[35]

Again, Herod stands out because his reign is so well documented, but the scarcer evidence for other client kings indicates that they followed the same approach. For Juba II, for instance, numismatic evidence suggests that the building programme for Iol–Caesarea also included a temple for the imperial cult. Gold coins show on the reverse a temple building with four columns at the front and the inscription AVGVSTI. Another issue from the same year (5/6 CE) depicts an altar, adorned with garlands and standing between two laurel trees. For a well-informed audience, the laurel trees and oak garland already indicated a connection to Augustus, yet here again, the message is left beyond doubt by the inscription LVCVS AVGVSTI (Fig. 3.2).[36] The examples of Judaea and Mauretania indicate a trend that is evidenced in other client kingdoms as well. The Bosporan kings, for example, served as chief priests of the local imperial cult, apparently *qua officio*, since Cotys I is referred to in an inscription as ἀρχιερεὺς τῶν Σεβαστῶν διὰ βίου.[37]

---

[31] Joseph. *BJ* 1.414; *AJ* 15.339. For the temple see esp. Holum, 2004: esp. 186–91; Holum, 2015.

[32] Joseph. *BJ* 1.414; *AJ* 16.136–41; cf. *AJ* 19.343.

[33] Roller, 1998: 209–12; Lichtenberger, 1999: 84–8; Netzer, 2006: 85–92; Kropp, 2009: 104–9.

[34] Joseph. *BJ* 1.404; *AJ* 15.363–4. Lichtenberger, 1999: 150–3; Netzer, 2006: 218–322; Kropp, 2009: 109–10.

[35] Philo, *Leg.* 157, 317; Joseph. *BJ* 2.197, 409, 415–16; *Ap.* 2.77.

[36] *CNNM* 144–65 = Alexandropoulos, 2000, reverse F1-F4, G1. Fishwick, 1985; Coltelloni-Trannoy, 1997: 187–94; Rives, 2001: 428; Suspène, 2015: 195.

[37] *CIRB* 41 (Cotys I); *CIRB* 42, 1047, 1118 (Rhescuporis II); *CIRB* 44, 1045, 1122 (Sauromates I). Nawotka, 1989: 335–6; Braund, 1997: 125.

Figure 3.2 Silver coin of Juba II. British Museum 1938,0510.187 (Alexandropoulos, 2000: 83). Obverse: Diademed head of Juba II, right; solid border. Inscription: REX IVBA. Reverse: Altar decorated with garlands and flanked by two laurels; beneath, a star; solid border. Inscription: LVCVS AVGVSTI. Photographs © The Trustees of the British Museum.

The introduction of the imperial cult in the eastern client kingdoms throws the dynamics between reverence paid to the emperor and the self-presentation of client rulers into sharper relief. Whereas the worship of Augustus started in the province of Asia and is most widely attested there,[38] it spread less rapidly in Syria and the neighbouring regions under direct Roman rule.[39] In fact, client kings appear as the main instigators of the imperial cult in the Near East.[40] These local processes were, of course, connected with each other, but there are major structural differences between the cult as established in provinces under direct Roman rule and those in the realms of client kingdoms. The emergence of the imperial cult in the east was facilitated by the long-standing traditions of ruler cult. Yet, in client kingdoms, the cult of Augustus (and his successors) did not fill a void left by the demise of Hellenistic empires.[41] Instead, a new authority was added that was superior to the local ruler.

---

[38] Cf., for instance, Cass. Dio 51.20.6–9.   [39] Butcher, 2003: 288–9; Kropp, 2009: 101.

[40] Cf. Bru, 2011: 287–93.

[41] This is not meant to imply that the imperial cult in the eastern provinces simply took the place and form of the previous ruler cults (as convincingly shown by Price, 1984: 23–47, 53–77; for the transitional process in cult organisation and priesthood cf. Frija, 2010). Nevertheless, the dynamics of imperial cult in the client kingdoms were strikingly different from those in Asia and other provinces. For the longevity of Hellenistic ruler cults beyond the demise of the respective dynasties and the provincialisation of their realms see Chankowski, 2010; Noreña, 2016. Noreña (esp. 96–7) explicitly compares the ongoing cults dedicated to Hellenistic kings within Roman provinces with the phenomenon of 'tiered monarchies' that is the focus of this chapter. The comparison is convincing, yet the widespread absence of ruler cults in client

The same superiority was already expressed by featuring the emperor's portrait on coins and naming cities after him, but the imperial cult gave this hierarchy an even more fundamental character. The fact that not the local king but the emperor received cultic reverence could be interpreted as diminishing the former's position. However, it appears once again that the imperial cult instead served to strengthen and support the position of client kings. It may even have eased the tension caused by the 'two-level sovereignty'. Cult devoted to the emperor made the hierarchy between him and the local king even more obvious, and it also clearly established that this distinction was not negotiable; in fact, the imperial cult clarified that the emperor and the respective local king were not to compare, let alone to compete. The emperor's elevation thus did not diminish the status of the local king but reaffirmed him as being appointed, sanctioned, and supported by a higher power. The two levels of authority were thereby set even further apart and a strict distinction was drawn that in the end fostered both forms of legitimacy, that of the emperor and that of the local king. The leading role that client kings assumed in the establishment and distribution of the imperial cult in the Near East thus did not contradict their royal status; it was a logical consequence of their own position between empire and kingship.

For client kings, the Roman Empire – and the goodwill of the present emperor – was their *raison d'être*, and the rapid and wide adoption of imperial models of representation shows that this fact could be neither hidden nor ignored. Yet the greater the empire and the more powerful and elevated the emperor appeared to be, the easier it was to integrate Rome and its *princeps* into royal self-presentation without harming the kings themselves. Propagating the emperor's power thus worked to the advantage of the emperor and client rulers alike. In turn, kings served as important catalysts in the process of establishing and disseminating the representation and reverence of the *princeps* across the east.

The Self-Presentation of Client Kings in their Own Realms

The presentation of the emperor and Roman power posed a challenge to client rulers, yet they also faced similar problems in their own royal representation. Client kings had to walk a fine line when communicating and emphasising their own, local legitimacy without undermining the

kingdoms and the prominence of the imperial cult instead, as discussed here, highlights the main political differences between provinces and dependent kingdoms.

authority of the emperor or evoking the notion that they might pose a potential threat to Roman rule. As in the cases discussed above, different client kings dealt with these challenges in different ways. Yet, again, the following examples indicate the value of this diverse set of evidence for the image and perception of the emperor at the fringes of the empire.

Principes et reges: *Client Kings in Portrait*

The influence that the image of the emperor had on the self-representation of client kings becomes immediately apparent in their own portraits, for which many of the dynasts quickly adopted and followed the imperial model. By the late Republican period, several Roman client kings had already begun to 'Romanise' their portraits. Prior to the Augustan era, this meant in particular departing from standard Hellenistic forms of royal representation and adopting the so-called veristic style instead. Most prominent in this context is the coinage of Ariobarzanes of Cappadocia and Tarcondimotus of Cilicia, whose portraits with their emphasis on age and individual facial features stood in sharp contrast to what until then had been the norm among Hellenistic rulers.[42]

However, the main stylistic turn in royal portraiture occurred under Augustus, when dependent rulers began to closely emulate the emperor's portrait in their own representation (cf. Fig. 3.1). For most client kings, statuary evidence is scarce, but portraits of the Mauretanian kings Juba II and Ptolemy show a strong resemblance to Augustus and other male members of his dynasty. The overall calm and reserved expression, the smooth, ageless faces, the characteristic Julio-Claudian hairstyle, and many more details show how strongly the representation was influenced by imperial portraits, an emulation that went far beyond simple fashion and *Zeitgeist*.[43] These portraits had the clear purpose of demonstrating the close connection of the respective king to the emperor and Rome, but they also depicted his own power. By representing themselves in the style of Augustus and his successors, local rulers integrated

[42] Cf. more extensively and with references to previous scholarship Smith, 1988b: 113; Kropp, 2013a: 51–3.

[43] For the Mauretanian kings see in particular Fittschen, 1974; Boube, 1990; Coltelloni-Trannoy, 1997: 161–5; Roller, 2003: 146–50; Landwehr, 2007 (arguing against the chronological reconstruction proposed by Fittschen); Teverson, 2015: 165–82. For a portrait from Samosata depicting, most probably, a member of the Commagenian dynasty in what appears as distinctively Augustan style see Fleischer (2008, arguing for Antiochus III) and Kropp (2013a: 85, suggesting Antiochus I instead). See also Smith, 1988a: 139–43; Smith, 1988b: esp. 495–7; Facella, 2005: esp. 101–2; Kropp, 2013a: 85–6.

Figure 3.3 Bronze coin of Rhoemetalces I. *RPC* I.1711. Obverse: Diademed head of Rhoemetalces I, head of Pythodoris, right; ΒΑΣΙΛΕΩΣ ΡΟΙΜΗΤΑΛΚΟΥ. Reverse: Bare head of Augustus, right; ΚΑΙΣΑΡΟΣ ΣΕΒΑΣΤΟΥ. Artwork: M. Hellström.

their rule into the broader imperial context and associated themselves symbolically with the emperor and his power.

Whereas such a choice is neither surprising nor exceptional, the adoption of the common Augustan *Zeitgesicht* could lead to potential complications when portraits of client kings were put side by side with a portrait of the emperor. This tension becomes obvious in several remarkable coins of the Thracian dynasty that feature the current *princeps* on the reverse and the present local king on the obverse (Fig. 3.3).[44] The two rulers are only distinguishable because of the inscription and the diadem that designates the local king. In fact, the diadem shows that the process of assimilation in image was neither complete nor a simple emulation. Almost all client kings maintained the diadem as the most distinctive symbol of their royalty. The direct juxtaposition of imperial and royal portraits presented both rulers – the emperor and the inferior king – in the same style, yet the latter was distinguished through the diadem. This difference in attribute appears as a paradox but is only an even more striking expression of the same dynamics discussed above for the honours paid to the emperor. Apparently, the separation of the local and imperial spheres was so deeply engrained that even the royal diadem was not perceived as an inversion of the hierarchy but rather as a cultural distinction. The tension could be eased by showing the king with a diadem and the emperor laureate. The

[44] Cf. Rhoemetalces I (*c.*22 BCE–12 CE): *RPC* I.1708–21; some issues (*RPC* I.1711–12) include his queen; *RPC* I.1708–10 conjoin the couple with Augustus and Livia on the obverse. Rhoemetalces II (19–36 CE): *RPC* I.1721 (with queen). Rhoemetalces III (38–*c.*46 CE): *RPC* I.1723–4.

images thus drew on the same cultural distinction yet made sure that the *princeps* was also appropriately adorned.

Such joined compositions of king and emperor never became the norm among client rulers.[45] However, the design was maintained at least among the Thracian rulers for several generations; if these types ever invited misinterpretations about the hierarchy between the two rulers depicted, such readings were kept secret enough not to invite suspicion or doubts at the imperial centre about the Thracians' loyalty. Other dynasties circumvented such a potentially troubling reading of their self-representation. Agrippa I of Judaea, for instance, clearly distinguished between the images of the imperial family and that of his own not through style but denomination: while the more valuable coins featured the emperor or one of his relatives, the king himself and his family members were depicted on lower-denomination coins.[46]

Clear distinctions like these prevented misreadings. Meanwhile, the combination of imperial modes of representation with royal regalia was apparently not perceived as undermining the emperor's authority or presenting him in an inappropriate light. Instead, the style of the portraits as such must have been recognised as distinctively imperial, as expressing a model that was deliberately and demonstratively emulated by the client king. The hierarchy was thus maintained and even underlined. Client kings hence played an important role in the process of creating, shaping, and promoting the image of the emperor. In turn, they capitalised on this new image and the visual possibilities it offered. Already in the first decades of Augustan rule, Roman imperial representation had become established and had been turned into a shared language of power. However, for this shared language to work appropriately, it had to be more than just a recognised marker of power and status. In the case of the client kings, the semantic system had to become more elaborate, including registers that were immediately identifiable as

---

[45] See, for example, coins of the Bosporan king Rhescuporis (*RPC* II.456–66) that show the king diademed and Domitian laureate. Coins of Polemo II of Pontus (38–64 CE) feature Polemo's portrait with a diadem and Claudius (*RPC* I.3813–15; *RPC* I.3820 adds the head of Nero to the obverse; *RPC* I.3827–35 has portraits of a diademed Polemo and laureate Nero; *RPC* I.3836–8 a diademed Polemo and laureate Britannicus). A coin of the tetrarch Philip featured Augustus and Philip both bareheaded, yet the distinction was made clear in the respective inscriptions, ΚΑΙΣΑΡΟC CEBACTOY and ΦΙΛΙΠΠΟΥ ΤΕΤΡΑΡΧΟΥ (*RPC* I.4938). A similar distinction was made on some Armenian coins that feature King Tigranes (III or V) adorned with diadem and tiara and a bareheaded portrait of Augustus. However, whereas Tigranes is described as ΒΑCΙΛΕΥΣ ΜΕΓΑC ΝΕΟC ΤΙΓΡΑΝΗC, Augustus' superiority is reinforced through the inscription ΚΑΙCΑΡ ΘΕΟC ΘΕΟΥ ΥΙΟC (*RPC* I.3841, cf. also *RPC* I.3843 by Artavasdes III or IV); see also Bendschus, 2018.

[46] Cf. Meshorer, 2001: 95.

different despite some visual similarities. The examples juxtaposing emperor and client king may have been rather extreme, but even in more cautious settings, the audience must have been expected to realise the hierarchy between an emperor and a king depicted in relatively similar ways.

Appropriation of Imperial Themes

The dynamics of appropriation can be further demonstrated with a few examples of dynastic representation among eastern rulers. After the death of Herod the Great in 4 BCE, Augustus divided his kingdom among three of his sons. Philip received a territory in the north of Judaea as tetrarch. In contrast to the principalities assigned to his brothers, Philip's tetrarchy had a predominantly non-Jewish population, and it is thus no surprise that Philip was the first Herodian ruler to have his own portrait as well as that of the emperor featured on his coins.[47] In establishing this new tradition, he followed Roman imperial models, as well as the example of other dynasts in the region. Philip was also the first ruler of the Herodian dynasty to honour Livia on coins, probably minted after her death in 29 CE.[48] When Philip died around 33/4 CE, his tetrarchy first came under the control of the Syrian governor; however, in 37 CE, Caligula appointed his friend and Philip's nephew, Agrippa I, as king over the former tetrarchy. The first coins that Agrippa issued as king closely followed his uncle's model, including one of the types honouring Livia. Agrippa's coin depicts a hand holding ears of grain and a vine branch on the reverse; Philip's coin features a similar hand with ears of grain.[49] Because both coins came from the same mint in Paneas/ Caesarea Philippi, the parallels were clearly deliberate. The similarities in design were also obvious on the obverse. Philip's coin had featured a bust of Livia, and Agrippa's type also showed a female portrait; yet his issue bears the inscription ΚΥΠΡΟC ΒΑCCΙ[ΛΙCCΑ].[50] Agrippa thus substituted Livia's effigy with an image of his own wife Cypros, the first Jewish queen ever to be depicted on a coin. A similar emulation of an imperial motif can be seen in

---

[47] Philip's brother, Herod Antipas, minted coins with the inscriptions ΓΑΙΩ ΚΑΙCΑΡΙ ΓΕΡΜΑΝΙΚΩ, ΓΑΙΩ ΚΑΙCΑΡ, or simply ΓΑΙΩ inscribed in a wreath on the reverse, the closest a Jewish tetrarch ruling over a predominantly Jewish population could come to featuring the emperor on his coins (at least up to the time of Agrippa I), *RPC* I.4934–7.

[48] Meshorer, 2001, no. 100 (jugate heads of Augustus and Livia), 107.

[49] Philip: Meshorer, 2001, no. 107; Meshorer *et al.*, 2013; Herodian dynasty no. 141; *RPC* I.4949. Agrippa I: Meshorer, 2001, 92, no. 114; Meshorer *et al.*, 2013, Herodian dynasty no. 149; *RPC* I.4975; *RPC* Suppl. 2 (2006), S-4975.

[50] *RPC* I.4975 (with erroneous reading of the inscription); Meshorer, 2001, no. 114 and Meshorer *et al.*, 2013, Herodian dynasty no. 149 have the inscription ΚΥΠΡΟC . . . ; *RPC* Suppl. 2 (2006), S-4975 supports the reading ΚΥΠΡΟC ΒΑCCΙ[ΛΙCCΑ]

another type of Agrippa I, also minted in the second year of his reign and from the same mint. This type shows Agrippa's portrait on the obverse and a youth on horseback with the inscription ΑΓΡΙΠΠΑ ΥΙΟΥ ΒΑΣΙΛΕΥΣ on the reverse.[51] The motif was presumably borrowed from imperial imagery; Caligula had his brothers Nero and Drusus Caesar depicted in a similar fashion.[52] The same dynamic of assimilation can be seen in Commagene, where Antiochus IV honoured his sons, Epiphanes and Callinicus, on coins with a similar design.[53] The broader shift among client kings to feature their close relatives on coins appears at first glance to contradict their political status and dependence on Rome. However, the ambiguity of dependence on the one hand and royal dignity on the other may have increased the desire for an enhanced dynastic representation of the rulers. More importantly, it also mirrored the formation and formalisation of dynastic representations in Rome and the empire.

The new symbolic and iconographic repertoire thus spread quickly and was apparently well understood and received by the various intended and implied audiences, including local subjects, other client kings, and the emperor himself. Whereas the visual (as well as the actual) language of imperial power offered client kings new tools and features for their own representation, the superiority of the *princeps* and imperial rule also deprived them of certain aspects that had been part of the standard royal repertoire in the Hellenistic period. As shown above, the imperial cult could be used to enhance and emphasise their own authority, yet it also meant that ruler cult for client kings themselves mostly ceased.[54] Interestingly, an episode during the reign of Agrippa I demonstrates that the emperor did not have a complete monopoly on links to the divine, as the king was still greeted as a god by the crowd in the theatre in 44 CE.[55]

---

[51] Meshorer, 2001, no. 113; *RPC* I.4974; Meshorer *et al.*, 2013, Herodian dynasty nos. 147–8.

[52] *RIC* I² Caligula 34, 42, 49. These types are dated to 39/40 and 40/1 CE; if the dating of the coin featuring Agrippa II to 38/9 CE is correct, it would thus predate the Caligula type. However, earlier examples may have existed, and the similarities are too striking to be ignored. For similar types featuring designated successors issued under Vespasian: Titus and Domitian (*RIC* I² Vespasian 54, 64, 1122, 1377, 1378) and Domitian alone (*RIC* I² Vespasian 372, 719, 888, 1480; with head of Titus on the obverse *RIC* I² Vespasian 418, 419, 455, 472, 473, 486, 487, 633, 1029, 1281).

[53] *RPC* I.3861, 3866.

[54] Several references in later sources suggest the existence of a ruler cult in Mauretania, but the evidence is too scarce to allow for definitive conclusions, let alone an analysis of its relationship with the imperial cult established by Juba II; cf. Tert. *Apol.* 24.7; Min. Fel. 24; [Cypr.] *Quod idola dii non sint* 2; Lactant. *Div. inst.* 1.15 6, 8; Isid. *Etym.* 8.11.1. The fragmentary inscription *CIL* 8.9342 has been reconstructed as referring to the Genius of Ptolemy, but the reading is far from certain. Cf. the discussion in Fishwick, 1972: 702; Coltelloni-Trannoy, 1997: 194–9; Rives, 2001: esp. 428–31.

[55] Joseph. *AJ* 19.343–6; Acts 12:21–2.

Although this was beyond doubt meant as an expression of admiration, not an actual act of spontaneous divinisation, the reaction of the audience to the impressive spectacle of the king's arrival in the theatre adorned with his royal regalia and clad in a shining garment still provoked a reaction that went back to Hellenistic ruler cult traditions.

Even if not meant as actual religious reverence, the flattery of Agrippa I by the theatre audience indicates again the fine line client kings had to walk. The combination of reverence for the emperor and propagation of local, royal power always remained a potential challenge. Rare coins minted by Agrippa I of Judaea and his brother Herod II, king of Chalcis, show the two kings crowning the emperor Claudius with wreaths (Fig. 3.4).[56] The image alludes to the role that both Herodians played in Claudius' accession during the tumultuous period after Caligula's assassination and was in all likelihood meant to emphasise the loyalty of the two kings, as well as their close friendship with the new emperor. However, as Andreas Kropp has shown, the composition drew on standard depictions of Roman emperors appointing inferior kings and thus reversed the common hierarchy among the persons depicted.[57]

Although such a potentially subversive reading presumably was not realised by the contemporary audience, the type still demonstrates the general volatility and risks every client king had to keep in mind. No imperial

Figure 3.4 Alloy coin of Herod of Chalcis. British Museum 1985,1002.1 (*RPC* I.4777). Obverse: Kings Herod of Chalcis and Agrippa I crown the emperor Claudius, who stands between them. Inscription: ΒΑΣΙΛ ΗΡΩΔΗΣ ΒΑΣΙΛ ΑΓΡΙΠΠΑΣ ‖ ΚΛΑΥΔΙΟΣ ΚΑΙΣΑΡ ΣΕΒΑΣΤΟΣ. Photograph © The Trustees of the British Museum.

[56] *RPC* I.4777; 4982.
[57] Cf. for instance *RPC* I.3629 (Germanicus crowning Artaxias). Kropp, 2013b; cf. Dahmen, 2010: 108; Vitale, 2017: 299–306.

objection against such a representation is known or can be reconstructed with certainty, yet some anecdotes from the reign of Caligula indicate the immanent risk that too presumptuous and ostentatious a self-presentation by dependent rulers could provoke. For instance, Suetonius reports that when a number of dynasts, who gathered on the Palatine for dinner, debated the nobility of their descent, the *princeps* interrupted with a quote from the *Iliad*: 'Let there be one Lord, one King.'[58] Along the same lines, Suetonius maintains that Caligula ordered Ptolemy of Mauretania to be assassinated because he had attracted the audience's attention when he entered the theatre in a purple cloak.[59] This is undoubtedly a rumour, yet the historicity of the charge is only secondary in this context. For Suetonius, it was imaginable that a Roman emperor might overreact to a king's royal splendour out of jealousy, even though it took a Caligula to act upon it.

Conclusions

The political dependency of client kings and the integration of their realms into the Roman Empire was a well-known reality from the very beginning of Augustan rule onwards. Nevertheless, the challenges associated with combining royal and imperial representation remained. The examples discussed above show that the two were not considered mutually exclusive; instead, they informed and influenced each other. Although client kings lost certain features of royal representation and legitimacy – such as the ruler cult – they also made use of the honour and reverence paid to the emperor for their own advantage. In representation in the client kingdoms and principalities in the east, these two levels of authority and power were only compatible because the emperor and client kings were not regarded as competitors, let alone rivals. In contrast to the provinces in the east, where the emperor filled a political and ideological void left by the former Hellenistic imperial powers, in client kingdoms, the Roman Empire and the *princeps* were grafted on to an already existing system at a higher, additional level. Client kings thus profited from, and even relied upon, the *princeps*' elevation, as is expressed most significantly in the institution of the imperial cult. With their strong promotion of the emperor's image, they then served as catalysts in the process of establishing and disseminating this image and the associated concept in other parts of the east.[60]

---

[58] εἷς κοίρανος ἔστω, εἷς βασιλεύς: Hom. *Il.* 2.204; Suet. *Calig.* 22.1.   [59] Suet. *Calig.* 35.1.
[60] For benefactions of client kingdoms outside of their own domains and their contribution to the emperor's image see Wilker, 2015.

On the other hand, client kings had to carefully balance the promotion of the empire and its emperor with their own royal legitimacy and representation. The vast majority of client rulers continued to employ various local and/or regional traditions of royalty and dynastic legitimacy. In addition, they adopted a style that was strongly influenced by imperial modes of representation. Adopting these new forms and styles emphasised their personal connection with the *princeps*. More importantly, they communicated power and authority. It is important to note that this 'imperial mode' remained only one register among others, although it quickly became dominant in most client kingdoms. We may assume that different media targeted different audiences; however, the representation of the emperor and royal portraits fashioned according to the imperial style on coins of all denominations prove that the imperial presence was not perceived as offensive to any social or cultural group of significance.[61]

After the beginning of the Augustan principate, imperial imagery not only spread rapidly but was also transformed into a language of power and authority that went beyond the *princeps* as an individual and could even be appropriated by client rulers with a distinctively different, inferior authority. In fact, reverence towards the emperor and the emulation of his image emerged as one of the few features that the vast majority of client kings shared, truly creating a shared language of power – and, in turn, presumably contributing to the formation of a group identity among the dynasts. At the same time, the dual integration of imperial imagery in the visual languages of power used by client kings, as the primary mode both for depicting the emperor himself and for their own self-representation, indicates that the intended audience(s) were expected to distinguish clearly and immediately between these two levels. This distinction required the existence of two separate registers of power, an imperial and a local one, that overlapped and were occasionally combined but never conflated. If they were, the client king had failed.

Bibliography

Alexandropoulos, J. 2000. *Les monnaies de l'Afrique antique: 400 av. J.-C.–40 ap. J.-C.* (Toulouse: Presses universitaires du Mirail).

[61] For instance, a coin of Juba II depicts the king in the Heraclean lion pelt (*CNNM* 226; *MAA* 172); even more prominent were the multiple references to Cleopatra Selene's Egyptian heritage in the general self-presentation of the queen. An issue of Agrippa I of Judaea features a panoply on the obverse (*RPC* I.4981); for an engraved ring featuring an Emesan king wearing an earring, although the rest of the portrait follows a common Augustan style, see Kropp, 2010: 201–4.

Bendschus, T. 2018. 'Tigranes V. und seine Münzen. Armenische Herrscherlegitimation des frühen 1. Jhdts. n. Chr. im Spiegel der numismatischen Zeugnisse', *NZ* 124: 9–54.

Boube, J. 1990. 'Une statue portrait de Ptolémée de Maurétanie à Sala (Maroc)', *RA* 1990: 331–60.

Bowersock, G. W. 1965. *Augustus and the Greek World* (Oxford: Clarendon).

Braund, D. 1984. *Rome and the Friendly King: The Character of the Client Kingship* (London: Croom Helm).

1997. 'Greeks and barbarians: the Black Sea region and Hellenism under the early empire', in Alcock, S. (ed.), *The Early Empire in the East* (Oxford: Oxbow Books), 121–36.

Bru, H. 2011. *Le pouvoir impérial dans les provinces syriennes: Représentations et célébrations d'Auguste à Constantin (31 av. J.-C.–337 ap. J.-C.)* (Leiden; Boston: Brill).

Burnett, A. 2011. 'The Augustan revolution seen from the mints of the provinces', *JRS* 101: 1–30.

Burrell, B. 2009. 'Herod's Caesarea on Sebastos: urban structures and influences', in Jacobson, D. M. and N. Kokkinos (eds.), *Herod and Augustus: Papers Presented at the IJS Conference, 21st–23rd June 2005* (Leiden; Boston: Brill), 217–33.

Butcher, K. 2003. *Roman Syria and the Near East* (London: British Museum).

Chankowski, A. 2010. 'Les cultes des souverains hellénistiques après la disparition des dynasties: formes de survie et d'extinction d'une institution dans un contexte civique', in Savalli-Lestrade, I. and I. Cogitore (eds.), *Des rois au prince: Pratiques du pouvoir monarchique dans l'Orient hellénistique et romain (IVe siècle avant J.-C.–IIe siècle après J.-C.)* (Grenoble: ELLUG), 271–90.

Coltelloni-Trannoy, M. 1990. 'Le monnayage des rois Juba II et Ptolémée de Maurétanie: image d'une adhésion réitérée à la politique romaine', *Karthago* 22: 45–53.

1997. *Le royaume de Maurétanie sous Juba II et Ptolémée (25 av. J.-C.–40 ap. J.-C.)* (Paris: CNRS).

Dahmen, K. 2010. 'With Rome in mind? Case studies in the coinage of client kings', in Kaizer, T. and M. Facella (eds.), *Kingdoms and Principalities in the Roman Near East* (Stuttgart: Franz Steiner Verlag), 99–112.

Facella, M. 2005. 'Φιλορώμαιος καὶ Φιλέλλην: Roman perception of Commagenian royalty', in Hekster, O. and R. Fowler (eds.), *Imaginary Kings: Royal Images in the Ancient Near East, Greece and Rome* (Stuttgart: Franz Steiner Verlag), 87–104.

Fishwick, D. 1972. 'The institution of the provincial cult in Roman Mauretania', *Historia* 21: 698–711.

1985. 'Le culte impérial sous Juba II et Ptolémée de Maurétanie: le témoignage des monnaies', *BCTH* 19: 225–34.

Fittschen, K. 1974. 'Bildnisse der mauretanischen Könige und ihre stadtrömischen Vorbilder', *Madrider Mitteilungen* 15: 156–73.

Fleischer, R. 2008. 'Augustusporträt und Klientelkönig: ein Bildnis des Antiochos III. von Kommagene', in Kreikenbom, D., K.-U. Mahler, P. Schollmeyer, and T. M. Weber (eds.), *Augustus – Der Blick von außen: Die Wahrnehmung des Kaisers in den Provinzen des Reiches und in den Nachbarstaaten* (Wiesbaden: Harrassowitz), 321–34.

Fraser, P. M. 1978. 'The kings of Commagene and the Greek world', in Schwertheim, E., S. Şahin, and J. Wagner (eds.), *Studien zur Religion und Kultur Kleinasiens: Festschrift für Friedrich Karl Dörner zum 65. Geburtstag* (Leiden: Brill), 359–74.

Frija, G. 2010. 'Du prêtre du roi au prêtre de Rome et au grand prêtre d'Auguste: la mise en place du culte impérial civique', in Savalli-Lestrade, I. and I. Cogitore (eds.), *Des rois au prince: Pratiques de pouvoir monarchique dans l'Orient hellénistique et romain (IVe siècle avant J.-C.–IIe siècle après J.-C.)* (Grenoble: ELLUG), 291–308.

Gruen, E. 2009. 'Herod, Rome, and the diaspora', in Jacobson, D. M. and N. Kokkinos (eds.), *Herod and Augustus* (Leiden; Boston: Brill), 13–28.

Hohlfelder, R. L. 2000. 'Beyond coincidence? Marcus Agrippa and King Herod's harbor', *JNES* 59: 241–53.

—— 2003. 'Images of homage, images of power: King Herod and his harbour, Sebastos', *Antichthon* 37: 13–31.

Hohlfelder, R. L., C. Brandon, and J. P. Oleson 2007. 'Constructing the harbour of Caesarea Palaestina, Israel: new evidence from the ROMACONS field campaign of October 2005', *IJNA* 36: 409–15.

Holum, K. G. 2004. 'Caesarea's temple hill: the archaeology of sacred space in an ancient Mediterranean city', *Near Eastern Archaeology* 67: 184–99.

—— 2015. 'The gods of Sebastos: King Herod's harbor temple at Caesarea', *Eretz-Israel* 31: 51*–68*.

Kahn, L. C. 1996. 'Herod's temple of Roma and Augustus at Caesarea Maritima', in Raban, A. and K. G. Holum (eds.), *Caesarea Maritima: A Retrospective after Two Millennia* (Leiden; Boston: Brill), 130–45.

Kropp, A. 2009. 'King – Caesar – God: Roman imperial cult among Near Eastern "client" kings in the Julio-Claudian period', in Blömer, M., M. Facella, and E. Winter (eds.), *Lokale Identität im Römischen Nahen Osten: Kontexte und Perspektiven* (Stuttgart: Franz Steiner Verlag), 99–150.

—— 2010. 'Earring, *nefesh* and *opus reticulatum*: self-representation of the royal house of Emesa in the first century AD', in Kaizer, T. and M. Facella (eds.), *Kingdoms and Principalities in the Roman Near East* (Stuttgart: Franz Steiner Verlag), 199–216.

—— 2013a. *Images and Monuments of Near Eastern Dynasts, 100 BC–AD 100* (Oxford: Oxford University Press).

2013b. 'Crowning the emperor: an unorthodox image of Claudius, Agrippa I and Herod of Chalkis', *Syria* 90: 377–89.

Landwehr, C. 2007. 'Les portraits de Juba II, Roi de Maurétanie, et de Ptolémée, son fils et successeur', *RA* 43: 65–110.

Lichtenberger, A. 1999. *Die Baupolitik Herodes des Großen* (Wiesbaden: Harrassowitz).

Lykke, A. 2013. 'Die Münzikonographie von Herodes Agrippa I. und ihre Beziehung zur römischen Bildsprache', in Lykke, A. (ed.), *Macht des Geldes – Macht der Bilder: Kolloquium zur Ikonographie auf Münzen im ostmediterranen Raum in hellenistisch-römischer Zeit* (Wiesbaden: Harrassowitz), 150–69.

Meshorer, Y. 2001. *A Treasury of Jewish Coins: From the Persian Period to Bar Kokhba* (Jerusalem: Yad Ben-Zvi).

Meshorer, Y., G. Bijovsky, and W. Fischer-Bossert 2013. *Coins of the Holy Land: The Abraham and Marian Sofaer Collection at the American Numismatic Society and the Israel Museum*, edited by D. Hendin and A. Meadows (New York: ANS).

Millar, F. 1996. 'Emperors, kings and subjects: the politics of two-level sovereignty', *SCI* 15: 159–73.

Nawotka, K. 1989. 'The attitude towards Rome in the political propaganda of the Bosporus monarchs', *Latomus* 48: 326–38.

Netzer, E. 2006. *The Architecture of Herod the Great Builder* (Tübingen: Mohr Siebeck).

Noreña, C. 2016. 'Ritual and memory: Hellenistic ruler cults in the Roman Empire', in Galinsky, K. and K. Lapatin (eds.), *Cultural Memories in the Roman Empire* (Los Angeles: Getty Publications), 86–100.

Price, S. 1984. *Rituals and Power: The Roman Imperial Cult in Asia Minor* (Cambridge; New York: Cambridge University Press).

Rives, J. B. 2001. 'Imperial cult and native tradition in Roman North Africa', *CJ* 96: 425–36.

Roller, D. W. 1998. *The Building Program of Herod the Great* (Berkeley: University of California Press).

2003. *The World of Juba II and Kleopatra Selene: Royal Scholarship on Rome's African Frontier* (London; New York: Routledge).

Salzmann, D. 2007. 'Zur Selbstdarstellung von Klientenherrschern im griechischen Osten', in Meyer, M. (ed.), *Neue Zeiten, Neue Sitten: Zu Rezeption und Integration römischen und italischen Kulturguts in Kleinasien* (Vienna: Phoibos), 47–53.

Schörner, G. 2011. 'Rom jenseits der Grenze: Klientelkönigreiche und der Impact of Empire', in Hekster, O. and T. Kaizer (eds.), *Frontiers in the Roman World: Proceedings of the Ninth Workshop of the International Network Impact of Empire* (Leiden; Boston: Brill), 113–31.

Schumacher, L. 2008. 'Glanz ohne Macht: Juba II. von Mauretanien als römischer Klientelkönig', in Kreikenbom, D., K.-U. Mahler, P. Schollmeyer, and T. M. Weber (eds.), *Augustus – Der Blick von außen: Die Wahrnehmung des Kaisers in den Provinzen des Reiches und in den Nachbarstaaten* (Wiesbaden: Harrassowitz), 141–60.

Schwentzel, C.-G. 2013. *Juifs et Nabatéens: Les monarchies ethniques du Proche-Orient hellénistique et romain* (Rennes: Presses universitaires de Rennes).

Smith, R. R. R. 1988a. *Hellenistic Royal Portraits* (Oxford: Clarendon Press).

1988b. '*Philorhomaioi*: portraits of Roman client rulers in the Greek east in the 1st century BC', in Bonacasa, N. and G. Rizza (eds.), *Ritratto ufficiale e ritratto privato: Atti della II Conferenza Internazionale sul Ritratto Romano* (Roma: Consiglio Nazionale delle Ricerche), 493–7.

Suspène, A. 2015. 'L'apport de la documentation numismatique à l'étude des foreign clientelae: le cas de Juba II de Maurétanie', in Jehne, M. and F. Pina Polo (eds.), *Foreign Clientelae in the Roman Empire: A Reconsideration* (Stuttgart: Franz Steiner Verlag), 185–207.

Teverson, R. H. 2015. Augustan Kings: The Art and Architecture of Herod the Great of Judaea and Juba II of Mauretania. PhD Diss., Yale.

Vann, R. L. 1991. 'The Drusion: a candidate for Herod's lighthouse at Caesarea Maritima', *IJNA* 20: 123–39.

Vitale, M. 2017. *Das Imperium in Wort und Bild: Römische Darstellungsformen beherrschter Gebiete in Inschriftenmonumenten, Münzprägungen und Literatur* (Stuttgart: Franz Steiner Verlag).

Votruba, G. F. 2007. 'Imported building materials of Sebastos harbour, Israel', *IJNA* 36: 325–35.

Wilker, J. 2008. '*Principes et reges*: Das persönliche Nahverhältnis zwischen Princeps und Klientelherrschern und seine Auswirkungen im frühen Prinzipat', in Coşkun, A. (ed.), *Freundschaft und Gefolgschaft in den auswärtigen Beziehungen der Römer (2. Jahrundert v. Chr.–1. Jahrhundert n. Chr.)* (Frankfurt am Main: Peter Lang), 165–88.

2015. 'Der Preis des Reiches: auswärtige Euergesien abhängiger Herrscher zur Zeit des frühen Prinzipats', in Baltrusch, E. and J. Wilker (eds.), *Amici – socii – clientes? Abhängige Herrschaft im Imperium Romanum* (Berlin: Edition Topoi), 91–121.

Wright, N. L. 2013. 'Ituraean coinage in context', *NC* 173: 55–71.

4 | *Publica numina*

Conspicuously Consuming the Imperial Image at Tomis

NANDINI B. PANDEY

> And you should never permit gold or silver images of yourself to be made,
> for they are not only costly but also invite destruction and last only a brief
> time; but rather by your benefactions fashion other images in the hearts of
> your people, images which will never tarnish or perish.
>
> Speech of Maecenas, Cass. Dio 52.35.3 (trans. Cary)

Overview

This volume's kaleidoscopic examination of Romans' and others' active
role in constructing imperial imagery challenges traditional notions of
what ideology is, whom it serves, and where it originates – even whether
images of power were understood in consistent or political ways by their
heterogeneous audiences. Such images find meaning in their consumption
as much as production, meaning that ultimately resides where Dio's
Maecenas would locate imperial divinity: in the hearts, minds, and practices of the people.[1] Yet the thoughts of individual subjects as they interacted with imperial ideology and its material instantiations remain
tantalisingly elusive. This chapter explores individual reception, that crucial yet ephemeral final stage in the formation of meaning, by turning to
Ovid's *Epistulae ex Ponto* 2.8. In purporting to elaborate the exiled poet's
thought process upon receiving silver images of the Caesars from Rome,[2]
this elegiac letter simultaneously deconstructs Romans' self-subjugating
fetishisation of imperial iconography and highlights their agency in vesting

---

[1] In Dio's fictional account, Maecenas urges Augustus not to permit temples or precious images of
himself, but instead focus on winning people's hearts through his good character and rulership:
in this way, 'the whole earth will be your hallowed precinct, all cities your temples, and all men
your statues, since within their thoughts you will ever be enshrined and glorified' (52.35.5, trans.
Cary).

[2] My analysis, inspired by Barthes on reader response, complements Gregory's brief 1994 survey
of historical evidence for responses to political imagery and attempts to address a gap in Zanker,
1990.

it with value. This literary source elucidates possibilities for the affective and cognitive processes that were constantly if invisibly unfolding around the various social, political, and material constructions of ideology examined throughout this collection. To many Roman subjects, the emperors lived *in* and *through* their material representations as *publica numina* (*Pont.* 2.8.67) who belonged to Rome as much as Rome belonged to them. Responding to these figures – whether in the public form of poetry or the private realm of their own thoughts – was therefore a crucial mode of political activity under empire, indeed one of the few available to all regardless of socio-economic status, gender, or distance from Rome.

Conspicuous Consumption in *Epistulae ex Ponto* 2.8

Ovid (43 BCE–17 CE), by many accounts the first truly Augustan poet, takes an unabashedly consumerist perspective on the opulent new buildings, public spectacles, and luxury goods that were flowing into the *caput mundi* under the Pax Augusta.[3] Though he writes for a literate elite, the poet frequently adopts an ignorant or over-eager narrative persona, parodying but also acknowledging the role of the illiterate masses in ideology formation.[4] As I argue elsewhere, he often fails to attach any ideological message at all to imperial representations, showing instead how they feed subjects' frivolous demands for sex, sport, and spectacle.[5] In *Ars amatoria* 1.177–228, for instance, he anticipates Gaius Caesar's triumph as an opportunity for flirtation, encouraging onlookers hoping to impress a potential mate simply to make up names for the images on parade: 'if you can, [say] their true ones, if not, something truthy' (*si poteris, vere, si minus, apta tamen*, 228).[6]

---

[3] On Rome's new cosmopolitanism see e.g. Edwards and Woolf, 2003 and Favro, 2005.

[4] Compare, e.g., *Tristia* 3.1 and discussion by Pandey (2011: 97–118 and 2018: 117–33). As Hardie notes (2002: 321), this is a 'mimetic poem', an Alexandrian form in which the speaker reacts to his changing environment, that also participates in the elegiac topoi of addresses to absent friends and epiphany.

[5] See Pandey, 2011: 144–9 and 2018 *passim*, with Hollis, 1977; Henderson, 2002; Boyle, 2003; and Beacham, 2005.

[6] Playing on Propertius' vision of himself and his girlfriend reading triumphal *tituli* at 3.4.11–19, this Ovidian scene seems to envision an illiterate observer's response perhaps more reflective of general audiences; see Pandey, 2018: 206–15 on the poem and Johnson and Parker, 2009 for literacy rates. Beard (2009: 184) views these lines as mocking the arbitrariness of the triumph's representational distinctions, asking 'who cares when the "real" conquest is the girl standing next to you?'

Ovid's detachment of sign from signified is no mere literary *jeu*. It points to the physical, social, and informational factors that delimited the crowd's interpretations of imperial imagery yet also sometimes liberated them from its mimetic claims. Such fissures between imperial representations and audience interpretations emerged across media and class. The copious material evidence for consumers' active role in remediating imperial imagery includes a silver skyphos from the Boscoreale hoard that translates a triumph of Tiberius into a high-status consumer good (Fig. 4.1).[7] The absence of inscriptions, omission of individuating details, and strong visual emphasis on the *triumphator* render it difficult to identify the specific occasion and leave a great deal of interpretive freedom to viewers, quite

Figure 4.1 Silver skyphos from the Boscoreale treasure depicting the triumph of Tiberius. Musée du Louvre. Photograph and original data provided by Réunion des Musées Nationaux / Art Resource, NY. Photograph: H. Lewandowski.

[7] Kuttner (1995: 194–8) speculates that the cups, hidden in a wine cellar during the eruption of Vesuvius in 79 CE, were made by the Ara Pacis atelier based on a monumental relief prototype.

literally placing the emperor's image within their hands.[8] It is up to the cup's users, in lieu of the original triumphal audience, to imagine the battles won, peoples conquered, and spoils plundered; to determine how (or whether) to connect the triumph scene on one side with the sacrifice on the other;[9] to construct, discuss, contest, or ignore the cup's meaning and message as they sip their wine. Even as they preserve Tiberius' memory, these elite viewers subject a grand state event to their own private uses, interpretations, and social constructions of identity within a sympotic context. Not unlike *Ars am.* 1.177–228, then, the Boscoreale cup permits, even necessitates, an imaginative inversion of the triumph's normative power dynamic, transferring ownership from *imperator* to citizen as consumer and enjoyer of this imperial image.

Ovid's interest in the social dynamics behind imperial meaning, particularly its susceptibility to appropriation and transformation from below, took on new depth and political heft after he was relegated to the Black Sea in 8 CE on the charge that the *Ars amatoria* encouraged adultery. The poet insists in *Tristia* 2 that he is innocent of any corrupting intention (345–60); it is readers who impose their own morals and meanings upon texts (253–312).[10] This self-defence is the literary equivalent of the economic idea that consumer demand drives the production and usage of goods. And it has fascinating implications for the emperor's image, which, thanks to an ongoing 'consumer revolution', was circulating ever more widely through words, images, and objects like the Boscoreale cups, often independently of centralised control, even as it gained symbolic potency.[11] As a complement to this volume's examination of imperial imagery's distributed authorship, then, the remainder of this chapter will show how Ovid conspicuously 'consumes' and thus deconstructs the emperor's image in *Pont.* 2.8 to dramatise subjects' role as co-creators of imperial ideology, even and

---

[8] Kuttner (1995: 152) argues based on the lack of identifying information that Tiberius had celebrated only his 8/7 BCE triumph at this point, while Künzl (1988, 1989) and Zanker (1990: 229) argue for the triumph of 12 CE, awarded in 8 CE; see Pandey, 2018: 190–3 for brief discussion.

[9] Kuttner identifies the bull scene as a *nuncupatio votorum* demonstrating Tiberius' *pietas* in discharging the correct rites before departure (1995: 11), while Huet (1996: 27–8) and Kleiner (1997, 2010) view it as a sacrifice upon his triumphant return. These divergent interpretations attest to the cup's interpretive malleability.

[10] On this poem and Ovid's exile see especially Nugent, 1990; Williams, 1994; Gibson, 1999; and McGowan, 2009.

[11] Through a process of distributed authorship analysed throughout this volume, with Russell especially relevant regarding iconographic potency. Greene (2008: 64–70) provides a helpful overview of 'consumerism' in ancient Rome; see also Woolf, 1998 on this 'consumer revolution' in Gaul and Morley, 2007 for trade in ancient Rome.

especially on Rome's geographic and political margins.[12] By adopting a naïve narrative persona whose desire for imperial contact has gone unsatisfied, Ovid shows how audiences imaginatively rendered the emperor a *praesens deus* ('present god') by commodifying, circulating, and consuming his image.[13] On another level, though, this persona provides a 'hermeneutic alibi' behind which the poet makes fun of imperial ideology and its provincial reception for urban readers' amusement.[14] The poem ultimately performs a *reductio ad absurdum* of all Roman subjects' self-subordination to dominant ideology through their economic and psychological interactions with objects that they themselves vest with power.[15]

Pont. 2.8, dated to 13 CE, offers Cotta Maximus extended thanks for sending silver likenesses of Augustus, Tiberius, and Livia from Rome (1–8):[16]

> redditus est nobis Caesar cum Caesare nuper,
>   quos mihi misisti, Maxime Cotta, deos,
> utque tuum munus numerum quem debet haberet,
>   est ibi Caesaribus Livia iuncta suis.
> argentum felix omnique beatius auro,   5
>   quod, fuerit pretium cum rude, numen habet.
> non mihi divitias dando maiora dedisses
>   caelitibus missis nostra sub ora tribus.

> There recently arrived for me a Caesar with a Caesar – the gods whom you sent me, Cotta Maximus; and so that your gift might have the number that

---

[12] With Davis, 2002, this analysis tries to complicate Habinek's view (1998: 151) that the exile poems construct model subjecthood and support imperial propaganda in the provinces; see also Evans, 1983: 10–13 and Habinek, 2002. My own emphasis on the emperor's absent presence and readerly hermeneutics owes much to Hinds, 1985; Casali, 1996; and Hardie, 2002. For the poet's rivalry with Augustus, see also Oliensis, 1997: 190; for Augustus as *deus praesens*, McGowan, 2009: 84; and for political criticism under empire, Ahl, 1984. I argue elsewhere (2018: 215–39) that *Tristia* 3.1 and 4.2 and *Pont.* 2.1 and 3.4 together create a sense of unfulfilled demand on the part of provincial subjects for news of a triumph, one that Ovid as *vates* is able to satisfy independently of information from Rome.

[13] For epiphany and the language of 'true' or 'present' godhood here, see Galasso, 1995: 350 and Helzle, 2003: 359; for the poem's illusion of presence, see Hardie, 2002: 318–25; and for the 'elision of persons and images', especially in late antiquity, see Elsner, 1998: 37. The fact that Ovid's epistles never receive recorded reply, from the emperor or other addressees, enhances the social and cultural isolation of which he complains.

[14] Hinds, 1988 uses this term for Ovid's attribution of undesirable meanings to reader interpretation rather than his own authorial intentions, especially in *Tristia* 2.

[15] Compare Mitchell's view of images as 'a ventriloquist's dummy into which we project our own voice' (2005: 140, and cf. Rowan in this volume), and contrast panegyrical readings of this poem (e.g. Galasso, 1995: 351).

[16] Cotta, consul of 20 CE, is also addressed in *Tr.* 4.5 and 5.9 and *Pont.* 1.5, 1.9, 2.3, 3.2, 3.5, 3.8. I view these images, the correspondence with Cotta, and Ovid's exile not necessarily as historical realities, but as literary constructions that have an effect on readers.

it ought, Livia is there, joined with her Caesars. Fortunate silver, more
blessed than all gold, because, though it was once rough metal, it has divine
might. You wouldn't have given me more by giving me riches than you do
by sending these triple divinities to my sight.[17]

Ovid's suggestion in the *Tristia* that his friends risk retribution simply by
corresponding with him adds a subversive patina to Cotta's gift, complicating
this poem's ostensible piety towards the imperial family.[18] The poet rejoices
in these images, he explains at 11–14, because they transport him back to
Rome, assuaging the sense of isolation that he elsewhere characterises as the
most punitive aspect of his exile. At *Pont.* 2.1, in fact, Ovid frames the dearth
of news from Rome as part of a deliberate imperial attempt to deprive him of
joy. On the other hand, in that poem, he celebrates news of a triumph
contrary to the emperor's intentions. 'Even though Caesar does not wish
any joys to touch me,' Ovid asserts, 'nevertheless he might wish this one thing
to be granted to all' (*nolit ut ulla mihi contingere gaudia Caesar,* | *velle potest
cuivis haec tamen una dari, Pont.* 2.1.7–8). Several lines later, he claims
a citizen's rights of ownership to the emperor's own 'joys' on the grounds
that this public figure can have nothing private (*gaudia Caesareae mentis pro
parte virili* | *sunt mea: privati nil habet illa domus, Pont.* 2.1.17–18).[19] Ovid's
defiantly patriotic enjoyment of the imperial image at *Pont.* 2.8 does something
comparable. This poem exploits Caesar's dual status as *res publica*, both as the
personification of 'the commonwealth' and as 'public property' (*Tr.* 4.4.15), by
exerting imaginative ownership over the emperor's representational
instantiation(s) in Tomis.

The form that these representations take remains perhaps deliberately
obscure, focusing attention instead on the narrator's imaginative response.
Most commentators assume Cotta's *imagines* (21) to be three small statues
or busts, citing later imperial analogues like the *simulacra* placed among
household Lares (Suet. *Vit.* 2.5) or legionary standards (Tac. *Ann.* 15.24.3;
Cass. Dio 63.25.1).[20] At times, though, Ovid's word choice suggests that the
likenesses are closely connected upon a single surface, for instance, at 3–4:
'and, so that your [singular] gift might have the [plural] number which it

---

[17] I use Richmond's 1990 Teubner text.

[18] See Oliensis, 1997. Gregory, 1994: 92 compiles evidence of the suspicion that would later attach
to private *imagines* of figures like Caesar's assassins.

[19] The flip side of Augustus' ownership of everything under the sun (*quodcumque est alto sub Iove,
Caesar habet*, 'whatever is under the lofty sky is Caesar's', *Fast.* 2.138) is that he, like the sun,
becomes public property, to be enjoyed at will by his subjects. Cf. *Tr.* 4.4.13, Galasso, 1995: 104,
and Pandey, 2020: 172–3.

[20] Galasso (1995: 343) and Helzle (2003: 359) discuss the possibilities; see below for the latter, and
for the former, *Fast.* 5.143–6, Waites, 1920, and Pollini, 2012: 332.

ought, Livia is there [with them, or on it?], joined with her Caesars'.[21] Such language conjures a relief on a medallion or coin, like the type featuring Julia flanked by Lucius and Gaius at Fig. 4.2; in Durham, Clare Rowan made an apt comparison with Ovid's address to the image of Janus struck on a coin at *Fasti* 1.189–254.[22] I will alternate among these various descriptors (images, statues, medallions) to preserve what I take to be a pointed ambiguity enhancing the gift's symbolic applicability to the consumption of imperial images in any form or medium.

Ovid does, however, specify that the material is silver, again subtly positioning these images on the wrong side of imperial policy. 'Although

Figure 4.2 Denarius of Augustus, 13 BCE. Obverse: AVGVSTVS DIVI F; head of Augustus, right, in oak wreath. Reverse: C MARIVS TRO III VIR; Gaius, Julia, and Lucius Caesar, heads right; wreath central above. *RIC* I^2 Augustus 405; *BMC* 109. Photograph © The American Numismatic Society.

---

[21] Note also Ovid's address to plural gods (*cavete*) as if they reside on a single image (*vestra figura*) at 63–4 and the apparent linkage of the Caesars' plural faces with a singular effigy at 60 (*quos dedit ars, vultus effigiemque colo*), though metrical constraints and the poetic transposition of singulars and plurals urge caution.

[22] The *Fasti* passage discusses the New Year's tradition of bringing token gifts known as *strenae* to one's patrons (Frazer, 1929: 114; Green, 2004: 95), which during the principate evolved into the popular presentation of small coins to the emperor, which he would then convert into religious offerings (cf. Suet. *Aug.* 57.1, *Calig.* 42; Mart. 8.33.11–12). This emblematises the emperor's role as universal patron and hints at his control over the conversion of precious metals via the mint, discussed below. *Fasti* 1 sets this whole process against the backdrop of Rome's decline from the Golden Age (1.191–226), which finds inverse measure in an increasingly gilded city thanks to imperial patronage. See Green, 2004: 98 for this Augustan tension; 109 for this passage as a brief history of Roman money; and 113, with Crawford, 1974: 719, for examples of the coin in question.

well aware that it was usual to vote temples even to proconsuls,' Suetonius
writes, Augustus 'would not accept one even in a province save jointly in
his own name and that of Rome. In the city itself he refused this honour
most emphatically, even melting down the silver statues which had been
set up in his honour in former times and with the money coined from
them dedicating golden tripods to Apollo of the Palatine' (*Aug.* 52, trans.
Rolfe).[23] At *RG* 24, Augustus himself boasts of removing eighty silver
statues of himself from the city after his Actian victory, suggesting a more
widespread suppression of precious metal portraiture as part of his
campaign to advertise his humility.[24] Cotta's gift, however, demonstrates
that silver statues of the emperor were being privately produced in Rome
and circulated to the provinces, in apparent defiance of this official
position. The inclusion of Livia's image, for that matter, cuts against
Augustus' evident efforts to minimise her role in visual culture, at least
in the city.[25] Thus, the gift that Ovid so effusively welcomes simultaneously highlights the disingenuousness and ineffectuality of the emper-
or's attempts to control the composition and circulation of his image,
from the *urbs* on outwards.[26]

Fetishising the Imperial Image

The emperor's subjects, Ovid demonstrates, do more than metamorphose him
into silver and mail him abroad against his expressed wishes; they can and do
imbue his material representations with value, even imaginative life, without
his knowledge or permission. The rest of the poem both indulges and deconstructs this subjective illusion, showing how the imperial image remains
vulnerable to the same quasi-magical thinking by which it ultimately exerts
power in the first place. While Ovid elsewhere revisits Rome on the wings of his
imagination,[27] at *Pont.* 2.8.9–20, his imagination brings the Caesars to Tomis:

[23] Compare Maecenas' above-quoted advice to Augustus in Cass. Dio 52.35.

[24] At least in the early principate; Cass. Dio 53.22.3 places the event in 27 BCE, and Pollini, 2012:
75 notes that no substantial minting of *denarii* occurred at the time (i.e., the silver was not
needed for bullion).

[25] In Durham, Clare Rowan noted Augustus' evident reluctance to feature Livia on monuments
and coins in the city, striking given the triumvirs' coins featuring their wives and Livia's greater
prominence in visual culture in the provinces and after Augustus' death. See also Kleiner, 2005:
255–60. Galasso (1995: 360–1) suggests Ovid's marked attention to Livia may reflect her
importance and assimilation with Juno and other female gods in the provinces.

[26] Analysed by Scott, 1931.

[27] E.g. at *Tr.* 4.2.57–60 and *Pont.* 1.8.33–8, 3.5.49–50 to speak with Cotta Maximus, and 4.4 and
4.9; see Williams, 2002: 236.

est aliquid spectare deos et adesse putare
    et quasi cum vero numine posse loqui.   10
quantum ad te, redii, nec me tenet ultima tellus,
    utque prius, media sospes in urbe moror.
Caesareos video vultus, velut ante videbam:
    vix huius voti spes fuit ulla mihi.
utque salutabam numen caeleste, saluto.   15
    quod reduci tribuas, nil, puto, maius habes.
quid nostris oculis nisi sola Palatia desunt?
    qui locus ablato Caesare vilis erit.
hunc ego cum spectem, videor mihi cernere Romam;
    nam patriae faciem sustinet ille suae.   20

It is something to view the gods and think them nearby, and to be able to speak with them as if with a real divinity. As far as was in your power, I've returned, and the ends of the earth no longer detain me, and as before, I linger safe in the middle of the city. I see the Caesars' faces as I used to see them before; scarcely did I have any hope of this prayer; and as I used to salute the heavenly power, I salute him; even should you grant my return, you have nothing greater, I think. What is lacking to my eyes except only the Palatine? That place will be worthless with Caesar removed. As I look upon him, I seem to myself to discern Rome; for he sustains the face of his own fatherland.

This flight of fancy is the natural culmination of the narrator's earlier, irrational overvaluation of the imperial *imagines*' worth: 'Fortunate silver, more blessed than all gold, because, though it was once rough metal, it has divine might' (5–6). There, the poet recognises the normative exchange value of silver and gold only to invert it (*argentum ... beatius auro*, 5).[28] This silver object has grown more precious than gold, and attained value beyond its raw material (*fuerit pretium cum rude*, 6), because it is crafted in the shape of the Caesars – now even begins to become the Caesars.

The narrator's comical conflation of the objects' material and ideological value makes a serious point: commodities like these portraits gain their value not through their materials' intrinsic worth, but from the labour that produced them, the social contexts in which they are consumed and exchanged, and the stories they travel with and inspire.[29] Coins are a classic example. Despite their lack of intrinsic

---

[28] Cf. *Pont.* 3.8.3 and Hor. *Epist.* 1.1.52, where gold is cheaper than virtue. Galasso (1995: 249) cites some examples of the wealth topos in poetry.

[29] With thanks to one of my anonymous readers for the latter phrase.

utility, a social contract imbues these pieces of metal with definite and fungible value when stamped with a particular image. Caesar's head was, of course, the validating image on Roman coins. Ovid's proclamation that this image is worth more to him than any riches and seems to imbue the very silver with divinity (*numen habet*, 6) thus parodies the human tendency to vest objects with emotional value as well as the tacit (il)logic behind the monetary system.[30] By assigning increasing *numen* to this numismatic image at 9–20, Ovid ironically anticipates a Late Antique tendency to value coins based on the size of the imperial portrait rather than the size, weight, or face value of the coin. A Constantinian ban on this practice (*Cod. Theod.* 9.22.1) suggests that currency speculators were able to prey on the kind of naïve thinking parodied by Ovid. The harsh punishments for this crime, including decapitation and consignment to flames, symbolically re-enact the process of (re)minting upon the perpetrator's body. These gruesome retaliations indicate the perceived gravity of usurping the emperor's authority over the coins that combined his 'face and veneration in one' (*in quibus nostri vultus ac veneratio una est*, 9.22.1).[31]

In *Pont.* 2.8, however, Ovid similarly detaches imperial image and authority by exploring subjects' freedom, however fallacious, to salute and venerate the emperor's face in his stead (*utque salutabam numen caeleste, saluto*, 15). Here, despite the obvious differences between Rome's largely agrarian economy and industrialised capitalist societies, Marx's theory of 'commodity fetishism' (*Warenfetischismus*) provides a useful comparison for Ovid's exploration of the social construction of imperial power through objects.[32] In *Das Kapital*, Marx critiques a transhistorical tendency to ascribe intrinsic value to commodities without regard for the human labour that creates them. Marx associates this phenomenon with the 'mist-enveloped regions of the religious world' wherein 'the productions of the human brain appear as independent beings endowed with life'. Indeed, like religion, commodity

---

[30] To use Gregory's sociological distinction (1994: 89), these images' power relies on 'affective' valuations which Ovid depicts as inseparable from subjects' 'cognitive' responses.

[31] I thank Rowan for the reference; cf. Howgego, 1995: 125–37 and Morley, 2007: 63. Gregory (1994: 95–6) compiles some examples of statues' almost magical surrogate power, e.g. Cassander's fear of a statue of Alexander (Plut. *Alex.* 74.6), Pliny's satisfaction in destroying images of Domitian (*Pan.* 52.4), and the crowd's symbolic execution of Cn. Piso via his statues (Tac. *Ann.* 3.14); compare Lucius Ennius' alleged *maiestas* for converting an imperial stater into silver plate (*Ann.* 3.70).

[32] This theory, and its expansions by Lukács, Žižek, and Debord, has yet to be applied systematically to the ancient world. Ray, 2009 lays groundwork for applying modern economic thought to ancient Rome, here consumer patterns in Pompeii; see also Walsh, 2014 on consumerism in Greek pottery.

fetishism encompasses a set of irrational beliefs and practices that drive socio-economic inequalities. Marx points by example to the shipwrecked Robinson Crusoe, who must apportion his time among various labours in proportion to their benefit for his survival. In a more complex society, of course, different people produce diverse goods and services for one another's consumption. But the exchange of these goods ultimately obscures the individual human labour that produced them and falsely focuses consumers' attention instead on the relationships between objects. Thus, as people acquire goods and status symbols beyond their subsistence needs, they value Fabergé eggs over fishing nets, and reward the silversmith more than the fisherman for an equal amount of labour – exacerbating their inequality while obscuring its injustice.

Pont. 2.8 dramatises its fictive narrator's analogous, self-subjugating, yet emotionally satisfying fetishisation of the imperial portrait. It is patently absurd that Ovid, in the ancient-day Robinson Crusoe scenario of exile,[33] would value silver portraits over the safety, warmth, and companionship he elsewhere vocally craves. Yet instead of directing his labour towards supplying these needs, he continues to subscribe to the economic and political myths that keep him in exile and maintain imperial dominance across empire (simultaneously satirising the elision of needs and wants that is one hallmark of consumerism).[34] *Pont.* 2.8 thus responds to and reverses Augustus' conversion of silver statues into golden tripods through the intermediary of coinage or bullion (Suet. *Aug.* 54; *RG* 24). This supposedly modest gesture, like Augustus' juxtaposition of the temple of Apollo Palatinus with his own home, paradoxically reinforced the emperor's super-human status: only he had the authority to turn silver into money whose purchasing power was undersigned by his own image. (The *Res gestae*, in turn, verbally rewinds this conversion to resuscitate the tripods' original form as a testament of popular acclaim.) *Pont.* 2.8 similarly converts the emperor's silver statues into something more valuable than gold: the divine presence of the emperor himself. But this transformation doubles as a demonstration of the poet's imaginative power as a consumer of imperial imagery – a power that, in contrast to Augustus' monopoly on the mint, Ovid shares with all Roman subjects.[35]

---

[33] Compare among others Little, 1990 on Ovid's exaggerations of the miseries of exile.

[34] For needs and wants, see Morley, 2007: 39–43 and Greene, 2008: 66; for the Roman 'consumer revolution', Woolf, 1998: 181–93 and Greene, 2008: 68–70.

[35] I am here of course oversimplifying the complicated question of coin circulation and manufacture in Rome and the provinces, for which see e.g. Howgego, Heuchert, and Burnett, 2005.

Ovid winks at his urbane audience, and continues to construct himself among them, through a self-satirical consumerist theophany that marks its own inadequacy as a means of personally interacting with the emperor and Rome from the provinces. '*It is something* to view the gods, and think them nearby, and to be able to speak with them *as if with a real divinity*', he announces, in words that simultaneously indicate the subjective and imperfect nature of these statuary gods' presence (9–10: emphasis mine). He similarly qualifies his statement to Cotta: '*as far as was in your power*, I've returned … and, as before, I linger safe in the middle of the city' (11–12).[36] So, too, the poet only *seems* to himself 'to discern Rome' at 19.[37] The fact that he nonetheless continues to fetishise these images points out the lack of viable alternatives for citizens hungry for a sense of imperial presence. At 15, for instance, the narrator performs upon these images the *salutatio* that used to define his social role and routine in Rome ('and as I used to salute the heavenly power, I salute him'; compare his nostalgia for this ceremony at *Pont.* 2.2.3 and 3.5.5). The narrator's self-delusive sense of epiphany grows so strong that, by 16, he seems to prefer these images over actual return. At 17–18, he jokes that he can see all of Rome but the Palatine, which anyway is 'worthless' (*vilis*) without Caesar. This recalls and reverses the Palatine's description elsewhere in elegy as 'golden' from its opulent decor and dedications (*aurea Phoebi | porticus*, Propertius 2.31.1–2). The narrator instead suggests, in another subversive display of patriotism, that Caesar's presence had given the Palatine its value, but has now been relocated to Tomis in the form of these images.

This logic satirises the quasi-mystical belief that a ruler's *numen* resides both in his human body and in its manifold mimetic avatars, from state-controlled coinage to consumer goods like Cotta's gift; the same thinking underpins the weaponisable interdependence of imperial statues and bodies implied in iconoclasm.[38] Blissfully ignoring the multiplicity and mass production of the imperial image, Ovid's naïve narrator continues to invest the silver medallion with singular, transcendent agency. Yet, at this point in the poem, he also transfers onto it the anger he had experienced from the real Augustus, marking his pathetic fallacy with a verb of deceit:

[36] *Quantum ad te redii* is Ehwald's sensible restoration; see Galasso, 1995: 351–2 for discussion.

[37] As Galasso points out (1995: 354), this device highlights desire's role in fuelling illusion; see also Hardie, 2002: 321, and compare Lucr. 4.760, Ov. *Her.* 19.59 and *Pont.* 4.4.27, and Pliny's own adoption of the phrase to imagine a Trajanic triumph at *Pan.* 17.1.

[38] Compare Kantorowicz, 1958 on 'the king's two bodies' in medieval culture. The question of reproduction and authenticity applies also to Ovid's poem, which had to be copied in order to circulate, spreads the author's voice among many readers, and eternalises a stream of thought that purports to be immediate.

fallor, an irati mihi sunt in imagine vultus, | torvaque nescioquid forma minantis habet? ('Am I mistaken or do I see an angry expression in his portrait, and does his grim face convey something of a threat?' 21–2; compare 2.8.71–6).[39] This passage thereby conducts an immanent proto-Marxist critique of imperial ideology formation: it shows how image and reality create feedback loops in the minds of subjects who further their own sociopolitical subordination by demanding, consuming, and empowering the signs of their oppressors.

Real and Ideal

As he directs his pleas to these present *imagines* in lieu of the absent emperor, Ovid explores how such objects may create a false sense of reality even as they serve as vessels of subjects' desires and projections (27–36):

> per patriae numen, quae te tibi carior ipso est,
>   per numquam surdos in tua vota deos
> perque tori sociam, quae par tibi sola reperta est,
>   et cui maiestas non onerosa tua est,　　　　　　30
> perque tibi similem virtutis imagine natum,
>   moribus adgnosci qui tuus esse potest,
> perque tuos vel avo dignos vel patre nepotes,
>   qui veniunt magno per tua iussa gradu,
> parte leva minima nostras et contrahe poenas,　　35
>   daque, procul Scythico qui sit ab hoste, locum.

By the divine might of our country, which is dearer to you than your own self, by the gods, never deaf to your prayers, by the companion of your bed, who alone is found to be your equal, and who does not find your greatness burdensome, and by your son, like you in his image of virtue, who can be recognised from his character to be yours, and by your grandsons, worthy either of their father or their grandfather, who advance with great steps by your commands, lighten and reduce my punishment by just a tiny part, and grant me a place which is far from the Scythian enemy.

Here, the narrator performs what appears to be an ideal reading of the Caesars' already idealised representations in silver, carefully worded to remind urban readers like Cotta of the misleading 'image of virtue' (31)

---

[39] Hardie suggests (2002: 322) that Ovid's use of *fallo* invites readers to join him in suspending disbelief; I find, rather, that it calls their attention to his self-deceptive thought process.

that they (along with poems like Ovid's) help sustain and circulate. Absent is any indication of the aging Augustus' decline from his youthful portrait types; any mention of his daughter and granddaughter Julia, exiled amidst sexual and political scandal in 2 BCE and 8 CE, respectively; suspicions that Livia was more than Augustus' 'equal' behind the throne (29–30) despite her low profile on urban monuments; and the dynastic troubles that finally resulted in Augustus' grudging adoption of her son Tiberius as his own (31) in 4 CE. These included the untimely deaths in 2 and 4 CE of the grandsons whose careers Augustus had accelerated 'with great steps' in hopes of their succession (33–4), years before Ovid departed Rome in 8 CE. His pretence not yet to have received the news in Tomis (note the present-tense *veniunt* at 34) enhances his intimation throughout the exile poems that provincial subjects live in an information vacuum, reliant on sparse, unreliable, and belated sources to construct their vision of Rome.[40] Such ignorance would explain the narrator's perception of a family resemblance between the silver Augustus and Tiberius as 'image[s] of virtue' (31), despite the two men's non-consanguinity and Tiberius' dubious moral repute.[41] His invocation of 'Caesar next to Caesar' (*Caesare proxime Caesar*, 37) similarly implies that the two are presented as serial iterations on this silver surface and in official accounts abroad.[42] The prayer that Tiberius may long 'be able to be a son' (*possis filius esse diu*, 42) raises the ironic possibility, for cynical readers, that Augustus might reconsider the adoption or that Tiberius would follow his precedent in styling himself *divi filius* ('son of a god') long after his death.[43] These evident misprisions illustrate the deceptive version of reality that generic, idealising imperial imagery manufactures in the minds of subjects with few other points of comparison.

Ovid crystallises this idea when, in looking upon the statues, he 'seems to see Rome itself, because the emperor sustains the face of his homeland' (*hunc ego cum spectem, videor mihi cernere Romam, | nam patriae*

[40] *Tr.* 3.12 and *Pont.* 3.4, discussed by Pandey, 2018: 215–39, are good examples. See also Millar, 1982 on the frontiers as an 'information barrier' and Lott, 2012: 339–40 on Augustus' cultivation of Gaius and Lucius' careers.

[41] See Miller 2004, 233. Compare Ovid's similar naturalisation of the succession at *Met.* 15 as if it were genealogical rather than adoptive, discussed by Pandey, 2013 and 2018: 74–82.

[42] Hardie (2002: 255) points out Ovid's repetition of the word *Caesar* to blur the bounds between these two men; see also this poem's first line and *Tr.* 2.230.

[43] Prayers for the emperor's long life were already becoming a trope (cf. Helzle, 2003: 367), here almost caricatured; Ovid is making a cliché of his own prior usage (e.g. at *Tr.* 2.57, 5.2.51, 5.5.61, 5.11.25–6). For rumours that, towards the end of his life, Augustus visited the exiled Agrippa Postumus and considered preferring him as heir, see Cass. Dio 56.30, Tac. *Ann.* 1.5, and Detweiler, 1970.

faciem sustinet ille suae, 19–20).[44] In literal terms, of course, the emperor's face looks nothing like Rome's. But the narrator's metonymic conflation of Augustus and Rome points out that both were known in the provinces through coins, temples, statues, prayers, and inscriptions linking their names and Genii.[45] Ovid's importunement of Caesar in the name of *virtus*, Tiberius, Gaius, and Lucius, all featuring prominently on coins, underscores the extent to which such images shape the imaginations and conceptual lexicons of subjects abroad. From their perspective, the emperor is visually synonymous with the 'divine might of your country, which is dearer to you than you yourself' (*patriae numen, quae te tibi carior ipso est*, 27, interlacing pronouns underscoring their conceptual interconnectivity).[46] The narrator's vision of foreign peoples, no less than Rome, depends on representations that reduce and report grand public ceremonies like the triumph to the provinces, much as the Boscoreale cup miniaturised a triumph for an elite Campanian consumer. His vision of 'wild Germany', personified as a 'slave with fearful expression', borne before 'triumphal horses' (*sic fera quam primum pavido Germania vultu | ante triumphantis serva feratur equos*, 39–40) emphatically envisions Germany as one of the provincial effigies reproduced on coins, reliefs, and statues throughout empire, as in the image of the kneeling barbarian at Fig. 4.3.[47] Through this Pontic flight of fancy spurred by the emperor's image, Ovid shows elite urban readers the formative, even warping effects of stock representations on provincial perceptions of Rome (41). At the same time, he demonstrates their shared complicity in creating the conditions that allowed such verbal and visual rhetoric to dominate Roman discourse, and in continuing to demand, produce, and consume it in the form of likenesses, and poems, like these.

[44] This literalises Cicero's *Phil.* 8.23 and revises it for more autocratic times (*senatus enim faciem secum attulerat auctoritatemque rei publicae*, 'for the senate bears with it the face and authority of the *res publica*'). Ovid explored the trope already in *Tr.* 5.2.49: *o decus, o patriae per te florentis imago* ('O ornament, O image of your homeland flourishing because of you').

[45] The emperor also sustains the appearance of his homeland economically through public expenditures. Hardie (2002: 320) additionally points out that the phrase encompasses the image's ability to 'play the part of' or 'wear the face of' Caesar (as in theatrical masks).

[46] Richmond, 1990 prints *numen*; Owen, 1984 [1915], *nomen*. The latter would add a different spin to the joke, connecting it with the iconographical and inscriptional association between Augustus and Roma.

[47] Compare the Augustan poets' generic or explicitly fictitious treatments of triumphal imagery, discussed by Pandey, 2018: 194–224 as a marker of their own mimetic reliance on imperial representations.

Figure 4.3 Denarius of Augustus, 12 BCE, Rome. Obverse: AVGVSTVS, bare head right. Reverse: L CANINIVS GALLVS IIIVIR with barbarian kneeling right and offering a vexillum. *RIC* I² Augustus 416; *BMC* 128. Photograph © The American Numismatic Society.

The Imperfection of Representation

It might not seem overly problematic, from an official point of view, for subject peoples to form false beliefs about the emperor and Rome, so long as they obey. But by emphasising the indirect relationship between imperial representations and realities, Ovid suggests a philosophical and ontological paradox behind imperial image transmission. At lines 9, 13, 17, and 19, Ovid had thrilled to 'see' the emperor via his images. At 53–62, he ascribes great power to the sight of the Caesars rather than the Caesars directly: it is the emperor's appearance rather than his command that spares the gladiator (53),[48] the sight of his face that brings help (54), and the vision of his likeness that cheers the exiled poet, 'as far as allowed' (*qua licet*, 55). This latter qualification, however, prompts meditation on imperial images' deficiencies as vessels of theophany (57–62):

> felices illi, qui non simulacra, sed ipsos
> quique deum coram corpora vera vident.
> quod quoniam nobis invidit inutile fatum,
> quos dedit ars, vultus effigiemque colo.   60
> sic homines novere deos, quos arduus aether
> occulit, et colitur pro Iove forma Iovis.

---

[48] Galasso, 1995: 369 cites other Ovidian passages on gladiatorial combat but cannot find independent testimony for this assertion, leading Helzle, 2003: 369 to favour the emendation *ad nutum* for *adventum*.

> Happy are they who see not the *simulacra*, but the gods themselves, and who see the true bodies of the gods before their eyes. Because unprofitable fate denies me that, I worship the faces and depiction that art has provided. Thus men come to know the gods, whom lofty heaven conceals, and worship the form of Jupiter in Jupiter's stead.

This discussion recalls the Platonic distinction between, say, a table's material instantiations and its true form (*Rep.* 596a–b). So too are representations of the emperor imperfect but indispensable intermediaries by which mortals may know and worship the divine (*colitur pro Iove forma Iovis*, 61–2). On the other hand, consumers' sensory perceptions of these representations may lead them to beliefs that contradict official 'truths'. Moreover, despite Augustus' refusal of personal worship in Rome, he is visually indistinguishable from the gods in the provinces: both appear only through *simulacra* (57, the usual term for cult statues) that functionally collapse the two.[49]

These *simulacra*, moreover, are subject to physical as well as interpretive indignities. In his conversation with Janus as featured on the old Republican *as* in *Fasti* 1, Ovid alludes to the wear and tear that obscures the god's stamped face: '*noscere me duplici posses sub imagine*', *dixit* | '*ni vetus ipsa dies extenuasset opus*' ("'You'd be able to recognise me under the double image," he said, "if old age itself had not worn out the design'", 231–2). But distance, as well as time, could erode: the fresh-struck faces of coins minted at Rome wore down, too, as they passed through various hands in circulating out to the frontiers. On a figurative level, even though Cotta's likenesses originate in Rome, they are described in well-worn terms that highlight the second-hand, indistinguishable quality of imperial representations as viewed from a provincial perspective. This is a liability of all serial mimeses, one that preoccupies the exiled poet given his own works' reliance on successive hands to copy and preserve them. He complains at *Tristia* 3.12, for instance, that his news of Rome depends on a tenuous rumour chain subject to ships' routes, winter weather, and unverified sailors' reports eagerly consumed by information-starved audiences (*fieri famae parsque gradusque potest*, 'he can become a part and passer-on of fame', 3.12.44). At *Pont.* 3.4, Ovid excuses his poetic mimesis of a triumph at 2.1 on the grounds that news reaches Tomis only vaguely and belatedly. News of Augustus' death and Tiberius' succession, too, would be subject to

---

[49] Cf. Galasso, 1995: 344–5 and 372 and, for the gods' and Caesar's shared absence, Hardie, 2002: 319. Ovid also refers to Augustus as *terrarum dominum* ('lord of the world', *Pont.* 2.8.26) despite the emperor's known dislike of the term (Suet. *Aug.* 53); see Wallace-Hadrill, 1982.

a time lag making it impossible for Ovid to tell whether the *simulacrum* of Augustus represented a living, dead, or deified emperor at the time of writing. The fact that this statue may very well be a *praesens deus* underscores the numinous power of images in the minds of subjects, as well as the high stakes of interpretive interventions like Ovid's.

On the one hand, then, the poet's (over-)attribution of divine agency to these statues from his credulous provincial persona re-enacts, in strikingly simplified terms, the range of social and political practices by which subjects at every social stratum all across empire fashioned themselves in submission to an imperial authority they experienced largely indirectly, through signs. But, with a comic twist at 63–70, Ovid demonstrates consumers' concomitant power to submit these signs, and via them the emperor, to unauthorised interpretations and (ab)uses:

> denique, quae mecum est et erit sine fine, cavete,
> ne sit in inviso vestra figura loco.
> nam caput hoc nostra citius cervice recedet,   65
> et patiar fossis lumen abire genis,
> quam caream raptis, o publica numina, vobis:
> vos eritis nostrae portus et ara fugae.
> vos ego complectar, Geticis si cingar ab armis,
> utque meas aquilas, < . . . . s>igna sequar.[50]   70

So beware that your likeness, which is here with me and will be without end, not stay in a hateful place. For sooner will my head recede from my neck and I suffer my eye to depart from my gouged cheeks, than I go without you, O public divinities, [and let you be] snatched away: you will be the haven and altar of my exile. I will embrace you, if I'm surrounded by Getic arms, and I'll follow you as my eagles and my standards.

Here, the narrator acts on his idea that the emperor is public property (*Tr.* 4.4.15; *Pont.* 2.1.17–18, etc.) by physically as well as hermeneutically appropriating the emperor's image for private purposes.[51] Clutching it to his chest and vowing never to let it go, he hilariously transfers his naïve conflation of image and person onto the Caesars himself when he urges them to rescue themselves, and hence him, from their wretched Pontic abode. (The same

---

[50] The various textual possibilities (*tutaque* or *vos ego signa*, emended by Korn to *ut mea signa*) make little difference.

[51] Compare his assertion at *Tr.* 4.2.62 that even the lowliest of Romans is entitled to enjoy 'so great' a public 'good' as news of the triumph, discussed above and by Pandey, 2018: 224 and 2020. The emperor, far from ruling an *imperium sine fine* as in *Aeneid* 1.279, is now subject *sine fine* (63) to the poet.

conflation would have grimmer consequences for the young man who, according to Cassius Dio 78.15.5, was sentenced to death for bringing a coin bearing Caracalla's face into a brothel, thus debasing the imperial person.)[52] On the other hand, the poet's subsequent promise that his 'head will ... recede from [his] neck' and his eye will 'depart from [his] gouged cheek' before he relinquishes these images again dismantles the illusion. It is the Caesars, not he, whose heads are severed from their bodies to feature on imperial coins and busts, and whose eyes are chiselled from statues for the gaze of viewers across empire.[53] The image of head sundered from body thus becomes an ironic emblem for the representations that embody imperial power across space and time yet elude his governing control. Ovid's vision of hiding from the Getes behind these tutelary deities drives home the culturally conditioned, subjective judgement behind his (over-)valuation of the imperial image. A savage race, concerned like Robinson Crusoe with mere survival, would hardly share the fetishistic thinking that vests this totemic shield with protective power in the narrator's imagination. At the same time, this flight of fancy evokes the worship of imperial *simulacra* among the legionary standards,[54] a real-world instance where fetishism played a pragmatic as well as symbolic role in undergirding the military might that enforced Roman power.

Publica numina

Ovid concludes *Pont.* 2.8 with a return to the pathetic fallacy, imagining that the images' features grow kindlier in response to his prayers – though he may 'deceive himself' or 'be made mockery of' by excessive 'desire' or 'hope' (*aut ego me fallo nimioque cupidine ludor | aut spes exilii commodioris adest*, 71–2).[55] This imaginative conversion of image into reality, now animated by the poet's wishful thinking to countermand Augustus' punitive intentions, is a fitting capstone to this poem's examination of the

---

[52] See Hekster, 2011: 2.

[53] Helzle, 2003: 372 calls these *adynata* 'besonders drastisch' – but my point is that they are not *adynata* in the realm of representation. Parallels include lovers' refusals of separation at Prop. 2.7.7–8 and Ov. *Her.* 16.155–6. The gouged-out eyes have clear tragic undertones, e.g. at *Aen.* 3.663, *Ars am.* 1.339, and Sen. *Oed.* 957.

[54] Tac. *Ann.* 15.24.3 and Cass. Dio 63.25.1; cf. also Tac. *Hist.* 1.41; Cass. Dio 59.27.3; Suet. *Tib.* 48.2, *Calig.* 14.3 and *Vit.* 2.4; Scott, 1930, 1931: 118, and Helgeland, 1988.

[55] Compare *Tristia* 1.2, where the storm seems to calm in response to the poet's prayers. Gregory (1994: 88) notes some (later) instances where imperial statues were thought to bear portentous power.

individual hermeneutic processes that were ultimately responsible for con-structing (or failing to construct) ideological meaning around the coins, statues, inscriptions, and built environments examined throughout this volume. *Pont.* 2.8 simultaneously deconstructs and reinforces the process by which the apparatuses of imperial power, to use Althusserian terms, gain meaning, value, and agency through mutually constitutive interactions with the subjects who demand and consume them. In Ovid's simultaneously naïve and knowing depiction, these intrinsically irrational interactions perpetuate subjects' psychosocial self-subjugation to dominant powers. Yet this poem's multivalence becomes a mirror for the intrinsic indeterminacy of all represen-tation, portraying consumers as powerful and at least partly autonomous co-creators of imperial meaning, even if they do not always realise it themselves.

The Ovidian narrator's imagined monologue, returned to Rome as textual coin in payment for Cotta's gift, itself becomes a consumer good exemplifying the liabilities of Rome's necessary reliance on representation to bridge the information gap between empire's centre and periphery, not to mention the 'reality gap' that thereby emerged between emperors and their 'perception by different layers of society'.[56] It is easy to see why this poetic reminder that the visually omnipresent, seemingly omnipotent emperor could not control his appearance within subjects' minds might appeal to Rome's literary elite as they redefined themselves in relation to Rome's new dominant force.[57] Later in the empire, however, fiction would become reality as subjects formed false perceptions based on real-world conflations of image with events. Elsewhere in this volume, Hellström illustrates the point with a story from Cassius Dio:

> On one occasion, when a great many images of Plautianus had been made (this incident is well worth relating) Severus was displeased at their number and caused some of them to be melted down, and in consequence a rumour spread to the cities that the prefect had been overthrown and had perished. So some of them demolished his images, an act for which they were later punished. *Epit. hist. Rom.* 76.14 (trans. Cary)

This anecdote vindicates Ovid's theme that the representations through which the emperor ruled belonged less to him than to his subjects, bore a bidirectional relationship with reality, and were subject to autonomous

---

[56] In Hekster's phrase (2011: 111). Cf. Bauman, 2007: 57 and Greene, 2008: 78 on consumers as themselves commodities. Underlying the whole rhetorical situation of exile is Ovid's professed desire to exchange verses for social capital and imperial forgiveness.

[57] Pandey, 2018: 87–92 discusses elegy as a reaction to this status shift in light of the Republican conception of *libertas* as freedom from domination; see also Miller, 2004.

animation and remediation. In the final analysis, the power of images in the age of Augustus, and beyond, stemmed from a socially conditioned yet remarkably democratic process of creative consumption that rendered the Caesars *publica numina* indeed.

Bibliography

Ahl, F. 1984. 'The art of safe criticism in Greece and Rome', *AJPh* 105: 174–208.

Appadurai, A. 1986. *The Social Life of Things: Commodities in Cultural Perspective* (Cambridge: Cambridge University Press).

Bauman, Z. 2007. *Consuming Life* (London: Polity Press).

Beacham, R. C. 2005. 'The emperor as impresario', in Galinsky, K. (ed.), *The Cambridge Companion to the Age of Augustus* (Cambridge: Cambridge University Press), 151–74.

Beard, M. 2009 (reprint). *The Roman Triumph* (Cambridge, MA: Harvard University Press).

Boyle, A. J. 2003. *Ovid and the Monuments: A Poet's Rome*. Ramus Monographs 4 (Bendigo, Victoria: Aureal Publications).

Brilliant, R. 1999. '"Let the trumpets roar!" The Roman triumph', in Bergmann, B. and C. Kondoleon (eds.), *The Art of Ancient Spectacle* (Washington, DC: National Gallery of Art), 221–9.

Brunt, P. A. 1990. *Roman Imperial Themes* (Oxford: Clarendon Press).

Cary, E. 1914–27. *Cassius Dio: Roman History*. Loeb Classical Library (Cambridge, MA: Harvard University Press).

Casali, S. 1996. '*Quaerenti plura legendum*: on the necessity of "reading more" in Ovid's exile poetry', *Ramus* 26: 80–112.

Crawford, M. 1974. *Roman Republican Coinage* (London: Cambridge University Press).

Davis, P. J. 2002. 'The colonial subject in Ovid's exile poetry', *AJPh* 123: 257–73.

Detweiler, R. 1970. 'Historical perspectives on the death of Agrippa Postumus', *CJ* 65: 289–95.

Dowling, M. B. 2006. *Clemency and Cruelty in the Roman World* (Ann Arbor: University of Michigan Press).

Edwards, C. and G. Woolf 2003. 'Cosmopolis: Rome the world city', in Edwards, C. and G. Woolf (eds.), *Rome the Cosmopolis* (Cambridge: Cambridge University Press), 1–20.

Elsner, J. 1998. *Imperial Rome and Christian Triumph: The Art of the Roman Empire* AD *100–450* (Oxford: Oxford University Press).

Evans, H. B. 1983. *Publica Carmina: Ovid's Books from Exile* (Lincoln: University of Nebraska Press).

Favro, D. 2005. 'Making Rome a world city', in Galinsky, K. (ed.), *The Cambridge Companion to the Age of Augustus* (Cambridge: Cambridge University Press), 234–63.

Frazer, J. G. 1929. *Publii Ovidii Nasonis Fastorum Libri Sex: The Fasti of Ovid.* Vol. 2: *A Commentary on Books I and II* (London: Macmillan).

Galasso, L. 1995. *P. Ovidii Nasonis Epistularum ex Ponto II* (Florence: le Monnier).

Gibson, B. 1999. 'Ovid on reading: reading Ovid. Reception in Ovid *Tristia* II', *JRS* 89: 19–37.

Green, S. J. 2004. *Ovid, Fasti 1: A Commentary.* Mnemosyne Suppl. 251 (Leiden: Brill).

Greene, K. 2008. 'Learning to consume: consumption and consumerism in the Roman Empire', *JRA* 21: 64–82.

Gregory, A. P. 1994. '"Powerful images": responses to portraits and the political uses of images in Rome', *JRA* 7: 80–99.

Habinek, T. 1998. *The Politics of Latin Literature: Writing, Identity, and Empire in Ancient Rome* (Princeton: Princeton University Press).

  2002. 'Ovid and empire', in Hardie, P. R. (ed.), *The Cambridge Companion to Ovid* (Cambridge: Cambridge University Press), 46–61.

Hardie, P. 2002. *Ovid's Poetics of Illusion* (Cambridge: Cambridge University Press).

Hekster, O. 2011. 'Imagining power: reality gaps in the Roman Empire', *BABesch* 86: 111–24.

Helgeland, J. 1988. 'Roman army religion', *ANRW* II.16.2, 1470–1505.

Helzle, M. 2003. *Ovids Epistulae ex Ponto: Buch I–II. Kommentar* (Heidelberg: Winter).

Henderson, J. 2002. 'A doo-dah-doo-dah-dey at the races: Ovid *Amores* 3.2 and the personal politics of the Circus Maximus', *ClAnt* 21: 41–65.

Hinds, S. E. 1985. 'Booking the return trip: Ovid and *Tristia* 1', *PCPhS* 31: 13–32.

  1988. 'Generalizing about Ovid', in Boyle, A. J. (ed.), *The Imperial Muse: Ramus Essays on Roman Literature of the Empire, to Juvenal through Ovid* (Victoria, Australia: Aureal), 4–31.

Hollis, A. S. (ed.) 1977. *Ovid: Ars Amatoria, Book 1* (Oxford: Oxford University Press).

Howgego, C. 1995. *Ancient History from Coins* (London: Routledge).

Howgego, C., V. Heuchert, and A. Burnett 2005. *Coinage and Identity in the Roman Provinces* (Oxford; New York: Oxford University Press).

Huet, V. 1996. 'Stories one might tell of Roman art: reading Trajan's Column and the Tiberius Cup', in Elsner, J. (ed.), *Art and Text in Roman Culture* (Cambridge: Cambridge University Press), 8–31.

Johnson, W. A. and H. N. Parker 2009. *Ancient Literacies: The Culture of Reading in Greece and Rome* (Oxford: Oxford University Press).

Kantorowicz, E. H. 1958. *The King's Two Bodies: A Study in Mediaeval Political Theology* (Princeton: Princeton University Press).

Kleiner, D. 2005. *Cleopatra and Rome* (Cambridge, MA: Harvard University Press).

Kleiner, F. 1997. Review of A. Kuttner, *Dynasty and Empire in the Age of Augustus: The Case of the Boscoreale Cups, JRA* 10: 377–80.

2010. *A History of Roman Art, Enhanced Edition* (Belmont, CA: Cengage Learning).

Künzl, E. 1988. *Der römische Triumph: Siegesfeiern im antiken Rom* (Munich: Beck).

1989. 'Der Kniefall des Tiberius: zu den beiden Kaiserbechern von Boscoreale', *AArchHung* 41: 73–9.

Kuttner, A. L. 1995. *Dynasty and Empire in the Age of Augustus: The Case of the Boscoreale Cups* (Berkeley: University of California Press).

Little, D. A. 1990. 'Ovid's last poems: cry of pain from exile or literary frolic in Rome?' *Prudentia* 21: 23–39.

Lott, J. B. 2012. *Death and Dynasty in Early Imperial Rome: Key Sources with Text, Translation and Commentary* (Cambridge: Cambridge University Press).

McGowan, M. M. 2009. *Ovid in Exile: Power and Poetic Redress in the Tristia and Epistulae Ex Ponto* (Leiden: Brill).

Millar, F. 1982. 'Emperors, frontiers, and foreign relations, 31 b.c. to a.d. 378', *Britannia* 13: 1–23.

Miller, P. A. 2004. *Subjecting Verses: Latin Love Elegy and the Emergence of the Real* (Princeton: Princeton University Press).

Mitchell, W. J. T. 2005. *What Do Pictures Want? The Lives and Loves of Images* (Chicago: University of Chicago Press).

Morley, N. 2007. *Trade in Classical Antiquity* (Cambridge: Cambridge University Press).

Nugent, G. 1990. '*Tristia* 2: Ovid and Augustus', in Raaflaub, K. and M. Toher (eds.), *Between Republic and Empire: Interpretations of Augustus and his Principate* (Berkeley: University of California Press), 239–57.

Oliensis, E. 1997. 'Return to sender: the rhetoric of *nomina* in Ovid's *Tristia*', *Ramus* 26: 172–93.

2004. 'The power of image-makers: representation and revenge in Ovid, *Metamorphoses* 6 and *Tristia* 4', *ClAnt* 23: 285–321.

Östenberg, I. 2009. *Staging the World: Spoils, Captives, and Representations in the Roman Triumphal Procession* (Oxford: Oxford University Press).

Owen, S. G. 1984 [1915]. *P. Ovidi Nasonis Tristium libri quinque, ex Ponto libri quattuor, Halieutica fragmenta*. Oxford Classical Texts (Oxford: Oxford University Press).

Pandey, N. B. 2011. Empire of the Imagination: The Power of Public Fictions in Ovid's Reader Response to Augustan Rome. PhD Diss., Berkeley.

2013. 'Caesar's comet, the Julian star, and the invention of Augustus', *TAPhA* 143: 405–49.

2018. *The Poetics of Power in Augustan Rome: Latin Poetic Responses to Early Imperial Iconography* (Cambridge: Cambridge University Press).

2020. 'Ovid on the *res publica*: public figures, information access, and inter-pretive liberty in Ancient Rome and modern America', in Nelsestuen, G. and D. Kapust (eds.), *From Polis to Urbs: Contemporary Directions in Roman Political Thought. Polis* 37: 123–44.

Pollini, J. 2012. *From Republic to Empire: Rhetoric, Religion, and Power in the Visual Culture of Ancient Rome* (Norman: University of Oklahoma Press).

Ray, N. 2009. Household Consumption in Ancient Economies: Pompeii and the Wider Roman World. PhD Diss., Leicester.

Richmond, J. A. 1990. *Ex Ponto Libri Quattuor* (Leipzig: Teubner).

Rolfe, J. C. (trans.) 1913–14. *Suetonius: The Lives of the Twelve Caesars* (Cambridge, MA: Harvard University Press).

Scott, K. 1930. 'Emperor worship in Ovid', *TAPhA* 61: 43–69.

1931. 'The significance of statues in precious metals', *TAPhA* 62: 101–23.

Veyne, P. 1988. 'Conduct without belief and works of art without viewers', trans. J. Ferguson, *Diogenes* 36: 1–22.

2002. 'Lisibilité des images, propaganda et apparat monarchique dans l'Empire romain', *RH* 304.1: 3–30.

Villefosse, H. de 1899. *Le trésor de Boscoreale* (Paris: Fondation Eugène Pilot).

Waites, M. C. 1920. 'The nature of the *lares* and their representation in Roman art', *AJA* 24: 241–61.

Walker, S. and A. Burnett 1981. *The Image of Augustus* (London: British Museum).

Wallace-Hadrill, A. 1982. '*Civilis princeps*: between citizen and king', *JRS* 72: 32–48.

1986. 'Image and authority in the coinage of Augustus', *JRS* 76: 66–87.

Walsh, J. 2014. *Consumerism in the Ancient World: Imports and Identity Construction* (New York: Routledge).

Williams, G. 1994. *Banished Voices: Readings in Ovid's Exile Poetry* (Cambridge: Cambridge University Press).

2002. 'Ovid's exile poetry: *Tristia, Epistulae ex Ponto*, and *Ibis*', in Hardie, P. (ed.), *The Cambridge Companion to Ovid* (Cambridge: Cambridge University Press), 233–45.

Woolf, G. 1998. *Becoming Roman: The Origins of Provincial Civilization in Gaul* (Cambridge: Cambridge University Press).

Woytek, B. 2015. '"*Hominem te memento!*": der mahnende Sklave im römischen Triumph und seine Ikonographie', *Tyche* 30: 193–209.

Zanker, P. 1990. *The Power of Images in the Age of Augustus*, trans. A. Shapiro (Ann Arbor: University of Michigan Press).

5 | Roman Emperors, Conquest, and Violence

Images from the Eastern Provinces

CAILLAN DAVENPORT

Introduction

Early in 68, the emperor Nero was forced to hurry back to Rome from Naples after disturbing messages reached him about the revolt of C. Julius Vindex in Gaul.[1] Suetonius writes that Nero's despair was lifted momentarily on the journey when he caught sight of a sculpted monument showing a Roman equestrian officer dragging a Gallic warrior by the hair.[2] This was probably one of many reliefs commemorating Romano-Gallic conflicts that had been created in Italy during the Republican period, when Rome first began to celebrate enemy defeats in this fashion.[3] By Nero's reign, such images were familiar commonplaces on the tombstones of Roman soldiers, such as that of the Thracian cavalryman Longinus Sdapeze, whose tombstone from Camulodunum shows him on horseback trampling his opponent to death.[4] This manner of representing the treatment of enemy combatants was not indigenous to Rome. Millennia earlier, Akkadian, Assyrian, and Egyptian kings had been depicted crushing their rivals underfoot or grasping them by the hair.[5] Indeed, throughout history it has been common for monarchical societies to depict their rulers in combat, for this was one way

[1] I am very grateful to Amy Russell and Monica Hellström for inviting me to be a part of this rewarding project and for their comments and feedback on the chapter. I would like to thank James Corke-Webster, who offered an immensely helpful formal response to my paper, and all participants in the Durham workshops who engaged thoughtfully and critically with my arguments. The final version has also benefited from the comments of Meaghan McEvoy and the anonymous readers for Cambridge University Press. The research and writing of this chapter have been supported by the Australian Research Council's Discovery Early Career Researcher Award funding scheme (project DE150101110). I am grateful to Charlotte Mann for her research assistance with the numismatic evidence.

[2] Suet. *Ner.* 41.2.
[3] Zanker, 1998: 68; Holliday, 2002: 74–5. For an example from Trier in Gaul, see Walter, 1993: 41–5.
[4] *RIB* I 201 = *CSIR* I.8, no. 48.
[5] See the Victory Stele of the Akkadian king Naram-Sin (Foster, 2016: 10–11, 200) and a relief of the Assyrian king Tiglath-pileser III from Nimrud showing him standing on an enemy's neck (Assante, 2017: 45–6). For the Egyptian motif, see Hall, 1986.

of recognising that a king was a king.[6] But no one would have seen the emperor Nero depicted crushing or smiting barbarians in Italy or the western provinces.

Roman imperial imagery did, of course, celebrate the conquest and subjugation of foreign peoples. We can see this on media as diverse as the temple of Apollo Sosianus, which depicts both a cavalry battle and Octavian's triumph of 29 BCE, and the Gemma Augustea, in which Augustus and his family preside over the restoration of world order after the subjugation of the barbarians.[7] Indeed, on the Gemma Augustea the actual violence of dragging a foreign woman by the hair is performed by a Roman officer, not by the *princeps* himself. The emperor was not personally depicted as an agent of violence maiming or crushing enemies on these or other images produced in the west during the Julio-Claudian period.[8] This is certainly true of what we call 'official' media, authorised and produced by the Roman state, such as coinage minted at Rome.[9] But it also seems to be the case with the range of 'unofficial' artistic works, like lamps, terracotta reliefs, and statuettes.[10] The absence of the subjugating emperor from the range of western media is noteworthy given that such an image could clearly be envisaged in literature.[11] In Ovid's *Tristia*, the poet imagines Tiberius' triumph over Germany, with the defeated nation sitting at his feet, offering her neck to the victorious general.[12]

[6] Fowler and Hekster, 2005: 12, 26; Oakley, 2006: 11–12, 41.

[7] Zanker, 1998: 68–70; Pollini, 2012: 183–4.

[8] See Kiss, 1989: 127–8, and on the elevated position of the emperor in combat scenes, see Hölscher, 2003: 6–7. The closest possible parallel is the Arch of Drusus the Elder erected by the emperor Claudius. The statuary group on top of the arch showed Drusus on horseback brandishing a spear, between two trophies, with barbarian captives (*RIC* I² Claudius 69). The 'images of subjugated peoples' (*signis devictarum gentium*) on the arch erected in honour of Germanicus in the Circus Flaminius (*Tab. Siar.* frag. (i), 10) do not appear to have been shown as recipients of violence. We only know that they were 'in the corners' (*in a[ngulis]*). See Lott, 2012: 217.

[9] For the use of the term 'official', see the Introduction; Noreña, 2011: 15–17, 200–18; Hekster, 2015: 30–4. One possible exception is the military *signum* from Niederbieber in Germany, which shows an emperor standing on a barbarian. It has been suggested that this is a Julio-Claudian emperor, but the iconography better fits the late Roman Empire (La Baume, 1977; Walter, 1993: 52–3).

[10] There are small statuettes found in the western provinces which do show barbarians beneath a foot, either of Victory or the emperor, but the agent is unknown. These are usually dated to the second and third centuries CE (Bieńkowski, 1928: 55–7; Levi, 1952: 31–2). 'Official' or 'unofficial' are useful shorthand terms, although neither is entirely satisfactory, as they do not capture the range of patrons and artists involved in the creation of these media, from moneyers at the Roman mint to non-imperial benefactors of public buildings; see Mayer, 2010: 112–17 on the agents involved in the production of images of Augustus, and Davenport, 2014: 45–59 on the late empire. See also the Introduction and Russell, Goldman-Petri, and Rowan in this volume.

[11] Depictions of the subjugated barbarians themselves were ubiquitous in the west (see the catalogue in Walter, 1993), but in this chapter I am concerned with images of the emperors personally conquering them.

[12] Ov. *Tr.* 2.4.43–6.

The lack of images of the emperor as a violent conqueror can be explained by the change in representation of the first *princeps* after 27 BCE. The generals of the triumviral period, including the young Caesar himself, had been portrayed as subjugators.[13] For example, a denarius of Sextus Pompeius depicted a statue of himself (or his father Cn. Pompeius Magnus) performing *calcatio* on the prow of a ship, a gesture which represented domination over the sea.[14] After the young Caesar had defeated Sextus Pompeius, a public statue was erected of him in a similar pose as a riposte to his vanquished enemy. This statue, as shown on a near-contemporary denarius, depicted the young general triumphant with his foot on the celestial globe, signifying his conquest of land and sea.[15] The most dramatic example of such imagery is an agate intaglio produced in the period 31–27 BCE. This shows the young Caesar being carried over the sea by hippocamps, whose hooves trample on a defeated rival, either Sextus Pompeius or Marcus Antonius.[16] These types of images disappeared as the youthful general became Augustus, a transition which ushered in a new style of artistic representation of the *princeps* as sole ruler over a pacified world.[17] The vision of the emperor as an agent of violence, personally vanquishing his opponents, did not reappear on coins and monuments in the west until the Flavian period. This new dynasty of emperors was depicted on horseback spearing an enemy or placing their foot on a defeated barbarian in the *calcatio* style.[18]

However, in two cities in the Roman province of Asia, Koula and Aphrodisias, members of the Julio-Claudian dynasty were shown in sculptural reliefs as violent agents of subjugation. Caligula is depicted at Koula riding on horseback against a female personification of Germany, while at Aphrodisias Claudius and Nero are represented spearing Britain and brutalising Armenia, respectively. Since these monuments differ iconographically from media such as Julio-Claudian coinage and the Gemma

---

[13] Earlier Republican parallels are rare. It is possible that the marble frieze at the top of the Column of L. Aemilius Paullus at Delphi depicted Paullus himself in combat, but this is uncertain and controversial. See Kähler, 1965: 17–18; Taylor, 2016: 564–5.

[14] *RRC* 511, 3a–c, as interpreted by Zanker, 1988: 40.

[15] *RIC* I² Augustus 256; Zanker, 1988: 39–41. For the idea of conquest *terra marique* in this period, see Cornwell, 2017: 87–97.

[16] Museum of Fine Arts, Boston, 27.733; Zanker, 1988: 97–8.

[17] This is a central theme of Zanker, 1988. See especially his comments on p. 33: 'Much that had happened between 44 and 27 had to be forgotten; the image of himself that Octavian promoted before this turning point is fundamentally different from that which he later conveyed so successfully as Augustus.'

[18] As Malone, 2009: 58 points out, this is a real and vital change in imperial iconography: 'The standard depiction of the emperor as armed and armoured is military, but not explicitly violent. Violence requires a level of activity and a relational, personal element, in that the violent action needs to be inflicted on some target.'

Augustea, the patrons and artists must have also drawn inspiration from other ideas and artistic themes of monarchical representation. Indeed, as Hekster (2015: 319–20) has shown, provincial representations of Roman emperors were not simply reactions to images produced by the imperial administration, but were also shaped by their own traditions.[19] The first part of this chapter examines the iconography of the Koula and Aphrodisias monuments in order to determine why these two Greek cities in Asia created such violent imperial images, and what their impact may have been on their local audiences.[20] In the latter part of the chapter, I examine a second group of images from the eastern provinces that show the emperor as the agent of violence. These are coins referring to Domitian enslaving Germany and Dacia from Prusias ad Hypium in Bithynia, a series of statues showing Hadrian crushing a barbarian underfoot, and terracotta and marble figures from Egypt portraying an emperor grasping a barbarian by the hair. These works of art were created in a period in which the Roman emperor was increasingly depicted on coinage and monuments at Rome riding into battle and trampling enemies underfoot.

I argue that all these images of the conquering emperor produced in the eastern provinces were influenced both by local and Roman concepts of rulership and artistic practices. The emphasis on the violent treatment of foreign peoples by the Roman emperors demonstrates that the patrons of these monuments sought to identify themselves with the civilised world of Rome, rather than the subjugated barbarian 'other'. The Roman emperor was thus envisioned as a protector of his people, and a guarantor of their safety and security. This conclusion is reinforced by the fact that these depictions draw on regional traditions, transforming the emperor into a more familiar figure. At the same time, however, it is likely that these images which dramatised the coercive power of the emperor reminded his subjects of his capacity to punish them as well.

Speared by Caligula

Caligula's German campaign of 39/40 was mocked as a disastrous farce by poets and historians alike.[21] He had to be content with an ovation to celebrate his suppression of the conspiracy of the governor Gaetulicus,

[19] See also Fowler and Hekster, 2005: 31–3 on the importance of distinguishing between parallel trends in imagery and deliberate appropriation.
[20] For the emphasis on the viewer, see Elsner, 1995: 1–3; Clarke, 2003: 9–12.
[21] Pers. 6.43–9; Suet. *Calig.* 43–8; Cass. Dio 59.21.2–23.6.

rather than for his military achievements against the German tribes.[22] However, there is a fragmentary relief from Koula in Lydia (part of the Roman province of Asia) which reveals rare contemporary recognition of Caligula's achievements in Germany.[23] The relief depicts a Roman man on horseback, carrying a spear in his right hand, which is aimed provocatively towards a woman standing with her hands behind her back (Fig. 5.1). The accompanying inscription shows that the figure on horseback is Caligula, and identifies the woman as the personification of Germania:

Γαίῳ Γερμανικῷ Αὐτο|κράτορι Καίσαρι καθιέρωται | πᾶς ὁ δημόσιος τόπος

The whole public place is dedicated to Gaius Germanicus Imperator Caesar.

Γερμα|νία

Germany

The combination of text and image presents a violent image of subjugation by the Romans, which encourages the viewer to see Caligula himself as the primary agent of conquest. It is the emperor who rears up on his horse and aims his spear at the female Germania; she stands largely placid and defenceless, her arms behind her back, helpless in the face of Caligula's weapon. The Koula monument contrasts with the vision of world domination secured through the *Pax Romana* in other artistic representations, such as the Gemma Augustea or the Grand Camée de France.[24] The low quality of the monument and the roughness of the inscription show that it was not erected with imperial sponsorship, but was a local creation, perhaps intended to mark out a 'special public area in commemoration of Caligula's German campaign'.[25] The text, which may have been added to a pre-existing relief, does not have Caligula's correct titulature.[26] The emperor's name was C. Caesar Augustus Germanicus; the use of Αὐτοκράτωρ instead may well be a replacement for Σεβαστός, or intended as a reference to an imperatorial acclamation for the German victory.[27] Cassius Dio notes that Caligula was hailed as *imperator* seven times in the course of his campaigns, and although there is no other official record of this, it does not mean that it is untrue.[28] The error may indicate that the creator(s) did not copy the titulature from an official proclamation of Caligula's German success; the monuments could have

---

[22] Suet. *Calig.* 49; Cass. Dio 59.23.2.
[23] *ILS* 8791 = *TAM* 5.1 235 = *IGRR* 4.1379; Mommsen, 1888; Boschung, 1989: 120–1 (no. 51).
[24] For the rather different imperial imagery on these large cameos, see Hölscher, 2003: 10–12, 16.
[25] Price, 1984: 84.   [26] Mommsen, 1888: 19.
[27] For Caligula's titulature, see Kienast, 1996: 85.   [28] Cass. Dio 59.22.2; Balsdon, 1934: 82.

Figure 5.1 Caligula and Germania relief from Koula. Museo d'Antichità J. J. Winckelmann, Trieste, Inv. Nr. 2228. Photograph © Civico Museo di Storia ed Arte, Trieste.

been created in response to oral reports, perhaps received from the provincial capital. The Koula relief forms a distinctly individual response to Caligula's German campaign, one which was not replicated elsewhere in the empire.[29]

Subjugated by Claudius and Nero

The second monument that demands our attention is the Sebasteion (imperial cult temple) at Aphrodisias, which was a free city within the province of Asia. The patrons of the Sebasteion were two wealthy families of Aphrodisias. The south portico, which includes the imperial reliefs I examine, came under the purview of Ti. Claudius Diogenes, his brother Attalus, and Attalus' wife, Attalis Apphion.[30] In the upper register of the

[29] Amphipolis in Macedonia minted two bronze coins showing Caligula on horseback (*RPC* I.1637–8). However, he is not charging at a victim or provincial personification, as on the Koula relief.

[30] Smith, 1987: 90, 2013: 19–21, 123.

Figure 5.2 Reliefs from the Sebasteion at Aphrodisias: (left) Claudius and Britannia and (right) Nero and Armenia. Photographs: G. Petruccioli, © New York University Excavations at Aphrodisias.

south portico, Claudius appears in heroic nudity, towering over the prostrate female figure of Britannia (Fig. 5.2, left).[31] He pulls her by the hair with his right arm; the left arm, no longer extant, would have originally held a spear aimed at the prostrate province. Britannia herself is helpless, her *chiton* falling off, exposing her right breast.[32] Smith (1987: 117; 2013: 146) suggested that the relief is designed to show Claudius on the point of killing Britannia. Other commentators have drawn attention to the gender dynamics inherent in the scene, arguing that the emperor is about to rape the subjugated province.[33]

The second relief shows Nero and the kingdom of Armenia, once again personified as a woman (Fig. 5.2, right).[34] Nero is also depicted heroically nude, hoisting up the defeated Armenia in such a way that her drooping torso is effectively caught between his outstretched thighs. Armenia wears a Phrygian cap, but is otherwise almost completely naked, her *chiton* hanging limply from her right shoulder, and covering only the top of the

---

[31] Smith, 2013: 145–7.   [32] Erim, 1982: 279–80; Smith, 1987: 116.
[33] Ferris, 2000: 56–8; Whittaker, 2004: 115; Vout, 2007: 25–6.   [34] Smith, 2013: 140–3.

thigh. Smith (1987: 118–19; 2013: 142) has highlighted the Hellenistic depictions of Achilles and Penthesilea that provide inspiration for the composition of this relief. On Smith's interpretation, the relief was designed to show that Nero would 'raise' and 'embrace' the conquered Armenia into the empire. Other scholars have suggested a different, more confrontational reading, which envisages the image as the aftermath of rape.[35] Vout (2007: 25, 48) in particular has questioned Smith's conclusion, given that the ancient viewer would have recognised that Penthesilea died in the original story.[36]

The portrayal of Claudius and Nero reflects local choices made by the patrons and artists in Aphrodisias itself: the imagery is quite distinct from that found elsewhere in the empire, even in the eastern provinces.[37] For example, at Cyzicus in Asia, the Roman citizens and the Cyzicenes erected a triumphal arch to commemorate Claudius' British victory. The inscription honouring the emperor uses triumphal language which is comparable to that found on Claudius' arch in Rome.[38] This similarity suggests that both inscriptions drew on the original *senatus consultum* which voted Claudius arches in Rome and Gaul.[39] The only other form of commemoration in the eastern provinces appears on silver coins minted at Caesarea in Cappadocia. These proclaimed Claudius' victory 'over the Britons' (DE BRITANNIS), which echoes themes promoted on issues produced at Rome.[40] These are conventional forms of celebration when compared to the Aphrodisias relief. Nero's Armenian success did not receive extensive recognition throughout the east, either. Direct references to military triumph on his provincial coinage are very rare, consistent with post-Augustan trends in this medium.[41] Once again, the main exception was Caesarea in Cappadocia, which minted silver hemidrachms featuring reverses depicting Victory and the legend APMENIAC.[42] The most notable monumental celebration of Nero's achievements outside Aphrodisias occurred at Athens. In 61/2, the Athenians rededicated

---

[35] Ferris, 2000: 58; Whittaker, 2004: 115–17.

[36] Smith, 1987: 119 argued that 'that meaning can be suspended here by the compositional adjustments that avoid a direct equation with the myth'.

[37] Smith, 1987: 135–6; 2013: 147.

[38] *CIL* 3.7061 = *ILS* 217 (Cyzicus); *CIL* 6.40416 = *ILS* 216 (Rome); Barrett, 1991: 12–13.

[39] Cass. Dio 60.22.1.   [40] *RPC* I.3625.

[41] Burnett, Amandry, and Ripollès, 1992: 45. The emperor could be depicted in military uniform, however, as on a leaded bronze coin from Amphipolis in Macedonia (*RPC* I.1641).

[42] *RPC* I.3644. Cf. 3645–6, which have images of Victory on the reverse but no legend. Burnett, Amandry, and Ripollès (1992: 555) suggest that APMENIAC 'must presumably stand for something like *Victoria Armeniaca*'.

the Parthenon to Nero using gilt-bronze letters on the temple.[43] Carroll
(1982: 67–74) has proposed that this was designed to commemorate
Nero's diplomatic successes in Armenia achieved through his legate
Domitius Corbulo. What is striking about these honours is their con-
servatism when compared to the violent depiction of Nero at
Aphrodisias.

Images and Interpretation

Where did the inspiration for the imperial images at Koula and
Aphrodisias come from, given that they were so different from other
contemporary representations of Caligula, Claudius, and Nero? They
were probably influenced to some extent by images of Hellenistic kingship,
which was founded on the idea of the ruler as an active warrior.[44] The
progenitor of this imagery was of course Alexander the Great, who was
depicted riding gloriously into battle on the sarcophagus of Abdalonymos
of Sidon and in the Alexandrian painting that served as the inspiration for
the 'Alexander Mosaic' in the House of the Faun at Pompeii.[45] His
Hellenistic successors adopted this type of imagery for their own victory
monuments, as shown by Attalus I's commemoration of his victories over
the Gauls with statue groups erected at Pergamon, Athens, and Delphi in
the third century BCE. The Galatomachy dedicated by Attalus I on the
Acropolis at Athens to celebrate his victory at the River Kaïkos showed the
king himself in battle against the Gauls.[46] The Attalid victors were also
depicted in two earlier monuments at the Sanctuary of Athena Nikephoros
at Pergamon and at Delphi.[47] The idea that a king should undertake
warfare in person underlies the depiction of Roman emperors as the agents
of conquest in both the Koula and Aphrodisias reliefs. In the case of the
Koula monument, we can posit an additional source of inspiration from
Greek funerary sculpture. The image of combat between a mounted rider
and an opponent features on reliefs as diverse as the Dexileos stele from
Athens and the funerary monument of the local dynast Uzebeemi at
Kadyanda in Asia Minor (both of the fourth century BCE).[48] It was this
manner of representing combat that inspired the creation of Roman victory

---

[43] *IG* II².3277 = *SEG* 32.251; Carroll, 1982: 16.   [44] Smith, 1988a: 49; Marvin, 2002: 217.
[45] Alexander sarcophagus: Hölscher, 1973: 189–96; Smith, 1988a: 634; Stewart, 1993: 294–306.
Alexander mosaic: Hölscher, 1973: 122–69; Stewart, 1993: 130–50; Cohen, 1997.
[46] Stewart, 2004: 189, 206–13.   [47] Marvin, 2002: 211; Stewart, 2004: 148, 191–2, 197, 209–12.
[48] Hölscher, 1973: 102–3, 108; Cohen, 1997: 28–35.

commemorations such as that seen by Nero on his journey from Naples to Rome, as well as tombstones of Roman cavalrymen like Longinus Sdapeze.

However, the conflict between emperors and personified provinces at Koula and Aphrodisias also marks a departure from Greek models and shows greater Roman influence at work. Personifications of cities and regions in female form had been a feature of Hellenistic art.[49] These representations were adopted in Rome in the form of paintings and images of conquered cities carried in the triumphs of Roman generals.[50] Republican and Augustan moneyers produced coins showing a single defeated captive under a trophy or a personified province offering supplication to a general.[51] The habit of showing defeated cities or countries in the triumphal ceremonies was a peculiarly Roman practice, since Hellenistic kings, despite their penchant for depicting themselves defeating rival peoples in battle, did not usually do so in allegorical terms. The Attalid monuments, for example, portrayed Attalus I fighting real Gauls, not tribal personifications.[52] The only example of a defeated personification of a region in Hellenistic art comes in the first-century BCE frescoes at the villa of P. Fannius Synistor at Boscoreale (which were themselves Roman copies of Macedonian court painting of the third century BCE). One panel depicts a female personification of Macedonia claiming Asia (another personified woman) as spear-won territory.[53] Therefore, the Koula and Aphrodisias images emphasised the personal agency of the emperor in keeping with ideas of Hellenistic kingship, but were also shaped by the Roman visual language of subjugated provinces.

The Koula and Aphrodisias monuments depart from the standard Roman artistic presentation of defeated regions by showing the emperor himself doing violence to them. For example, the way in which Nero hoists up the brutalised Armenia at Aphrodisias contrasts with the Via Cassia terracotta relief, which shows Julius Caesar extending his hand to raise up the seated Roma.[54] The spectacle of the female body being violated by the emperor himself on the Aphrodisias reliefs, and the anticipation of such treatment at Koula, is the defining difference that sets these images apart from other contemporary depictions of imperial conquest. The mistreatment of the female bodies of Germany, Britain, and Armenia functions as a potent metaphor for the power of the Roman

---

[49] Toynbee, 1934: 7–11.   [50] Holliday, 2002: 104–14.

[51] Holliday, 2002: 115–16; Cody, 2003: 105–6, 114–15.   [52] Smith, 1988b: 70–1.

[53] Smith, 1994: 109–12. This interpretation is widely accepted (see also Holliday, 2002: 114–15; Stewart, 2014: 71–4).

[54] Barden Dowling, 2006: 24–5; Pollini, 2012: 144.

emperor.[55] Such a message would have resonated for the viewers of these monuments. In the Roman world, as in all ancient societies, people were accustomed to see punishment meted out through the mistreatment of the human body.[56] Our monuments can be seen as provincial celebrations of the martial prowess of the Roman emperor and his ability to control and subjugate foreign lands.[57] Contemporary texts composed by Greek-speaking easterners, such as Philo's *Embassy to Gaius* and the inscription on the *Stadiasmus Patarensis* in Lycia, celebrate the Roman emperor both as the bringer of peace and as a protector.[58] The commemorative impulse behind the dedication of a special public place to Caligula at Koula suggests that the patrons wished to identify themselves with the conquering Romans and their emperor, rather than the bound figure of Germany, a far-off land which most of the city's inhabitants would never have visited.

A slightly different, but complementary, argument can be made about the patrons of the Sebasteion at Aphrodisias. The citizens of Aphrodisias, a free city with immunity from taxation, envisioned themselves as allies rather than subjects of Rome.[59] The monument can thus be read as a tribute to the Roman emperor as an equal of the Aphrodisians. This is the same message as that conveyed by the Athenians when they rededicated the Parthenon to Nero. They assimilated their past success against the Persians, commemorated by the erection of the Parthenon, with Nero's own against the Armenians. The difference between the Parthenon inscription for Nero and the Sebasteion is that the former is largely traditional, whereas the imperial reliefs at Aphrodisias break with commemorative practices in the west by showing the emperor violating female bodies. Britannia and Armenia appear as bare-breasted women, and are thus inherently constructed as different and 'other' from civilised society – Rome and Aphrodisias.[60] The fact that the composition of these reliefs

---

[55] For the use of the human body for ideological purposes, see Scarry, 1985, and for violence towards bodies acting as a symbol of political control in the ancient world, see Kyle, 1998: 11; Gleason, 2001: 74, 78.

[56] Foucault, 1979. See Zimmermann, 2006: 355–7 on popular understanding of the meanings of violent imagery.

[57] For barbarians representing chaos as opposed to order, see Zanker, 1998: 72.

[58] Philo, *Leg.* 145–7 on the peace of Augustus; *SEG* 51.1832 = 57.1560 on the gratitude of Lycians for their protection by Claudius.

[59] Smith, 2013: 313.

[60] See Rogers, 2003: 84–6 on the image of the bare-breasted female. Vout, 2007: 31–2 has argued that such a viewpoint privileges the male viewer, but we must remember that one of the patrons of this part of the Sebasteion, Attalis Apphion, was a woman. It is problematic to assign views to individuals based solely on their gender.

draws inspiration from Hellenistic sculpture serves to assimilate the Roman emperor into the regional context, transforming him into a more familiar figure to the local viewer.

This interpretation of the monuments does not exclude other, more unsettling readings. We cannot discount the possibility that viewers, however much they might have wanted to identify themselves with Rome, saw a little of the subjugated provinces in themselves. For all Greeks were themselves at one time outside the orbit of Roman control.[61] The Roman process of incorporating new peoples into their empire involved rituals of bodily mistreatment and execution to mark their conquest, followed by their integration via provincialisation and grants of citizenship.[62] The violence of conquest therefore marked a moment of transition for provincials. The images of Caligula, Claudius, and Nero served as a reminder of the continuing coercive power of the Roman emperor when people transitioned from opponents to subjects. His representatives, the provincial governors, had the authority to deliver capital sentences and a range of other punishments to those who transgressed the laws.[63] For low-status individuals, these penalties would have included shameful treatment of their bodies similar to that suffered by the female provinces.[64]

The Koula and Aphrodisias images are thus the product of multiple iconographical influences and encourage a multiplicity of readings about the place of these cities in the Roman world. The images draw on representations of monarchs from the Hellenistic kingdoms, but they are also influenced by Roman representation of captured provinces in the form of female personifications. In their portrayal of the emperor himself as the agent of violent subjugation, the Koula and Aphrodisias patrons deviate from other representations of Roman conquest to produce a striking new conception of the emperor. Through such monuments, they position themselves as allies and supporters of Rome and its civilising process, and show the futility of resistance to Roman power. This message, I would argue, was enhanced by the fact that these images do not replicate images produced at Rome and in the west, but draw on regional conceptions of military leadership and representations of conflict. At the same

---

[61] This reading is inspired by the discussion of Clarke, 2003: 38–41 on outsiders and insiders, and the integration of new peoples into the *imperium Romanum*, on Trajan's Column. Cf. Smith, 2013: 313, who has argued in his discussion of the Aphrodisias reliefs that 'the Roman conquest of Greece is, if not forgotten, out of sight, out of mind, anyway irrelevant'.

[62] Bryen, 2014: 136.

[63] Note especially Dio Chrys. *Or.* 46.14 on the deeds and misdeeds of Greek communities being reported to the governors.

[64] See Garnsey, 1970: 136–41.

time, however, these images had the capacity to remind viewers of their own subordination to the emperor, in both the past and the present.

Imperial Innovations

The Flavian period marked a watershed in the representation of the Roman emperor. The mint at Rome began to produce *capta* coin types showing a defeated province for the first time since the late first century BCE.[65] In 72/3, the mint issued the first reverse design of the 'charging horseman' type, depicting Titus on horseback spearing an opponent; the same image subsequently featured on bronze coins of Domitian produced in 85–9.[66] An *aureus* of Titus was also produced in 70 showing the personification of Virtus putting his foot on a defeated foe in the *calcatio* style.[67] These new types are limited in number, but their issue represents a significant innovation in imperial imagery. In 89, Domitian celebrated a joint triumph over both the Chatti and Dacians, and was honoured with an equestrian statue in the forum. The statue depicted his horse crushing the personification of the Rhine, a scene subsequently reproduced on coinage.[68] This imagery was taken up by later emperors. Trajan's coinage issued at Rome to celebrate his Dacian victories depicted him standing on the head of a subjugated Dacian.[69] One particular type shows Trajan standing on a podium, with two defeated barbarians extending their hands towards him.[70] It has been suggested that such an image was probably based on a now lost statue from Rome.[71] These images reveal a fundamental shift in the presentation of the emperor from a monarch presiding over the pacification of the world to a martial leader who personally crushed barbarian bodies.

Such shifts can be seen in the representation of rulers of other ancient states. For example, on the Behistun relief, created in the sixth or fifth century BCE, the Persian king Darius stands on the chest of his defeated rival Gaumata. This scene was unparalleled in Achaemenid Persian art, though the *calcatio* imagery had been common in the earlier Assyrian Empire.[72] Its re-introduction under Darius was designed to make a statement about the king's authority. In the case of the change in Roman imperial iconography, it is probable that the Flavian dynasty

---

[65] Levi, 1952: 10–11; Cody, 2003.

[66] *RIC* II² Vespasian 429–30 (Titus), Domitian 280; Malone, 2009: 59.

[67] *RIC* II² Vespasian 1537 (Titus); Malone, 2009: 61.

[68] Stat. *Silv.* 1.1.50–1; *RIC* II² Domitian 797.   [69] *RIC* II Trajan 210, 489.

[70] *RIC* II Trajan 551.   [71] Levi, 1952: 16–17.   [72] Root, 1979: 185, 196–226.

chose to be depicted differently from their Julio-Claudian predecessors. The triumph over Judaea secured by Vespasian and Titus, and the resulting *pax* secured by this victory, was a key part of Flavian image-making.[73] Domitian was particularly concerned to be seen as a military leader in the vein of his father and brother. He took to the field late 82 or early 83 for a campaign against the Chatti on the Rhine, for which he was awarded a triumph and the *cognomen ex virtute* of *Germanicus*, the first reigning emperor to be so honoured.[74] This was followed by the Dacian Wars in 84/5 and 86, which again saw Domitian campaign in person and celebrate another triumph.[75] Further campaigns against the Chatti and the Dacians in 89 resulted in a double triumph in Rome later that same year.[76] These military activities were commemorated on coinage issued by the imperial mint at Rome, as well as on issues by select communities in the Greek east.[77] The equestrian statue at Rome showing Domitian crushing the Rhine underfoot emphasised his martial ability to the people of the capital. Once such imagery had been introduced into the imperial repertoire, many of Domitian's successors continued to depict themselves crushing barbarian peoples in official media, a trend which increased from the third century onwards.[78] In the remainder of this chapter we will see how representations of Flavian, Antonine, and Severan emperors in the eastern provinces paralleled the imagery found at Rome, but, like the monuments at Koula and Aphrodisias, also demonstrated substantial variety and innovation.

Enslaved by Domitian

The city of Prusias ad Hypium in Bithynia minted two coin types to celebrate Domitian's campaigns. The reverse of the first coin, a 24 mm bronze, shows a standing captive with her hands bound behind her back (Fig. 5.3, left). The legend ΔΕΔΟΥΛΟΜΕΝΗ ΣΕΒΑ ΔΟΜΙΤΙΑΝΩ, with ΓΕΡΜΑΝΙΑ in the field, explicitly identifies the bound woman as a personification of Germany.[79] The reverse legend is an adaptation of GERMANIA CAPTA, as featured on

---

[73] See Noreña, 2003, with Cornwell, 2017: 121–53 on the connection between peace and victory in the imperial age.

[74] Jones, 1992: 128–31.   [75] Jones, 1992: 138–9.   [76] Suet. *Dom.* 6.1; Jones, 1992: 150–2.

[77] For Rome, see Carradice, 1993. For the east, see Burnett, Amandry, and Carradice, 1999: 33, 35–6.

[78] See Malone, 2009.

[79] *RPC* II.685. The Greek is not quite correct. We would expect ΔΕΔΟΥΛΩΜΕΝΗ for the perfect passive participle (Babelon, 1917: 26 n. 1).

Figure 5.3 (left) Bronze coin from Prusias ad Hypium celebrating Domitian's German victory. (right) Brass coin from Prusias ad Hypium celebrating Domitian's Dacian victory. Photographs: K. Dahmen, © bpk / Münzkabinett, Staatliche Museen zu Berlin [18268526/18268527].

Domitian's coins minted at Rome in 85 and 87.[80] The second coin is a 23 mm brass, which has a reverse type featuring a kneeling captive with her hands tied behind her back (Fig. 5.3, right). The reverse legend is ΔΕΔΟΥ ΣΕΒ ΔΟΜΙΤΙΑΝΩ, with ΓΕΤΙΚΗ in the field.[81] This refers to Domitian's Dacian victories, using the term Γετική/Γέται for Dacia/Dacians.[82] The mint-masters were being especially innovative in striking this coin type, given that Domitian's own coinage did not use a *Dacia capta* legend.[83] The Bithynian coins were issued as part of a single series, either in 86, the same year as Domitian's first triumph over the Dacians, or 89, when Domitian celebrated his double triumph over both the Germans and Dacians.[84]

The language of the Greek reverse legends deserves particular comment. The Latin verb *capio* ('I capture') has been translated by the Greek δουλόω ('I enslave'). The English translations of the legends would be 'Germany enslaved by the emperor Domitian' and 'Dacia enslaved by the emperor Domitian'.[85] But this was not the only possible way of translating the Latin

---

[80] *RIC* II² Domitian 274, 351, 397, 463, 525, 632; Babelon, 1917: 26. See Cody, 2003: 112 for discussion of the iconography of the Roman types.

[81] *RPC* II.686.

[82] For the Getae and the Dacians commonly being regarded as the same people, see Cass. Dio 67(66).6.2; Strabo 7.3.12–13 (304–5).

[83] Dräger (1993: 133 n. 33) argues that the Germania coin type was struck in 83, and the Getike coin type separately in 86, in response to separate victory celebrations. Burnett, Amandry, and Carradice (1999: 94–5), however, suggest that all the Bithynian coins were struck in 86, or possibly in 89 after the double triumph that year.

[84] Burnett, Amandry, and Carradice, 1999: 95, 106.   [85] *LSJ* s.v. δουλόω 1.

terminology of conquest into Greek. Two denominations of bronze coins minted by Roman officials at Caesarea in Judaea to celebrate the suppression of the Jewish revolt by Vespasian and Titus provide a point of comparison.[86] On these, the Latin term *Iudaea capta* ('Judaea has been captured') is rendered as ΙΟΥΔΑΙΑΣ ΕΑΛΩΚΥΙΑΣ ('the Jews have been captured').[87] The Greek verb ἁλίσκομαι ('I am conquered, caught') is the most straightforward translation of the Latin passive form *capior*.[88] The mint-masters of Prusias ad Hypium, however, decided that a verb of enslavement was a better way of articulating Domitian's subjugation of these foreign peoples. The reverse legends on the coins emphasise the emperor's personal role in the enslavement, as shown by the dative of the agent ΔΟΜΙΤΙΑΝΩ(Ι) in both cases.[89] The language chosen by the mint-masters stands in contrast to the official rhetoric of the Roman imperial administration, which studiously avoided the language of slavery in referring to provincials.[90]

If the Roman imperial state did not commonly use the rhetoric of slavery, how did the mint-masters of Prusias ad Hypium decide upon the text of their reverse legend? It is probable that they were influenced by contemporary Greek political discourse. Greek authors and intellectuals of this period often used the 'master–slave' paradigm as a way of conceptualising their own ambivalent relationship with the Roman state, urging their fellow Greeks not to become slaves to Rome.[91] On these coins, the minters applied the rhetoric of slavery as a way of conceptualising Roman domination over Germany and Dacia, rather than over the Greeks themselves. This was a discourse that would be familiar to the viewers and users of the coins they produced. By employing such terminology, the minters were identifying themselves with the conquering Roman emperor, not with the plight of the barbarians, in a similar fashion to the Koula and Aphrodisias reliefs.

---

[86] Burnett, Amandry, and Carradice, 1999: 317.

[87] *RPC* II.2310–13. For the portrayal of Judaea as a subjugated barbarian nation, rather than a Roman province, on coins minted at Rome, see Cody, 2003: 107–11.

[88] *LSJ* s.v. ἁλίσκομαι (defective passive) 1.

[89] The dative of the agent is used in Greek after a perfect or pluperfect passive form of a verb (Goodwin, 1892: 252).

[90] Lavan, 2013: 218–35. The exception is Nero's famous speech granting freedom to Greece, in which he describes the generosity of his benefaction: 'For you were enslaved either to foreigners or to each other' (ἢ γὰρ ἀλλοτρίοις ἢ ἀλλήλοις ἐδουλεύσατε; *IG* VII.2713, l. 16). In this formulation, the provincials of Achaia were effectively slaves to Rome before Nero's grant because they paid tax (Lavan, 2013: 235–6). Note also Philostratus' fictional *Life of Apollonius of Tyana* 5.41, in which the sage writes a letter to Vespasian, who rescinded Nero's decision, bluntly telling the emperor: 'You have enslaved Greece' (Ἐδουλώσω τὴν Ἑλλάδα).

[91] Swain, 1996: 172, 176 (on Plutarch), 201–2, 209, 218–19 (on Dio Chrysostom); Lavan, 2013: 8–9.

However, as with these earlier monuments, the coins could also have served as reminders of the coercive power of the emperor over all his subjects, whether they were German, Dacian, or Bithynian. Therefore, the designs of Prusias ad Hypium responded to celebrations of Domitian's campaigns at Rome, but the mint-masters chose to commemorate these wars in a different way from coins produced by the imperial administration, using the political discourse of slavery familiar to their local Greek audience.

Crushed by Hadrian

The late first and early second centuries saw the appearance of a new statue type depicting the Roman emperor as a conqueror. The 'sitting barbarian' type features a sculptured representation of a small captive, the representative or personification of a region or people, crouched at the emperor's feet.[92] The earliest known example is a statue of Vespasian from the Metroon at Olympia. This shows the emperor towering over a small Jewish woman, the personification of Judaea, who kneels at his feet with her hands tied behind her back.[93] The patron of this monument – perhaps the priest of the imperial cult – thought it fitting that Vespasian be represented as a conqueror of Judaea, a depiction that stood in contrast with the other Julio-Claudian imperial statues in the cult complex without 'sitting barbarians'. There are also two examples of statues of Trajan in such a pose: one from the Stoa of the Library of Pantainos in the Athenian Agora showing a Dacian at his feet, and another from the theatre at Perge with a female captive.[94] The statue from Athens may have been erected in response to one of Hadrian's visits to the city, as a way of showing honour to the emperor's deified father. Stewart (2004: 163–4) has argued that the depiction of the Dacian captive was directly inspired by the images of the Gauls in the Attalid statue group on the Acropolis. Although all these 'sitting barbarian' statues are found in Greece and Asia Minor, and one, at least, may have drawn inspiration from Attalid iconography, the composition of the conflict between king and opponent is quite different from Hellenistic precursors. Stewart (2004: 177) has described the message of the

[92] Karanastasi, 2012/13: 339–41.
[93] Hitzl, 1991: 52–5. This is not to say that emperors had not been depicted with small barbarians in other artistic contexts, such as the reliefs at Aphrodisias (see Smith, 2013: 128–31). This discussion refers to a specific type of free-standing statues.
[94] Athens: Shear, 1973: 404–5; Stewart, 2004: 177–8. Perge: Karanastasi, 2012/13: 341.

Athens Trajan as 'quintessentially Roman, reducing the rich Attalid narrative of battle's ebb and flow to a simple statement of fact'.

There is a famous statue type of the emperor Hadrian, commonly called the 'Athenian agora–Olympia type' or the 'eastern Hadrianic breastplate type', examples of which have been found in Greece, Crete, Asia Minor, Syria, and North Africa.[95] It shows Hadrian in military dress wearing a breastplate depicting Athena, who is flanked by winged Victories and standing on the she-wolf suckling Romulus and Remus.[96] There are many variations of the 'Athenian agora–Olympia type', one of which shows Hadrian accompanied by the 'sitting barbarian' figure. There are four examples of this type from Asia Minor and Greece, and one from Ammaedara in the province of Africa Proconsularis.[97] The statue of Hadrian from Africa can be connected in pose and composition with examples found at Herakleion and Kissamos on Crete.[98] It is probable that these statues were manufactured in the east, and at least one example shipped to Africa.[99] But we should be wary of seeing all images of emperors with barbarians as the product of eastern workshops. There is a statue of an emperor (perhaps Trajan) from the theatre at Arausio in Gaul, in which he is depicted with a small barbarian figure.[100] From Pula, in the Italian province of Venetia and Histria, comes the feet of an imperial statue with a barbarian wearing trousers. This may depict Hadrian with an Illyrian captive, commemorating the campaigns in the Danubian region early in his reign.[101] Therefore, we can say that although our eastern versions of the 'sitting barbarian' statue type may have been inspired by Hellenistic images (as Stewart suggests), the representation also had wider appeal throughout the empire.

One important variation of the 'Athenian agora–Olympia type' of Hadrian utilises more violent iconography: it shows the emperor performing the act of *calcatio colli* on a subjugated figure. A statue from the theatre of Hierapytna in Crete depicts Hadrian with his left foot trampling on a diminutive female captive; although his right arm no longer survives, it probably held a lance or sword aimed at the prostrate figure (Fig. 5.4).[102] The pose recalls the image of Claudius conquering Britannia from Aphrodisias, as the original relief there also featured the emperor

---

[95] Gergel, 2004; Bergmann, 2010; Spawforth, 2012: 255–61; Karanastasi, 2012/13.

[96] There are, however, variations even in the breastplate design (Karanastasi, 2012/13: 332–4).

[97] Gergel, 2004: 374; Karanastasi, 2012/13: 326.   [98] Gergel, 2004: 381; Bergmann, 2010: 267.

[99] See the comments of Gergel, 2004: 386.

[100] Walter, 1993: 30–1. This has been incorrectly restored to represent Augustus. Note also the base for a statue of an emperor with two provinces from the villa at Chiragan, tentatively dated to the Trajanic/Hadrianic period (Walter, 1993: 57–8).

[101] Bieńkowski, 1912.   [102] Gergel, 2004: 378; Spawforth, 2012: 256.

Figure 5.4 Statue of Hadrian from Hierapytna. Photograph: Arachne FA104-03, © Arachne Images Database, http://arachne.uni-koeln.de/item/marbilder/7770388.

brandishing a spear. Further statues showing Hadrian in this same aggressive pose can be reconstructed from fragments now in museums at Antalya in Turkey and the Piraeus in Greece.[103] There may also be an example attested in the Roman province of Mauretania Tingitana, based on the fragment of an imperial knee found in the region.[104]

---

[103] Gergel, 2004: 374; Spawforth, 2012: 256; Karanastasi, 2012/13: 324, 338.
[104] Karanastasi, 2012/13: 327–8, 366.

Recent studies have dated the 'Hierapytna type' with the emperor engaging in *calcatio colli* to the beginning of Hadrian's reign.[105] It has been suggested that it may have been designed as a visual representation of the Roman triumph over Parthia, which Hadrian celebrated on Trajan's behalf after his predecessor's death, as well as the other military successes at the beginning of his reign.[106] There were serious Jewish revolts throughout North Africa and Egypt in 116/17.[107] Hadrian received recognition for restoring peace in the region, as seen on building inscriptions from Cyrene.[108] Such events would have had particular resonance for Crete, which was part of the same province as Cyrene. But the commemorative impulse may have been a more general one, motivated by a desire to see Hadrian both as a conqueror and a protector. The Cretans not only erected the statue of Hadrian in the theatre at Hierapytna, but also a number of additional examples of 'Athenian agora–Olympia type' statues of the emperor in other cities on the island.[109] Despite the possible presence of a *calcatio colli* statue in Mauretania, the type was most likely the product of a workshop in the Greek world.[110] The decision to represent Hadrian crushing a barbarian underfoot, rather than simply showing the captive sitting at his feet, was a provocative innovation in this part of the empire, as all previous examples of this imagery are known from statues and coins from Rome (as I discussed above). The origin and inspiration of the violent imagery eludes precise identification. The sculptors could have been stimulated by images of imperial *calcatio colli* represented on coins minted at Rome, or they may have been inspired by the same ideas about kingship and violence that helped to shape the Koula and Aphrodisias monuments.

The fact that imperial statues featuring the emperor with a 'sitting barbarian' can be found in Arausio, Pula, and North Africa suggests the wide appeal and circulation of such iconography throughout the empire beyond the provinces of the Greek east. They allow us to detect continuity in the representation of Trajan and Hadrian, showing that both emperors were portrayed as active military leaders, despite the latter's abandonment of his predecessor's conquests in the east.[111] By the second century, the emperor-as-subjugator image was an accepted element of imperial representation in a wide range

[105] Gergel, 2004: 377–8; Karanastasi, 2012/13: 334–7.   [106] Gergel, 2004: 383–6.
[107] Gergel, 2004: 384; Opper, 2008: 70–2; Karanastasi, 2012/13: 342–8.
[108] Birley, 1997: 152; Ziosi, 2010. If the statue does celebrate Hadrian's quashing of the Jewish revolt, it parallels the creation of the 'sitting barbarian' type for Vespasian in celebration of his earlier victory in Judaea.
[109] Karanastasi, 2012/13: 348. Hadrian may have visited the island himself in 123 (Birley 1997: 153).
[110] Karanastasi, 2012/13: 357.   [111] Vout, 2003: 457; Opper, 2008: 69–72.

of media, from coins issued by Rome and the Greek provincial mints to statuary and monuments in Rome and the provinces. The 'Hierapytna' statue type of Hadrian should be seen as a particularly violent and aggressive example of this wider iconographical trend created by an eastern workshop. It is important to point out that this specific representation of Hadrian was designed to appeal to a Greek audience. The presence of Athena supported by the she-wolf suckling Romulus and Remus on Hadrian's breastplate emphasises that his subjugation of foreign enemies was for the benefit of the Graeco-Roman world at large.

Power and Protection

A particularly interesting example of local traditions shaping the representation of the Roman emperor in the second and third centuries can be seen in a group of small terracotta figurines from Egypt. These depict a bearded figure in military dress, probably a Roman emperor, who faces the viewer front-on, while holding a barbarian by the hair and pointing a sword aggressively at his or her throat. They were probably intended as votive offerings or for use in household shrines (Fig. 5.5, left).[112] The terracottas are iconographically very similar to a larger, marble relief also from Egypt, now in the Liverpool World Museum. This depicts a left-facing emperor (whose features are very similar to those of Caracalla), brandishing a sword in his right hand, and grasping a bearded and hirsute captive with his left (Fig. 5.5, right).[113]

The production of the terracotta images has been connected with Egyptian gratitude for Hadrian's actions in suppressing the Jewish revolts, though there are many other candidates among emperors of the second and third centuries.[114] Over time, however, such statuettes may have lost their association with a specific emperor, and instead have come to represent *the* emperor in a timeless sense.[115] As Bailey (1996: 210) has suggested, the design could be a 'more general type brought forward by Egyptian coroplasts whenever a victory needed to be celebrated'. If the terracottas are Hadrianic, they are completely different to other images of emperors produced in this period, as the emperor dragging a barbarian by the hair

[112] Bailey, 1996: 207–10. The terracotta depicted here is from the British Museum (1983,0723.1). It is 17.5 cm high, 10.5 cm wide, and 5 cm deep. Similar small terracotta statues are attested in Berlin, Moscow, Athens, and Boston.
[113] This relief is in the World Museum at Liverpool (1971.80). It is 50 cm in height, and 35 cm in width. See Vermeule and von Bothmer, 1959: 163; Kiss, 1989: 129–30; Riccomini and Porciani, 2014: 500–4.
[114] Bailey, 1996: 208–10; Karanastasi, 2012/13: 350–4.   [115] See also Rowan in this volume.

Figure 5.5 Egyptian figurines of emperors with captives: (left) Terracotta emperor with captive. British Museum 1983,0723.1. Photograph © Trustees of the British Museum. (right) Marble emperor with captive. World Museum, Liverpool, Inv. Nr. 1971.80. Photograph © National Museums, Liverpool.

does not commonly appear on coins minted by imperial mints until late antiquity.[116] Given their origin in Egypt, these terracotta depictions, as well as the larger marble relief discussed above, are more likely to be inspired by imagery from Near Eastern societies, notably Pharaonic Egypt, where both kings and gods were depicted in such poses.[117] This influenced the portrayal of the Roman emperor in Egypt: for example, Titus, Domitian, and Trajan were depicted smiting enemies at the temple of Khnum in Latopolis.[118] The composition of the Egyptian images is different from the examples of conquering emperors from Koula, Aphrodisias, Prusias ad Hypium, and Hierapytna, but they convey the same fundamental message: the emperor himself is the violent agent of conquest.

---

[116] Levi, 1952: 25–6; Malone, 2009: 62, 66. He points out that the earliest example is a coin of Caracalla, which shows Victory dragging a captive by the hair on the reverse (*RIC* IV Caracalla 172). Emperors themselves are not depicted on imperial coinage dragging captives until the Tetrarchic period (e.g. *RIC* VI Siscia 153–4 (Severus II and Maximinus Daza)).

[117] Kiss, 1989; Bailey, 1996: 207. Sometimes scholars have mistakenly identified representations of the god Antaios as Roman emperors (Bailey, 2005). For the Egyptian motif, see Hall, 1986.

[118] Bowman, 1986: 38.

The manufacture of the terracottas for personal use in household shrines or as votives showed popular acceptance of, and gratitude for, an emperor who personally subjugated their enemies in order to protect his people, just like a Pharaoh. The continuity in imagery from the Pharaonic period made the emperor seem more familiar to the local Egyptian audience – as *their* king and protector – rather than an autocrat in far off Rome, who had no concern for their defence. But the assimilation of Roman emperors to Pharaohs emphasised that their fearsome power could also be turned on the people of Egypt themselves if circumstances demanded it. The inhabitants of Alexandria discovered this to their horror when many of them were massacred in December 215 during Caracalla's violent reprisals against them (either for their insults towards him, rioting, or both).[119] Indeed, if the Liverpool marble relief does depict Caracalla, then it would have served as a graphic reminder that the Roman emperor held the power of life and death over all men and women, both outside and inside the empire.[120]

Conclusion

The images discussed in this chapter, from sculptures and reliefs to coins and terracottas, all depict the Roman emperor as the agent of violent conquest, personally subjugating enemy peoples. In the case of the Koula and Aphrodisias monuments, these images predate the appearance of such scenes in Italy and the western provinces. Their different iconography reflects the choices made by patrons and artists, who were influenced by both Hellenistic and Roman traditions, but who also sought to create new and provocative images of imperial power. Even when the Roman emperor began to be depicted subjugating and crushing barbarians in person on coins and monuments at Rome, provincial representations of his military power could still draw on other ideas and themes relevant to local audiences, as shown by the coins from Prusias ad Hypium and the use of the discourse of slavery. The 'Hierapytna Hadrian' statue type, while produced during a period in which it was more common for statues of emperors to be accompanied by barbarians, was nevertheless innovative in its use of the *calcatio colli* motif in eastern statuary. The best example of local traditions continuing to shape the representation of the Roman emperor can be seen

---

[119] Cass. Dio 78(77).22.1–23.4; Herodian, 4.8.6–9.8; SHA *M. Ant.* 6.2–3; Harker, 2008: 133–8.

[120] See Riccomini and Porciani, 2014: 504–10, who argue that the 'Liverpool type', and a similar marble depiction of an emperor in Torino, portray Caracalla in the two years immediately after the Alexandrian massacre.

in the small Egyptian statues, both those in terracotta and marble, which clearly draw upon Pharaonic motifs. Although all of the monuments and images in this chapter were created in the eastern provinces, it would be misleading to say that they represented a consistently 'eastern' or 'Greek' way of representing emperors. I have, for example, noted quite different responses to Claudius' British victories and Nero's achievements in Armenia, and not all provincial coinage alluded to Domitian's German wars through the language of subjugation and slavery. I have instead identified different 'moments' of innovative imperial representation, which were shaped by a multiplicity of local and Roman ideas about the personal role of kings in warfare. Yet these monuments were all inspired by the same underlying discourse, that the aggression and domination of the Roman emperor over enemies was to be celebrated. The creation of these images by provincials allowed them to identify themselves with the Roman conquerors, not the subjugated foreigners, reassuring them of their place within the Roman world. This was reinforced by the fact that the representations drew on local commemorative practices and motifs, making the emperor seem more familiar to the regional viewer. As with all messages, however, this came with a potential sting in the tail – the emperor who protected his subjects could also punish them.

Bibliography

Assante, J. 2017. 'Men looking at men: the homoerotics of power in the state arts of Assyria', in Zsolnay, I. (ed.), *Being a Man: Negotiating Ancient Constructs of Masculinity* (London: Routledge), 42–82.

Babelon, E. 1917. 'Quelques monnaies de l'empereur Domitien (*Germania Capta*)', *RN* Series 4, 21: 25–44.

Bailey, D. M. 1996. 'Little emperors', in Bailey, D. M. (ed.), *Archaeological Research in Egypt*. Journal of Roman Archaeology Supplementary Series 19 (Ann Arbor: Journal of Roman Archaeology), 207–13.

2005. 'Antaios, an Egyptian god in Roman Egypt: extracting an iconography', in Sanader, M. and A. Rendić-Miočević (eds.), *The Proceedings of the 8th International Colloquium on Problems of Roman Provincial Art* (Zagreb: Golden Marketing tehnička knjiga), 389–98.

Balsdon, J. P. V. D. 1934. *The Emperor Gaius (Caligula)* (Oxford: Clarendon Press).

Barden Dowling, M. 2006. *Clemency and Cruelty in the Roman World* (Ann Arbor: University of Michigan Press).

Barrett, A. A. 1991. 'Claudius' British victory arch in Rome', *Britannia* 22: 1–19.

Bergmann, B. 2010. 'Bar Kochba und das Panhellenion: die Panzerstatue Hadrians aus Hierapytna/Kreta (Istanbul, Archäologisches Museum Inv. Nr. 50) und der Panzertorso Inv. Nr. 8097 im Piräusmuseum von Athen', *MDAI(I)* 60: 203–89.

Bieńkowski, P. 1912. 'Über eine Kaiserstatue in Pola', *WS* 34: 272–81.

1928. *Les Celtes dans les arts mineurs gréco-romains avec des recherches iconographiques sur quelques autres peuples barbares* (Krakow: Jagiellonian University).

Birley, A. R. 1997. *Hadrian: The Restless Emperor* (London: Routledge).

Boschung, D. 1989. *Die Bildnisse des Caligula* (Berlin: Gebr. Mann Verlag).

Bowman, A. K. 1986. *Egypt after the Pharaohs, 332 B.C.–A.D. 642* (Berkeley; London: University of California Press).

Bryen, A. 2014. 'Histories of violence: notes from the Roman Empire', in Campbell, R. (ed.), *Violence and Civilization: Studies of Social Violence in History and Prehistory* (Providence, RI: Joukowsky Institute of Archaeology), 125–51.

Burnett, A., M. Amandry, and I. Carradice 1999. *Roman Provincial Coinage: Volume II* (London; Paris: British Museum).

Burnett, A., M. Amandry, and P. P. Ripollès 1992. *Roman Provincial Coinage: Volume I* (London; Paris: British Museum).

Carradice, I. 1993. 'Coin types and Roman history: the example of Domitian', in Price, M., A. Burnett, and R. Bland (eds.) *Essays in Honour of Robert Carson and Kenneth Jenkins* (London: Spink), 161–75.

Carroll, K. K. 1982. *The Parthenon Inscription*. Greek, Roman and Byzantine Studies Monographs 9 (Durham, NC: Duke University).

Clarke, J. R. 2003. *Art in the Lives of Ordinary Romans: Visual Representation and Non-Elite Viewers in Italy, 100 B.C.–A.D. 315* (Berkeley; London: University of California Press).

Cody, J. M. 2003. 'Conquerors and conquered on Flavian coins', in Boyle, A. J. and W. J. Dominik (eds.), *Flavian Rome: Culture, Image, Text* (Leiden: Brill), 105–13.

Cohen, A. 1997. *The Alexander Mosaic: Stories of Victory and Defeat* (Cambridge: Cambridge University Press).

Cornwell, H. 2017. *Pax and the Politics of Peace: Republic to Principate* (Oxford: Oxford University Press).

Davenport, C. 2014. 'Imperial ideology and commemorative culture in the eastern Roman Empire, 284–250 CE', in Dzino, D. and K. Parry (eds.), *Byzantium, its Neighbours and its Cultures*, Byzantina Australiensia 20 (Brisbane: Australian Association for Byzantine Studies), 45–70.

Dräger, M. 1993. *Die Städte der Provinz Asia in der Flavierzeit: Studien zur kleinasiatischen Stadt- und Regionalgeschichte* (Frankfurt: Peter Lang).

Elsner, J. 1995. *Art and the Roman Viewer: The Transformation of Art from the Pagan World to Christianity* (Cambridge: Cambridge University Press).

Erim, K. T. 1982. 'A new relief showing Claudius and Britannia from Aphrodisias', *Britannia* 13: 277–81.

Ferris, I. M. 2000. *Enemies of Rome: Barbarians through Roman Eyes* (Stroud: Tempus).

Foster, B. R. 2016. *The Age of Agade: Inventing Empire in Ancient Mesopotamia* (London: Routledge).

Foucault, M. 1979. *Discipline and Punish: The Birth of the Prison* (New York: Vintage Books).

Fowler, R. and O. Hekster 2005. 'Imagining kings: from Persia to Rome', in Fowler, R. and O. Hekster (eds.), *Imaginary Kings: Royal Images in the Ancient Near East, Greece, and Rome* (Stuttgart: Franz Steiner), 9–38.

Garnsey, P. D. A. 1970. *Social Status and Legal Privilege in the Roman Empire* (Oxford: Clarendon Press).

Gergel, R. A. 2004. 'Agora S166 and related works: the iconography, typology, and interpretation of the eastern Hadrianic breastplate type', in Chapin, A. P. (ed.), *XAPIΣ: Essays in Honor of Sara A. Immerwahr*, Hesperia Supplements 33 (Athens: American School of Classical Studies at Athens), 371–409.

Gleason, M. 2001. 'Mutilated messengers: body language in Josephus', in Goldhill, S. (ed.), *Being Greek under Rome: Cultural Identity, the Second Sophistic and the Development of Empire* (Cambridge: Cambridge University Press), 50–85.

Goodwin, W. W. 1892. *A Greek Grammar* (Boston: Ginn and Company).

Hall, E. S. 1986. *The Pharaoh Smites his Enemies: A Comparative Study* (Munich: Deutscher Kunstverlag).

Harker, A. 2008. *Loyalty and Dissidence in Roman Egypt: The Case of the Acta Alexandrinorum* (Cambridge: Cambridge University Press).

Hekster, O. 2015. *Emperors and Ancestors: Roman Rulers and the Constraints of Tradition* (Oxford: Oxford University Press).

Hitzl, K. 1991. *Olympische Forschungen: Die Kaiserzeitliche Statuenausstattung des Metroon* (Berlin: De Gruyter).

Holliday, P. J. 2002. *The Origins of Roman Historical Commemoration in the Visual Arts* (Cambridge: Cambridge University Press).

Hölscher, T. 1973. *Griechische Historienbilder des 5. und 4. Jahrhunderts v. Chr.* (Würzburg: Konrad Triltsch).

    2003. 'Images of war in Greece and Rome: between military practice, public memory, and cultural symbolism', *JRS* 93: 1–17.

Jones, B. W. 1992. *The Emperor Domitian* (London: Routledge).

Kähler, H. 1965. *Der Fries vom Reiterdenkmal des Aemilius Paullus in Delphi* (Berlin: Gebr. Mann Verlag).

Karanastasi, P. 2012/13. 'Hadrian im Panzer: Kaiserstatuen zwischen Realpolitik und Philhellenismus', *JDAI* 127/8: 323–91.

Kienast, D. 1996. *Römische Kaisertabelle* (Darmstadt: Wissenschaftliche Buchgesellschaft).

Kiss, Z. 1989. 'Représentations de barbares dans l'iconographie romaine impériale en Égypte', *Klio* 71: 127–37.

Kyle, D. 1998. *Spectacles of Death in Ancient Rome* (London: Routledge).

La Baume, P. 1977. 'Signumscheibe und Merkurrelief von Niederbieber', *BJ* 177: 565–8.

Lavan, M. 2013. *Slaves to Rome: Paradigms of Empire in Roman Culture* (Cambridge: Cambridge University Press).

Levi, A. C. 1952. *Barbarians on Roman Imperial Coins and Sculpture* (New York: American Numismatic Society).

Lott, J. B. 2012. *Death and Dynasty in Early Imperial Rome* (Cambridge: Cambridge University Press).

Malone, C. W. 2009. 'Violence on Roman imperial coinage', *JNAA* 20: 58–72.

Marvin, M. 2002. 'The Ludovisi Barbarians: the Grand Manner', in Gazda, E. K. (ed.), *The Ancient Art of Emulation: Studies in Artistic Originality and Tradition from the Present to Classical Antiquity* (Ann Arbor: University of Michigan Press), 205–23.

Mayer, E. 2010. 'Propaganda, staged applause, or local politics? Public monuments from Augustus to Septimius Severus', in Ewald, B. C. and C. F. Noreña (eds.), *The Emperor and Rome: Space, Representation, and Ritual* (Cambridge: Cambridge University Press), 111–34.

Mommsen, T. 1888. 'Relief aus Kula', *MDAI(A)* 13: 18–22.

Noreña, C. F. 2003. 'Medium and message in Vespasian's *templum Pacis*', *MAAR* 48: 25–43.

2011. *Imperial Ideals in the Roman West: Representation, Circulation, Power* (Cambridge: Cambridge University Press).

Oakley, F. 2006. *Kingship: The Politics of Enchantment* (Oxford; Malden, MA: Blackwell).

Opper, T. 2008. *Hadrian: Empire and Conflict* (London: British Museum).

Pollini, J. 2012. *From Republic to Empire: Rhetoric, Religion, and Power in the Visual Culture of Ancient Rome* (Norman: University of Oklahoma Press).

Price, S. 1984. *Rituals and Power: The Roman Imperial Cult in Asia Minor* (Cambridge: Cambridge University Press).

Riccomini, A. M. and L. Porciani. 2014. 'Su una statuetta con imperatore e barbaro nel museo di antichità di Torino', *ArchClass* 65: 499–512.

Rogers, R. 2003. 'Female representation in Roman art: feminizing the provincial "other"', in Scott, S. and J. Webster (eds.), *Roman Imperialism and Provincial Art* (Cambridge: Cambridge University Press), 69–93.

Root, M. C. 1979. *The King and Kingship in Achaemenid Art* (Leiden: Brill).

Scarry, E. 1985. *The Body in Pain: The Making and Unmaking of the World* (Oxford: Oxford University Press).

Shear, T. L. Jr. 1973. 'The Athenian agora: excavations of 1972', *Hesperia* 42: 359–407.

Smith, R. R. R. 1987. 'The imperial reliefs from the Sebasteion at Aphrodisias', *JRS* 77: 88–138.

1988a. *Hellenistic Royal Portraits* (Oxford: Oxford University Press).

1988b. 'Simulacra gentium: the *ethne* from the Sebasteion at Aphrodisias', *JRS* 78: 50–77.

1994. 'Spear-won land at Boscoreale: on the royal paintings of a Roman villa', *JRA* 7: 100–28.

2013. *The Marble Reliefs from the Julio-Claudian Sebasteion (Aphrodisias 6)* (Darmstadt; Mainz: Philipp von Zabern).

Spawforth, A. J. S. 2012. *Greece and the Augustan Cultural Revolution* (Cambridge: Cambridge University Press).

Stewart, A. 1993. *Faces of Power: Alexander's Image and Hellenistic Politics* (Berkeley; London: University of California Press).

2004. *Attalos, Athens, and the Akropolis: The Pergamene 'Little Barbarians' and their Roman and Renaissance Legacy* (Cambridge: Cambridge University Press).

2014. *Art in the Hellenistic World: An Introduction* (Cambridge: Cambridge University Press).

Swain, S. 1996. *Hellenism and Empire: Language, Classicism, and Power in the Greek World, A.D. 50–250* (Oxford: Oxford University Press).

Taylor, M. J. 2016. 'The battle scene on Aemilius Paullus' Pydna monument: a re-evaluation', *Hesperia* 85: 559–76.

Toynbee, J. M. C. 1934. *The Hadrianic School: A Chapter in the History of Greek Art* (Cambridge: Cambridge University Press).

Vermeule, C. and D. von Bothmer 1959. 'Notes on a new edition of Michaelis: ancient marbles in Great Britain', *AJA* 63: 139–66.

Vout, C. 2003. 'A revision of Hadrian's portraiture', in Erdkamp, P., O. Hekster, G. de Kleijn, S. T. A. M. Mols, and L. de Blois (eds.), *The Representation and Perception of Roman Imperial Power* (Amsterdam: J. C. Gieben), 442–57.

2007. *Power and Eroticism in Imperial Rome* (Cambridge: Cambridge University Press).

Walter, H. 1993. *Les Barbares de l'Occident Romaine: Corpus des Gaules et des provinces de Germanie* (Paris: Les Belles Lettres).

Whittaker, C. R. 2004. *Rome and its Frontiers: The Dynamics of Empire* (London: Routledge).

Zanker, P. 1988. *The Power of Images in the Age of Augustus*, trans. A. Shapiro (Ann Arbor: University of Michigan Press).

1998. 'Die Barbaren, der Kaiser und die Arena: Bilder der Gewalt in der römischen Kunst', in Sieferle, R. P. and H. Breuninger, *Kulturen der Gewalt: Ritualisierung und Symbolisierung der Gewalt in der Geschichte* (Frankfurt; New York: Campus Verlag), 53–86.

Zimmermann, M. 2006. 'Violence in late antiquity reconsidered', in Drake, H. A. (ed.), *Violence in Late Antiquity* (Aldershot: Ashgate), 343–57.

Ziosi, F. 2010. 'Sulle iscrizioni relative alla ricostruzione di Cirene dopo il "tumultus Iudaicus", e sul loro contesto', *ZPE* 172: 239–48.

6 | Court Politics and Imperial Imagery in the Roman Principate

BENJAMIN KELLY

In essence, this chapter is concerned with a single question: what role did the Roman imperial court play in the genesis of imperial imagery intended for public display?[1] By 'court' I have in mind the social world surrounding the emperor – the circle of people who had reasonably regular personal contact with him, either in the form of verbal (or physical) interaction, or in the context of the provision of domestic or security services.[2] The court in this sense generally included (but was not necessarily limited to): members of the emperor's immediate family; freedman and (later) equestrian secretaries such as the *ab epistulis*, the *a libellis*, and the *a rationibus*; prominent senators (but by no means the whole senate); domestic servants; and members of the bodyguard units. Depending on the tastes of a particular emperor and whether he was at Rome or travelling, the constellation of people around him would change, making the boundaries of the court ever fluid.[3]

Under the influence of the sociologist Norbert Elias[4] and historians of early modern Europe inspired by him, political historians of the Roman Principate over the last two decades have begun the serious study of the Roman court as a distinct social 'figuration' (to use Elias's term).[5] This has yielded important insights into the sociology of political decision-making, insights that allow us to move beyond formal constitutional and

[1] I am grateful to the editors for their incisive and constructive comments on this chapter, and for suggestions made by the participants at the Durham workshop in May 2017 and by audiences in Toronto and St John's, NL. Many thanks also to Carly Murdoch and Christopher Dawson, who served as research assistants on the project. This research was supported by the Social Sciences and Humanities Research Council of Canada.

[2] Although the Latin word *aula* was roughly coextensive with the modern word 'court' (or *Hof*, *cour*, or *corte*), it lacks the precision needed to use it as a category of scholarly analysis. I therefore use 'court' as an etic, not an emic term here.

[3] For discussions of the definition of 'court' in the Roman context, see Wallace-Hadrill, 1996: 285; Winterling, 1999: 2, 195–203; Acton, 2011: 104; Kelly, forthcoming.

[4] See Elias, 1969 = 1983.

[5] See especially Wallace-Hadrill, 1996; Winterling, 1997, 1999; Hurlet, 2000; Laeben-Rosén, 2005; Paterson, 2007; Acton, 2011; Bang, 2011; Wallace-Hadrill, 2011; Schöpe, 2014; Michel, 2015.

administrative categories – 'senate', 'emperor', 'equestrian secretaries', etc. – and to appreciate better how power worked in practice. The 'court studies' approach has made clear the ways that power and advancement often depended on access to and influence with the emperor; it has shown how the lines of patronage that determined the allocation of resources often ran through the members of the court to the emperor; and it has suggested that both the emperor and his 'courtiers' were engaged in a constant process of trying to control each other[6] – in mutual 'domestication', to use another of Elias's terms. The study of the court has also had important implications for understanding how the image of an emperor (in the non-visual sense) was created, since the court lifestyle and ceremonial could help generate and augment a certain public perception of his reign.

But the turn towards 'court studies' in political history has had little discernible impact on the study of imperial imagery intended for 'public' display – by which I mean coin iconography and artworks set up in civic spaces, usually in monumental contexts. True, it has long been suspected that fashions generated in court circles were then adopted by private individuals outside of the emperor's milieu in wall paintings, funerary monuments, and statuary.[7] Various surviving cameos, such as the Gemma Augustea, have also been suspected of having been 'court art'.[8] In her important 2008 discussion of the commissioning of imperial portrait types, Jane Fejfer did suggest in passing that new prototypes were perhaps generated by private workshops 'competing in showing their loyalty to the court' and possibly influenced by 'general ideological trends emerging from the court'.[9] But the role of the court in the generation of public imperial imagery – either in the sense of depictions of the emperor or in the broader sense of images laden with ideology supportive of the regime – has not been discussed in any detailed and systematic way.

In this chapter, I therefore consider this issue. I begin with the question of whether the study of the court as a distinct and coherent social figuration can throw light on the difficult question of who commissioned, designed, and approved public imperial imagery. In the main part of the chapter, I suggest another angle of attack: that even if the question of agency will always remain elusive, we can see how court politics set the limits of the

---

[6] See Bang, 2011.

[7] Zanker, 1987: 267–8, 283, 290–3 = 1988: 267, 283, 291–5; Wallace-Hadrill, 1996: 292; 2008: 357–8; Winterling, 1999: 76–82; Michel, 2015: 55.

[8] Zanker, 1987: 234 = 1988: 233.

[9] Fejfer, 2008: 416, cf. 419. Some of Winterling's works on the imperial court are cited by Fejfer, so one can perhaps see there the beginnings of the influence of 'court studies' on the field of art history.

possible for whoever did commission, design, and approve the artworks in question. To illustrate this, I examine a detailed case study of an especially problematic kind of imperial image, namely depictions of the emperor in the presence of his bodyguards. I argue that as the influence at court of guard units and their commanders waxed and waned, it became more or less possible to display publicly depictions of a monarch surrounded by his guards.

Who Commissioned, Designed, and Approved Imperial Imagery?

A 'court studies' approach can never tell us precisely which individuals were the main driving forces in commissioning, designing, and approving particular imperial images intended for public display. The Roman literary sources are notoriously reticent about this process. Official inscriptions such as the one adorning Trajan's Column tell us who dedicated a monument,[10] but such formalities may mask a more complex story – or even positively mislead. And, of course, we lack the sort of detailed documentary sources that would give us the full story.[11]

   In the absence of hard data, educated guesses must prevail. Take, for example, the assumptions that run through the most important work of the last generation on Roman imperial imagery, Paul Zanker's *Augustus und die Macht der Bilder*. Some public artworks, Zanker assumes, were designed by 'the senate'.[12] At other times, he senses, it was the 'inner circle' of Augustus that generated imagery.[13] Sometimes, 'Augustus' made key decisions about imperial imagery, Zanker assumes[14] – although he is often

---

[10] *CIL* 6.960.

[11] In contrast, for example, to France under Louis XIV, where we can see in detail how the king's public image was crafted by particular courtiers: see Burke, 1992: 49–59. On the general lack of evidence about the commissioning of imperial portraits, see Fejfer, 2008: 408.

[12] Zanker, 1987: 130 = 1988: 123 (the sacrificial procession on the Ara Pacis), 1987: 191 = 1988: 187 (the Parthian Arch of 19 BCE), 1987: 219 = 1988: 217–18 (the costumes of 'Gaius' and 'Lucius' on the Ara Pacis). For a very strong claim that 'the senators' 'designed' the Ara Pacis, see Armstrong, 2008: 352.

[13] Zanker, 1987: 180 = 1988: 176 (on the image of 'Pax' – or Ceres or Tellus or Venus or Italia – depicted on the Ara Pacis and on the cuirass of the Prima Porta statue).

[14] See, for example, Zanker's comments on Augustus' personal involvement in the creation of the new portrait type that was used from 27 BCE (1987: 104 = 1988: 98). For a similar set of assumptions about the controlling hand of Constantine in the ideological programme in the area of the Arch of Constantine, see Marlowe, 2006. Prototypes of statues of the emperor have also been seen as commissioned by the emperor himself: see Fejfer, 2008: 503 n. 156 for literature.

careful to add that the emperor perhaps had advisors.[15] Other authors are less circumspect about the role of the emperor. For instance, some treatments of the Ara Pacis have seen Augustus as playing a heavily *dirigiste* role in the design of the altar's imagery.[16]

What the study of the court encourages us to do is blur the boundaries between such conventional categories of 'senate', 'emperor', and 'inner circle', and to be suspicious of the notion of hermetically sealed sites of decision-making. Analysis of the circle surrounding the emperor highlights the complexity of the ties that cut across institutional divisions and status categories from the very start of the Principate. When important decisions were made by people other than the emperor, they were still usually courtiers, and their strategies were shaped by court relationships and by the overarching need for the emperor's favour.

The imperial court and the senate were never separate worlds.[17] The two most important social practices of court life, the morning *salutatio* and the evening *convivium*, are known to have involved members of the senate (and their families) from the start.[18] A string of dynastic marriages allowed Augustus to integrate scions of several senatorial families into the *domus Augusta*, which formed the kernel of his court.[19] Further, senators always featured prominently amongst the *amici* of the emperor; equestrian favourites and freedman confidants may loom large in the (often sensational) reports of some reigns, but prosopographical research has highlighted that senators routinely enjoyed special proximity to the emperor.[20] These senatorial *amici* were not necessarily mere social companions: as the membership of the emperor's *consilium* became increasingly institutionalised, there was always a strong expectation that leading senators would have a major role.[21]

Thus, imagining the decision-making process of either emperor or senate as distinct from the other is less attractive in the light of the constant communication between emperor and leading senators on all manner of

---

[15] Zanker, 1987: 198, 215 = 1988: 195, 212 (on the 'portrait gallery' in the Forum of Augustus).

[16] See Conlin, 1997: 11–25 for a useful taxonomy of the literature on the design and execution of the Ara Pacis.

[17] Cf. Wallace-Hadrill, 1996: 301: ' . . . it is wrong to represent the senators as a coherent group, either socially or politically. They were as much creatures of the court as imperial freedmen.'

[18] *Salutationes*: Suet. *Aug.* 53, *Galb.* 4; Cass. Dio 54.30.1, 56.26.2–3, 57.11.1. *Convivia*: Cass. Dio 57.12.5–6; cf. Suet. *Aug.* 74.

[19] Hurlet, 2000: 128–9.

[20] Wallace-Hadrill, 1996: 291–2; Hurlet, 2000 (on the courts of Augustus and Tiberius); Michel, 2015: 16, 133–61 (on the court of Claudius). Winterling's analysis of the *amici Caesaris* (1999: 161–91) should now be read in the light of the work of Hurlet and Michel.

[21] Eck, 2000: 199–202.

matters, political and otherwise. There is no reason to suppose that decisions about major public artworks would have been any different. Furthermore, the notion that the emperor's decisions could sometimes be entirely independent seems unlikely in the light of the constant processes of influence, persuasion, and 'domestication' that were intrinsic to court life. Rather, the study of the court tends to support Ronald Syme's dictum that '[i]n all ages, whatever the form and name of government, be it a monarchy, republic, or democracy, an oligarchy lurks behind the façade'.[22] In other words, no monarch is an island.

When it comes to imperial imagery on coins, the issue is even more complex, as has been demonstrated by the lengthy debate about who was responsible for choosing designs.[23] The 'emperor' and 'senate' have sometimes been seen as the creators of particular images,[24] but there is also the complication that those who operated the mint might have had a role; possible actors include: the *a rationibus* (the freedman – and, from the late first century, equestrian – secretary with ultimate control over financial affairs); the *tresviri monetales* (junior senators whose office persisted from the Republic right into the third century); the equestrian *procurator monetae* (attested from the time of Trajan);[25] and the *optio et exactor auri argenti et aeris* (an imperial freedman). We do not know whether any or all of these officials were indeed central in the creation of coin imagery. But in view of who these men were, it is implausible that if they did make decisions about coin imagery, they did so in splendid isolation. As junior senators, the *tresviri* hoped for the imperial favour needed to progress further along the senatorial *cursus*.[26] Imperial freedmen and equestrian administrators were not workers in a 'rational-legal' bureaucracy where merit alone determined advancement: the emperor's favour – obtained directly or through brokers at court – was important for their career advancement;[27] and the intense disfavour of the emperor was likely to be

---

[22] Syme, 1939: 7.

[23] Important contributions include Sutherland, 1959; Levick, 1982; Sutherland, 1986; Wallace-Hadrill, 1986; Howgego, 1995: 67–72; Duncan-Jones, 2005: 460–71; Beckmann, 2012: 415–18; Mander, 2012: 30–3.

[24] For instance, Gibson (2013: 118, 125) asserts that the PRAET RECEPT type of Claudius (discussed below, pp. 136–7) was part of a 'political manifesto Claudius issued' at the start of his principate, and that it is highly likely that the 'figurative model' of the coin was ordered by the emperor himself.

[25] Peachin, 1986.

[26] Loyalty towards and favour from the emperor (obtained either directly or through patrons) were amongst the factors governing promotion on the senatorial *cursus*: see Eck, 2002: 136–43; on *monetales* specifically, cf. Wallace-Hadrill, 1986: 79, 84.

[27] Saller, 1982: 79–116; Eck, 2002: 143–9.

terminal for a career – or worse. The fact that all of the minting officials were enmeshed in a web radiating out from the emperor means that true independent decision-making would have been a dangerous act. The context in which these men worked would have encouraged conservatism and a tendency to involve the emperor in decisions, or at least members of an inner court circle whose close access allowed them to know his mind.[28]

Court Politics and Imperial Imagery: The Emperor and his Bodyguards

An understanding of the Roman court as a distinct and coherent social figuration is not just helpful in the negative sense that it restrains overly rigid assumptions about decision-making processes. I would like to suggest that a consideration of court politics can help us to understand why certain imagery was possible in some periods but not in others. This I illustrate with an extended case study: images of the emperor in the presence of members of his guard units. My basic method here is to use what we know from literary sources about court politics and the changing influence of guard units to interpret the patterns visible in this kind of image of the emperor. Of course, to a reader of a sceptical bent it might seem naïve to use biographies and narrative histories written well after the events they describe to learn about the politics of the imperial court. But in fact, the patterns in the imagery align very well with the claims in the literary evidence. This supports the basic picture that the written sources offer of the cycles of influence at court.

The starting point of my analysis is the fact that the image of the emperor in the presence of his bodyguards was always politically sensitive, and therefore possible only in certain periods. The connection between bodyguards and tyranny had deep roots in Greek culture, as is visible in traditions about the Athenian tyrant Pisistratus.[29] The notion that bodyguards (especially foreign bodyguards) are the mark of the tyrant and that good kings do not need them is present in several extant works of Greek political philosophy.[30] The Roman reception of these mentalities is clearly

---

[28] The point made here has some kinship with Levick's argument that the moneyers chose coin images to please an audience of one: the emperor (Levick, 1982). This has been criticised for too readily discounting the notion that coin imagery aimed to persuade the population at large (Sutherland, 1986; Wallace-Hadrill, 1986: 68), but there is still some truth in the basic idea that the moneyers' choices could not have been truly independent of the emperor.

[29] Hdt. 1.59, 1.64; Plut. *Sol.* 30; [Arist.] *Ath. Pol.* 14; Solon, fr. 11 (ed. Gerber).

[30] Xen. *Hier.* 5.3, 6.4–5, 6.10–11, 8.10; cf. 2.8; Isoc. *Ad Nicolem* 21.

displayed in Seneca's *De clementia*, where bodyguards are treated with distinct ambivalence;[31] in Pliny's *Panegyric*, which attacks Domitian's supposed preoccupation with security;[32] and in Marcus Aurelius' *Meditations*, where Antoninus Pius is lauded for showing that it is possible to live in a court (*aule*) without bodyguards (*doryphoreseis*).[33] Reports in literary histories and biographies lambasting emperors who supposedly had too much security[34] and praising those who were not heavily guarded[35] might not be entirely accurate, but they at any rate illustrate the attitudes of the Roman elite. For Romans of the early empire, memories would also have persisted of the Republican prohibition on the exercise of military command within the *pomerium*, which had effectively made the city a demilitarised zone. The early emperors therefore had to try to negotiate between the pragmatic need for a bodyguard and the problematic status of such guards in the eyes of their fellow citizens, especially senators still enthralled by Republican liberties. One can see Augustus attempting such a negotiation: although he created nine praetorian cohorts, he only allowed three of them to be in Rome at once, and these were scattered through the city, not concentrated in a visible way.[36]

Guard Units and the Emperor on Coinage

In view of the fact that guard units were potentially controversial, it is scarcely any wonder that in the coinage of Augustus and Tiberius there is no hint of the existence of guard forces, let alone portraits of the emperor in their presence.[37] This changed, however, in the later Julio-Claudian period. For 37/8, 39/40, and 40/1, there are sestertii from the Roman mint with a reverse depicting Caligula on a tribunal addressing five figures in military dress (e.g. Fig. 6.1).[38] These are clearly soldiers of the praetorian cohorts, since the reverse legend reads ADLOCVT(io) COH(ortium), making it unlikely that these were meant to be legionary soldiers – none of whom would have been stationed in Italy in 37/8 in any case. Furthermore, as is clear from the Vienna specimen in Fig. 6.1, the middle shield has some kind of multi-legged creature depicted. A published photo of a better-preserved

---

[31] Sen. *Clem.* 1.12.3, 1.13.1–2, 1.13.5, 1.19.6.   [32] Plin. *Pan.* 49.   [33] M. Aur. *Med.* 1.17.3.

[34] Suet. *Claud.* 35; cf. Cass. Dio 60.3.2–3; Suet. *Dom.* 14. To judge from Zonaras' *Epitome* (7.10.1), Cassius Dio portrayed the hated Tarquinius Superbus as constantly surrounded by bodyguards.

[35] Cass. Dio 65(66).10.5; Suet. *Vesp.* 12; Cass. Dio 68.15.4–6; Hdn. 1.2.4.

[36] Suet. *Aug.* 49, *Tib.* 37; Tac. *Ann.* 4.2.

[37] There is a coin from Bilbilis in Spain with a reverse honouring Sejanus (*RPC* I.398), but it is his consulship in 31 that is being honoured, not the fact that he was praetorian prefect.

[38] *RIC* I² Gaius/Caligula 32, 40, 48.

Figure 6.1 Sestertius of Caligula. *RIC* I² Gaius 32. Photograph courtesy of the Kunsthistorisches Museum, Vienna, MK RÖ 5257.

specimen of the same type that was once in the private collection of Franz Trau in Vienna makes it clear that two of the three shields have scorpions on them.[39] This tends to confirm the identification of the soldiers as praetorians, since we know from the tombstone of a praetorian by the name of M. Pompeius Asper that praetorian standards had scorpions on them,[40] and it appears that this motif was not shared by legions or auxiliary units, which had other heraldic animals.[41] The praetorian scorpion has long been recognised as a reference to Tiberius,[42] who was born under the astrological sign of Scorpio, and who first concentrated the praetorian guard in its own camp in Rome, thus giving it a full corporate identity.[43]

That such an image became possible under Caligula is surely linked to the role of the praetorian prefect Macro in ensuring that emperor's accession.[44] The literary sources claim that Macro encouraged Tiberius to favour Caligula as a successor,[45] and then had Tiberius' will (which named

[39] Gilhofer und Ranschburg, Wien, 1935: no. 342; see too Rossi, 1967: 27.

[40] *CIL* 14.2523 = *ILS* 2662. For images, see Domaszewski, 1885: 31, fig. 5; Rankov, 1994: 25.

[41] Domaszewski, 1909: 1–15; Töpfer, 2011: 20–5. There is a scorpion on the shield in the lower register of the Gemma Augustea, but this should not be taken as evidence that Roman units aside from the praetorians shared the scorpion motif. The distinctive shape of the shield is best paralleled in mythological depictions of Amazons, not by real historical armour (Bastet, 1979; Prückner, 1997: 121); in any case, the shield is almost certainly part of the *tropaeum*, where one would expect enemy armour. Most scholars take the scorpion on the Gemma to be a reference to Tiberius' zodiac sign, complementing the reference to Capricorn, Augustus' birth sign, in the upper register: Simon, 1988: 156–61; Pollini, 1993: 266; Prückner, 1997: 121. Bastet (1979) sees the Amazon shield and its scorpion as referring to Tiberius' activities in the east in 20 BCE.

[42] Domaszewski, 1909: 14.   [43] Tac. *Ann.* 4.2; Suet. *Aug.* 49, *Tib.* 37.

[44] See generally Barrett, 2015: 76.   [45] Philo, *Leg.* 32–8.

Gemellus as joint heir) declared void by the senate.[46] There were even rumours that he had helped to hasten the demise of the ailing emperor.[47] Upon his succession, Caligula addressed the praetorians and gave them a substantial donative, and the *adlocutio* type could refer to this[48] – although it is unlikely that this large donative was literally paid in bronze.[49] Macro's fall from grace in 38 did not spell the end of Caligula's dependence on the guard. In 39–40, he believed he was the target of various conspiracies involving members of the senatorial order and even his own sisters.[50] It was with the protection of several cohorts of praetorians that he marched north during the tense period when he was (allegedly) threatened by the plot(s) of Gaetulicus and Lepidus.[51] In this fragile security situation, it would have been clear to everyone near the centre of power how strongly the emperor relied on the praetorians for his continued survival. The *adlocutio* type of 37 could therefore be recycled in 39/40 and 40/1. This sort of frank image of the monarch and his bodyguard might have prompted unease amongst any senators moving in court circles, but they now lacked the influence to do anything about it.

Under Claudius, two reverse types associated the emperor with the praetorians even more explicitly. One type carries a depiction of the walled praetorian camp, on which appears the inscription IMPER RECEPT.[52] This can be expanded in various ways, but the meaning is clear: it refers to the acceptance of the emperor by the praetorians.[53] The second type has the legend PRAETOR RECEPT,[54] which again can be expanded in various ways,[55] but must essentially refer to the acceptance of the praetorians by

---

[46] Cass. Dio 59.1.2. It has also been inferred by modern scholars that the praetorians must have acclaimed Caligula *imperator* soon after the death of Tiberius, and before the senate accepted him as emperor: see Barrett, 2015: 76, 102 n. 18.

[47] Tac. *Ann.* 6.50; Cass. Dio 58.28.3.

[48] On the other hand, there is always the chance that such scenes depict what have been called 'pseudo-events' – that is, scenes with an aura of plausibility that had nevertheless not happened, or not in the way depicted. The category is deployed by Burke (1992: 11, 126, 199), adopting (and adapting) one proposed by Boorstin, 1962.

[49] Łuć, 2011: 231–4, citing additional literature. On the question of whether the issue was minted to pay the donative, see Barrett, 2015: 104 n. 56. It is perhaps difficult to imagine the donative, which amounted to 2,000 sestertii (Cass. Dio 59.2.1), being literally paid in sestertii rather than a larger denomination. For general doubts about the minting of special issues for donatives and *congiaria*, see Millar, 2004.

[50] Barrett, 2015: 129–50 for references and analysis.   [51] Suet. *Calig.* 43.

[52] *RIC* I² Claudius 7, 19, 25, 36 (aureus); *RIC* I² Claudius 8, 20, 26, 37 (denarius).

[53] For the different possibilities, see Łuć, 2011: 236, with bibliography. The main contenders are: IMPER(ator) RECEPT(us), IMPER(atore) RECEPT(o), and IMPER(atoris) RECEPT(us).

[54] *RIC* I² Claudius 11, 23, 29 (aureus); 12, 24 (denarius).

[55] For the different possibilities, see Łuć, 2011: 236, with bibliography. The main contenders are: PRAETOR(ianus) RECEPT(us), PRAETOR(iani) RECEPT(i), and PRAETOR(ianis) RECEPT(is).

Figure 6.2 Aureus of Claudius. *RIC* I² Claudius 23. Photograph courtesy of the American Numismatic Society, ANS 1967.153.114.

the emperor. Depicted on the reverse are a praetorian standard-bearer and the emperor clasping hands (Fig. 6.2).

These images were made possible by the continuing – perhaps even escalated – importance of the guard in Claudius' court. Famously, it was the praetorians who had found this unpromising candidate in the imperial residence following the murder of Caligula and taken him to the *castra praetoria* to be acclaimed – thus thwarting attempts by the senate to gain control of the situation.[56] The coins clearly allude to these events.[57] Both types were initially issued in 41/2. The IMPER RECEPT type was then reissued in 43/4, 44/5, and 46/7, and the PRAET RECEPT type in 43/4 (Fig. 6.2) and 44/5. This is a clear reflection of the ongoing importance of the praetorians in Claudius' regime;[58] the events of 41 and also the discovery of two conspiracies against Claudius' life in 42 had resulted in a higher level of security around the person of the emperor than was the case under Tiberius and Augustus.[59]

[56] Suet. *Claud.* 10; Cass. Dio 60.1.2–3; Joseph. *AJ* 19.212–47.
[57] The obvious connection between the praetorian types and the circumstances of Claudius' accession has often been observed; see, for example, Wolters, 2003: 187; Hekster, 2007: 351; Łuć, 2011: 234–7.
[58] The figure of Claudius on the PRAET RECEPT issue has been seen as standing between the standard-bearer and the coin's viewer, implying to any senator seeing it that the emperor was a 'conduit' between senate and praetorians (Gibson, 2013: 121–5). This seems forced: the act of clasping hands requires the figures' bodies to be turned, but their faces are in profile; there is no real sense that the emperor stands between the viewer and the praetorian.
[59] For the conspiracies of Appius Junius Silanus, see Tac. *Ann.* 11.29; Suet. *Claud.* 37, 39; Cass. Dio 60.14.2–15.1; for those of Annius Vinicianus and A. Camillus Scribonianus, see Plin. *Ep.* 3.16; Tac. *Ann.* 12.52; Suet. *Claud.* 13, 35, *Otho* 1; Cass. Dio 60.15. See Suet. *Claud.* 35 for the security measures.

Figure 6.3 Sestertius of Nero. *RIC* I² Nero 135. Photograph courtesy of the American Numismatic Society, ANS 1995.11.1559.

Clear depictions of the emperor with his bodyguards also appear on Neronian coins. Three reverse types are relevant here, all of them dated to the last years of Nero's principate (64–8). Firstly, there is the type with the legend DECVRSIO and the depiction of a horseman and two foot soldiers.[60] In a second, closely related type, the legend DECVRSIO is combined with the depiction of two mounted figures.[61] It has been argued that the type commemorates a specific occasion in 51 on which Nero personally led a drill (*decursio*) of the praetorian guard,[62] although we could be dealing with a 'pseudo-event',[63] confected with the memory of the drill in 51 in mind. A third Neronian type has the legend ADLOCVT COH,[64] or ADLOCVT COH SC,[65] and depicts the emperor haranguing three armed men, two of whom are holding standards, with another figure standing behind him (Fig. 6.3). There has been debate about whether *Germani corporis custodes* or praetorians are depicted in this scene.[66]

The ancient sources claim that under Nero, two praetorian prefects, Sex. Afranius Burrus (*pr. pr.* 51–62) and Ofonius Tigellinus (*pr. pr.* 62–8), were extremely influential at court. Moreover, especially following the very serious and extensive Pisonian conspiracy of 65, it would have been apparent to all just how much Nero owed his continuing survival to the

---

[60] *RIC* I² Nero 105–8, 174–7, 395.   [61] *RIC* I² Nero 163–73, 395–7, 436–7, 507–9, 577–82.

[62] Suet. *Nero* 7, with Rossi, 1996: 143, *contra* Speidel, 1994: 27. Tac. *Ann.* 12.41 could refer to the same occasion.

[63] Cf. n. 48 above.   [64] *RIC* I² Nero 95–7.

[65] *RIC* I² Nero 130–6, 371, 386–8, 429, 489–92, 564–5.

[66] *Germani*: Rossi, 1967: 27–38, accepted by Bellen, 1981: 50–2; Rankov, 1994: 32; cf. Rossi, 1996: 142–3. Praetorians: Charles, 2005: 962 n. 18.

loyalty of his security forces. It is no accident, therefore, that both the *decursio* and *adlocutio* types appear in the last years of Nero's principate.

It must be stressed that with the coins of Caligula, Claudius, and Nero depicting the emperor and his guard, we shall never know which individuals designed and approved these coin types. Nor can we know their precise motives. We can certainly speculate. The *adlocutio* type of Nero could have been ordered by a grateful and relieved emperor to honour the role of the German bodyguard or praetorians in repressing the Pisonian conspiracy.[67] There could, indeed, have been an intention to make the image sufficiently ambiguous that members of either unit could see themselves depicted. On the other hand, perhaps we should see the type as having been ordered by Tigellinus to remind any surviving malcontent senators of the strong relationship between emperor and guardsmen. Or perhaps an ambitious young moneyer chose the designs to ingratiate himself with the emperor or the praetorians. However we imagine the specific intentions behind these images, what is clear is that they were only possible due to the strong position of guard units at the court of Nero.

From the accession of Vespasian through to the age of the Severans, with one exception (below, pp. 140–1), there are no coins that depict the emperor in the presence of guard units or, indeed, even hint at the existence of these units.[68] This I would connect to the less influential position of the emperor's bodyguard in the Flavian and Antonine periods. The *Germani corporis custodes* were abolished by Galba.[69] Eventually, either under Domitian or Trajan, the *equites singulares* were established, forming a new guard unit. They were recruited from auxiliary units on the Rhine–Danube frontier, and so the majority of its members were ethnically Germanic too.[70]

The praetorians, for their part, survived the demise of the Julio-Claudians, but the literary sources give the impression that in the crisis of 68–9 they blotted their copybook. Led by their prefect C. Nymphidius Sabinus, the praetorians are said to have turned against Nero at the last, provoking his suicide. They were then implicated in the mutiny against Galba that led to his murder and the accession of Otho.[71] When Vespasian finally won the civil war, he brought the praetorian guard to heel. He

---

[67] Tac. *Ann.* 15.58–61, 72.

[68] The praetorians are mentioned on the coinage of two of the emperors of 69, but the designs shy away from depicting the emperor with his guards. The CONCORDIA PRAETORIANORVM and FIDES PRAETORIANORVM reverse types of Vitellius do not depict the emperor himself, just Concordia (*RIC* I² Vitellius 19 (Tarraco)) and two clasped hands (*RIC* I² Vitellius 55 (Lugdunum)) respectively. Cf. *RIC* I² Civil Wars 118, 121 (both Gallia).

[69] Suet. *Galb.* 12.   [70] Speidel, 1994: 81–6.

[71] Tac. *Hist.* 1.24–41; Suet. *Galb.* 16–20; Plut. *Galb.* 23–7.

appears to have pruned the number of praetorian cohorts, which had briefly swollen to sixteen under Vitellius, back to nine, as it had been under Augustus.[72] The urban troops received only a token donative of 100 sestertii on Vespasian's accession.[73] Perhaps most importantly, to ensure the complete loyalty of a force that despite its lack of influence still had the potential to be dangerous, Vespasian appointed as prefects his son, Titus, and M. Arrecinus Clemens, the brother of Titus' first wife, Arrecina Tertulla. Vespasian himself, we are told, lived with minimal security (or at any rate he created the impression that he did),[74] presumably in reaction to the view that the good monarch does not need protection from his fellow citizens.

Whilst Vespasian's steps put the praetorians in check, the guard then overplayed its hand in the crisis of 96–8. Not only were there rumours of complicity in the murder of Domitian by the two praetorian prefects of the day,[75] but in 97, the rank and file of the praetorians mutinied against Nerva and demanded the punishment of the assassins of Domitian, to whose memory the guard remained loyal.[76] On the accession of Trajan, the retribution was swift: Cassius Dio reports that the prefect Casperius Aelianus and the troops who supported him in the mutiny against Nerva were summoned by Trajan who 'put them out of the way', which could refer either to exile or execution.[77] It seems likely that to this unstable context belongs the decision to institute the *equites singulares* as a counterweight to the fractious praetorians.

In short, under the Flavians and Trajan, praetorian prefects and their men had nothing of the outsized influence that their predecessors enjoyed in the age of Caligula, Claudius, and Nero. The guard had not been responsible for the accession of the Flavians or Trajan, and it had been repeatedly cut down to size due to its malign behaviour in 68–9 and 96–7. Influence at court had returned to those who favoured the vision of the *civilis princeps* – above all, members of the senatorial order. It is therefore unsurprising that the emperor does not appear alongside his praetorians on a coin again until a type with the reverse legend COH (or COHORT) PRAETOR SC was minted late in the principate of Hadrian as part of a series of coins honouring different military units around the empire.[78] It is striking that this image of the emperor conducting an *adlocutio* before

---

[72] *CIL* 16.21 = *ILS* 1993, with Bingham, 2013: 54, 161 n. 14.   [73] Cass. Dio 64(65).22.2.

[74] Cass. Dio 65(66).10.5; Suet. *Vesp.* 12.   [75] Cass. Dio 67.15.2.

[76] Plin. *Pan.* 6.1; Cass. Dio 68.3.3.

[77] Cass. Dio 68.5.4. In Dio's Greek, the phrase ἐκποδὼν ἐποιήσατο could either refer to killing (cf. Cass. Dio 57.22.2) or to exile (cf. Cass. Dio 38.15, 17, 30).

[78] *RIC* II Hadrian 908–11.

the praetorians almost certainly coincides with the tenure of the influential praetorian prefect Q. Marcius Turbo, who reportedly was distinguished for his ferocious work ethic during Hadrian's twilight years.[79]

Guard Units and the Emperor on Relief Sculpture

When we turn to relief sculpture, images of guard units in the presence of the emperor turn out to be difficult to locate – much more so than on coins under the last three Julio-Claudians. In the Appendix to this chapter, I have listed the major attempts at such identifications in the modern literature, and have given an outline of the complicated (and often fragile) criteria that military equipment specialists have employed in this process.

The first conclusion to be drawn from this excursion into the technical world of Roman military equipment studies is that there are no plausible candidates on public relief sculptures for the *Germani corporis custodes* of the Julio-Claudian period. As for the *equites singulares*, several identifications have been made, but their basis is little more than the fact that the figures in question are horsemen in the presence of the emperor. The absence of any clear depictions of such forces is not surprising, since they were not only bodyguards, but also of predominantly 'barbarian' origin, and hence doubly problematic for a ruler wanting to escape insinuations of tyranny.

As for praetorians, the labours of military equipment specialists have yielded a few cases in which one can reasonably see guardsmen depicted in the presence of the emperor on public relief sculptures. These cases are, however, all from the 90s or later, and their presence has a somewhat faint and equivocal quality about it. One is tempted to theorise that the differences between media might account for the lack of Julio-Claudian examples; unlike coins, relief sculptures cannot use text to identify figures in a scene, for example. But a more straightforward explanation relates to the unequal survival of evidence: most of the major extant public relief sculptures in the public spaces of Rome are from the Flavian period and later; from the late Julio-Claudian period, there are few surviving relief scenes of a genre in which soldiers would be included.

In the great relief sculptures of the second century, artists had no problem signalling the presence of praetorians in a scene without the use of text if they (or their patrons) desired it.[80] One signalling device was the scorpion motif, which, as we have seen, is widely agreed to have been unique to the praetorians.

---

[79] Cass. Dio 69.18. The end date of Turbo's prefecture is not securely known, but most likely fell in the last year or so of Hadrian's life.

[80] There is, however, little to recommend Durry's hypothesis that praetorians on relief sculptures would have had their own colour scheme, which is invisible now that the paint has weathered

Figure 6.4 Puteoli relief: (left) Pennsylvania Fragment. (right) Detail. Photograph courtesy of the Penn Museum, Image #152738, Object MS4916.

On this basis, one can identify as praetorians the soldiers in the Puteoli relief (Fig. 6.4), who (it is plausibly assumed) accompanied the emperor – although damage to the scene means that he is now missing. Soldiers on part of the Great Trajanic Frieze, now incorporated into the Arch of Constantine, also sport the scorpion on their cheekpieces and shields (Fig. 6.5). The presence of the scorpion on shields on these two monuments and also on the *adlocutio* coin of Caligula is congruent with an anecdote in Tacitus' *Histories*, which assumes that praetorian shields were noticeably different from those of legionaries.[81]

There is a second reasonably firm criterion on which praetorians can be identified on relief sculptures: their standards. Military specialists, helped partly again by the tombstone of the praetorian M. Pompeius Asper, have established that praetorian standards were distinct from those of legions (see the Appendix, with n. 107). This has allowed the identification of praetorian units in reliefs on

off (1938: 233). This is based on Durry's sense that praetorians were important enough to deserve distinctive dress, not on any actual evidence.
[81] Tac. *Hist.* 3.23; cf. Rankov, 1994: 20–1 and Tac. *Hist.* 1.28.

Figure 6.5 (left) Section of the Great Trajanic Frieze. Photograph courtesy of Bridgeman Images. (right) Detail. Photograph courtesy of the DAI Rome, D-DAI-ROM 86.362 (F. Schlechter).

Figure 6.6 Trajan's Column, Scene LXXV. Photograph courtesy of DAI Rome, D-DAI -ROM 89.746 (K. Anger).

Trajan's Column (e.g. Scene LXXV, Fig. 6.6), the Great Trajanic Frieze, the *decursio* on the base of the Column of Antoninus Pius, and (possibly) on the *submissio* relief of Marcus Aurelius, also now part of the Arch of Constantine.

Also relevant here are the standards on the Severan Arch of the Argentarii, which are clearly praetorian; this monument does not quite have rank-and-file praetorians depicted with the emperor, but the standards are juxtaposed with images of Severus and his family, and the praetorian prefect Plautianus was probably depicted in a scene prior to his fall from grace.[82]

One can fairly conclude that there was an intention in these various artworks to depict praetorian guardsmen in the presence of the emperor, or to associate them with the emperor, in the case of the Arch of the Argentarii. How does this fit with the sense that one obtains from the literary sources that in the late first and second centuries the praetorians lacked the influence that their predecessors had enjoyed in the later Julio-Claudian court? Here it is worthwhile to consider how different audiences might have received these images. Praetorians themselves, we can assume, would have known that the scorpion was a motif peculiar to their unit and would have been able to recognise their own standards and shields. For them the reliefs would signal their importance to the emperor and, since most of these were scenes of battles and campaigns, acknowledge their valour in war. A second group, namely any senators or equestrians who had spent part of their careers as army commanders, can reasonably be assumed to have had a sufficiently detailed knowledge of military paraphernalia to make sense of such images. One could even speculate that reminding members of the elite – particularly those with a military background – that the emperor was heavily protected by body-guards was an intention of the designer of these images.

It is difficult to believe, however, that for ordinary inhabitants of the city of Rome (or Puteoli for that matter) such insignia would have been meaningful. In the surviving reliefs, praetorians are mainly depicted in scenes alongside legionaries and auxiliary soldiers. Knowing which troops in these scenes belonged to which units would have required a sophisticated knowledge of military dress that could only be developed by extensive contact with a variety of legionary and auxiliary units, yet no such units were stationed in Italy in the first two centuries. More likely, the ordinary viewer of such scenes would have seen nothing more specific than *milites*. This is apparently confirmed by the fact that an unaltered section of the Great Trajanic Frieze with praetorian standards and scorpion motifs was affixed to the Arch of Constantine, even though the praetorians had supported Constantine's rival, Maxentius, at the Battle of the Milvian Bridge. The meaning of the scorpion and this particular kind of standard cannot, therefore, have been common knowledge.

---

[82] Cf. below, pp. 146–7.

One should also consider the original physical context of the images in question. We do not know the original location of the Great Trajanic Frieze,[83] but Trajan's Column is still *in situ*. The lowest scene in which praetorians with standards appear is VIII, which stands a little over 8 m above ground level; the rest appear at various points on the remaining 30 m of the column.[84] It is quite possible that someone actively looking for praetorian standards and who stood in the correct place on a balcony of one of the two adjacent libraries could have found what he was looking for.[85] But a casual viewer on ground level is likely to have just seen 'standards' without being able to distinguish those of the praetorian units from the many legionary standards on the column. A similar visibility issue pertains to the praetorian motif on the Puteoli frieze. If there is merit in the conjecture that the frieze was originally located on the attic of a monumental arch, then the scorpion in question would have been especially hard to detect, since it is roughly 3 × 6.5 cm in size and carved in low relief on the shield of a figure in the background.[86] To be sure, the scorpion could theoretically have been distinguished by an especially bright paint, now vanished. But why carve a motif in low relief if the intention is to highlight it?

Our conclusion, therefore, must be that for different audiences, depictions of the emperor in the presence of his guardsmen would have meant different things. The casual viewer, unversed in military insignia, would have surely seen generic soldiers in the presence of the emperor. Only the soldiers themselves – and perhaps members of the elite with military experience – would have seen something more specific.

A Model: Court Politics and the Limits of the Possible

One powerful metaphor for understanding monarchical courts in different times and places has been the court as arena of competition.[87] Very commonly, the social world surrounding monarchs was populated by competing individuals and groups. Some monarchs were adept at playing off these competitors against each other, but weaker ones were often trapped

---

[83] It is usually suggested that the frieze was once located somewhere in the Forum of Trajan. Holloway's theory (1985: 265–7, 2004: 31–2) that it was once part of an altar located in Asia Minor does not convince.

[84] For the dimensions of the column, see Coarelli, 2000: 21–8.

[85] On the question of the visibility of the friezes, see Coarelli, 2000: 19–21.

[86] Flower, 2001: 640–2, citing earlier literature.   [87] Duindam, 2016: 210–14.

by whichever group was in the ascendency, and rendered virtually impotent or reduced to the status of just another player. In the life of any monarchical system – and indeed in the life of an individual ruler – the power of particular court groups waxed and waned, depending on the psychology and changing capabilities of rulers.[88]

The metaphor of the monarchical court as an arena of competition is an attractive one for the Roman case.[89] Inter alia, the senatorial elite, equestrian secretaries, imperial freedmen, and guard units all faced each other in an arena of competition where the ultimate goal was influence with the emperor. More ephemeral cliques also formed around particular individuals – for example, potential successors to the reigning emperor. Different groups had distinct interests and visions of how imperial power should be exercised and represented.

This constant competition, I suggest, had an impact on decisions about imperial imagery, just as it had impacts on decisions concerning other matters. My claim is not that if a group or an individual was influential at court, this guaranteed a particular kind of imperial imagery. Decisions about imagery were made for all manner of reasons, not all of them necessarily rational; we are not dealing with some kind of artistic vending machine, where a given input guaranteed a particular output.[90] Rather, court politics opened up new possibilities, or closed off old ones when it came to this decision-making process.

This can be seen with the images of the emperor and his guard units discussed above: the emperor's decisions, and those of courtiers (and potentially others), about such images were connected with the influence the praetorians had at court. I would also suggest that my model has explanatory power in instances where powerful courtiers fell spectacularly from grace, with the result that their images were physically defaced or erased as part of a process of *damnatio memoriae*. The fate of imagery of the two most powerful praetorian prefects, Sejanus and Plautianus, illustrates this. We hear that when the influence of these men with Tiberius and Septimius Severus respectively was at its zenith, large numbers of statues were publicly erected.[91] Sejanus' bronze statues, so Cassius Dio seems to imply, were even paired with those of Tiberius.[92] In neither case should we assume that this was done on the direct

---

[88] Duindam, 2016: 223–4, 292.   [89] Cf. Wallace-Hadrill, 1996: 300; Hurlet, 2000: 136.

[90] For this reason, I am sceptical about the possibility raised – albeit not unequivocally endorsed – by Fejfer (2008: 416) that design decisions about imperial portraits in sculpture workshops were influenced by 'general ideological trends emerging from the court': the process may not have been so direct.

[91] Tac. *Ann.* 3.72.3; Cass. Dio 58.2.7, 58.4.4, 76(75).14.6–7.   [92] Cass. Dio 58.4.4.

orders of the prefect or his emperor; indeed, the initiative could well have come from outside the court as a response to configurations of power at the centre. Dio believed that the senate, equestrian order, tribes, and 'leading men' (*andres protoi*) were all responsible for the thicket of statues of Sejanus that grew up,[93] and he also reports that the senate, as well as the populaces of cities (*demoi*) and individuals were behind those for Plautianus.[94] When the influence with the emperor enjoyed by both men abruptly ended, the widespread public display of their images became impossible. The populace of the city of Rome (*ho demos*) obliged by toppling Sejanus' images there,[95] and we are also told that all the images of Plautianus were destroyed following his fall.[96] Evidence for the *damnatio* of the latter has been seen in the deliberate removal of the head of a prominent figure in a siege scene on the north-west panel of the Arch of Septimius Severus. Plautianus and his daughter, Plautilla, have also apparently been removed from a sacrifice scene on the Arch of the Argentarii.[97]

A change in the configuration of court politics did not necessarily result in the spectacular destruction of particular types of imperial images, but could simply halt their creation. This point is well illustrated by the case of the Younger Agrippina.[98] Agrippina had been amongst the first living imperial women to be depicted on a Roman coin and expressly identified by its legend, when she appeared on a coin of her brother Caligula.[99] Then, as the influential fourth wife of Claudius, she also became the first living imperial woman to be given a clear portrait in profile, appearing in multiple types in the last years of Claudius' reign.[100] Her powerful influence with her son Nero in the opening years of his principate is reflected in an extraordinary obverse type from 54 in which busts of Agrippina and Nero face each other without anything in the composition to suggest hierarchy.[101] A hint of hierarchy reappears in a type from 55, in which Nero and Agrippina are depicted jugate, with the emperor in the foreground.[102] But then coin depictions of Agrippina abruptly cease. The striking fact is that it is precisely to 55 that the ancient sources date Agrippina's loss of influence at the court of Nero.[103] To be sure, Nero did not have his mother murdered until 59, but

---

[93] Cass. Dio 58.2.7. [94] Cass. Dio 76(75).14.6–7. [95] Cass. Dio 58.11.3; Juv. 10.58–64.

[96] Cass. Dio 76(75).16.5. [97] Varner, 2004: 161–3.

[98] On numismatic depictions of the Younger Agrippina, see Wood, 1999: 289–95.

[99] *RIC* I² Gaius/Caligula 33, 41. [100] *RIC* I² Claudius 75, 80–1, 103, 117, 119.

[101] *RIC* I² Nero 1–3. [102] *RIC* I² Nero 6–7.

[103] Tac. *Ann.* 13.12–14, 18; Cass. Dio 61.7.1–3; cf. Suet. *Nero* 34; see too Levick (1982: 109) on images of Agrippina on Neronian coins and their disappearance: 'The iconography was intended to reflect the actual state of affairs at court, and to conform to the conception of it held by the ruling clique.' Wood (1999: 265) has suggested that the prominent presentation of an

whoever was making decisions about coin designs – and we do not know who this was – clearly recognised that from 55 Agrippina's position at court was sufficiently weak that it would be wise to cease depicting her on coins.[104]

If my suggestion about the nexus between court politics and imperial imagery has explanatory power, there is a final point to be made: the line between the impossible and possible was not always a sharp one, and could be deliberately blurred to suit the circumstances. This emerges from my analysis of the praetorians in relief sculpture. In the second century, as we have seen, the praetorian guard was in a less influential position, making unequivocal depictions of guardsmen in the presence of the emperor problematic: no emperor would himself authorise one, and nobody with the slightest knowledge of court politics would risk doing so either.

At the same time, however, the crises of the first century had demonstrated the latent danger that the guard posed to the emperor. For much of the second century, it was like some old god, slumbering beneath a volcano, who needed to be appeased. The praetorians might have lost their influence in the world of court politics, but they were still armed men in physical proximity to the emperor – and could therefore theoretically murder him if sufficiently enraged. The solution hit upon by whoever designed the great public reliefs of the period was to acknowledge the praetorians' relationship with the emperor, but only in the context of military campaigns or imperial journeys well away from Rome,[105] thus avoiding any unfortunate associations of tyrants menacing their fellow citizens with bodyguards. The visual cues used to signal their presence in these scenes were so faint that only the cognoscenti could grasp them.

Conclusion

At the centre of power in the Roman Principate was not just an emperor but a monarchical court. Our attempt to understand the social dynamics of

imperial woman on a coin might have been controversial, and the practice was stopped when it was recognised as harmful to the regime. This is not, however, sufficient in itself to explain why it was precisely after 55 that this happened.

[104] Lusnia (1995: 129–30) has suggested a similar argument in relation to Julia Domna: that her image became scarce on coinage in 202–5, when the praetorian prefect Plautianus, who was hostile to her, had great influence at court. However, hoard evidence shows that her *pietas*-type coin (*RIC* IV Septimius Severus 572–4), conventionally dated to 204, was minted in significant quantities (Rowan, 2011: 250–1). There is also the problem that the chronological sequence of Julia Domna types for the period 195–211/12 is based mainly on Lusnia's sense of the artistic phases rather than hard chronological markers.

[105] Cf. Busch, 2011: 27–8.

Roman imperial imagery can be enriched by taking this fact into account. The relationships, pressures, and struggles of the court must have impinged on the creation of imperial images, just as they did on decisions regarding other political questions. The realities of court society encourage us to add nuance to hypothetical reconstructions of who commissioned, designed, and approved imperial images. On closer inspection, ostensibly independent sites of decision-making – 'senate', 'inner circle', 'moneyers', 'emperor' – turn out to be deeply interconnected, due to constant face-to-face interactions, the overwhelming importance of the emperor's favour, and the constant attempts of emperor and 'courtiers' to control each other.

Moreover, courts tend to be unstable, with the influence and power of different individuals and groups ebbing and flowing, and the Roman court was no exception. Whilst a particular configuration of power at court never guaranteed particular images, it did set limits to what was possible. As such configurations changed, so did the feasibility of depicting certain individuals in major works of 'public' art. Such changes also helped to move the line between the possible and the impossible when it came to images of the emperor himself, as we can see with images of the emperor in the presence of guard units. Furthermore, when dealing with controversial topics like this, artists and their patrons could exploit the fact that viewing is always a subjective experience, conditioned by the viewer's background knowledge and assumptions. Different audiences could therefore be encouraged to see different things in the same image.

APPENDIX: GUARD UNITS IN THE PRESENCE OF THE EMPEROR IN RELIEF SCULPTURE OF THE PRINCIPATE

In the table below, I list the major attempts to identify guard units in the presence of the emperor in relief sculptures from the Principate. It must be stressed that these identifications rest on a number of different criteria, of which all but the first two are open to serious doubt:

i) **Scorpion motifs.** Scorpion motifs on shields and helmets are usually accepted as firm indicators of praetorians.[106]

ii) **Standards.** Praetorian standards are securely characterised by combinations of the following: *coronae murales*, *vallares*, or *navales*; *phalerae cum imaginibus*; and perhaps images of eagles with wings stretched to the side.[107]

iii) **Attic-style helmets.** This was probably an artistic convention used for both praetorians and legionaries in imitation of Hellenistic depictions of soldiers, not a reflection of the actual equipment of Roman soldiers.[108]

iv) **Cuirasses.** The two main types of cuirass – the mail cuirass (*lorica hamata*) and the scale cuirass (the so-called *lorica segmentata*) – were both worn by legionaries, so armour cannot distinguish praetorians.[109]

v) **Shield shapes.** Both praetorians and legionaries seem to have used curved, rectangular shields, as well as oval shields, so shield shapes cannot be used to identify praetorians.[110]

vi) **Proximity to the emperor.** The emperor might interact with urban cohorts, legionaries, and auxiliaries. Soldiers in the presence of the emperor need not be praetorians or *equites singulares*.

---

[106] Charles, 2002: 673, citing earlier literature.
[107] Domaszewski, 1885: 56–69; Töpfer, 2009: 288, 2011: 66, 91–9.
[108] Rankov, 1994: 20; Charles, 2002: 672–3.   [109] Charles, 2002: 669–77.
[110] Bishop and Coulston, 2006: 91.

Relief	Date	Location	Unit	Identification Criteria	Identified by
Lost Augustan monument (depicted on the Boscoreale cup I:2)	Augustus (late?)	Louvre, Bj 2366	Praetorians	Proximity to emperor; armour	Villefosse, 1899: 138 with n. 1; Kuttner, 1995: 94 with n. 1; *disputed by Durry, 1938: 218.*
Cancellaria reliefs, Frieze A	Domitian	Musei Vaticani, Museo Gregoriano Profano, 13389–13391	Praetorians	Proximity to emperor; shields; weaponry	Durry, 1948: 328–33; Rankov, 1994: 46–8; Bingham, 2013: 76, 184 n. 197; *disputed by Magi, 1945: 81–2.*
Puteoli reliefs	Domitian	MS 4916 University of Pennsylvania Museum + Pergamonmuseum in Berlin, Sk 887	Praetorians	Scorpions on shields	Durry, 1948: 329, 332; Rankov, 1994: 52–3; Flower, 2001: 636.
The Great Trajanic Frieze	Trajan	Arch of Constantine	Praetorians	Scorpions on shields and cheekpieces; standards	Durry, 1938: 213; Rankov, 1994: 53–5; Töpfer, 2011: 323–4 (cat. SR 7.2–3); *disputed by Leander Touati, 1987: 44–8.*

(cont.)

Relief	Date	Location	Unit	Identification Criteria	Identified by
Trajan's Column, Scenes VIII, XXIII, XXIV, XL, XLII, LI, LIII, LIV, LXIII, LXXV, LXXXVI, LXXXVII, XCVIII, CII, CIV, CVI, CXVIII	Trajan	Rome	Praetorians	Standards	Töpfer, 2011: 313 (cat. SR 3.3), 314 (cat. SR 6.6), 315 (cat. SR 6.9, 6.10), 316 (cat. SR 6.11, 6.14), 317 (cat. SR 6.15, 6.16, 6.18), 318 (cat. SR 6.19), 319 (cat. SR 6.23, 6.24), 320 (cat. SR 6.26–8), 321 (cat. SR 6.30, 6.33, cf. Coarelli, 2000: 173), 322 (cat. SR 6.37).
Trajan's Column, Scenes LVIII, LXXXIX, XCVII, CI	Trajan	Rome	*Equites singulares*	Horsemen near the emperor	Speidel, 1994: 44–5, 119; Coarelli, 2000: 166.
Tropaeum Traiani, Metope XXXVI (Florescu, 1965)	108/9	Tropaeum Traiani, Adamklissi	Praetorians, *equites singulares*	Proximity to emperor	Richmond, 1967: 34 (praetorians); Speidel, 1994: 14 (*equites singulares*); *disputed by* Durry, 1938: 218; Rossi, 1996: 144; Charles, 2004.
Anaglypha Traiani/Hadriani: debt-burning relief	Trajan or Hadrian	Curia, Rome	Praetorians	Proximity to emperor	Hammond, 1953: 145; Torelli, 1982: 91 (praetorians or *urbanici*); Flower, 2001: 642 n. 104; *disputed by* Rüdiger, 1973: 168–9 (legionaries).

			Praetorians	Proximity to emperor	
Adlocutio of Hadrian	Hadrian	Palazzo dei Conservatori, formerly Arco di Portogallo		Proximity to emperor	Flower, 2001: 642 n. 104.
Decursio scene	Antoninus Pius	Column of Antoninus Pius	Praetorians, *equites singulares*	Proximity to emperor; standards	Speidel, 1994: 50 (*equites singulares*); Töpfer, 2011: 331 (cat. SR 14); Flower, 2001: 642 n. 104 (praetorians), Gabelmann, 1984: 176, 196.
Column of M. Aurelius, Scene LXII	176 or 180	Column of Marcus Aurelius	*Equites singulares*	Dress; proximity to emperor	Speidel, 1994: 51.
Column of M. Aurelius, Scene LXXII	176 or 180	Column of Marcus Aurelius	*Equites singulares*	Proximity to emperor	Speidel, 1994: 33, 50; *disputed by* Rossi, 1996: 144.
Column of M. Aurelius, Scene LXXIV	176 or 180	Column of Marcus Aurelius	*Equites singulares*	Proximity to emperor	Speidel, 1994: 33, 50; *disputed by* Rossi, 1996: 144.
Profectio of Marcus Aurelius	Marcus Aurelius	Arch of Constantine	*Equites singulares*	Proximity to emperor	
Submissio to Marcus Aurelius	Marcus Aurelius	Arch of Constantine	Praetorians	Standards	Gabelmann, 1984: 175; *doubted by* Töpfer, 2011: 341 (cat. SR 18.5).
Clementia scene of Marcus Aurelius	Marcus Aurelius	Palazzo dei Conservatori, Rome	Praetorians	Proximity to emperor; helmet	Rankov, 1994: 58; Flower, 2001: 642 n. 104.

Bibliography

Acton, K. 2011. 'Vespasian and the social world of the Roman court', *AJPh* 132: 103–24.

Armstrong, G. E. 2008. 'Sacrificial iconography: creating history, making myth, and negotiating ideology on the Ara Pacis Augustae', *Religion and Theology* 15: 340–56.

Bang, P. F. 2011. 'Court and state in the Roman Empire: domestication and tradition in comparative perspective', in Duindam, J., T. Artan, and M. Kunt (eds.), *Royal Courts in Dynastic States and Empires*. Rulers and Elites 1 (Leiden; Boston: Brill), 103–30.

Barrett, A. A. 2015. *Caligula: The Abuse of Power*, 2nd ed. (London; New York: Routledge).

Bastet, F. L. 1979. 'Der Skorpion auf der Gemma Augustea', in Kopcke, G. and M. B. Moore (eds.), *Studies in Classical Art and Archeology: A Tribute to Peter Heinrich von Blanckenhagen* (Locust Valley, NJ: J. J. Augustin), 217–23.

Beckmann, M. 2012. 'Trajan and Hadrian', in Metcalf, W. E. (ed.), *The Oxford Handbook of Greek and Roman Coinage* (Oxford: Oxford University Press), 405–22.

Bellen, H. 1981. *Die germanische Leibwache der römischen Kaiser des julisch-claudischen Hauses*. Abhandlungen der Geistes- und Sozialwissenschaftlichen Klasse 1981.1. (Wiesbaden; Mainz: Franz Steiner).

Bingham, S. 2013. *The Praetorian Guard: A History of Rome's Elite Special Forces* (Waco, TX: Baylor University Press).

Bishop, M. C. and J. C. N. Coulston 2006. *Roman Military Equipment from the Punic Wars to the Fall of Rome*, 2nd ed. (Oxford: Oxbow Books).

Boorstin, D. 1962. *The Image: Or, What Happened to the American Dream?* (New York: Atheneum).

Burke, P. 1992. *The Fabrication of Louis XIV* (New Haven; London: Yale University Press).

Busch, A. W. 2011. *Militär in Rom: Militärische und paramilitärische Einheiten im kaiserzeitlichen Stadtbild*. Palilia 20. (Wiesbaden: Reichert).

Charles, M. B. 2002. 'The Flavio-Trajanic *miles*: the appearance of citizen infantry on Trajan's Column', *Latomus* 61: 666–95.

2004. 'Trajan's guard at Adamklissi: infantry or cavalry?', *Historia* 53: 476–89.

2005. 'Further thoughts on the Flavio-Trajanic *miles*: unarmoured guardsmen on the column?', *Latomus* 64: 959–68.

Coarelli, F. 2000. *The Column of Trajan*, trans. C. Rockwell (Rome: Editore Colombo).

Conlin, D. A. 1997. *The Artists of the Ara Pacis: The Process of Hellenization in Roman Relief Sculpture* (Chapel Hill; London: University of North Carolina Press).

Domaszewski, A. 1885. *Die Fahnen im römischen Heere*. Abhandlungen des Archäologisch-Epigraphischen Seminares der Universität Wien 5 (Vienna: C. Gerold's Sohn).

    1909. *Abhandlungen zur römischen Religion* (Leipzig; Berlin: Georg Olms).

Duindam, J. 2016. *Dynasty: A Global History of Power, 1300–1800* (Cambridge: Cambridge University Press).

Duindam, J., T. Artan, and M. Kunt (eds.) 2011. *Royal Courts in Dynastic States and Empires*. Rulers and Elites 1 (Leiden; Boston: Brill).

Duncan-Jones, R. 2005. 'Implications of Roman coinage: debates and differences', *Klio* 87: 459–87.

Durry, M. 1938. *Les cohortes prétoriennes* (Paris: De Boccard).

    1948. 'Sur l'armement prétorien', *RA* 29/30: 326–33.

Eck, W. 2000. 'The emperor and his advisers', in Bowman, A. K., P. Garnsey, and D. Rathbone (eds.), *The Cambridge Ancient History*, Vol. 11: *The High Empire, AD 70–192*, 2nd ed. (Cambridge: Cambridge University Press), 195–213.

    2002. 'Imperial administration and epigraphy: in defence of prosopography', in Bowman, A. K., H. M. Cotton, M. Goodman, and S. Price (eds.), *Representations of Empire: Rome and the Mediterranean World*. Proceedings of the British Academy 114 (Oxford: Oxford University Press), 131–51.

Elias, N. 1969. *Die höfische Gesellschaft* (Darmstadt; Neuwied: Luchterhand) [= 1983. *The Court Society*, trans. E. Jephcott (New York: Pantheon)].

Fejfer, J. 2008. *Roman Portraits in Context*. Image and Context 2. (Berlin; New York: De Gruyter).

Florescu, F. B. 1965. *Das Siegesdenkmal von Adamklissi: Tropaeum Traiani* (Bucharest: Verlag der Akademie der Rumänischen Volksrepublik; Bonn: Habelt).

Flower, H. 2001. 'A tale of two monuments: Domitian, Trajan, and some praetorians at Puteoli (*AE* 1973, 137)', *AJA* 105: 625–48.

Gabelmann, H. 1984. *Antike Audienz- und Tribunalszenen* (Darmstadt: Wissenschaftliche Buchgesellschaft).

Gibson, A. G. G. 2013. '"All things to all men": Claudius and the politics of AD 41', in Gibson, A. G. G. (ed.), *The Julio-Claudian Succession: Reality and Perception of the 'Augustan Model'* (Leiden; Boston: Brill), 107–32.

Gilhofer und Ranschburg, Wien. 1935. *Sammlung Franz Trau: Münzen der römischen Kaiser* (Vienna; Lucerne: Gilhofer und Ranschburg).

Hammond, M. 1953. 'A statue of Trajan represented on the "Anaglypha Traiani"', *MAAR* 21: 127–83.

Hekster, O. 2007. 'The Roman army and propaganda', in Erdkamp, P. (ed.), *A Companion to the Roman Army* (Chichester; Oxford; Malden, MA: Wiley-Blackwell), 339–58.

Holloway, R. R. 1985. 'The spolia of the Arch of Constantine', *NAC* 14: 261–72.

2004. *Constantine and Rome* (New Haven; London: Yale University Press).

Howgego, C. 1995. *Ancient History from Coins* (London; New York: Routledge).

Hurlet, F. 2000. 'Les sénateurs dans l'entourage d'Auguste et de Tibère: un complément à plusieurs synthèses récentes sur la cour impériale', *RPh* 74: 123–50.

Kelly, B. forthcoming. 'Introduction', in Kelly, B. and A. Hug (eds.), *The Roman Emperor and his Court: ca. 30 BC–ca. AD 300*, Vol. 1: *Historical Essays* (Cambridge: Cambridge University Press).

Kuttner, A. L. 1995. *Dynasty and Empire in the Age of Augustus: The Case of the Boscoreale Cups* (Berkeley: University of California Press).

Laeben-Rosén, V. 2005. Age of Rust: Court and Power in the Severan Age (188–238 AD). Diss. Uppsala.

Leander Touati, A.-M. 1987. *The Great Trajanic Frieze: The Study of a Monument and of the Mechanisms of Message Transmission in Roman Art*. Acta Instituti Romani Regni Sueciae Series in 4°, 45 (Stockholm: Svenska institutet i Rom).

Levick, B. 1982. 'Propaganda and the imperial coinage', *Antichthon* 16: 104–16.

Łuć, I. 2011. 'The military coins of Caligula and Claudius: the types *ADLOCVT. COH., IMPER. RECEPT.* and *PRAETOR. RECEPT.*', in Ruciński, S. (ed.), *Studia Lesco Mrozewicz ab amicis et discipulis dedicata* (Poznań: Instytut Historii UAM), 231–8.

Lusnia, S. S. 1995. 'Julia Domna's coinage and Severan dynastic propaganda', *Latomus* 54: 119–40.

Magi, F. 1945. *I rilievi flavi del Palazzo della Cancelleria* (Rome: Presso la Pontificia accademia romana di archeologia).

Mander, E. 2012. *Coining Images of Power: Patterns in the Representation of Roman Emperors on Imperial Coinage, A.D. 193–284* (Leiden; Boston: Brill).

Marlowe, E. 2006. 'Framing the sun: the Arch of Constantine and the Roman cityscape', *ABull* 88: 223–42.

Michel, A.-C. 2015. *La Cour sous l'empereur Claude: les enjeux d'un lieu de pouvoir*. Aulica: L'Univers de la cour (Rennes: Presses universitaires de Rennes).

Millar, F. G. B. 2004. 'Cash distributions in Rome and imperial minting', in Cotton, H. M. and G. Rogers (eds.), *Rome, the Greek World, and the East*, Vol. 2: *Government, Society, and Culture in the Roman Empire* (Chapel Hill; London: University of North Carolina Press), 89–104.

Pani, M. 2003. *La corte dei Cesari fra Augusto e Nerone* (Rome; Bari: Laterza).

Paterson, J. 2007. 'Friends in high places: the creation of the court of the Roman emperor,' in Spawforth, A. J. S. (ed.), *The Court and Court Society in Ancient Monarchies* (Cambridge: Cambridge University Press), 121–56.

Peachin, M. 1986. 'The *Procurator Monetae*', *NC* 146: 94–106.

Pollini, J. 1993. 'The Gemma Augustea: ideology, rhetorical imagery, and the creation of a dynastic narrative', in Holliday, P. J. (ed.), *Narrative and Event in Ancient Art* (Cambridge: Cambridge University Press), 258–98.

Prückner, H. 1997. 'Die Stellung des Tiberius: Vorschlag für eine Ergänzung der Gemma Augustea', in Erath, G., M. Lehner, and G. Schwarz (eds.), *Komos: Festschrift für Thuri Lorenz zum 65. Geburtstag* (Vienna: Phoibos), 119–24.

Rankov, B. 1994. *The Praetorian Guard* (Oxford; New York: Osprey Publishing).

Richmond, I. A. 1967. 'Adamklissi', *PBSR* 35: 29–39.

Rossi, L. 1967. 'La Guardia Pretoriana e Germanica nella monetazione Giulio-Claudia', *RIN* 15: 15–38.

———— 1996. '"Riding for Caesar" can't win 'em all: conflicting iconography of the imperial guard on Roman coins and monuments', *RIN* 97: 141–8.

Rowan, C. 2011. 'The public image of the Severan women', *PBSR* 79: 241–73.

Rüdiger, U. 1973. 'Die Anaglypha Hadriani', *Antike Plastik* 12: 161–74.

Saller, R. P. 1982. *Personal Patronage under the Early Empire* (Cambridge: Cambridge University Press).

Schöpe, B. 2014. *Der römische Kaiserhof in severischer Zeit (193–235 n. Chr.).* Historia Einzelschriften 231. (Stuttgart: Franz Steiner).

Simon, E. 1988. *Augustus: Kunst und Leben in Rom um die Zeitenwende* (Munich: Hirmer).

Speidel, M. P. 1994. *Riding for Caesar: The Roman Emperors' Horse Guards* (Cambridge, MA: Harvard University Press).

Sutherland, C. H. V. 1959. 'The intelligibility of Roman imperial coin types', *JRS* 49: 46–55.

———— 1986. 'Compliment or complement? Dr Levick on imperial coin types', *NC* 146: 85–93.

Syme, R. 1939. *The Roman Revolution* (Oxford: Oxford University Press).

Töpfer, K. 2009. 'Zur Funktion der Bildnismedaillons an römischen Feldzeichen', in Busch, A. W. and H.-J. Schalles (eds.), *Akten der 16. Internationalen Roman Military Equipment Conference (ROMEC), Xanten, 13.–16. Juni 2007.* Xantener Berichte: Grabung – Forschung – Präsentation 16 (Mainz: Philipp von Zabern), 283–90.

———— 2011. *Signa militaria: Die römischen Feldzeichen in der Republik und im Prinzipat.* Monographien des Römisch-Germanischen Zentralmuseums 91 (Mainz: Schnell und Steiner).

Torelli, M. 1982. *Typology and Structure of Roman Historical Reliefs* (Ann Arbor: University of Michigan Press).

Varner, E. R. 2004. *Mutilation and Transformation: damnatio memoriae and Roman Imperial Portraiture* (Leiden; Boston: Brill).

Villefosse, H. de 1899. *Le trésor de Boscoreale.* Monuments et Mémoires publiés par l'Académie des inscriptions et belles-lettres, Fondation Eugène Piot 5 (Paris: Ernst Leroux).

Wallace-Hadrill, A. 1986. 'Image and authority in the coinage of Augustus', *JRS* 76: 66–87.

1996. 'The imperial court', in Bowman, A. K., E. Champlin, and A. Lintott (eds.), *The Cambridge Ancient History*, Vol. 10: *The Augustan Empire: 43 BC–AD 69*, 2nd ed. (Cambridge: Cambridge University Press), 283–308.

2008. *Rome's Cultural Revolution* (Cambridge: Cambridge University Press).

2011. 'The Roman imperial court: seen and unseen in the performance of power', in Duindam, J., T. Artan, and M. Kunt (eds.), *Royal Courts in Dynastic States and Empires.* Rulers and Elites 1 (Leiden; Boston: Brill), 91–102.

Winterling, A. 1997. 'Hof ohne "Staat": Die *aula Caesaris* im 1. und 2. Jahrhundert n. Chr.', in Winterling, A. (ed.), *Zwischen 'Haus' und 'Staat': Antike Höfe im Vergleich.* Historische Zeitschrift Beihefte 23 (Munich: R. Oldenbourg), 91–112 [= 2009. 'A court without "state": the *aula Caesaris*', in Winterling, A., *Politics and Society in Imperial Rome*, trans. K. Lüddecke (Chichester; Oxford; Malden, MA: Wiley-Blackwell)].

1999. *Aula Caesaris: Studien zur Institutionalisierung des römischen Kaiserhofes in der Zeit von Augustus bis Commodus (31 v. Chr.–192 n. Chr.)* (Munich: R. Oldenbourg).

Wolters, R. 2003. 'Die Geschwindigkeit der Zeit und die Gefahr der Bilder: Münzbilder und Münzpropaganda in der römischen Kaiserzeit', in Weber, G. and M. Zimmermann (eds.), *Propaganda-Selbstdarstellung-Repräsentation im römischen Kaiserreich des 1. Jhs. n. Chr.* Historia Einzelschriften 164 (Stuttgart: Franz Steiner), 176–204.

Wood, S. 1999. *Imperial Women: A Study in Public Images, 40 BC–AD 68* (Leiden; Boston; Cologne: Brill).

Zanker, P. 1987. *Augustus und die Macht der Bilder* (Munich: C. H. Beck) [= 1988. *The Power of Images in the Age of Augustus*, trans. A. Shapiro (Ann Arbor: University of Michigan Press)].

Local Aspirations and Statues of Emperors in Roman North Africa

MONICA HELLSTRÖM

The subject of this chapter is statues of emperors raised in the most densely urbanised part of Roman North Africa, during the first three centuries CE. The hundreds of towns in this area, which roughly corresponds to Africa Vetus, engaged prolifically with the imperial 'statue habit', filling their public spaces with dedications to a long row of emperors (Fig. 7.1). The phenomenon is remarkably intense from a global perspective, and also in many ways *sui generis*: it did not abate towards the end of the second century (as it did elsewhere), it penetrated down to village level,[1] and it showed an unusual level of initiative on the part of private individuals (about a fifth of the sample).[2] The images themselves were mainly of bronze (as in all regions outside Italy) and have for the most part perished,[3] but many inscribed bases have survived, and it is these that form my main material. Compared to imperial statues dedicated by communities,[4] for which the inscriptions tend to be brief and uninformative, those raised by individuals offer a wealth of information which can shed much-needed light on how these monuments functioned.

My focus is on what they communicated and to whom, and what relationship(s) they represent to the emperors on display. I argue that (at least in this area) they carried multiple messages and embodied multiple relations, some locally defined, some with a wider scope, but none that connected emperors to locals in any straightforward way, either as top-down propaganda or as bottom-up loyalty statements.[5] While both emperors and locals had vested interests in them, and while they played a key role in disseminating imperial ideology, the imperial statues in Roman North African

---

[1] Højte, 2005: 92, 96–7.

[2] More than seventy items, or 18 per cent of the inscriptions in my sample that are complete enough to disclose something about the agent. On this being unique to Africa: Højte, 2005: 186.

[3] Højte, 2005: 45–7. We thus have little by which to discuss iconography or style, or spatial relations, seeing that few bases (or plaques mounted on them) were found *in situ*.

[4] Here, statues of emperors rather than statues produced in the imperial period.

[5] See Introduction, pp. 5–10; specifically on African imperial statues, Hurlet, 2000; Polley, 2004/5 [2007].

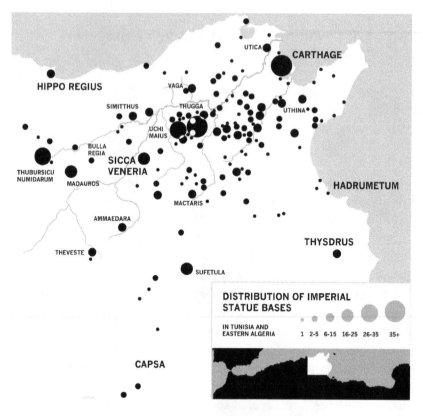

Figure 7.1 Map of the study area. The dots represent the number of bases retrieved at each location. The concentration in the riverine zone is misleading; the eastern littoral was the most populated in antiquity and remains so today. Survival in some small towns such as Thugga and Madauros is favoured by large-scale excavations, while the opposite obtains for Carthage. Artwork: M. Hellström.

towns were generated by local processes that had little directly to do with emperors. The emperor's influence over (and interest in) them was indirect, limited to manipulating content and regulating access in the broadest sense.

Inscriptions from more than 600 statue bases and fifty arches dedicated to emperors have survived from the area, dating from Augustus to the Valentinians.[6] More than forty have been retrieved from the perfectly ordinary (but well-excavated) town of Thugga alone, and many middling towns would have housed similar numbers. For major colonies such as Sicca Veneria, Hippo Regius, Hadrumetum, or Thysdrus – not to mention

---

[6] After this, imperial statues were only raised in Rome and Greece; Højte, 2005: 103. The sample is culled from the *CIL* 8 series, *ILTun.*, *ILAfr.*, *ILAlg.* 1–2, and African collections referenced in the *Année épigraphique*. When the stone is lost and there is no description, the inscription itself usually helps distinguish between monumental altars, statue bases, and building inscriptions.

Carthage – we must envision many more. Some caveats apply: most of the material comes from small inland towns, while (continuously inhabited) major cities present frustratingly little, and often in too fragmentary a state to be of much use. The loss of much of the record from Carthage is particularly lamentable, as the situation in this metropolis no doubt differed from that of the villages in its hinterland.[7] Each town, moreover, had its own version of the practice, perpetuating different elements in stone for posterity. Even so, there is enough homogeneity to allow for some generalisations as to who raised the statues, and to give us an idea of why.

Local Agents, Local Aims

That the emperor or imperial officials were directly involved can be excluded at once: all monuments were raised on the initiative of locals. Fejfer and Højte both note that this tendency is global, and underscore that imperial statues should be seen as honorific, and of a kind with statues to other dignitaries.[8] As such, they were the end product of local political processes, testifying to the stature not only of the honoree but also of the honouring bodies. Far and beyond, the most frequent such bodies are the town senates (or *ordines decurionum*), which is no doubt also the case for bases that omit such information. The *populus* also had political roles in African towns (if not to the extent seen in the Greek east), as did other civic institutions such as the *curiae*, but not in the sphere of raising statues to emperors, which comes across as very exclusive.[9] As a general tendency, the more significant the town, the larger a proportion of imperial statues raised by the *ordines*, as are all surviving examples from large and wealthy cities such as Carthage and the Julian colony Sicca Veneria. By contrast, private agents dominate in some smaller towns such as Madauros, through several

---

[7] Carthage has produced more than twenty (unreadable) fragments, which is more than any other location, but only sixteen texts from which something useful can be made out – and these, too, are in comparatively bad shape. Many of the bases from the area *in toto* are too fragmentary to be attributed to an emperor, and have not been included in the study.

[8] Fejfer, 2008: 420–1, 381; Højte, 2005: 90 ' . . . the economic, social and political factors that governed the erection of imperial portrait statues were the same as those regulating the erection of honorary statues of other individuals'. Inscriptions are tied to the public sphere; cult statues and statues in private settings were not usually inscribed: Højte, 2005: 119–20.

[9] Zuiderhoek, 2013, 2014, on the prominent role of the δῆμος in the Roman east. Dawson, 2016 shows how vivid the sub-curial political life of African towns could be. Its only exponents among imperial monuments, however, are a statue of Claudius by the *senatus populusque* (*AE* 1935.32, Hippo Regius), and one of Septimius Severus by the *populus Sustritanus* (*CIL* 8.25937, Sustri). The *populus* is absent also from building inscriptions: Saastamoinen, 2010b.

generations. Dedicators no doubt emulated earlier texts in the public spaces of their towns, creating internally homogenous samples but no region-wide regularity. Consistent, however, is the elevated social horizon of the dedicators. Bases that disclose their status reveal that between 75 and 80 per cent held the highest honours in the *ordines*: the majority were *flamines*, but many were also *duumviri* and aediles. Of those who fall outside this norm, all but one are of higher status still.[10]

Bases commissioned by *ordines* are sparing of detail, often with the author abbreviated as DDPP, *d(ecreto) d(ecurionum) p(ecunia) p(ublica)*, in line with the conventions for honouring other persons who do not belong to the community.[11] It is thus surprising to find that the bases set up by individuals provide a wealth of intimate details, in a manner otherwise associated with honouring locals. They disclose not only the authors' names but also their careers and families, as well as the process that generated the statues, including their price. Some also describe the festivities that accompanied their dedication, and how these were paid for. The mention of cost is almost unique for Africa, and, in Africa, unique to statues of emperors.[12] This type of information seems rather pointless if we envision the statues as an interchange between locals and emperors, few of whom ever visited the area.[13] Nor can it be put down to bragging (only), seeing that the cost of most statues is fairly modest;[14] while beyond the means of *humiliores*, it presented no difficulties for the social stratum involved. What the payments, and the statues, represent are stages in the careers of the authors. In African towns we see a consistent association between raising imperial statues and fulfilling the obligations for a local

---

[10] Of seventy-two imperial statue bases raised by individuals, seventeen do not disclose the status of the dedicator. Most of their inscriptions follow conventions that make clear that they held some manner of local magistracy. Three knights and a *dendrophoros* are known from fragments of texts that likely also included local positions. Ten outliers by eight authors feature one governor and two *curatores rei publicae*, a tribune, a prefect of a cohort and an imperial procurator at Simitthus (where the imperial marble quarry looms large), and one *decemvir stlitibus iudicandis* with personal ties to Pius. The only 'humble' dedicator is a Mancian farmer raising a statue on an imperial estate; however, such *cultores* are known to hold decurionates in nearby towns and his sub-curial status should not be taken for granted.

[11] Dawson, 2016: 85–8, 304–33, with brief, uninformative inscriptions for emperors and what he brands 'imperial elites', in this context often the proconsuls. Honours to locals described both honoree and dedicating body in much more detail. So also Hellström, 2014: 92–3; the higher the status of the patron of a building project, the less information was provided.

[12] Statues to private local individuals mention that they were raised by public funds or collations by groups of citizens, but not precisely how much they cost.

[13] See below, n. 62.

[14] Items in my cache range from 2,000–12,000 HS. Højte, 2005: 55 on the cost globally ranging from 3,000–8,000 HS, of which roughly half went to the manufacture.

honos such as the duumvirate or the flaminate, for which a fee was required to the *res publica* or *aerarium*. This pattern accounts for almost all privately raised statues from *c.*100 CE onward, when the practice first appears.[15] It is no coincidence that the costs of the statues correspond remarkably well to the required *summa honoraria* or *(summa) legitima*.[16]

One way or another, the fee for local offices is central to the texts (when these are complete enough to disclose anything about money). The fee appears to be the standard unit of assessment, as in cases where the text states that the endeavour cost twice the sum for office. In some cases it explicitly contributed to the raising of the statue (and some others are suggestive of the same procedure),[17] while other texts claim that the fee

---

[15] My sample so far: *ILTun.* 460 (Ammaedara); *CIL* 8.14370 (Avedda); *AE* 1978.854 (Belalis Maior); *ILAfr.* 451; *AE* 2004.1874; *AE* 2004.1875; *AE* 2005.19876 (Bulla Regia); *AE* 1957.77 (Cillium); *CIL* 8.17408 (*in nomine*, Hippo Regius); *CIL* 8.00622 (Mactaris); *CIL* 8.16873; *ILAlg.* 1.2087; *ILAlg.* 1.2088; *ILAlg.* 1.2089; *ILAlg.* 1.2092; *ILAlg.* 1.2095 (Madauros); *CIL* 8.1576 (Musti); *AE* 1995.1657 (Pagus Mercurialis); *CIL* 8.14755 (Sicilibba); *ILAfr.* 68 (Sidi Bou Ali); *AE* 1942/3.98; *AE* 1992.1797; *CIL* 8.23004; *ILAfr.* 300 (Sutunurca); *CIL* 8.1401 (*in nomine*, Thignica); *ILTun.* 714; *ILTun.* 718 (Thuburbo Maius); *CIL* 8.26517; *CIL* 8.26529; *ILAfr.* 561; *AE* 1904.115 (*in nomine*, Thugga); *CIL* 8.26250; *CIL* 8.26351; *CIL* 8.26255 (for the base, the council paying for the statue, Uchi Maius); *CIL* 8.12005 (Vazi Sarra); *AE* 1961.199; *AE* 1992.1803 (Vina); *CIL* 8.10833 (Zattara); *CIL* 8.895 (Ziqua). An arch inscription from Vazi Sarra (*CIL* 8.23749) adds that the builder had also raised a statue of Septimius Severus to obtain his flaminate.

[16] This is the most common interpretation of the practice, promoted by Richard Duncan-Jones (e.g. 1974: 82–8, 147–9) and followed by most observers; see (for Italy) Lomas, 2003: 39; (for Africa) Wesch-Klein, 1990: 39–41, more recently Højte, 2005: 53, esp. n. 127; Dawson, 2016: 15.

[17] E.g. twin texts from Sutunurca (*AE* 1942/43.9; *ILAfr.* 300, Pius); *ILAfr.* 300: *Divo Hadriano patri | Imp(eratoris) Caes(aris) T(iti) Aeli Hadr(iani) Antonini | Aug(usti) Pii pontif(icis) max(imi) trib(unicia) | potest(ate) VIIII co(n)s(ulis) IIII p(atris) p(atriae) | Germanus Passi Germani f(ilius) | Sutunurc(ensis) ob honorem flam(onii) perp(etui) | Quintae f(iliae) suae ex HS IIII mil(libus) legitim(is) | statuam divi Hadriani et L(uci) Aeli Caes(aris) | adiectis a se HS MDXXV n(ummum) d(ecreto) d(ecurionum) s(ua) p(ecunia) f(ecit) et | ob dedicationem viscerationem et | gymnasium populo dedit.* The statue was raised from the *summa legitima* of 4,000 HS, to which the author Germanus added 1,525 HS of his own. At Thigibba Bure (*AE* 1999.1845, Severus Alexander), a man promised to raise a statue on account of the edition of *missilia* (that is, gifts distributed at celebrations) and the *summa* due for his quaestorship, and at Thuburbo Maius (*ILTun.* 714, Pius), another promised to make a bronze statue for 2,000 HS, on account of his quinquennial duumvirate, beyond the 3,000 HS for the office. A *flamen* at Uchi Maius (*CIL* 8.26255, Septimius Severus) made the base for a public imperial statue from the *summa* of his office, and also paid for the ceremonies; for this being a sought-after privilege rather than an obligation, Dawson, 2016: 190. An inscription from Vina (*AE* 1992.1803, Pius), claims that the author had raised a statue for his sufetate for 10,000 HS, a sum reached by amplifying the *summa legitima* due for the office. A fragment from Bulla Regia (*AE* 2004.1876, Septimius Severus) seems to state that a statue was raised from both *pecunia sua* and the *summa honoraria* for a duumvirate; and a silver statue at Hippo Regius (*CIL* 8.17408, Hadrian) was promised, as it seems from the *legitima* 10,000 HS with another 7,000 added of the author's own money. At Zattara (*CIL* 8.10833, Septimius Severus), a man raised a statue on account of his magistership with a sum of of 2,400 HS, adding 1,000 of his own, suggesting that the first sum was stipulated,

had been paid in advance to the *res publica*.[18] In such cases, the formula 'on account of the office' (*ob honorem*) is not tied to the erection of the statue but to the payment, and there is no text in which it is clearly used to express pride in the new position itself; it seems to have a more bureaucratic sense related to the process of attaining the position, at least in this context.[19] The payment may well have been used to fund the erection of the statue, which some texts suggest could be handled by the *ordines* from sums contributed by their members, likely along with the many statues raised by the council in its own name.[20] Imperial statues could serve as campaigning promises, and some texts show that the *summa honoraria* covered (at least part of) their cost once the office was reached.[21] Some monuments were raised for the offices of others, which speaks against the idea that they were raised *post facto* in thanks for an office (seeing that the office holders did not actually raise them) but rather suggests that they formed part of reaching said office (as did, clearly, statues promised

perhaps as a fee. This might be supported by a text from Biniana (*CIL* 8.76, Commodus) according to which a statue was built using 2,000 HS contributed by the author's father (and transferred by the decree of the *ordo*), *super* the *summa legitima* for the flaminate, to which more money still was added by the author.

[18] Musti (*CIL* 8.1576, Septimius Severus), and two texts from Bulla Regia (*ILAfr.* 451; *AE* 2004.1874, Septimius Severus), mentioning payments to the *res publica* of 5,000 and 6,000 HS for the duumvirate and the quinquennial duumvirate; furthermore, two texts from Madauros (*ILAlg.* 1.2088–9, Septimius Severus) state that the *summa honoraria* had been paid to the fisc in advance, *prius* (although the latter states that the statue was raised with funds added to the *summa legitima*). The formula is rare; texts on other imperial statue bases from Madauros do not contain it, and the only parallels in Africa Proconsularis are three bases at Giufi (*CIL* 8.858, 862–3, to Victory and Apollo, third century) which were likely raised together. One suspects it was underscored because it was not the standard procedure.

[19] Sutunurca (*AE* 1992.1797, Pius), the formula referring to the payment, not the erection of the statue, as also in *AE* 2004.1874 and *ILAlg.* 1.2088 mentioned in n. 18 above.

[20] A long text from Ammaedara lists promises, payments, and works on account of offices, including 10,000 HS for the quinquennial duumvirate (likely), as well as money paid to the *res publica* on account of the flaminate for works on a theatre, which were apparently administered centrally. The same seems likely for another text from Sutunurca (*ILAfr.* 303, Marcus), according to which a statue was raised for someone else's flaminate, but the author also paid 1,000 HS to the fisc *ob dedicationem* for a distribution of meat. Suggestive is a text from Bulla Regia (*AE* 2004.1875, early Severan) mentioning that the author of the statue paid the fee to the *res publica* and also, according to a promise, from what was left and his own generosity, set up the base. One might feasibly argue that the text refers to what was left of the payment after the statue was set up.

[21] E.g. the texts from Bulla Regia, Hippo Regius, Thigibba Bure and Thuburbo Maius mentioned in n. 17 above and from Ammaedara mentioned in n. 20, two from Thignica (*AE* 1992.1818; *CIL* 8.1401, Septimius Severus), two from Madauros (*ILAlg.* 1.2087 and 2089, Septimius Severus), and one each from Thugga (*CIL* 8.26529, Marcus), Kudiat Setieh (*CIL* 8.17258, Septimius Severus), and Cillium (*AE* 1957.77, Pius), where a man promised for 12,000 HS to raise statues on account of his aedilitate, and made a silver image to supplement his promise. In others cases the statues appear to have been raised in addition to the fee.

during campaigns).[22] To pay for the dedication ceremonies of someone else's statue could also qualify the donor for office, and was presented in the same way.[23]

The phenomenon makes for long (and exceedingly dry) texts full of technical detail, in which career advancement has pride of place. Many of the statues were instrumental to the *cursus honorum* of their makers, which shows how deeply imperial honorific monuments and priesthoods were integrated with local political structures. This formed part of a wider phenomenon by which not just statues of emperors but all forms of *sacra* (e.g. shrines, altars, arches, and divine statues) were tied to local paths of advancement, in accordance with set conventions. Shrines (to emperors or otherwise) were raised in connection with honorary priesthoods held after the completion of the local *cursus honorum*, while statues to emperors and gods were often tied to duumvirates.[24] Conventions could differ between towns, as at Madauros, where imperial statues were systematically erected for the aedilitate,[25] but all imperial arches erected by private individuals were raised 'on account of' flaminates.[26]

---

[22] E.g., the texts from Thigibba Bure and Sutunurca mentioned in nn. 17–21 above, and another from Sutunurca (*CIL* 8.24003, Marcus) according to which a man adopted a nephew in lieu of a son and paid for his decurionate with money that seems to have paid for equestrian statues.

[23] E.g. the example from Uchi Maius mentioned in n. 17 above, where the base was made on account of an office but the statue was public. At Pagus Mercurialis (*AE* 1995.1657, Septimius Severus) the *pagani* set up a statue for *divus Pertinax* from 5 (thousand) and 333 HS, with three times the *summa honoraria* of the flaminate of two men who, on account of their flaminates, provided gifts and spectacles at the dedication ceremonies: *Divo* | [*P*(*ublio*)] *Helvio Pertinaci Aug*(*usto*) *Pio p*(*atri*) *p*(*atriae*) | *pagani Pagi Mercurial*(*is*) | *veterani Medelitan*(*i*) | *ponend*(*um*) *curaver*(*unt*) *ex* HS *VCCC*|*XXXIII n*(*ummis*) *cum tertis summae* | *honorar*(*iae*) *flamoni*(*i*) *perpet*(*ui*) | *C*(*ai*) *Mithri Gemini et M*(*arci*) *Vibi Fe*|*licis qui ob hon*(*orem*) *flam*(*onii*) *sui perp*(*etui*) | *magg*(*istris*) *flaminib*(*us*) *sportul*(*as*) *et de*|[*cu*]*riis singulis binos aureos* | [*et*] *gymna*[*sium*] *biduo populo de*|*der*(*unt*) *d*(*ecreto*) *p*(*aganorum*).

[24] E.g. a statue of Mars (*CIL* 8.895, as protector of Gordian III) raised at Ziqua by two aediles on account of office and in compensation for (presumably promised) *missilia*. One to Minerva (*ILAlg*. 1.1236, Thubursicu Numidarum) was promised for one office but appears to have paid for several, albeit paid to the *res publica*: *Miner*[*vae*] | *Aug*(*ustae*) *sacr*(*um*) | *Q*(*uintus*) *Vetidius Pa*[*p*(*iria*)] | *Iuvenalis Q*(*uinti*) *Vetidi* | *Felicis f*(*ilius*) *statuam* | *quam ob honorem* | *aedil*(*itatis*) *amplius ad* | *summam honora*|*riam pollicitus est* | *ex* HS *V* (*milibus*) *intra an*|*num honoris sui* | *posuit inlatis a se* | *rei p*(*ublicae*) *flamoni*|*um* HS *VI mil*(*ibus*) *ob* | *decurionatum* | HS *IIII mil*(*ibus*) *ob aedi*|*litatem* HS *IIII* | *mil*(*ibus*) *dedicavit*.

[25] *ILAlg*. 1.2087–9, 2092, 2095.

[26] The transaction is explicit in the case of eleven of twenty-two arches raised by individuals; e.g. *CIL* 8.16441 (Zama Maior, Hadrian); *AE* 2004.1674 (Limisa, Marcus Aurelius); *ILAlg*. 1.1255 (Thubursicu Numidarum, Septimius Severus). On the high proportion of *ob honorem* projects in Africa, Wesch-Klein, 1990.

Regional Ambitions and Intercity Rivalries

Imperial honorific statues by private individuals thus read as a veritable 'who's who', displaying privileged access to the most powerful images available as well as to local political structures. The same roles were played by other imperial *sacra* such as altars, arches, and *sacella*, raised by the same high-status agents and forming part of the same celebratory matrix, which not only set the *ordines* apart but also made their internal hierarchy visible.[27] Imperial trappings helped elevate a community, as in imperial town titles (as per *CIL* 8.1487, a statue to Gallienus raised by the *res publica coloniae Liciniae Septimiae Aureliae Alexandrianae Thuggae*) or the names of local voting units (*curia Ulpia, curia Nervia, curia Antoniniana*, etc.),[28] but the same vocabulary and imagery also provided the scope for promoting individuals in what appears a happy marriage between the ambitions of the *ordines* and those of its individual members. The many imperial priesthoods are a leaf out of the same book, representing ornaments for the individuals who held them but also for their towns. As Adelina Arnaldi has argued, the number of *flamines* a town could sport marked its significance: the grander cities had flaminates to specific emperors, including long-dead *divi*, while lesser towns only had generic ones, *nudi dicti*.[29]

The connection to emperors, by contrast, seems slight. That many imperial monuments were raised by *flamines* has less to do with any expectations tied to imperial priesthood than with the flaminate's position at the top of the local civic hierarchy. For one, the relationship was not exclusive – *duumviri* and aediles also raised them – and the *flamines* dominate all construction of *sacra*, imperial or not.[30] In analogy to what Margaret Laird has observed for *Augustales*, there is no apparent correlation between imperial priests and imperial shrines; in fact, temples with an imperial bent were more often raised by *ordines*.[31] The key to understanding the phenomenon lies rather in regional politics, within which both towns and their leading individuals vied for prominence.

---

[27] Fejfer, 2008: 381 notes that in provincial urban spaces (as opposed to Rome), statues of emperors mingled with local notables, further adding to the status of the latter.

[28] For the naming of *curiae*, see Dawson, 2016: 127.

[29] Arnaldi, 2010. On the African flaminate, Bassignano, 1974; Pflaum, 1976. Jonathan Rives (1995: 48–9) regards the position as municipal rather than religious.

[30] Hellström, 2014. To name but two among numerous examples, a shrine to Caelestis by a family of imperial priests (*CIL* 8.993, Carpis), and one to Pluto (*AE* 1968.594, Musti).

[31] Laird, 2015: 7. Especially Capitolia, e.g. at Althiburos (*CIL* 8.1824, Commodus), Avedda (*CIL* 8.14369, Caracalla), Biracsaccar (*CIL* 8.12286, Pius), Hr el Gonai (*ILAlg.* 1.1097, Severus Alexander), Segermes (*CIL* 8.906, Diocletian), Sustri (*CIL* 8.25935, Gordian III), and Thuburbo Maius (*ILTun.* 699, Marcus).

The area was characterised by an intricate web of dependencies and much interregional interaction. At the top of its hierarchies lay *Colonia Iulia Karthago*, which had been granted an enormous territory, the so-called *pertica*, that embraced a host of peregrine *civitates* as well as enclaves of Carthaginian citizens, *pagi*, often in conjunction with dependent communities.[32] There were also independent *municipiae* and *coloniae* with their own elite networks; at the top, these local networks often overlapped with those of Carthage, which were famous for their wealth and power.[33] These overlapping networks made for several career paths for ambitious Africans. The pinnacle for wealthy *pagani* was to enter the illustrious *ordo* of Carthage, where the entry levels were forbiddingly expensive.[34] For notables in independent towns it was apparently more common to strive for regional positions such as the provincial flaminate, procuratorial posts in the *res privata* (which for obvious reasons was much present in the area), or equestrian and even senatorial positions.[35] Common to all these goals, however, was that a local *cursus honorum* had to be completed first, which meant reaching the local flaminate. The pivotal role of this office, poised between the local and the regional, helps explain both why it was so desired and why it was so often flaunted in the inscriptional record.

Competition and Control

The social dynamics of the African *cursus honorum* is the most important interpretative context for the unique way that statues of emperors there

---

[32] On the *pertica*, Poinssot, 1962; Aounallah, 2010a; for its spatial extent, and a similar arrangement in Cirta and Sicca Veneria, Aounallah and Maurin, 2008: 232, 247. On *pagi*, Picard, 1969–70, Aounallah, 2010b: 1615–24.

[33] On the so-called 'African oligarchy', a small number of (often senatorial) families that dominated the *ordo* of Carthage, fabulously wealthy and with networks that spanned the province and beyond, Corbier, 1982; Hugoniot, 2006. That not only individuals but families competed is seen in the numerous benefactions made 'on account of' the offices of relatives, or under the label *in nomine*, which is always followed by the names of close kin. What, exactly, it represented is obscure, but it was no casual procedure; e.g. *CIL* 8.1401, Thignica, finished in the name of self, siblings, and children by the son of a man who had promised it in his own and his children's name. The siblings are included in respect of the father's arrangement. Edmondson, 2006: 274 suggests it implies promotion of offspring, perhaps as *praetextati* in the council, but women are also featured, making this less likely.

[34] For the exorbitant cost and high prestige of Carthaginian offices, see Duncan-Jones, 1974, chh. 3–4; Hugoniot, 2006: 398–400, 394–7; Bel Kahia Karoui, 2010: 1573.

[35] E.g. T. Flavius Macer, completing his *cursus honorum* at Ammaedara and moving on to posts in the *res privata* (honoured at Hippo Regius and Calama, *CIL* 8.5351; *ILAlg*. 1.3992), and P. Mummius Saturninus, honoured as *sacerdos Africae* at Limisa in Byzacena (*CIL* 8.12039) after a career at Furnos Maius.

showcased their authors. At the most basic level, local elites erected them in pursuit of magistracies, testifying to goals reached but also aiding their future ambitions. Furthermore, intercity rivalries were fuelled by imperial monuments: the bigger, the more plentiful, and the more up to date the images, the more they showcased the community as one of wealth and connections. The situation is thus in many ways local in character, and calls to mind the intense competition for *neokoroi* in the eastern *koina*, to the point that a town could request that another town would *not* receive one (as in the case of Beroia, in competition with Thessaloniki).[36] But there are points where central authorities become involved. Burrell notes that imperial shrines and monuments were not an obligation but an eagerly sought privilege, and ties the handling of the petitions to urban, not religious, imperial policy.[37] Cassius Dio makes this clear in the speech by Maecenas in which he exhorts the emperor to be sparing of such grants; if he is, 'all towns will be your temples, all men your statues'.[38] Otherwise the communities would exhaust their resources on monuments useless to them, for the sake of peer-to-peer competition.[39] To manage imperial honorifics thus played an important role in maintaining local power balances, and because imperial images were so closely tied to local power, controlling access to images was part of controlling access to power.

The emperor thus had a clear interest in managing the spread of honorifics. But power and images were managed differently at different social levels, and the statues considered in this chapter were not subject to direct imperial control. The need to curb the demand of local elites for imperial paraphernalia seems to have been felt mainly in the most important cities, with less control in evidence at the municipal level.[40] Rather than the emperors themselves, it seems likely that the proconsuls managed the (apparently numerous) petitions for imperial monuments in the hundreds of tiny African towns. Occasional traces of such a procedure survive, suggesting that the proconsuls' engagement with the urban spaces of the towns in their care could be minute, albeit not for the most part announced

---

[36] Burrell, 2004: 279.   [37] Burrell, 2004: 283.

[38] Cass. Dio 52.35.5. Dio no doubt had contemporary emperors in mind, who were prone both to accept such honours and to meddle with the status of towns. It may particularly have smarted that Severus stripped Dio's home town Nicaea of its neokorate and favoured its arch-rival Nikomedia, in the aftermath of the war with Niger.

[39] Cass. Dio 52.30.3; 52.35.3–4; also 53.37.9, where he advises him not to allow them to go beyond their means, 'even if they offer prayers to your power, safety and fortune'.

[40] Burrell, 2004: 282, on the proliferation of imperial shrines and monuments in municipalities, and 284, on how from Hadrian even neokorates were granted to municipalities.

in inscriptions.[41] A rare example comes from Vazi Sarra, where a local big shot had built two sanctuaries to Aesculapius and Mercury (the latter probably serving as the town's *macellum*), and, according to an inscription, transferred an equestrian statue of a *deus* into the basilica of one of them, a move that was authorised by the proconsul.[42] Seeing that neither Aesculapius nor Mercury was represented on horseback, the statue in question no doubt depicted an emperor.

Such rare glimpses of a petition–response process are perhaps best seen as attempts to brag, showcasing contacts with the proconsul, rather than as traces of a consistent procedure.[43] That it could be desirable to flaunt such contacts is suggested by the practice of lending some glamour to dedication ceremonies for buildings and monuments by having someone of higher status officiate; by the end of the second century this usually meant the proconsul.[44] We should not assume that African communities were at liberty to raise statues of emperors entirely as they wished, or that imperial authorities were unaware of them, yet there is little to suggest that the attitude was restrictive. There is every reason to suspect that grants were given rather freely, seeing the mass of monuments that crowded African towns. The towns must have come across as glimmering forests of imperial statues, which were not removed but accumulated. Although no assemblages survive complete from this area, the study by Gerhard Zimmer and Gabriele Wesch-Klein on Cuicul and Thamugadi provides an indication, as do the well-preserved urban spaces in Aphrodisias.[45] It was in any case forbidden to remove them.[46]

---

[41] At Calama (*CIL* 8.5367), the placement of a statue to a local man by his sons is approved by two successive proconsuls, and affirmed by the *curator rei publicae*, and at Bulla Regia (*AE* 1962.184b) another *curator rei publicae* authorises the erection of a statue to a local man. For what it's worth, Wilmanns resolved P P (e.g. *CIL* 8.955, *CIL* 8.1314) as *p(ermissu) p(roconsulis)* for many statues in the first edition of *CIL* 8, rather than the more common *p(ecunia) p(ublica)*.

[42] *CIL* 8.11999. For the *macellum*, Fentress, 2007.

[43] Fejfer, 2008: 421 suggests similar reasons behind petitioning the emperor directly for permission. She questions that such permissions were necessary; however, constraints clearly applied to higher-status individuals and locations. Cf. 389, on the exclusivity of permissions to raise imperial statues in Rome.

[44] A practice in evidence especially at Thugga in the first century, e.g. *CIL* 8.26464+26603; *CIL* 8.11519; *CIL* 8.1478; *ILAfr.* 558. Proconsuls dedicating at Avita Bibba (*CIL* 8.800), Thuburbo Maius (*ILTun.* 699), Mactaris (*CIL* 8.11799), Musti (*CIL* 8.1582), Thubursicu Numidarum (*ILAlg.* 1.1230–2). It remains rare in the area, reserved for grand projects such as aqueducts or Capitolia, in contrast to western Numidia where the legate of the Third Augusta dedicated all manner of buildings in the role of honorary patron.

[45] Zimmer and Wesch-Klein, 1989. For Aphrodisias, Smith, 2006. See also the letter to Orcistus, below, n. 55.

[46] Højte, 2005: 111.

The most frequent location was the forum with adjacent basilicas and council buildings and, especially in the west, major thoroughfares, while in eastern towns they often appeared in baths, theatres, and sanctuaries.[47] Arches adorned crossroads, or functioned as gates in imaginary city walls.[48] Imperial paraphernalia thus marked the community as a town proper, by highlighting signal urban features and showcasing the *ordo* as responsible for their erection. They were thus necessary for the towns' prestige, and while eastern towns often had several statues to the same emperor, their western counterparts went for all-inclusive displays.[49] It was not uncommon to dedicate to *divi* (8.3 per cent in Højte's global assessment), including those from previous dynasties. Bases of emperors who suffered *damnatio memoriae* were more often recut as their predecessors than their successors.[50] Augustus received new statues still in the third century, and in Thugga, statues to Augustus, Trajan, Hadrian and a (non-specified) Antoninus, all as *divi*, were erected as a group.[51] Statues to *divi* were no doubt related to the practice of assigning flaminates to *divi*, which are attested (and perhaps were installed) long after the death of the emperor in question; priests to *divus Vespasianus* are attested under Pius and to *divus Traianus* under Severus Alexander.[52]

The statues and priesthoods gave a sense of continuity, of a temporal depth that anchored the town in a past it did not necessarily have: while of royal Berber origin, Thugga did not become a municipality until 206 CE. Fejfer reports an interesting case from Palestrina, where *colossi* of Augustus and a Faustina had been manufactured together, but the emperor had been cut in Augustan style.[53] Such antiquarianism perhaps answered to the

---

[47] Højte, 2005: 112–17.
[48] This was particularly useful in this *inermis* region where the towns lacked city walls. Arches have a parallel in *tetrakionia* in the east, which straddled major crossings, and which begin appearing under the Antonines; see Boyer, 1995; Thiel, 2002.
[49] Højte, 2005: 114.
[50] Højte, 2005: 58–60. Removing one element of a title could suffice. Recutting the base in this manner was more common in the east, while in the west it was often simply discarded.
[51] *CIL* 8.26517; *ILAfr.* 556; *CIL* 8.26521–3. Højte, 2005: 135 mentions a similar assemblage at Tarraco in Spain, and another that honours the whole Flavian dynasty, after the death of Domitian. Frédéric Hurlet's argument (2000: 330) that statues to *divi* were promised to living emperors who then died before they were completed does not seem to fit with the evidence. The one instance is a *colossus* to Lucius Verus dedicated *post mortem*, as a pair with one to Marcus Aurelius (*CIL* 8.26529, Thugga). Most statues raised through *pollicitatio* were to living emperors. E.g. *CIL* 8.14370 (Avedda, Septimius Severus); *AE* 1999.1845 (Thigibba Bure, Severus Alexander). On *divi* statues also Fejfer, 2008: 392–3.
[52] Flamen of *divus Traianus*, and also to other *divi*: *CIL* 8.14447 (Henchir Bir el Afu); of *divus Vespasianus* under Antoninus Pius: *CIL* 8.26604 (Thugga).
[53] Fejfer, 2008: 393.

expectation that his image should look a certain way, but it also offered a means to retroject the community's identity as a town. Furthermore, the series of statues evoked a stable, well-ordered world, especially if the statues were placed paratactically in colonnades. Emblazoned across the bases – literally as contributors to this continuum – were the leading members of the community, forming a seriality as established as that of the emperors. Many *civitates*, *municipia*, and even *coloniae* are known only through stray finds of such monuments, which reveal full-blown, well-grounded honorific practices. The amount of resources and space that the towns saw fit to spend on imperial monuments is simply astounding.[54]

This investment may to some extent be explained by the role the monuments played not only in regional rivalries, but in preparing for petitions for enhanced civic status. That the monumental makeup supported such a case is clear from the rescript of Constantine to Orcistus, in which the emperor approvingly mentions the *forum statuis veterum principum ornatum* among the features that recommended the town.[55] Admittedly, the phrases about buildings and statues of old emperors are coloured by sentimentality and may not reflect the real reasons why the petition was granted, but it is well known that such cases were supported by a community's perceived past, and aligning its history with that of the principate by marking its public spaces with a series of imperial monuments was a way to underscore its relevance.

Emperors and the Imperial Statue Habit

As for the emperors, one might assume that their attitude towards such statue displays was positive; the practice is one of the most visible exponents of empire, and the aggregate of previous emperors supported the prevailing order. Even so, there is little evidence for how they viewed the phenomenon in Africa, or anywhere else. Literary testimonies to the relation between emperors and imperial statues are mostly topical, and on a closer look, not well grounded; it was common to ascribe a desire for statues to 'bad' emperors and make 'good' ones reject them, but descriptions do not square with the physical evidence.[56] Some insight may be

---

[54] E.g. the *civitas* Maragui Sara (*ILTun.* 614) raising a statue to Caracalla, or *CIL* 8.5276a–b from (otherwise unknown) Koubba, grandiloquently honouring a *duumvir* for gladiator games.

[55] *CIL* 3.7000 (= *FIRA*² 1.95), lines 26–7; see also Feissel, 1999.

[56] Højte, 2005: 51. His study shows that the assertions in literature that Gaius, Nero, Domitian, Commodus, and Caracalla not only did not decline but actively promoted statues in precious

gained from between the lines of these passages by Cassius Dio on the 'image war' between Septimius Severus and Plautianus:

> 76.16: On one occasion, when a great many images of Plautianus had been made (this incident is well worth relating) Severus was displeased at their number and caused some of them to be melted down, and in consequence a rumour spread to the cities that the prefect had been overthrown and had perished. So some of them demolished his images, an act for which they were later punished.
>
> 76.14: Among other things, his statues and images were not only far more numerous but also larger than theirs [the emperors'], and this not alone in outside cities but in Rome itself, and they were erected not merely by individuals or communities but by the very senate. All the soldiers and the senators took oaths by his Fortune, and all publicly offered prayers for his preservation (trans. Cary).

We learn that what primarily mattered to the emperor were statues in Rome, while in peripheral communities they were of interest mainly as bulk, and Dio does not expect the emperor to keep continuous track of them. The link they represented between emperor and town seems rather weak, but could be mobilised in a political crisis. What is more, the crisis is a metropolitan, rather than an African one: Severus is concerned with the ambitions of his prefect, not a potential provincial revolt. The part of Africa here concerned – no doubt in particular the propertied social stratum involved with imperial monuments – became wealthy from being part of the empire and was unlikely to wish to revolt against it per se. On the other hand, they may plausibly have been affected by the war between Septimius Severus and Clodius Albinus, who hailed from Hadrumetum (a town much closer to home than Lepcis Magna), or the fall of Plautianus, whose family had networks in the area.[57] An inscription on a base from Sicca Veneria is unusually direct, raised in the wake of the uncovering of 'plots of public enemies', *detectis insidiis hostium publicorum*, which likely refers to Plautianus.[58] But Sicca Veneria was an important city in an area defined

---

metal to themselves are not borne out by material evidence. Extant silver and gold statues portray Tiberius, Trajan, and Vespasian, emperors who are all described as rejecting such extravagances: Suet. *Tib.* 26; Tac. *Ann.* 3.18.2; Suet. *Vesp.* 23.3; Plin. *Pan.* 52. Højte claims further (p. 61) that the notion that Domitian promoted statues to himself of any kind is unfounded. The same caution is due for monuments mentioned by Herodian and in the *Historia Augusta*.

[57] A statue to Albinus as emperor has been found at Agbia (*CIL* 8.1549). On the elites of Hadrumetum as intertwined with those of Carthage, Corbier, 1982.

[58] *CIL* 8.1628, although it appears to have been raised some years after his fall.

by imperial concerns; its elites mattered, and imperial representatives dwelt there who might care. The mass of hick towns that dotted the African landscape would have been too minor to merit such attention; nor is it likely that their inhabitants expected any.

There is, in fact, very little to suggest that the texts on the bases aimed to communicate with emperors at all. The texts on the bases do not express any sentiments for the princes honoured. Technical details concerning private persons dominate the texts, listing appointments over which emperors had no influence: the primary aims were local, as were the agents and audiences. Even the way the imperial cult was organised locally was up to the *ordo*, and the non-homogeneity of the practice confirms that it was not governed by any universal command (or strongly formulated expectation).[59] Dates of erection do not correlate with events tied to emperors such as accessions, birthdays, jubilees, or triumphs – seeing the sheer numbers involved, it is natural that some items should date to years when something notable occurred in the lives of emperors, yet chronological coincidences are few, and never explicit – and only three statues in the entire cache, private or civic, celebrate a specific victory.[60]

There is no concentration in towns that housed imperial bureaux, or major roads along which emperors and imperial officials could be expected to travel.[61] Nor is there any relation to imperial presence: only three emperors ever visited and none left any monumental traces, either in terms of benefactions by emperors or monuments by locals.[62] The area had no camps to recommend it (such as Lambaesis in Numidia)[63] or ties to the imperial family (as did, famously, Lepcis Magna), and no reciprocity is in evidence. Only one imperial personage is attested as in any way invested with the area, Marcus Aurelius' daughter Vibia Sabina: she was honoured

---

[59] Dawson, 2016: 158–9.

[60] *AE* 1913.46 (Althiburos, Caracalla); *CIL* 8.26242a (Uchi Maius, Septimius Severus and sons); *CIL* 8.965 (Siagu, Septimius Severus). This mirrors the global situation, according to Højte, 2005: 118, 145–65, who cites the poor evidence for statues on accession (most were raised in the second or third year of rule, after which they petered out), jubilees, or triumphs. The precision is low; all statues that mention the date of erection are Italian; Højte, 2005: 78–9. Fejfer, 2008: 411–16 rejects the notion of 'celebratory' types.

[61] For instance, Hippo Regius, Theveste, Thysdrus, Leptiminus, and Hadrumetum housed imperial bureaux, but did not attract any concentrations of statues beyond other towns.

[62] Hadrian, Septimius Severus, and Maximian visited; see Guédon, 2006. A bridge 'by' Hadrian at Ammaedara was built five years earlier than his visit. Proconsuls, legates, or curators appear as authors only at the turn of the fourth century, but even then the vast majority of monuments are raised by locals. On the weak ties between imperial presence and benefactions generally, Højte, 2005: 170–1.

[63] Several emperors – present or not – posed as builders in the camps of the Third Augusta at Lambaesis, among them the notoriously stationary Antoninus Pius (e.g. *CIL* 8.2653).

as patroness at Calama, but not until the reign of Caracalla, and not accompanied by statues to her imperial family (or any information as to the nature of her patronage).[64] Entirely unique is a *decemvir stlitibus iudicandis* and tribune of the Third Augusta who honoured Pius for favours to him personally, no doubt a way to show off locally.[65] Carthage may have been a different matter, but if emperors had direct dealings with the city (as is known for construction), this does not appear to have trickled down to its hinterland.[66]

    The phenomenon of imperial statue erection in our area thus does not seem to fit with the usual explanations for how imperial monuments in provincial communities related to emperors, most of which are predicated on ideas of a direct exchange between the two. They clearly do not fit the notion of active, top-down command,[67] nor the more common 'loyalty' models whereby locals seek to confirm their obedience and/or enthusiasm for the ruler, perhaps in pursuit of benefactions.[68] African statues have not seldom been treated as tokens of enthusiasm for a prince, particularly for Septimius Severus,[69] but at least in the area here treated the emperor was neither their author nor their audience. In view of their explicit (and rather prosaic) aims as benefactions *ob honorem*, and the fact that at least imperial priesthoods, if not also imperial monuments, were unavoidable for those with ambitions beyond the community, interpreting African statues of emperors as heartfelt and spontaneous expressions of enthusiasm for a ruler becomes problematic. One also needs to keep in mind the many statues dedicated to *divi*, who could not easily reciprocate. They may have been an echo of a native, Numidian practice; at least two monuments were raised by king Micipsa to his deceased father Masinissa, inscribed in local

---

[64] *AE* 1978.841. Her husband Anthistius Burrus was born not far away, at Thibilis.

[65] *CIL* 8.27776, Althiburos.

[66] Pius built at Carthage, according to Paus. 8.43.4; Fronto, *Grat. act. pro Carth.* Maximian built baths there, according to Aur. Vict. *Caes.* 39.45, Jer. *Chron.* 270g.

[67] Rejected by Fejfer, 2008: 421, who treats them as set up on local initiative.

[68] Hurlet, 2000, Kuhoff, 2006, and Polley, 2004/5 [2007] all treat them as raised in close communication with the emperors. Moralee (2004: ch. 1 *passim*, esp. 18, 24–35) argues for a more intimate (and top-down) relation, mediated by monuments and orchestrated by governors who directed and dedicated construction to emperors, organised prayers for them, and had these inscribed on buildings. He relates this to the Hellenistic practice of praying for the health of rulers, and treats attempts at local ostentation as secondary to the aim of expressing loyalty and participation. This close bond, he argues, became lost in the third century, as is manifest through the gradual disappearance of 'salutary formulas'. He does not recognise that this is a result of the gradual disappearance of the building inscriptions that featured them. Nor are there signs that governors were directly involved in the ways he suggests. Africa had no comparable tradition, and the *pro salute* formula only appears there in the second century.

[69] E.g. Polley, 2004/5 [2007]: 147.

alphabets.[70] But the messages conveyed had at least as much to do with Micipsa's claim to power among the living as with appeasing the powerful dead. With statues to dead emperors one suspects that the purposes are more ornamental, and similar to that of a statue to Gaius Marius raised by a *flamen* at Thuburnica in order to promote his wife, on the same pattern as imperial statues.[71] It showcased a glamorous connection to the general (supposedly the town's founder), but no attention or benefaction was expected in return. This was the case also with statues to *divi*, and, I propose, the mass of statues to living emperors as well. It is doubtful that they even knew about their existence.

It seems more prudent to view the attitude of the emperor (or at least a Severan emperor) towards his provincial statues as a mix of passive monitoring and active manipulation. Given the high demand, imperial monuments provided a low-effort means for emperors to influence local power negotiations, either by applying restrictions, or, if bulk was a thing desired, by adopting a permissive attitude. But the details of how such decisions were carried through was left to local initiative. Burrell describes such a trajectory for the neokorates, which went from signs of extraordinary standing to something every reasonably important town could boast, with the result that major cities jockeyed for two or more. One means to maximise visibility was to multiply the number of imperial personages to be honoured, as seen in the many African family groups of Septimius Severus, Julia Domna, and their sons, and another was to increase the length of imperial titles. Cassius Dio lampooned Commodus for his absurd titles, which may represent a jab at his own (not clearly beloved) patron Septimius Severus, whose titles were much worse.[72] The peak comes with Caracalla, honoured in Giufi near Carthage with 158 words.[73] The labour and cost of cutting this in stone was comfortably left to the Giufitani, but the visual outcome was to frame Caracalla as the crown of a succession of ever better, ever more victorious rulers, the sum total of all his forebears.

The proliferation of early Severan statues in Africa has often been viewed as a sign of their especial popularity there, but this is not clear for the region

---

[70] At Thugga (*RIL* 2 = *KAI* 101), and the Royal Numidian altar at Simitthus, a grand marble hilltop monument in Hellenistic style, on display in the museum at Chimtou.

[71] *AE* 1951.81.   [72] Cass. Dio 73.15.1–5, especially how he presented himself in letters.

[73] *AE* 2003.1986 (a shrine to Minerva), leaving fifteen words to anything else. This can be compared to all four tetrarchs, for whom eleven words sufficed. It is clear that titles were devised at the centre; changes are global and sudden, and after 217 they retract to pre-Antonine lengths, from an average of eighty-seven words to twelve. Horster, 2001: 76–98, table 3.1; Saastamoinen, 2010a: 83–5.

here concerned.[74] It may have just as much to do with a policy of open access, seen also in how Septimius' and Julia Domna's images appear on coins.[75] His statues, *nota bene*, dominate the record in central Italy as well, where there is no reason to assume that he was a favourite. One may note that Septimius Severus' images are the first that were clearly mass-produced.[76]

Monuments and Messages

To conclude, what appears to be a conversation between two parts, the emperor and provincial elites, represents instead a platform used by both parties to serve their own ends, without direct interaction between them.[77] Local elites used them to achieve local goals, competing at the individual, kin, and community levels in terms that at times were surprisingly explicit. Certain emperors recognised and exploited this practice, without directly engaging with the locals who raised them but instead remaining content with a passive approach, at least beyond large cities and military camps. Emperors could and did intervene in the use of their images, but mainly in response to emerging situations, and not obviously with local provincial populations in view.

Statues of emperors carried the potential for multiple messages, some explicit and immediate, others more indirect, variously mobilised depending on the sociopolitical circumstances. For the locals who raised them, imperial monuments and priesthoods were more than ornaments: they helped define communities internally and externally, providing an international honorific *koine* that allowed for comparisons across regions and hierarchies. This civic–imperial framework has parallels in other treatments in this volume, notably by Nicolas Tran on associations in which advancement was also marked by imperial honorifics in ways that emulated townhood. The practice is mirrored in African estate villages, dedicating imperial monuments and appointing leaders in imitation of civic practices, such as a statue to Septimius Severus raised *ob honorem* by

---

[74] The potentially conflicted position of elites in the area during his civil wars has already been mentioned; moreover, it is generally assumed that his relation to Carthage was hostile, seeing that his municipalisation strategies dismantled its *pertica*, and so, presumably, curtailed its considerable power. So Poinssot, 1962: 72; Gascou, 1972: *passim*; Hugoniot, 2006: 398; Briand-Ponsart and Hugoniot, 2006: 72, 96–7. Birley, 1989: 147 claims it was 'cut down to size'.
[75] Harl, 1996: 109–11.   [76] Fittschen, 2010: 235–7.
[77] This is also the situation described by Rives, 1995: 61–3, both parties benefiting from the process, in consensus but not direct cooperation.

a *magister*.[78] In the case of Africa the immediate concerns for the agents were near at hand, and highly specific. Those who raised the statues were not 'provincials' in a general sense; their exact positions mattered and conditioned their use of images in ways that did not, necessarily, reflect the wishes of all members of their communities (or members of their own class elsewhere). The primary audience consisted of peers, the secondary audience, perhaps, of the community at large. Only the tertiary (at best) audience were the emperors, who did not appoint either *flamines* or Carthaginian councillors, and who could have no possible interest in the types of texts that dominate the bases, concerned with heirs adopted and moneys translated from one relative or local bursary to another.[79] But beyond these outspoken aims they had other roles which were no less important: they underscored the urban nature of a community and displayed the resources it could muster; they connected it to the world and aligned it with imperial time; finally, they reinforced the authority of the *ordo*, and by extension of the emperors, who were the ultimate guarantors of said authority, wealth, and *urbanitas*.

Bibliography

Aounallah, S. 2010a. *Pagus, castellum et civitas: Études d'épigraphie et d'histoire sur le village et la cité en Afrique romaine* (Paris: Ausonius).

 2010b. 'Le pagus en Afrique romaine'. *AfrRom* 18: 1615–30.

Aounallah, S. and L. Maurin 2008. 'Pagus et civitas Siviritani', *ZPE* 167, 227–50.

Arnaldi, A. 2010. 'Osservazioni sul flaminato dei *Divi* nelle province africane', *AfrRom* 18: 1645–65.

Bassignano, M. S. 1974. *Il flaminato nelle province romane dell'Africa* (Rome: Bretschneider).

Bel Kahia Karoui, T. 2010. 'Édiles et édilité en Afrique Proconsulaire et en Numidie', *AfrRom* 18, 1565–614.

Birley, A. R. 1989. *Septimius Severus the African Emperor* (London: Routledge).

Boyer, J. E. 1995. The Roman Tetrakionion at Ancient Aprhodisias: An Analysis, Documentation and Reconstruction Program. MA thesis, University of Pennsylvania (Philadelphia).

Briand-Ponsart, C. and C. Hugoniot 2006. *L'Afrique romaine de l'Atlantique à la Tripolitaine: 146 av. J.-C.–533 ap. J.-C.* (Paris: Armand Colin).

---

[78] *CIL* 8.10833, at Zattara.
[79] E.g. *CIL* 8.26517 from Thugga, or *CIL* 8.24003 from Sutunurca, with long descriptions of strictly local matters concerning offices and family.

Burrell, B. 2004. *Neokoroi: Greek Cities and Roman Emperors* (Leiden; Boston: Brill).

Christol, M. 2008. 'La procuratelle du patrimonie de Lepti Minus.' *AfrRom* 17: 2037–79.

Corbier, M. 1982. 'Les familles clarissimes d'Afrique proconsulaire (Ier–IIIe siècle)', in *Epigrafia e ordine senatorio: atti del Colloquio internazionale AIEGL su epigrafia e ordine senatorio, Roma, 14–20 maggio 1981*. Tituli 5 (Rome, Storia e Letteratura), 685–754.

Dawson, C. D. 2016. Intimate Communities: Honorific Statues and the Political Culture of the Cities of Africa Proconsularis in the First Three Centuries CE. PhD. Diss., York University.

Duncan-Jones, R. P. 1974. *The Economy of the Roman Empire* (Cambridge: Cambridge University Press).

Edmondson, J. 2006. 'Cities and urban life in the western provinces of the Roman Empire, 30 BCE–250 CE', in Potter, D. S. (ed.), *A Companion to the Roman Empire* (Malden, MA: Blackwell), 250–80.

Feissel, D. 1999. 'L'*Adnotatio* de Constantin sur le droit de cité d'Orcistus en Phrygie', *Antiquité Tardive* 7: 255–67.

Fejfer, J. 2008. *Roman Portraits in Context* (Berlin; Boston: De Gruyter).

Fentress, E. 2007. 'Where were African *nundinae* held?' in Gosden. C., H. Hamerow, P. de Jersey, and G. Lock (eds.), *Communities and Connections: Essays in Honour of Barry Cunliffe* (Oxford: Oxford University Press), 125–41.

Fittschen, K. 2010. 'The portraits of Roman emperors and their families', in Ewald, B. C. and C. F. Noreña (eds.), *The Emperor and Rome: Space, Representation, and Ritual* (Cambridge: Cambridge University Press), 221–46.

Gascou, J. 1972. *La politique municipale de l'empire romain en Afrique proconsulaire de Trajan à Septime-Sévère*, CEFR 8 (Rome, École française de Rome).

Guédon, S. 2006. 'Les voyages des empereurs romains en Afrique jusqu'au IIIe siècle', *AfrRom* 16: 689–720.

Harl, K. W. 1996. *Coinage in the Roman Economy* (Baltimore: Johns Hopkins University Press).

Hellström, M. 2014. Public Construction under Diocletian: A Study of State Involvement in Construction in Roman Era Towns in Present Day Tunisia and Eastern Algeria. Diss., Columbia University (New York).

Højte, J. M. 2005. *Roman Imperial Statue Bases: From Augustus to Commodus* (Aarhus: Aarhus University Press).

Horster, M. 2001. *Bauinschriften römischer Kaiser: Untersuchungen zu Inschriftenpraxis und Bautätigkeit in Städten des westlichen Imperium Romanum in der Zeit des Prinzipats* (Stuttgart: Steiner).

Hugoniot, C. 2006. '*Decuriones splendidissimae coloniae Karthaginis*: les décurions de Carthage au IIIe siècle', in Quet, M.-H. (ed.), *La 'crise' de l'Empire romain de Marc Aurèle à Constantin: mutations, continuités, ruptures* (Paris: Presses de l'Université Paris-Sorbonne), 385–416.

Hurlet, F. 2000. 'Pouvoir des images, images du pouvoir impérial: la province d'Afrique aux deux premiers siècles de notre ère', *MEFRA* 112: 297–364.

Kuhoff, W. 2006. 'Die monumentale Repräsentation römischer Kaiser in Afrika', *AfrRom* 16: 2241–62.

Laird, M. 2015. *Civic Monuments and the Augustales in Roman Italy* (New York: Cambridge University Press).

Lomas, K. 2003. 'Public building, urban renewal, and euergetism,' in Lomas, K. and T. Cornell (eds.), *Bread and Circuses* (London; New York: Routledge), 28–45.

Moralee, J. 2004. *For Salvation's Sake: Provincial Loyalty, Personal Religion, and Epigraphic Production in the Roman and Late Antique Near East* (New York: Routledge).

Papi, E. 2004. 'A new golden age? The northern *Praefectum urbi* from the Severans to Diocletian', in Swain, S. and M. Edwards (eds.), *Approaching Late Antiquity: The Transformation from Early to Late Empire* (Oxford; New York: Oxford University Press), 53–81.

Pflaum, H.-G. 1976. 'Les flamines de l'Afrique romaine', *Athenaeum* 54: 152–63.

Picard, C. 1969/70: 'Le *pagus* dans l'Afrique romaine', *Karthago* 15, 1–12.

Poinssot, C. 1962. 'Immunitas perticae Carthaginiensium', *CRAI* 106.1, 55–76.

Polley, A. R. 2004/5 [2007]. 'Usurpations in Africa: ruler and ruled in the third century crisis', *AJAH* n.s. 3/4: 143–70.

Rives, J. B. 1995. *Religion and Authority in Roman Carthage from Augustus to Constantine* (Oxford: Oxford University Press).

Saastamoinen, A. 2010a. The Phraseology and Structure of Latin Building Inscriptions in Roman North Africa. PhD Diss., Helsinki.

   2010b. 'The common people in North African building inscriptions', *AfrRom* 18: 1631–44.

Smith, R. R. R. 2006. *Roman Portrait Statuary from Aphrodisias*. Aphrodisias 2 (Mainz am Rhein: Philipp von Zabern).

Thiel, W. 2002. 'Tetrakionia: Überlegungen einem Denkmaltypus tetrarchischer Zeit im Osten des Römischen Reiches', *AntTard* 10: 299–326.

Wesch-Klein, G. 1990. *Liberalitas in rem publicam: private Aufwendungen zugunsten von Gemeinden im römischen Afrika bis 284 n. Chr.* (Bonn: Habelt).

Zimmer, G. and G. Wesch-Klein 1989. *Locus datus decreto decurionum: zur Statuenaufstellung zweier Forumsanlagen im römischen Afrika* (Munich: Verlag der Bayerischen Akademie der Wissenschaften).

Zuiderhoek, A. 2013. 'Cities, buildings and benefactors in the Roman East', in Dickenson, C. P. and O. M. van Nijf (eds.), *Public Space in the Post-Classical City: Proceedings of a One Day Colloquium Held at Fransum, 23rd July 2007* (Leuven; Paris; Walpole, MA: Peeters), 173–92.

   2014. 'Controlling urban public space in Roman Asia Minor,' in Bekker-Nielsen, T. (ed.), *Space, Place and Identity in Northern Anatolia*. Geographica Historica 29 (Stuttgart: Steiner), 99–108.

8 | The Altar of P. Perelius Hedulus in Carthage and the Social Aspects of Provincial Image-Making

MEGAN GOLDMAN-PETRI

Introduction

In the winter of 1916 the French excavator Charles Saumagne discovered an altar decorated with imperial images in Carthage (Fig. 8.1).[1] The foundations of a larger shrine and an inscribed marble plaque were found in close proximity to the altar, and all are believed to be associated with the *templum* dedicated to the *Gens Augusta* by Publius Perelius Hedulus described in the text of the plaque (Fig. 8.2):[2]

> *Genti Augustae | P(ublius) Perelius Hedulus sac(erdos) perp(etuus) | templum solo privato | primus pecunia sua fecit.*

> To the Augustan family, Publius Perelius Hedulus, a *sacerdos perpetuus*, was the first to build a shrine on his private property and at his own expense.[3]

The artistic quality and iconographic sophistication of this provincial altar equal those of monuments in the capital. It is decorated with finely carved relief panels on all four sides, which depict sacrifice at an altar; Apollo with cithara, seated on a griffin and extending a palm towards a tripod; Aeneas' flight from Troy; and Roma seated on a pile of arms and armour proffering a victoriola towards an altar piled high with a cornucopia, banded globe, and caduceus (Figs. 8.3–6). The altar and its images, moreover, appear to be a very familiar expression of Augustan

---

[1] Excavation: Saumagne, 1924: 179; Poinssot, 1929; Deneauve, 1979: 42–4. Cf. Rives, 1995: 55. The altar is currently on display at the Musée National du Bardo in Tunis.

[2] Saumagne, 1924; Deneauve, 1979. Without first-hand analysis of the archival materials, I proceed on the basic assumption that these connections between altar, inscription, and shrine are sound. It is worth noting here, however, that what are now interpretations a century old are in need of future reinvestigation.

[3] For original publication of the inscription see Cagnat, 1913. The plaque measures 0.75 m × 2.10 m × 0.10 m and was found in a secondary context in a room of an atrium-style house, known as the House of Ariadne, located in close proximity to the shrine. Further publications: Saumagne, 1924; L. L. Sebaï, 2005: cat. no. 59; *ILAfr.* 353; *ILTun.* 1046; *ILPB* 7.

Figure 8.1 Altar of the *Gens Augusta*, Carthage. Tunis, Musée National du Bardo Inv. no. 2125. Photograph: P. Radigue.

Figure 8.2 Dedicatory inscription for the *templum Gentis Augustae* commissioned by P. Perelius Hedulus. Reproduced from Cagnat, 1913: 684.

Figure 8.3 Panel with a scene of sacrifice from the Altar of the *Gens Augusta*.
Photograph: P. Radigue.

ideology.[4] Each image individually celebrates the Augustan regime and
seems to derive from official models in Rome: the sacrifice is conducted
according to Roman custom with covered head (*capite velato*); Augustus
strongly associated himself with the god Apollo; and the Roma and Aeneas
panels are believed to copy decorative elements of well-known Augustan
monuments, respectively, the Ara Pacis Augustae and the Forum
Augustum. In addition, the altar's decorative scheme follows the same
principles informing the design of the Ara Pacis Augustae, but on
a reduced scale: the imperial images are displayed in discrete panels and
each image is rendered in a different representational mode – historical
(sacrifice, Fig. 8.3), allegorical (Roma, Fig. 8.4), legendary (Aeneas, Fig.
8.5), mythological (Apollo, Fig. 8.6). Like its imagery, the resplendent
marble from which the altar is carved also has imperial associations; it is

---

[4] Zanker, 1988: 315: 'virtually a textbook summary of Roman official iconography'. Schörner,
2009: 'Ein gutes Beispiel für die direkte Abhängigkeit von Rom und die Übernahme ganzer
Dekorationsschemata ist der Gens Augusta-Altar aus Karthago, der ein explizit stadtrömisches
Bildprogramm nicht nur hinsichtlich der mythologischen Szenen, sondern auch in Bezug auf die
Wiedergabe eines Opfers mit dezidiert hauptstädtischer Ikonographie zeigt.' For similar
assessments, see Poinssot, 1929; Hölscher, 1984: 31; Simon, 1986: 224, fig. 251; Rives, 1995: 53–7;
Beard, North, and Price, 1998: 333; Dardenay, 2007: 160; Joyce, 2015: 18.

Figure 8.4 Roma panel from the Altar of the *Gens Augusta*. Photograph: P. Radigue.

believed to come from the quarries at Luna in central Italy that were under the direct control of the emperor. The altar is dedicated to an Augustan divinity, the *Gens Augusta*, and seems to have been a site devoted to emperor worship. Finally, the patron of the altar, P. Perelius Hedulus, was in the brick business and likely a freedman; he was thus a member of a social class believed to be the most eager adopters of imperial imagery and the most active agents in its propagation through the construction of sacred dedications to the emperor.[5]

This altar is typically interpreted as an exemplum of one of the most notable features of Augustan art, the seemingly instantaneous dissemination and reproduction of imperial images across the empire. Indeed, the altar has been said 'to attempt to recreate Augustan Rome in Carthage'.[6] Using Hedulus' altar as a case study, this chapter explores how this might have happened – in other words, how it is that an altar in colonial Carthage could be covered with images that look as if they were designed and sculpted in Rome – and concludes that explanations in terms of 'imitation' or direct transmission from centre to periphery are unnecessary.

[5] Zanker, 1988: 305.   [6] Beard, North, and Price, 1998: 333.

Figure 8.5 Aeneas panel from the Altar of the *Gens Augusta*. Photograph: P. Radigue.

In this chapter, I first re-date the altar to the Claudian period on the basis of the appearance of *gens Augusta* in the epigraphic record. The altar and its imagery are then examined within a local context of dedications to imperial cult and located within the decentralised networks by which images associated with imperial institutions circulated. Rather than a straightforward example of Augustan image dissemination, I argue that the altar had no direct relationship to a particular Roman model, contending instead that the images on this altar were designed in Carthage and reflect the interplay between local social dynamics and imperial ideology. The chapter therefore not only challenges current models of imperial image circulation, but also reconsiders the underlying causes behind the appearance of 'Roman-looking' architectural forms and decoration across the empire, a phenomenon known as *imitatio urbis*.

Hedulus' Altar and Models of Imperial Image Dissemination

Despite a widespread belief that counterparts in the capital directly influenced the altar's images, modern scholars have, nevertheless, regularly

Figure 8.6 Apollo panel from the Altar of the *Gens Augusta*. Photograph: P. Radigue.

acknowledged that the altar has novel features that also distinguish it from its models. Scholarly explanations of these novel features have reflected changing theories of acculturation in Roman studies. In their earliest iterations, approaches to the study of image transmission were premised on the idea that provincial art sought to replicate art in the centre precisely, and that images flowed from the centre out to the periphery.[7] Under this transmission model, novel features of provincial art are 'deviations' and are attributed to distance from the capital, that is, to provincial artists either unfamiliar with imperial images or not skilled enough to reproduce the image quality seen at the capital. In the last twenty years the transmission model has been largely replaced by a reception one, which shifts attention and interest towards the provincial and personal transformations of the source image.[8] The reception model is bottom-up; it understands provincial art as a product of interaction or negotiation between the art, culture,

---

[7] Romanisation models are now outdated. For discussion, see Versluys, 2014.

[8] The focus on the receiver is part of a broader turn towards the application of theories of globalisation to the Roman world: Hingley, 2005; Naerebout, 2008; Witcher, 2014; Pitts and Versluys, 2015. Similarly, on the value of creolisation for the study of Roman provincial art, Webster, 2001.

and institutions of Rome and local contexts. According to this model, novel features are 'adaptations' or 'constructive (re-)interpretations' and can be the result of the importance and endurance of local artistic traditions and institutions, or the aesthetic tastes and ideological preferences of patrons.

Even if these recent approaches largely do away with a vision of the imperial court forcefully imposing ideological imagery on a passive provincial public, and, in fact, now assign a great deal of agency and creativity to local actors, they are still focused on explaining how patrons like Hedulus transformed 'Roman'/'centre'/'imperial'/'state' models. And they continue to regard his altar as an imitation and response to ideas and images generated at the capital.[9]

In what follows, I attempt to construct an alternative approach to the study of imperial image circulation by treating the production of images as a distributed process. Rather than taking images in isolation and looking for potential analogues in Roman Italy, I seek to understand them in relation to the holistic context of Hedulus' shrine, local contexts of elite competition at Carthage, and the circulation of persons, materials, and the concepts and language of imperial cult in the ancient Mediterranean.[10]

Situating the Altar

The altar and shrine stood at the point where the decumanus maximus reached the foot of the eastern slope of the Byrsa hill, the heart of the ancient Roman colony of Carthage (Fig. 8.7). They were built above foundations associated with a major re-terracing project of the hill undertaken during the reign of Augustus, establishing a *terminus post quem* for the shrine. An early imperial date accords with what little we know about Publius Perelius Hedulus himself. He seems to have been in the brick business; his nomen and cognomen are attested on a series of brickstamps that were recovered among the archaeological remains of a brick and tile workshop in Carthage.[11] The particular rectangular shape of these bricks suggests that they date to the first century CE.[12] Two of the brickstamps associated with Hedulus also bear the name of an imperial freedman, C. Julius Antimacus, another brick producer

[9]   See in particular Rives, 1995: 56.
[10] This approach builds upon recent attention to methodological issues in the study of Roman provincial art; see Scott and Webster, 2003; Alcock, Egri, and Frakes, 2016.
[11] Hedulus' brickstamps: *CIL* 8.22632.72. For brickstamps more broadly, see Helen, 1975. On hierarchies within the brick business (e.g. *dominus*, *officinator*): Setälä, 1977; Bodel, 1983.
[12] On the dates of the brickstamps: Helen, 1975; Bodel, 1983.

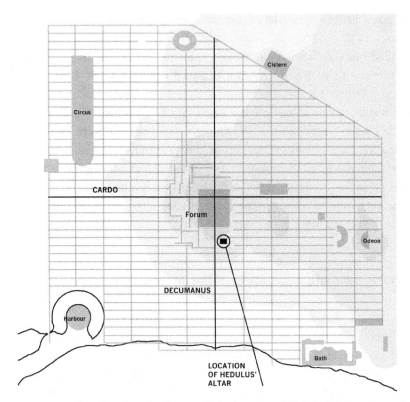

Figure 8.7 Plan of ancient Carthage with the location of Hedulus' shrine. Artwork: M. Hellström (after B. Bouret).

known from brickstamps found in Rome.[13] Brick production and distribution was a thriving industry in a city that underwent significant reconstruction of its monumental core during the reign of Augustus.[14] For this building activity, brick and materials were brought in from Italy on account of their superior quality.[15] It appears that, initially, Hedulus had a partnership with a known Italian producer of bricks, who was perhaps his agent.[16] At some unknown

---

[13] Brickstamps with the names of both Hedulus and Antimacus: *CIL* 8.22632.65. Bricks stamped with Antimacus' name found in the capital and in Italy: *CIL* 15.1202. Cf. Cagnat, 1913; Rives, 1995: 55; McCarty, 2011: 219 no. 79.

[14] On the staggering transformation of the Byrsa under Augustus: Deneauve, 1990.

[15] Likely on return cargoes for foodstuffs from Africa; so Gros, 1990; Rakob, 2000. The composition of return cargoes has become a subject of scholarly interest; e.g. Rice, Wilson, and Schörle, 2012. For Carthage and the brick and tile industry, see Russell, 2012 and 2014. He argues that bricks were not simply cheap ballast for return cargoes but that Italian bricks were sought after for their greater size and strength.

[16] *Contra* Rives (1995: 55), who proposes that Antimacus emigrated to Carthage to partner with Hedulus. Evidence for vertical integration: Broekaert, 2016. For the claim that freedmen usually continue to work as agents for their *patronus*, see Ruffing, 2016.

later point his business relationship with Antimacus ceased and Hedulus became a brick-producer in his own right.

The shrine's dedicatory inscription informs us that Hedulus built his *templum* on his own property and financed it with his own funds (*solo privato | primus pecunia sua fecit*). Archaeologists have uncovered two large residential buildings on the same city block where the altar and marble plaque were found. Also recovered from the site were three tiles bearing Hedulus' name, which raises the possibility that he may have owned one or both of the houses.[17] Together these archaeological remains suggest that the freedman and wealthy brick-entrepreneur Hedulus set up a substantial shrine consisting of a magnificent altar and small temple to the *Gens Augusta* in his own front yard.[18]

Gens Augusta and a Redating of the Altar

The altar has generally been assigned to the latter half of the reign of Augustus.[19] The divine dedicatee of the Carthaginian *templum*, however, might prompt us to consider a later Julio-Claudian date. The collective noun *gens Augusta* does not strike us as unusual because of its similarity to both *gens Iulia* and *domus Augusta*. *Gens Augusta*, however, is entirely unattested in Rome. Dedications to this Augustan abstraction have only been found in Corinth and Achaea. In the Greek-speaking parts of the empire, *genos Sebaston* developed as a Greek translation for the Latin *domus Augusta*.[20] *Genos* appears to have been the preferred translation over *oikos Sebaston*, although both are attested. The concentration of *gens Augusta* dedications in Corinth, a Roman colony in Greece, suggests that it is a translation of the Greek version of *domus Augusta*, *genos Sebaston*, back into Latin.[21]

The phrase *domus Augusta* is first epigraphically attested in the capital in connection with a statuary group commemorating Tiberius, Livia, Germanicus, and Drusus the Younger erected in the area of the Circus Flaminius. The group was dedicated in 15 CE, early in the reign of the emperor Tiberius.[22] The Greek translation *genos Sebaston*, however, is only attested in Achaea under Caligula, at a time when the emperor was

---

[17] The archaeological excavations are well reviewed in M. Sebaï, 2005.
[18] For this interpretation: Rives, 1995: 55 with earlier scholarship.
[19] Rives, 1995: 55–7; Beard, North, and Price, 1998: 333.   [20] Kantiréa, 2007.
[21] West, 1931: 15–17, no. 17. See also Hallett, 2004: 442.
[22] On the statuary group in the Circus Flaminius: Flory, 1996.

fashioning a new Julio-Claudian dynastic line and championing Antonia Minor as its matriarch. It continued to be employed through the reign of Claudius. An inscription discovered in Corinth near the Julian Basilica on the agora probably came from a statue group visualising this new dynastic line.[23] On a white marble slab is engraved:[24]

> TIBERIO ANT[oniae ---]
> CAESARI AVGV[stae ---]
> GENTI AVGVSTAE [---]

The sculpted ensemble featured Tiberius Gemellus, adopted by Caligula upon his accession, and Antonia Minor, the emperor's grandmother. The inscription is broken on the right side, suggesting that originally the statue group included more members of the imperial family.[25] The entire statue group was dedicated to the *gens Augusta*. The reference to Antonia as Augusta has informed the *communis opinio* which dates the statue group's dedication to March or April of 37 CE.[26]

Either this Latin translation of the Greek calque on *domus Augusta* developed simultaneously and independently in Corinth and Carthage as a result of their similar links to cities of the central Mediterranean; or, the concept of the *gens Augusta* was a region-specific phenomenon that reached Hedulus from Greece.[27] Both explanations, however, make more sense in a world where the phrase *genos Sebaston* was already widely used. There is thus a strong possibility that the altar should be dated to the Claudian period at the earliest. Even if it is Augustan, the fact that it could so easily be later should discourage us from reflexively thinking of the altar as a product of imitation of state monuments in Rome. Furthermore, Hedulus' *templum Gentis Augustae* differs from other dedications to the *domus Augusta*, *genos Sebaston*, and *gens Augusta*. These phrases typically accompany statuary groups featuring multiple imperial persons. In contrast, *Gens Augusta* appears to have been the divinity worshipped at Hedulus' shrine, which has no parallels either in Rome or

---

[23] The other inscription is too fragmentary to allow for any conclusions regarding the monument: *D[ivo? ---]RI[---]C[---] | Ca[esari? ---] | [ge]nt[i Au]gusta[e ---] Augus[t ---]*. Kent, 1966: 39, no. 71 (= Corinth VIII.3, 71 pl. 9).

[24] West, 1931: 15–17, no. 17 (= Corinth VIII.2, 17).   [25] Hallett, 2004: 442; Kantiréa, 2007: 73.

[26] Caligula conferred the title Augusta on Antonia shortly before her death on 1 May 37 CE. (Title: Suet. *Calig.* 15.2; Cass. Dio 59.3.4. Date of death: *Fasti Ostienses*.)

[27] Both Corinth and Carthage had been sacked in 146 BCE, refounded as Roman colonies by Julius Caesar in 44 BCE, and then rebuilt under Augustus. As Purcell (1995) has argued, the new Carthage echoed not only Rome but also the rebuilt Corinth.

the Greek east. Redating the *templum Gentis Augustae* to the Claudian or Neronian period offers new insight into how Hedulus' project relates to an innovative contemporary culture of euergetism associated with emperor worship in Carthage.

The Sacred Landscape of Imperial Cult in Carthage

Prominent Carthaginians, and their counterparts in smaller cities, found expression for their ambitions in the construction of imperial shrines.[28] Few traces of sacred dedications to the emperor have survived from Carthage itself, which has thwarted our ability to reconstruct both the visual and cultic milieu of which Hedulus' *templum Gentis Augustae* was a part. From what has been preserved, we can deduce that imperial cult in the colony may have centred on the summit of the Byrsa at the temple of Concord and possibly also at a basilica where statues believed to represent members of the imperial family, Julia and Gaius Caesar, were discovered.[29]

A number of building inscriptions from towns and cities in Carthage's immediate hinterland provide useful comparative evidence for the sacred landscape of the colonial capital.[30] The inscriptions attest that building activity associated with the imperial cult was intense, with multiple cultic structures clustered within close proximity to one another in central locations. In addition, the dedicators represent a wide range of social classes, including Roman citizens, native elite, and freed persons – both men and women.

There also seems to have been a mixture of private and public sacred dedications to the emperor. Carried out *solo privato* and *sua pecunia*, Hedulus' shrine seems to have been an individual project without any connection to established civic institutions. This has led some modern scholars to question the shrine's legal status.[31] While the evidence for

---

[28] The epigraphic record is particularly abundant for the reign of Claudius. Inscriptions from other towns in the hinterland attest to further imperial dedications; *ILS* 6797: a vow of an altar to Divus Augustus and the emperor Claudius in 48 CE by a *flamen divi Augusti*, Julius Venustus. *CIL* 8.14727: fragmentary inscription from Ghardimaou which mentions a dedication by a *flamen Augusti* in 52 CE.

[29] See Gros, 1990: 561–4. Gros argues that a complex for the imperial cult was located on the southern part of the Byrsa hill. He has suggested a monumental complex such as a *forum adiectum* or an Augusteum or Caesareum, and believes that the statues may have been housed in the early judicial basilica, in a *sacellum*, or even in a porticoed gallery like that of the Forum of Augustus in Rome.

[30] Discussions of these building inscriptions can be found in Saastamoinen, 2000; Rives, 2001; Saastamoinen, 2008a, 2008b; Sterrett-Krause, 2012.

[31] Following Rives, 1995: 56 no. 83.

how negotiations with the *decuriones* played out is lost, this should not lead us to believe that Hedulus' shrine was not *sacer*, or not officially public cult. The *templum Gentis Augustae* actually fits into a pattern of local notables establishing cult places on their private property on or immediately outside of major public spaces across the empire in the first century CE.[32] In some instances benefactors built public cult on private property as a means of maintaining control over the cult, and, in others, as a result of an inability to acquire public space, either because they had failed to obtain permission from the *ordo* or due to overcrowding. Finally, it is unclear how much these legal distinctions may have mattered. Given the centrality of the shrine's location, its construction in marble, and the characteristically 'Augustan' imagery decorating the altar, it would have been difficult for someone walking around Carthage to make a distinction between Hedulus' shrine and imperial cult places funded by more eminent figures in the community.

We have some sense of at least one of these other monuments. The existence of another altar covered with imperial images is suggested by two marble relief panels, one now in the Louvre and the other in Algiers, which were discovered together in an area immediately outside of the

Figure 8.8 Relief depicting the goddess Tellus, Carthage. Musée du Louvre MA 1838, NIII 975. Photograph © DEA / A. DAGLI ORTI/De Agostini via Getty Images.

[32] On cults built *solo et sua pecunia*: Van Andringa, 2015.

Figure 8.9 Relief depicting three standing figures typically identified (from left to right) as Venus Genetrix with Eros, Mars Ultor, and a deceased Julio-Claudian prince, Carthage. Musée National des Antiquités, Algiers. Photograph: M. Goldman-Petri.

city's street grid (Figs. 8.8–9).[33] The imagery similarly appears to imitate official state monuments and sculptural groups in Rome; the Louvre panel is thought to be a copy of the Tellus on the east facade of the Ara Pacis, while the panel in Algiers supposedly reproduces the cult statues displayed in the temple of Mars Ultor in the Forum of Augustus. The lost altar has, in fact, been called the 'Carthaginian Ara Pacis' in the scholarship.[34] The iconography of the Algiers relief has informed the consensus view that the lost altar was likely built under Nero. Therefore, this altar and Hedulus' may have been roughly contemporary in date. We cannot say which altar came first or anything about the particular social competition engaged in through their construction, but these panels do demonstrate that there was a rich image culture in Carthage that may have more directly informed Hedulus' decorative choices.

[33] The following discussion of the panels derives from Fishwick, 2014.   [34] Brent, 2010: 32.

Social Dynamics in the Local Context

Hedulus' self-presentation in his shrine's dedicatory inscription provides a glimpse of some of the competitive social dynamics driving the appearance of imperial imagery across the empire. Beginning with his name: Hedulus' cognomen is likely a Latin transliteration of the Greek *hedulos*, 'the sweet one' or 'sweety'.[35] His Greek cognomen together with the absence of patronymics in the formal presentation of his name has suggested to modern scholars that he was a freedman or the son of a freedman. Some scholars have claimed that Hedulus was ethnically Greek, but there is little to support such a claim beyond his Greek cognomen.[36] And even this is flimsy evidence, since it is well known that Romans developed a penchant for giving their slaves of diverse ethnic origins Greek names.[37] An inscription from a late Republican funerary monument in Rome mentions a number of freedmen who share his nomen, Perelius, and also have Greek cognomina.[38] Hedulus, therefore, may have come to Carthage from Italy, perhaps even from Rome itself.

Hedulus was one of a small group of freedmen benefactors of the imperial cult in Africa Proconsularis in the later Julio-Claudian period. In the nearby town of Thugga, some 100 km south-west of Carthage, a freed couple, Marcus Licinius Tyrannus and his wife, Licinia Prisca, made several prominent dedications. They collaborated together with their *patronus*, Marcus Licinius Rufus, to finance and build a *cella* with porticoes to Ceres Augusta.[39] Tyrannus alone also restored and beautified a temple dedicated to the emperor Tiberius, which had originally been built by his patron's grandmother, Viria Rustica, but had recently been destroyed by fire.[40] Licinia Prisca was a *flaminica perpetua* of the local imperial cult in

---

[35] All other known attestations of the cognomen Hedulus or its early imperial variants occur with slaves and freedmen. Cf. Solin, 1982: 878; Rives, 1995.

[36] Following Solin, 1982: 878.

[37] On Greek names for slaves and freedmen: Gordon, 1924; Taylor, 1961: 125–8; Solin, 1996. On Greek cognomina for slaves of eastern and western origins: Treggiari, 1969; Coles, 2017.

[38] *CIL* 1².3016a: *M(arcus) Perenn[ius] C(ai) l(ibertus) | Menopantus | P(ublius) Perelius C(ai) l(ibertus) Philotaerus | P(ublius) Maelius Sex(ti) l(ibertus) Philomusus || Pere[---] Stratonice | M(arcus) Perelius M(arci) l(ibertus) Isoc[---] | M(arcus) Fuurius M(arci) l(ibertus) | Antimacus || in fr(onte) [p(edes)] XVIII | in ag(ro) [p(edes) ---].*

[39] Saint-Amans, 2004: 285–6 no. 12; *CIL* 8.26603; *ILTun.* 1433; *AE* 1969–70, 649.

[40] *DFH* 65–7, no. 25: *Imp(eratori) Ti(berio) Caesari A[ugusto sacr]um | curatore L(ucio) Vergilio P(ubli) f(ilio) Ru[fo ---]G dato Viriae | P(ubli) f(iliae) Rusticae aviae M(arci) Licini [Rufi flam(inis) perp(etui) Aug(usti) | C(oloniae) C(oncordiae)] I(uliae) K(arthaginis) | M(arcus) Licinius M(arci) l(ibertus) Tyrannus patronus pa[gi --- ign]e consumptas | restituit aedem et statu[a]s corruptas exornavit opus intestinu[m refecit curatore | M(arco) Licinio P]riscillo f(ilio).*

Thugga; she is the only freedwoman known to have held this position. Possibly as a payment (*summa honoraria*) for her priesthood, she built and dedicated a temple to Venus Concordia in her own right. This couple held offices and erected edifices on the same terms as Roman citizens.[41] They and other freedmen like them in the hinterland seem to have enjoyed a greater degree of independence because the attention of their freeborn, Roman patrons was focused on the larger metropolitan centre of Carthage. For their part, freedmen appear to have derived social capital from their Carthaginian connections; their dedicatory inscriptions regularly include the names of their patrons and the magistrates who travelled to Thugga to officially consecrate their benefactions.

That freedmen benefactions were likely more numerous in the hinterland sets Hedulus' *templum Gentis Augustae* in Carthage further apart. Hedulus operated in the provincial capital itself, where he competed with men like the patron of Tyrannus and his wife, Marcus Licinius Rufus, who was a Roman citizen of equestrian rank and priest of the imperial cult. Unlike other freedmen, Hedulus omits not only his status as a *libertus*, but also the name of his patron. And, since he makes no mention of public office, it has also been suggested by James Rives that he may have also omitted the name of the magistrate needed to officially recognise the shrine as public cult. Caution is required here, however: it is difficult to discern the degree to which the epigraphic customs of Thugga extended to Carthage; moreover, Hedulus may have operated with an unusual degree of independence in his local context if his patron was based in Italy.[42]

An especially striking feature of Hedulus' self-presentation is his claim to be a *sacerdos perpetuus* of the *Gens Augusta*. Although the provincial cult of Augustus himself may not yet have been installed in Africa Proconsularis, the local, civic cult certainly was, and was for the most part represented by a *flamen*.[43] Both *flamen* and *sacerdos* were common designations for imperial priests across the empire, but Hedulus' title

---

[41] There is a growing body of evidence indicating that in the early empire, especially in the provinces, freedmen held public positions as eminent as *duumvir* and aedile, for which see Coles, 2017; cf. Le Glay, 1990a, 1990b. For comparanda, see the rich study of freedman office holders in Corinth by Millis, 2014.

[42] On the unique situation of euergetism in Thugga: Briand-Ponsart, 2003: 241.

[43] The provincial cult had been established in 30 BCE in Asia Minor and in 12 BCE in the Three Gauls, but is not attested in Africa until 70–1 CE, when a number of inscriptions testify to a *flamen provinciae Africae Augusti*. Marcus Licinius Rufus is, in fact, among the earliest attested priests associated with imperial cult in North Africa. Cf. Rives, 1995: 51–63; Fishwick, 2002: 130.

departs from what was a clear regional preference.[44] There are reasons to suspect that he had bestowed it on himself, as an attempt to distinguish his position from the municipal flaminate in Carthage and align it with the most impressive priesthoods in the city (which were sacerdotal).[45] *Perpetuus*, 'for life' or 'eternal', was an honour bestowed upon a select group of *flamines* after their annual term had ended. It signified that the person maintained the rank of *flamen*, although they no longer held the office. *Flamen perpetuus* was the highest honour in a municipal career. The use of *perpetuus* in this instance, however, is odd. The *sacerdos Gentis Augustae* was not an annually elected priesthood. Indeed, the only person who ever seems to have held the position in Carthage was Publius Perelius Hedulus. *Perpetuus* appears simply to have been tacked on to raise the status of the priesthood Hedulus created for himself.

Hedulus piles on the superlatives in other ways as well. He says he is *primus*, but of what is unclear: the first to have built a *templum* to this particular divinity, the *Gens Augusta*; to have built a shrine on his private property; or, to have built a religious site for the worship of the emperor? Moreover, it is difficult to ascertain the extent to which *primus* is a serious claim or a boastful exaggeration. The placement of *primus* so that it aligns with *P. Perelius Hedulus* and *templum* on the far left side of the plaque suggests that, whether true or not, the self-made and ambitious Hedulus sought to emphasise his claim to be 'first'.[46]

The Physical Altar

All the aspects of Hedulus' *templum Gentis Augustae* examined thus far – his choices of divine dedicatee, the shrine's location in the urban fabric, the title of his priesthood, the language of the dedicatory inscription – suggest that its design was primarily conceived in relation to other imperial cult sites in Carthage. Apart from the images, the only thing still linking Hedulus' altar directly to state monuments in Rome is its purported construction in Luna marble. Certainly by the time of Tiberius, if not already under Julius Caesar, the quarries at Luna were imperial property. This fact has led scholars to suggest that the distribution of Luna marble

---

[44] Hemelrijk, 2005: 139–44 with scholarship. Generally, *sacerdos* was favoured in Italy and Spain.

[45] Particularly the *sacerdos* of Ceres. McIntyre (2016: 84) suggests that Hedulus may have proclaimed himself *sacerdos* without permission from the *ordo*. On the provincial priesthood in Africa: Fishwick, 1981.

[46] On *primus*: Fishwick, 1996.

around the Mediterranean was expressly managed to encourage and shape monumental building in the periphery,[47] and to understand architecture built from Luna outside of the capital as forms of *imitatio urbis*, attempts to transform provincial centres into miniature versions of Rome.

First and foremost, the attribution of the altar's marble to the quarries at Luna is not certain.[48] Two major quarries of white marble were located on the eastern coast of Algeria at Djebel Filfila and Cap de Garde, and evidence for activity in the quarries dates back to the second century BCE. While isotopic analysis of column shafts of the third and fourth centuries CE has shown that marble from the Algerian quarries was being shipped to Italy and Tunisia, we do not have a clear sense of circulation patterns in the early empire. The marble from these quarries has distinctive grey striations.[49] Similar striations run across many of the relief panels of Hedulus' altar. The marble composition of the quarries in Algeria and Carrara, however, are incredibly variable, and it cannot be known for certain without further investigation from where the marble of the *Gens Augusta* altar originated. But it should be noted that the very assignment of the marble to the Luna quarries has no firm foundation and may be based entirely on our assumptions about the circulation of imperial imagery.

Furthermore, even if the marble is, indeed, from Luna, imperial control may be a mirage. The significance of imperial ownership of the Luna quarries remains underexplored. Was control motivated purely by economic incentives and management of a finite valuable resource? Or did control extend to approval of the form and content of constructions in Luna marble? Evidence for prefabrication of individual architectural elements, such as column capitals, has been identified at the quarries.[50] There is an obvious logic to such prefabrication since it allowed for reduction in shipping costs and a concentration of skilled marble workers at Luna.[51] But there is no evidence that indicates this prefabrication included iconographic elements. While the provenance of the marble presents the

---

[47] Fant, 1988 and 1993; Pensabene, 2002, 2004, and 2013.

[48] J. Röder suggested that the Algiers relief may have been carved from marble from the Djebel Filfila quarries in Algeria. His observation is cited in Kraus, 1979: 245.

[49] The following discussion of marble from the Algerian quarries is derived from Hermann *et al.*, 2012.

[50] On the Luna quarries: Fant, 1988; Pensabene, 2004 and 2013. There is little evidence for the official regulation of the marble trade before the second century CE when a *procurator marmorum* is first attested. Cf. Fant, 1993.

[51] On the similarity of architectural elements found in fora Augusta across Italy and the Latin west: Goldbeck, 2015.

potential for centralised control and influence, there is plenty of evidence to the contrary.

Excavations of shipwrecks along the south-western coast of France have shown that in addition to large shipments of marble from Italy to major provincial ports, there may have been a good deal of short-distance, small-scale trade of Luna marble.[52] Several of these ships date to the first century CE. Generally, six to seven blocks of Luna marble have been found on each ship.[53] The blocks are square and rectangular in shape. There is no standardised size, but the faces of the square blocks have an average area of approximately 1.50 m^2, a size roughly equivalent to that of Hedulus' altar. Most importantly, all the blocks are unworked, clear evidence that the imperial quarries were not distributing worked pieces. Rather, there seems to have been a market for unworked marble blocks of relatively small size ideally suited for a variety of monumental forms – statue bases, altars (both funerary and public), and so on. The merchants of these ships most likely picked up their cargo from the port at Massalia (modern Marseilles), whether excess marble stored in warehouses or specially commissioned, and then transported it short distances along the coast to capitalise on the demand for marble in construction projects across southern Gaul. Such maritime excavation of the North African coastline has yet to be comprehensively undertaken, but what little has been discovered suggests a similar pattern of stone trade with activity at multiple socio-economic levels. This decentralised and multilevel circulation of Luna marble thus raises questions about the directness and unmediated nature of this material link to Rome.

Consequences for the Images

In the light of this discussion, does it still make sense to talk about the relationship between the images on this Carthaginian altar and images in Rome in terms of imitation – to imagine that all imperial images originated in Rome? What do we mean when we say that Hedulus' altar is a quotation or a copy of a state monument?[54] The Roma panel of Hedulus'

---

[52] Russell, 2012 with bibliography.

[53] Scholarship generally reports stone cargo in total tonnes rather than the size of individual blocks. The following observations of the blocks of Luna marble are deduced from the excavation reports of the shipwrecks Saintes-Maries 18, 21, and 22 in Long, 1999. Cf. Russell, 2012: 534.

[54] Rives, 1995: 53: 'the altar does more than simply employ these great Augustan images: it also deliberately evokes their prototypes in Rome'; Beard, North, and Price, 1998: 331: 'Two altars

altar (Fig. 8.4) and the Louvre Tellus panel from the other lost altar in Carthage (Fig. 8.8) are the proverbial smoking guns for the imitation model. As two panels from two different altar monuments, which exhibit visual correspondences with panels that adorned the east facade of the Ara Pacis, they have been taken as definitive proof that provincial images were modelled on those in Rome and that the altars in Carthage even competed for the best or most convincing allusion to state monuments in the capital.

The current model informing interpretations of the images on the Carthaginian altars is that articulated by Paul Zanker, who argues that imperial images were created at the centre, where they had clear political or ideological meanings, and, like the pervasive acanthus, they then spread and trickled everywhere.[55] The ingenuity of the imperial images designed under the Augustan regime was that they were easily adaptable and appealing because they symbolised generic messages of cultural prosperity and religious piety universally applicable to the diverse cultures and peoples of the Roman Empire. It was only as imperial images spread from Rome and were replicated in private contexts and on non-elite objects, Zanker argues, that they were gradually disassociated from their original political meanings and developed personal meanings or simply became fashionable (i.e. meaningless).

The Roma panel, therefore, as Zanker has proposed, simplifies its Roman model by reducing a message conveyed across two panels on the east facade of the Ara Pacis (Tellus and Roma) onto a single panel (Fig. 8.4). The Carthaginian composition also transforms its state model from a lofty allegorical message of war and peace into a 'pedestrian' message of commerce: the idyllic pastoral scene of Pax (or Tellus) has been replaced by her attributes, symbols of prosperity: a cornucopia, caduceus, and globe. Roma now proffers victory to a representation of the wealth of the new *imperium*.[56] In this instance, the transformations, which also constitute innovative adaptation of their model, reflect and serve Hedulus' personal interests as a freedman who has benefited directly from the new social and economic opportunities of the Augustan Age.

The Louvre Tellus Panel similarly transforms its supposed prototype (Fig. 8.8). While the central motif of the Louvre panel does indeed resemble

from the *colonia* of Carthage illustrate the different ways in which images of (and derived from) Rome might be represented and constructively interpreted in a *colonia*.'
[55] Zanker, 1988, especially ch. 8, 'The Roman Empire of Augustus: imperial myth and cult in east and west'; Wallace-Hadrill, 2008: 313–55.
[56] Zanker, 1988: 315; followed by Beard, North, and Price, 1998: 333 and Cornwell, 2017: 172–3.

the composition on the east facade of the Ara Pacis Augustae, depicting the goddess surrounded by marsh elements, animals, and birds, the figures on either side of the central matronly divinity are noticeably different: the goddess in the Ara Pacis panel is accompanied by two nymphs and in the Louvre Relief she is flanked on her right by Poseidon, represented as a bearded male figure emerging from the sea, and on her left by a female figure shown only from the chest up, holding a torch, who is thought to represent Kore. The association with Poseidon and Kore clearly identifies the goddess on the Louvre panel as Demeter. The cult of Demeter had enjoyed widespread popularity in Carthage since its introduction in the fourth century BCE and the representation of the earth goddess on the Louvre panel has been connected to a revival of the cult in a new guise as the cult of the Cereres after the re-foundation of the city under Augustus.[57] The transformations have thus been attributed to a desire to make a Roman/Augustan image of the earth goddess more legible and relevant for a Carthaginian audience.

The imitation model suggests that the patrons or artists of these altars intended that the images would be recognised as allusions, and that they derived at least part of their meaning from the viewer's recognition of the quotation. In practical terms, this treats an image as a copy in the same sense that a Roman statue is a copy of a Greek original. But is this a useful analogy? We have an understandable tendency to interpret images in terms of their relationship to other images, as well as to see these effects as part of the intent of the work of art. Commissioners of statues could expect that a certain subset of their viewers had 'taste' and would recognise the famous original behind the copy, as a result of the creation of artistic canons and critical discourses on art and their viewers' knowledge of them. Was this, however, the case with architectural monuments and their decorative image programmes? Do the images on state monuments at Rome consti-tute a canon, which provincial patrons making dedications in honour of the emperor sought to copy? Hedulus' altar corresponds stylistically to state monuments in Rome: it is built in marble and dedicated to an Augustan divinity. But is it therefore necessary to assume that it is or is intended to be a copy of the Ara Pacis?

Treating Hedulus' altar as a copy places the onus on modern scholars to reconstruct the ways in which Hedulus or his artist could have come to

---

[57] The cult was officially introduced in Carthage in 396 BCE (Diod. Sic. 4.77.4–5). On Demeter cult in Carthage: Picard, 1984. On the Roman cult of the Cereres in Carthage: Fishwick and Shaw, 1978.

know Rome and its visual culture.[58] Scholars have proposed a wide range of hypotheses, including that Hedulus, through his involvement in the building trade and contacts in Italy, commissioned the monument directly from Rome or Italy, hired a Roman artist, or sent a local artist to copy images on state monuments in the capital. Artists' networks could, of course, have played an important role in the spread of imperial imagery, whether images moved with travelling artists,[59] or through media, such as artists' workbooks, the existence of which has often been conjectured.[60] While we can assume that the artist of Hedulus' altar was highly skilled, the question should not be how he knew the monuments of Rome, but whether or not such knowledge was even needed to produce this altar.

There is, in fact, no good reason to assume that these images come from Rome. Over a century of *Quellenforschung* on the image programme of the Ara Pacis Augustae has shown that almost every image on the altar had an antecedent in the larger image culture of the Hellenistic Mediterranean.[61] The imagery found on the Ara Pacis also circulated outside its context on the state monument; therefore, the same image culture from which Augustus or the senate derived the image programme of the Ara Pacis was available to a much wider public. Rather than explaining novel features as deviations from or adaptations of Roman originals, we might see the images on the Ara Pacis and those on the Carthaginian altars emerging independently out of a shared image culture.

The Louvre Tellus relief presents evidence for a further challenge to, rather than, as scholars have typically proposed, substantiating proof of Rome-centred models. Barbara Spaeth has proposed a lost Hellenistic prototype, which she and others have assigned to Alexandria, as the model informing both the Ara Pacis and Louvre Tellus panels.[62] Under the assumption that a paradigmatic reference to a famous source is an intentional aspect of the monument, the question then becomes by what route the image travelled to Carthage. But it seems as likely that the image

---

[58] Beard, North, and Price, 1998: 331: 'It is likely that the altar was produced locally, in Carthage, though we do not know how knowledge of the Roman monuments was disseminated.'

[59] Evidence for artists travelling for commissions in Luna marble is extremely slight. See Russell, 2014: 333–6.

[60] On pattern-books and workshop organisation: Stauffer, 2008; Schmidt-Colinet, 2009; Clarke, 2010. On the Artemidorus Papyrus as a workbook: Settis, 2008; Elsner, 2009.

[61] The literature is vast. Some key studies include, but are by no means limited to, Borbein, 1975 on the form and decoration of earlier Greek altars; Galinsky, 1996 on Greek precedents for the altar's entire image programme; Billows, 1993, Conlin, 1997, Holliday, 2002 on procession scenes; and Castriota, 1995 and Sauron, 2000 on plant and vegetal imagery. Bordignon, 2010 provides a thorough summary of the history of scholarship.

[62] Torelli, 1982; Spaeth, 1994.

reached Carthage directly via Alexandria, or the Greek east more broadly, as that it did so from Rome. The fact that we might imagine other significant sources for the motif, and the impossibility of deciding between them, suggests that the idea of quotation itself should be called into question. This may simply be a standard form for an earth- or fecundity-related divinity.

The goddess Roma too need not have a geographical origin in Rome. Roma was a universal aspect of imperial cult, east and west.[63] From the second century BCE, cults of the goddess proliferated in the Greek east in response to Roman conquest. What is more, since 29 BCE, imperial cult had taken the form of the joint worship of Roma and Augustus.[64] Although no other early images of Roma survive, there is no reason to believe that the Ara Pacis had a monopoly on the representation of the goddess. We do not need to propose that these familial resemblances result from direct descent. The very universal presence of the goddess in imperial cult makes the possibility of another prototype highly plausible. We should thus see Roma and Tellus as variants of a commonly diffused image type without determinant genetic relationships to state monuments in the centre.[65]

The potential 'sources' of the other images comprising the altar's decorative programme also pose problems for the imitation model. Images of Aeneas' flight from Troy were similarly ubiquitous (Fig. 8.5).[66] The motif was widespread both in major and minor forms: sculpture in the round, sculptural relief panels on provincial state monuments, domestic wall-paintings, lamps, terracotta statuettes, and coins. Moreover, the image had a long life, dating as early as the fifth century BCE, before Caesar and then Augustus employed it as the symbol of the legendary origins of the *gens Iulia*.[67]

The fact that images of Aeneas, Roma, and Tellus appeared on monuments in both Rome and Carthage actually introduces more interesting questions about why certain images 'travelled' more than others. Does an image appear with higher frequency in the archaeological record because it was used in the decorative programme of a major monument in the capital, or because it best visualised an ideological message? The image of Apollo

[63] On the early development of imperial cult: Price, 1984; Hänlein-Schäfer, 1985; Fishwick, 1987; Galinsky, 1996; Gradel, 2002. On the cult of Roma specifically: Mannsperger, 1974; Fayer, 1976; Mellor, 1981.

[64] Cass. Dio 51.20.6–8. For interpretation, see Gradel, 2002: 73–6; Koortbojian, 2013: 228–9.

[65] Discussions of visual composition in relation to language are long-standing. Cf. Hölscher, 2004.

[66] Fuchs, 1973; de la Barrera and Trillmich, 1996; Dardenay, 2010.

[67] See *LIMC* I, s.v. 'Aineias' (F. Canciani) for the earlier Greek and Etruscan examples.

demonstrates that it was certainly sometimes the latter. Apollo was a personal divinity of Augustus and the presence of the god on the altar represents an ideologically charged choice. While Hedulus' image of Apollo Citharoedus recalls a very popular Hellenistic statuary group, it has no parallels, as far as we know, on state monuments in Rome (Fig. 8.6).[68] The particular portrayal of Apollo on Hedulus' altar, seated on a griffin with his lyre and extending a laurel branch in his outstretched arm towards a tripod, actually shows the greatest affinity with a motif featured on gold staters struck by the Hellenistic king Pharnaces II of the Bosporus.[69] On the one hand, the image, like that of Tellus, attests to the endurance of pre-Roman image cultures in Carthage. On the other, the image, likely selected personally by Hedulus or his artist, suggests the degree to which provincials were capable of reproducing the sophisticated ideological logic of the Augustan regime independent of the emperor and his court.[70]

Finally, the scene of sacrifice prompts us to consider the extent to which the artist of a provincial monument could compose an image without a model. For obvious reasons, scenes of sacrifice are incredibly common features of altar dedications. The likeness among the surviving compositions is extraordinary: a *togatus capite velato* performs a *praefatio*, a preliminary libation, at an altar surrounded by attendants who carry ritual implements, a flute player, and a *victimarius* leading a bull. The resemblance is so close that Otto Brendel proposed that all derived from a single Italic model which established the artistic conventions for depicting Roman sacrifice.[71] The sacrifice represented on Hedulus' altar departs from the canonical example: the *victimarius* usually leads the bull towards the altar opposite the sacrificant, rather than standing behind him; and, many more attendants are typically shown in a tighter grouping around the altar, so as to fill out the composition. While the image does not replicate the most prominent Italic examples, it does not necessarily depart from the lived experience of Roman sacrifice; all the necessary ritual elements of Roman sacrifice are there: the togate sacrificant with covered head, the altar, the *patera* with incense and wine to invite the gods to the sacrifice

---

[68] An early imperial altar from the theatre in Arles represents the figures from this very grouping in relief on three of its faces; see Espérandieu, 1907: 117–18, no. 138; Sauron, 1991, 1994: 545–6; Carrier, 2005–6: 377–81.

[69] Golenko and Karyszkowski, 1972.

[70] Simon, 1978; *LIMC* II, s.v. 'Apollon' (O. Palagia). On Roman copies of the statuary group of Apollo and Marsyas and their potential meaning: Newby, 2016: 70–9. Some scholars have suggested a close parallel with the Avellino relief in the Museum of Fine Arts, Budapest: Poinssot, 1929; Strong and Strong, 1992; followed by Davies, 2011: 219 no. 10.

[71] Brendel, 1930.

(*praefatio*), the double-flute player (*tibicen*) making the musical accompaniment, attendants to assist the sacrificant, and the animal victim. On the one hand, the 'deviations' of the Carthaginian version suggest that if images were generated in the capital, they may not have circulated equally across the empire. On the other hand, they demonstrate that the similarity of sacrificial compositions may reflect the uniformity of Roman religious culture as much as a culture of artistic imitation, with the prescriptiveness of Roman ritual ensuring a kind of visual consistency.

If we do away with the old circulation models, many of the novel features of the panels' composition could be easily attributed to the personal preferences of the patron or artist. For example, modern scholars have often characterised the sacrificial scene on Hedulus' altar as 'clumsy', with an overcrowding of figures in the right half of the visual field (Fig. 8.3).[72] While symmetry and balance might be characteristics of relief panels on other altars or monuments, or simply reflect our own aesthetic preferences and expectations, they do not describe the designs of the artist who executed the reliefs of the *Gens Augusta* altar. This artist, in contrast, favoured strong, raking diagonals running from the top right to three quarters of the way towards the left. The Carthaginian altar's departure from canonical Roman models served to align the head of the protagonist of the image, the togate sacrificant, possibly a portrait of Hedulus, with the diagonal. While creating pronounced asymmetries, this formal choice did not result in inelegant compositions. Taking the artist's choices under more serious consideration better explains the disposition of the figures. In the same vein, the unique arrangement of the Apollo panel (Fig. 8.6) seems to have been specifically composed for its setting on this altar monument in order to create a visual parallelism with the Roma panel directly opposite it (Fig. 8.4).[73] Many of the so-called 'departures' may result from the artist's desire to create a unified visual presentation across the four sides of the altar.

Direct imitation of images on Roman monuments certainly occurred, and it is not impossible that Hedulus and the patron of the Louvre-Algiers altar competed for social capital among Carthage's most elite and aesthetic-minded audiences by seeking to incorporate allusions to the Ara Pacis in individual panels of much larger image programmes. Yet, this type of image relationship, I argue, should not be the default. This presentation

---

[72] For the scene's similarity to Roman models: Beard, North, and Price, 1998: 333–4; McCarty, 2011: 218–19. On the canonical composition: Brendel, 1930. On the composition's clumsiness: Ryberg, 1955.

[73] Beard, North, and Price, 1998: 333.

of alternative sources for the images on Hedulus' altar demonstrates that in every case, including Roma, an image need not point specifically back to the Ara Pacis, Augustus, or Rome. To assume that the capital was the only source for imperial images, or the only means by which images could acquire imperial ideological meanings, in fact, underestimates the extent and complexity of both circulation networks and the image culture of the early empire.

Conclusion: The Limits of Imperial Control

Hedulus' cult to the *Gens Augusta* aligns with broader trends in ruler cult across the empire. The epigraphic record attests to *sacerdotes* and *flamines* (*perpetui* and not) of the *domus Augusta*, *domus divina*, and *Augustorum*, as well as *flaminicae Augustarum*. There was even an *archierus*, a relatively rare Greek loan word meaning 'chief priest', of the *domus Augusta in perpetuum*.[74] This evidence attests that people across the empire seem to have received the memo concerning the new imperial ideology: Augustus is now to be worshipped together with his family, conceived in both a horizontal (Augustus, his wife, and the members of the imperial family) and vertical manner (the living emperor and his divinised predecessors). But the sheer multiplicity and variety of responses suggests that to a large degree the incorporation of these new ideologies into the infrastructure of ruler cult was being worked out locally on the ground across the empire by people who were attentive or attuned to ideological messaging from the centre but who were also responding to local concerns and constraints.

Why should the process of assembling images have been any different? To read the altars in Carthage as miniature versions of the Ara Pacis reflects art-historical and archaeological biases towards seeing extant works of art in relation to other extant works, and towards privileging Rome as the centre of creativity and artistic ingenuity. By focusing on the images and their sources, it may be that we have been asking the wrong questions. The images on Hedulus' altar are inseparable from the material history of its construction and design, and from the local social dynamics of early imperial Carthage. We should no longer be exclusively exploring the ways in which images with their associated ideological meanings get from

---

[74] West, 1931: no. 68; Spawforth, 1994: 218. On the establishment of provincial ruler cult in Achaea: Fishwick, 2002: 127–32.

Rome to Carthage, but the ways in which material and social networks interact to produce and reproduce imperial ideology in local contexts.

Bibliography

Alcock, S. E., M. Egri, and J. F. D. Frakes (eds.) 2016. *Beyond Boundaries: Connecting Visual Cultures in the Provinces of Ancient Rome* (Los Angeles: Getty).

Ando, C. 2000. *Imperial Ideology and Provincial Loyalty in the Roman Empire* (Berkeley: University of California Press).

Bassignano, M. S. 1974. *Il flaminato nelle province romane dell'Africa* (Rome: Istituto di Storia Antica II).

Beard, M., J. North, and S. R. F. Price 1998. *Religions of Rome*, Vol. 1 (New York; Cambridge: Cambridge University Press).

Bendlin, A. 1997. 'Peripheral centres – central peripheries: religious communication in the Roman Empire', in Cancik, H. and J. Rüpke (eds.), *Römische Reichsreligion und Provinzialreligion* (Tübingen: Mohr Siebeck), 35–68.

   2001. 'Rituals or beliefs? "Religion" and the religious life of Rome', *SCI* 20: 191–208.

Bernard, H., J. C. Bessac, P. Mardikian, and M. Feugère 1998. 'L'épave romaine de marbre de Porto Nuovo', *JRA* 11: 53–81.

Billows, R. 1993. 'The religious procession of the Ara Pacis Augustae: Augustus' supplicatio in 13 B.C.E.', *JRA* 6: 80–92.

Bodel, J. P. 1983. *Roman Brick Stamps in the Kelsey Museum* (Ann Arbor: University of Michigan Press).

Borbein, A. H. 1975. 'Die Ara Pacis Augustae: Geschichtliche Wirklichkeit und Programm', *JDAI* 90: 242–66.

Bordignon, G. 2010. *Ara Pacis Augustae* (Venice: Cafoscarina).

Boschung, D. 2003. 'Die stadtrömischen Monumente des Augustus und ihre Rezeption im Reich', in Noelke, P., F. Naumann-Steckner, and B. Schneider (eds.), *Romanisation und Resistenz in Plastik, Architektur und Inschriften der Provinzen des Imperium Romanum* (Mainz: Philipp von Zabern), 1–12.

Brendel, O. 1930. '*Immolatio boum*', *MDAI* 45.3–4: 196–226.

Brent, A. 2010. *Cyprian and Carthage* (Cambridge: Cambridge University Press).

Briand-Ponsart, C. 2003. 'Thugga et Thamugadi: exemples des cités africaines', in Cébeillac Gervasoni, M. and L. Lamoine (eds.), *Les élites et leurs facettes: les élites locales dans le monde hellénistique et romain* (Rome: École française de Rome), 241–66.

Broekaert, W. 2016. 'Freedmen and agency in Roman business', in Wilson, A. and M. Flohr (eds.), *Urban Craftsmen and Traders in the Roman World* (Oxford: Oxford University Press), 222–53.

Cagnat, R. 1913. 'Un temple de la Gens Augusta à Carthage', *CRAI* 57.9: 680–6.

Carrier, C. 2005–6. 'Sculptures augustéennes du théâtre d'Arles', *Revue archéologique de Narbonnaise* 38–9: 365–96.

Castrén, P. 1975. *Ordo Populusque Pompeianus: Polity and Society in Roman Pompeii.* Acta Instituti Romani Finlandiae 8 (Rome: Bardi).

Castriota, D. 1995. *The Ara Pacis Augustae and the Imagery of Abundance in Later Greek and Roman Imperial Art* (Princeton: Princeton University Press).

Clarke, J. R. 2010. 'Model-book, outline book, figure book: new observations on the creation of near-exact copies', in Bragantini, I. (ed.), *Atti del X Congresso Internazionale dell'Association Internationale pour la peinture murale antique, Napoli 17–21 Settembre 2007* (Naples: Istituto Universitario Orientale di Napoli), 203–14.

Coles, A. 2017. 'Between patronage and prejudice: freedman magistrates in the late Roman Republic and Empire', *TAPhA* 147: 179–208.

Conlin, D. A. 1997. *Artists of the Ara Pacis: The Process of Hellenization in Roman Relief Sculpture* (Chapel Hill: University of North Carolina Press).

Cornwell, H. 2017. *Pax and the Politics of Peace: Republic to Principate* (Oxford: Oxford University Press).

Dardenay, A. 2007. 'Le rôle de l'image des *primordia Vrbis* dans l'expression du culte imperial', in Nogales, T. and J. González (eds.), *Culto Imperial: política y poder* (Rome: 'L'Erma' di Bretschneider), 153–72.

    2010. *Les mythes fondateurs de Rome: images et politique dans l'Occident romain* (Paris: Picard).

Davies, S. H. 2011. 'An Augustan-period altar at Carthage: freedman status and Roman provincial identity', in Martin, S. and D. Butler, *It's Good to be King: The Archaeology of Power and Authority. Proceedings of the 41st (2008) Annual Chacmool Archaeological Conference, University of Calgary, Alberta, Canada* (Calgary: Chacmool Archaeological Association), 213–24.

de la Barrera, J. L. and W. Trillmich 1996. 'Eine Wiederholung der Aeneas-Gruppe vom Forum Augustum samt ihrer Inschrift in Mérida (Spanien)', *MDAI(R)* 103: 119–38.

Deneauve, J. 1979. 'Les structures romaines de Byrsa: historique des recherches', in Lancel, S. (ed.), *Byrsa I: Mission archéologique française à Carthage; rapports préliminaires des fouilles (1974–1976)*, Collection de l'École française de Rome 41.1 (Rome: École française de Rome), 41–55.

    1990. 'Le centre monumental de Carthage: un ensemble cultuel sur la colline de Byrsa', in Lancel, S. (ed.), *Carthage et son territoire dans l'antiquité: Actes du IVᵉ colloque international sur l'histoire et l'archéologie de l'Afrique du Nord*, Vol. 1 (Paris: Comité des travaux historiques et scientifiques), 143–55.

Dowling, M. B. 2006. *Clemency and Cruelty in the Roman World* (Ann Arbor: University of Michigan Press).

Elsner, J. 2009. 'P. Artemid.: the images', in Brodersen, K. and J. Elsner (eds.), *Images and Texts on the Artemidorus Papyrus* (Stuttgart: Franz Steiner Verlag), 43–6.

Espérandieu, E. 1907. *Recueil général des bas-reliefs, statues et bustes de la Gaule romaine*, vol. 1 (Paris: Imprimerie nationale).

Estienne, S. 2010. '*Simulacra deorum* versus *ornamenta aedium*: the status of divine images in the temples of Rome', in Mylonopoulos, J. (ed.), *Divine Images and Human Imaginations in Ancient Greece and Rome*. Religions in the Graeco-Roman World 170 (Leiden; Boston: Brill), 257–71.

Fant, J. C. 1988. 'The Roman emperors in the marble business: capitalists, middle-men, or philanthropists?' in Herz, N. and M. Waelkens (eds.), *Classical Marble: Geochemistry, Technology, and Trade*. Nato ASI Series 153 (Dordrecht: Springer), 147–58.

   1993. 'Ideology, gift, and trade: a distribution model for Roman imperial marbles', in Harris, W. V. (ed.), *The Inscribed Economy*. Journal of Roman Archaeology Supplement 6 (Providence: Journal of Roman Archaeology), 145–70.

Fayer, C. 1976. *Il culto della dea Roma: origine e diffusione nell'Impero* (Pescara: Trimestre).

Fishwick, D. 1981. 'From *flamen* to *sacerdos*: the title of the provincial priest of Africa Proconsularis', *BCTH* 17: 337–44.

   1987. *The Imperial Cult in the Latin West*, Part 1: *Studies in the Ruler Cult of the Western Provinces of the Roman Empire*, 2 vols. (Leiden: Brill).

   1996. 'The origins of Africa Proconsularis, III: the era of the Cereres again', *AntAfr* 32: 13–36.

   1998. 'The provincial priesthood of L. Calpurnius Augustalis', *AntAfr* 34: 73–82.

   2002. *The Imperial Cult in the Latin West*, Vol. 3: *Provincial Cult*, Part 1: *Institution and Evolution* (Leiden: Brill).

   2014. 'Iconography and ideology: the statue group in the temple of Mars Ultor', in Fishwick, D., *Cult Places and Cult Personnel in the Roman Empire* (Farnham: Ashgate), 63–94.

Fishwick, D. and B. Shaw 1978. 'The era of the Cereres', *Historia* 27: 343–54.

Fittschen, K. 1976. 'Zum angeblichen Bildnis des Lucius Verus im Thermen Museum', *JDAI* 86: 214–52.

Flory, M. B. 1996. 'Dynastic ideology, the *domus Augusta*, and imperial women: a lost statuary group in the Circus Flaminius', *TAPhA* 126: 287–306.

Franklin, J. L. 2001. '*Pompeis Difficile Est*': *Studies in the Political Life of Imperial Pompeii* (Ann Arbor: University of Michigan Press).

Fuchs, W. 1973. 'Die Bildgeschichte der Flucht des Aeneas', *ANRW* I.4: 615–32.

Galinsky, K. 1996. *Augustan Culture* (Princeton: Princeton University Press).

Garnsey, P. 1981. 'Independent freedmen and the economy of Roman Italy under the principate', *Klio* 63: 359–71.

Goldbeck, V. 2015. *Fora augusta: Das Augustusforum und seine Rezeption im Westen des Imperium Romanum*. Eikoniká: Kunstwissenschaftliche Beiträge 5 (Regensburg: Schnell und Steiner).

Golenko, K. V. and P. J. Karyszkowski 1972. 'The gold coinage of King Pharnaces of the Bosporus', *NC* ser. 7, 12: 25–38.

Gordon, M. L. 1924. 'The nationality of slaves under the early Roman Empire', *JRS* 14: 93–111.

Gradel, I. 2002. *Emperor Worship and Roman Religion* (Oxford: Oxford University Press).

Gros, P. 1990. 'Le premier urbanisme de la Colonia Julia Carthago: mythes et réalités d'une fondation césaro-augustéenne', in *L'Afrique dans l'Occident romain (Ier siècle av. J.C.–IVe siècle ap. J.C.)*. Publications de l'École française de Rome 134 (Rome: École française de Rome), 547–73.

Hallett, C. H. 2004. Review of D. Boschung, *Gens Augusta: Untersuchungen zu Aufstellung, Wirkung und Bedeutung der Statuengruppen des julisch-claudischen Kaiserhauses*, Gnomon 76.5: 437–45.

Hänlein-Schäfer, H. 1985. *Veneratio Augusti: Eine Studie zu den Tempeln des ersten römischen Kaisers*. Archaeologica 39 (Rome: Bretschneider).

Helen, T. 1975. *Organization of Roman Brick Production in the First and Second Centuries: An Interpretation of Roman Brick Stamps* (Helsinki: Suomalainen Tiedeakatemia).

Hemelrijk, E. A. 2005. 'Priestesses of the imperial cult in the Latin west: titles and functions', *AC* 74: 137–70.

Herrmann, J. J. Jr, D. Attanasio, R. H. Tykot, and A. van den Hoek 2012. 'Characterization and distribution of marble from Cap de Garde and Mt. Filfila, Algeria', in Gutiérrez Garcia-Moreno, A., P. Lapuente Mercadal, and I. Rodà de Lllanza (eds.), *Interdisciplinary Studies on Ancient Stone: Proceedings of the IX Association for the Study of Marbles and Other Stones in Antiquity (ASMOSIA) Conference (Tarragona 2009)* (Tarragona: Institut Català d'Arqueologia Clàssica), 300–9.

Hingley, R. 2005. *Globalizing Roman Culture: Unity, Diversity and Empire* (London: Routledge).

Hodder, I. 2012. *Entangled: An Archaeology of the Relationships between Humans and Things* (Oxford: Wiley-Blackwell).

Holliday, P. J. 2002. *The Origins of Roman Historical Commemoration in the Visual Arts* (New York; Cambridge: Cambridge University Press).

Hölscher, T. 1984. *Staatsdenkmal und Publikum: vom Untergang der Republik bis zur Festigung des Kaisertums in Rom* (Konstanz: Universitätsverlag Konstanz).

— 2004. *The Language of Images in Roman Art* (Cambridge: Cambridge University Press).

Hurst, H. 2010. 'Understanding Carthage as a Roman port', in Keay, S. and G. Boetto (eds.), *Ostia and the Ports of the Roman Mediterranean: Contributions from Archaeology and History. 17th AIAC International Congress of Classical Archaeology* (Rome: Bollettino di Archeologia Online), 49–68.

Joyce, L. B. 2015. 'Roma and the virtuous breast', *MAAR* 59/60: 1–49.

Kantiréa, M. 2007. *Les dieux et les dieux augustes: le culte impérial en Grèce sous les Julio-claudiens et les Flaviens: études épigraphiques et archéologiques.*

Meletemata (Kentron Hellenikes kai Romaikes Archaiotetos) 50 (Athens: Research Centre for Greek and Roman Antiquity, National Hellenic Research Foundation).

Kent, J. H. 1966. *Corinth: Results of Excavations Conducted by the American School of Classical Studies at Athens*, Vol. 8, Part 3: *The Inscriptions 1926-1950* (Princeton: American School of Classical Studies at Athens).

Koortbojian, M. 2013. *The Divinization of Caesar and Augustus: Precedents, Consequences, and Implications* (Cambridge: Cambridge University Press).

Kraus, T. 1979. 'Zum Mars Ultor-Relief in Algier', in Kopcke, G. and M. B. Moore (eds.), *Studies in Classical Art and Archaeology: A Tribute to Peter Heinrich von Blanckenhagen* (Locust Valley: J. J. Augustin): 239–45.

Laird, M. 2015. *Civic Monuments and the Augustales in Roman Italy* (Cambridge: Cambridge University Press).

Le Glay, M. 1985. 'Les premiers temps de Carthage romaine: pour une révise des dates', *BCTH* 19B: 235–48.

   1990a. 'Évergétisme et vie religieuse dans l'Afrique romaine', in *L'Afrique dans l'Occident romain (Ier siècle av. J.C.-IVe siècle ap. J.C.)*. Publications de l'École française de Rome 134 (Rome: École française de Rome), 77–88.

   1990b. 'La place des affranchis dans la vie municipale et dans la vie religieuse', *MEFRA* 102: 621–38.

Long, L. 1999. 'Carte archéologique: Camargue et Rhône', *Bilan scientifique – Département des recherches archéologiques subaquatiques et sous-marines*: 41–6.

Lott, J. B. 2004. *The Neighborhoods of Augustan Rome* (Cambridge: Cambridge University Press).

   2014/15. 'The earliest Augustan gods outside Rome', *CJ* 110: 129–58.

Manders, E. 2012. *Coining Images of Power: Patterns in the Representation of Roman Emperors on Imperial Coinage, A D 193–284*. Impact of Empire 15. (Leiden: Brill).

Mannsperger, D. 1974. 'ROM.ET.AVG. Die Selbstdarstellung des Kaisertums in der römischen Reichsprägung', *ANRW* II.1: 919–96.

McCarty, M. 2011. 'Representations and the "meaning" of ritual change: the case of Hadrumetum', in Chaniotis, A. (ed.), *Ritual Dynamics in the Ancient Mediterranean: Agency, Emotion, Gender, Representation*. Heidelberger althistorische Beiträge und epigraphische Studien 49 (Stuttgart: Steiner), 197–228.

McIntyre, G. 2016. *A Family of Gods: The Worship of the Imperial Family in the Latin West* (Ann Arbor: University of Michigan Press).

Mellor, R. 1981. 'The goddess Roma', *ANRW* II.17.2: 950–1030.

Millis, B. W. 2014. 'The local magistrates and elite of Roman Corinth', in Friesen, S. J., S. James, and D. Schowalter (eds.), *Corinth in Contrast: Studies in Inequality* (Leiden: Brill), 38–53.

Mouritsen, H. 1988. *Elections, Magistrates, and Municipal Élite: Studies in Pompeian Epigraphy* (Rome: Bretschneider).

2005. 'Freedmen and decurions: epitaphs and social history in imperial Italy',
    JRS 95: 38–63.

Naerebout, F. G. 2008. 'Global Romans? Is globalisation a concept that is going to
    help us understand the Roman empire?', *Talanta* 38/9: 149–70.

Newby, Z. 2016. *Greek Myths in Roman Art and Culture: Imagery, Values and
    Identity in Italy, 50 BCE–AD 250* (Cambridge: Cambridge University Press).

Noreña, C. 2011. *Imperial Ideals in the Roman West: Representation, Circulation,
    Power* (Cambridge: Cambridge University Press).

Pensabene, P. 2002. 'Il fenomeno del marmo nel mondo romano', in De Nuccio, M.
    and L. Ungaro (eds.), *I marmi colorati della Roma imperiale* (Venice:
    Marsilio), 3–67.

    2004. 'La diffusione del marmo lunense nelle province occidentali', in
    S. F. Romallo (ed.), *La decóracion arquitectónica en las ciudades romanas
    de occidente* (Murcia: Universidad), 421–43.

    2013. 'Il marmo lunense nei programmi architettonici e statuari dell'Occidente
    romano', in Garcia-Entero, V. (ed), *El marmor en Hispania: explotación, uso
    y difusión en época romana* (Madrid: UNED), 17–48.

Petersen, L. H. 2006. *The Freedman in Roman Art and Art History* (Cambridge:
    Cambridge University Press).

Picard, C. 1984. 'Demeter et Kore à Carthage: problèmes d'iconographie', *Kokalos*
    28–9 [1982/3]: 187–94.

Pitts, M. and M. J. Versluys (eds.) 2015. *Globalisation and the Roman World:
    Perspectives and Opportunities* (Cambridge: Cambridge University Press).

Poinssot, L. 1913–16. 'Inscriptions de Thugga découvertes en 1910–1913',
    NouvArch 21: 1–227.

    1919. 'Les fouilles de Dougga en 1919 et le quartier du forum', *NouvArch* 22:
    133–98.

    1929. *L'autel de la Gens Augusta à Carthage*. Notes et documents publiés par la
    Direction des antiquités et arts 10 (Paris; Tunis: Protectorat français;
    Gouvernement tunisien).

Pollini, J. 2012. *From Republic to Empire: Rhetoric, Religion, and Power in the Visual
    Culture of Ancient Rome* (Norman: University of Oklahoma Press).

Price, S. R. F. 1984. *Rituals and Power: The Roman Imperial Cult in Asia Minor*
    (Cambridge: Cambridge University Press).

Purcell, N. 1995. 'On the sacking of Carthage and Corinth', in Innes, D., H. Hine,
    and C. Pelling (eds.), *Ethics and Rhetoric: Classical Essays for Donald Russell
    on his Seventy-Fifth Birthday* (Oxford: Oxford University Press), 133–48.

Rakob, F. 2000. 'The making of Augustan Carthage', in Fentress, E. (ed.),
    Romanization and the City: Creation, Transformations, and Failures.
    Journal of Roman Archaeology Supplement 38 (Portsmouth, RI: Journal
    of Roman Archaeology), 73–82.

Rice, C., A. Wilson, and K. Schörle 2012. 'Roman ports and Mediterranean con-
    nectivity', in Keay, S. (ed.), *Rome, Portus and the Mediterranean,*

Archaeological Monographs of the British School at Rome 21 (London: British School at Rome), 367–92.

Richardson, L. 1988. *Pompeii: An Architectural History* (Baltimore: Johns Hopkins University Press).

Rives, J. B. 1995. *Religion and Authority in Roman Carthage from Augustus to Constantine* (Oxford: Oxford University Press).

——— 2001. 'Imperial cult and native tradition in Roman North Africa', *CJ* 96: 425–36.

Rose, C. B. 1997. *Dynastic Commemoration and Imperial Portraiture in the Julio-Claudian Period* (Cambridge: Cambridge University Press).

Rowe, G. 2002. *Princes and Political Cultures: The New Tiberian Senatorial Decrees* (Ann Arbor: University of Michigan Press).

Ruffing, K. 2016. 'Driving forces for specialization: market, location factors, productivity improvements', in Wilson, A. and M. Flohr (eds.), *Urban Craftsmen and Traders in the Roman World* (Oxford: Oxford University Press), 115–31.

Russell, A. 2016. *The Politics of Public Space in Republican Rome* (Cambridge: Cambridge University Press).

Russell, B. 2012. 'Shipwrecks and stone cargoes: some observations', in Gutiérrez Garcia-Moreno, A., P. Lapuente Mercadal, and I. Rodà de Lllanza (eds.), *Interdisciplinary Studies on Ancient Stone: Proceedings of the IX Association for the Study of Marbles and Other Stones in Antiquity (ASMOSIA) Conference (Tarragona 2009)* (Tarragona: Institut Català d'Arqueologia Clàssica), 533–9.

——— 2014. *The Economics of the Roman Stone Trade* (Oxford: Oxford University Press).

Ryberg, I. S. 1955. *Rites of the State Religion in Roman Art* (Rome: American Academy in Rome).

Saastamoinen, A. 2000. 'Some remarks on the development of the style of Roman building inscriptions in Roman North Africa', *AfrRom* 13: 1684–94.

——— 2008a. The Phraseology and Structure of Latin Building Inscriptions in Roman North Africa. PhD Diss: Helsinki.

——— 2008b. 'Some observations on the authorship of building inscriptions', *AfrRom* 17: 237–52.

Saint-Amans, S. 2004. *Topographie religieuse de Thugga (Dougga)* (Bordeaux: Ausonius).

Saumagne, C. 1924. 'Notes de topographie Carthaginoise: la colline Saint-Louis', *BCTH* 5B: 177–93, 629–47.

——— 1979. 'Le métroon de Carthage et ses abords', manuscript published posthumously by Ennabli, A., J. Deneauve, P. Gros, and S. Lancel, in Lancel S. (ed.), *Byrsa I: Mission archéologique française à Carthage; Rapports préliminaires des fouilles (1974–1976)* (Rome: École française de Rome), 283–310.

Sauron, G. 1991. 'L'espace sacrificiel dans les civilisations méditerranéennes de l'Antiquité', in *L'espace sacrificiel dans les civilizations méditerranéennes de l'Antiquité. Actes du colloque, Maison de l'Orient, Lyon 4–7 juin 1988* (Paris: De Boccard): 205–16.

1994. *Quis deum? L'expression plastique des idéologies politiques et religieuses à Rome.* Bibliothèque des Écoles françaises d'Athènes et de Rome 285 (Rome: École française de Rome).

2000. *L'Histoire végétalisée: ornament et politique à Rome* (Paris: Picard).

Scheid, J. 2005. *Quand faire, c'est croire* (Paris: Aubier).

2007. 'Le sens des rites: l'exemple romain', in Bonnet, C. and J. Scheid (eds.), *Rites et croyances dans les religions du monde romain: huit exposés suivis de discussions.* Entretiens Hardt 53 (Geneva: Fondation Hardt), 39–63.

Schmidt-Colinet, A. 2009. '"Musterbücher" statt "Meisterforschung": zum Verständnis antiker Werkstattstrukturen und Produktionsprozesse', *JRA* 22: 787–92.

Schörner, G. 2006. 'Opferritual und Opferdarstellung im römischen Kleinasien: ein Testfall für das Zentrum-Peripherie-Modell', in Erdkamp, P., O. Hekster, G. de Kleijn, S. T. A. M. Mols, and L. de Blois (eds.), *The Impact of Imperial Rome on Religions, Ritual and Religious Life in the Roman Empire* (Leiden: Brill), 138–49.

2009. 'Bild und Vorbild: Nordafrika – Rom – Kleinasien', in Cancik, H. and J. Rüpke (eds.), *Die Religion des Imperium Romanum: Koine und Konfrontationen* (Tübingen: Mohr Siebeck), 249–71.

Scott, S. and J. Webster (eds.) 2003. *Roman Imperialism and Provincial Art* (New York: Cambridge University Press).

Sebaï, L. L. 2005. *La colline de Byrsa à l'époque romaine: étude épigraphique et état de la question.* Karthago: Revue d'archéologie méditerranéenne 26 (Paris: CEAM).

Sebaï, M. 2005. 'La romanisation en Afrique, retour sur un débat. La résistance africaine: une approche libératrice?' *Afrique et Histoire* 3: 39–56.

Setälä, P. 1977. *Private domini in Roman Brick Stamps of the Empire: A Historical and Prosopographical Study of Landowners in the District of Rome* (Helsinki: Institutum Romanum Finlandiae).

Settis, S. 1988. 'Die Ara Pacis', in W. D. Heilmeyer, E. La Rocca, and H. G. Martin (eds.), *Kaiser Augustus und die Verlorene Republik: Eine Ausstellung im Martin-Gropius-Bau Berlin 7. Juni–14. August 1988* (Mainz: Philipp von Zabern), 400–26.

2008. 'Il contributo del papiro alla storia dell'arte antica', in Gallazzi, C., B. Krämer, and S. Settis (eds.), *Il papiro di Artemidoro* (Milan: LED, Edizioni Universitarie di Lettere Economia Diritto), 576–616.

Severy, B. 2000. 'Family and state in the early imperial monarchy: the *Senatus Consultum de Pisone Patre*, Tabula Siarensis, and Tabula Hebana', *CP* 95: 318–37.

Simon, E. 1978. 'Apollo in Rom', *JDAI* 93: 202–27.

1986. *Augustus: Kunst und Leben in Rom um die Zeitenwende* (Munich: Hirmer).

Smadja, E. 1980. 'Remarques sur les débuts du culte impérial en Afrique sous le regne d'Auguste', in *Religions, pouvoir, rapports sociaux.* Collection de l'Institut des sciences et techniques de l'antiquité 32. Annales littéraires de l'Université de Besançon 237 (Paris: Les Belles Lettres), 151–69.

Smith, R. R. R. 2013. *The Marble Reliefs from the Julio-Claudian Sebasteion.* Aphrodisias 6 (Mainz: Philipp von Zabern).

Solin, H. 1982. *Die griechischen Personennamen in Rom, II.* CIL Auctarium (New York: De Gruyter).

  1996. *Die stadtrömischen Sklavennamen. Ein Namenbuch I-III.* Forschungen zur antiken Sklaverei, Beiheft 2 (Stuttgart: Franz Steiner).

Spaeth, B. S. 1994. 'The goddess Ceres in the Ara Pacis Augustae and the Carthage relief', *AJA* 98: 65–100.

Spawforth, A. J. 1994. 'Corinth, Argos, and the imperial cult: Pseudo-Julian, *Letters* 198', *Hesperia* 63: 211–32.

  1996. 'Roman Corinth: the formation of a colonial elite', in Rizakis, A. D. (ed.), *Roman Onomastics in the Greek East: Social and Political Aspects* (Athens: Research Centre for Greek and Roman Antiquity, National Hellenic Research Foundation), 167–82.

Stauffer, A. 2008. *Antike Musterblätter: Wirkkartons aus dem spätantiken und frühbyzantinischen Ägypten* (Wiesbaden: Reichert).

Steinby, M. 1993. L'organizzazione produttiva dei laterizi: un modello interpretativo per l'instrumentum in genere?' in Harris, W. V. (ed.), *The Inscribed Economy: Production and Distribution in the Roman Empire in the Light of Instrumentum Domesticum.* Journal of Roman Archaeology Supplement 6 (Portsmouth, RI: Journal of Roman Archaeology), 139–43.

Stemmer, K. 1978. *Untersuchungen zur Typologie, Chronologie, und Ikonographie von Panzerstatuen* (Berlin: Gebrüder Mann).

Sterrett-Krause, A. E. 2012. The Impacts of Private Donations in the Civic Landscapes of Roman Africa Proconsularis. PhD Diss: Cincinnati.

Strong, D. and R. Strong 1992. *Roman Art*, 3rd ed. (New Haven: Yale University Press).

Taylor, L. R. 1961. 'Freedmen and freeborn in the epitaphs of imperial Rome', *AJPh* 82: 113–32.

Torelli, M. 1982. *Typology and Structure of Roman Historical Reliefs* (Ann Arbor: University of Michigan Press).

Treggiari, S. 1969. *Roman Freedmen during the Late Republic* (Oxford: Oxford University Press).

Van Andringa, W. 2009. *Quotidien des dieux et des hommes: la vie religieuse dans les cités du Vésuve à l'Époque Romaine.* Bibliothèque des Écoles françaises d'Athènes et de Rome 337 (Rome: École française de Rome).

  2011. 'Architecture et archéologie d'un lieu de culte romain: le temple de Fortune Auguste à Pompéi', in Quantin, F. (ed.), *Archéologie des religions antiques: contributions à l'étude des sanctuaires et de la piété en Méditerranée (Grèce, Italie, Sicile, Espagne)* (Pau: Presses de l'Université de Pau et des pays de l'Adour), 141–50.

  2012. 'Statues in the temples of Pompeii: combinations of gods, local definition of cults and the memory of the city', in Dignas, B. and B. Smith (eds.),

Historical and Religious Memory in the Ancient World (Oxford: Oxford University Press), 83–115.

2015. "'*M. Tullius . . . aedem Fortunae August(ae) solo et peq(unia) sua*": private foundation and public cult in a Roman colony', in Ando, C. and J. Rüpke (eds.), *Public and Private in Ancient Mediterranean Law and Religion, University of Erfurt 3–5 July 2013* (Erfurt: De Gruyter), 99–113.

Vermeule, C. C. 1959. *The Goddess Roma in the Art of the Roman Empire* (Cambridge, MA: Sprink).

Versluys, M. J. 2014. 'Understanding objects in motion: an archaeological dialogue on Romanization', *Archaeological Dialogues* 21: 1–64.

Walker, S. 1988. 'From west to east: evidence for a shift in the balance of trade in white marbles', in Herz, N. and M. Waelkens (eds.), *Classical Marble: Geochemistry, Technology, and Trade*. Nato ASI Series 153 (Dordrecht: Springer), 187–96.

Wallace-Hadrill, A. 2008. *Rome's Cultural Revolution* (Cambridge: Cambridge University Press).

Weaver, P. R. C. 1972. *Familia Caesaris: A Social Study of the Emperor's Freedmen and Slaves* (Cambridge: Cambridge University Press).

1998. 'Imperial slaves and freedmen in the brick industry', *ZPE* 122: 238–46.

Webster, J. 2001. 'Creolizing the Roman Provinces', *AJA* 105: 209–25.

Weinstock, S. 1960. 'Pax and the Ara Pacis', *JRS* 50: 44–58.

West, A. B. 1931. *Corinth: Results of Excavations Conducted by the American School of Classical Studies at Athens*, Vol. 8, Part 2: *Latin Inscriptions 1896–1926* (Cambridge, MA: American School of Classical Studies at Athens).

Wightman, E. M. 1980. 'The plan of Roman Carthage: practicalities and politics', in Pedley, J. G. (ed.), *New Light on Ancient Carthage* (Ann Arbor: University of Michigan Press), 29–46.

Witcher, R. E. 2014. 'Globalisation and Roman cultural heritage', In Pitts, M. and M. J. Versluys (eds.), *Globalisation and the Roman World: World History, Connectivity and Material Culture* (Cambridge: Cambridge University Press), 198–222.

Zanker, P. 1970–1. 'Über die Werkstätten augusteischer Larenaltäre und damit zusammenhängende Probleme der Interpretation', *BCAR* 82: 147–55.

1988. *The Power of Images in the Age of Augustus* (Ann Arbor: University of Michigan Press).

1999. *Pompeii: Public and Private Life* (Cambridge, MA: Harvard University Press).

Zevi, F. and C. Valeri 2008. 'Cariatidi e clipei: Il foro di Pozzuoli', in La Rocca, E., P. León, and C. Parisi Presicce (eds.), *Le due patrie acquisite: Studi di archeologia dedicati a Walter Trillmich* (Rome: 'L'Erma' di Bretschneider), 443–64.

9 | *Imagines et tituli*

Epigraphic Evidence of Imperial Imagery in Meeting Places
of Roman Professional *corpora*

NICOLAS TRAN

A few years ago, a group of French archaeologists, art historians and
epigraphers developed a research programme called *Signa et Tituli*.[1] Its
purpose was a better historical understanding of Roman societies during
the High Empire and it has resulted in the publication of several conference
proceedings. One of them deals with meeting places of Roman associations,
especially in southern Gaul.[2] In the wake of this achievement, some scholars involved in the programme continued to develop the same line of
research with Spanish archaeologists.[3] In both cases, our interdisciplinary
dialogue tried to make up for our frustrations and lack of evidence, as
epigraphers facing textual documents without archaeological context, or as
archaeologists confronted with mute remains. This chapter is
a continuation of this research and focuses on the imagery produced by
Roman *collegia*, in relation to imperial ideology and representations.[4]
These images are much less well preserved than the inscriptions which
mention them; we cannot study one without the other. Hence, this chapter
looks at the epigraphy of imperial imagery in meeting places occupied by
a few professional *corpora*: those that gathered local boatmen who worked
in major riverine ports or seaports of the Roman west. On the one hand,
this case study allows detailed analyses, based on a selection amongst the
huge number of inscriptions engraved by Roman associations. On the
other, this documentation is rich enough to shed light on the layout of
associations' headquarters.

The development of Roman *collegia* or *corpora* was at its apogee during
the second century and the early third century.[5] Modern historians qualify
many of those associations as 'professional', because they gathered

---

[1] I am very grateful to Amy Russell and Monica Hellström for their kind invitations to Durham,
their inspiring comments and their linguistic corrections.
[2] Agusta-Boularot and Rosso, 2014.   [3] Rodríguez *et al.*, 2016.   [4] See also Rosso, 2013.
[5] In Ostia, the *collegium fabrum tignuariorum* probably existed from 60 CE, but the earliest
evidence about other professional associations dates back to the beginning of the second century.
In a few cities, like Narbo Martius for instance, evidence on workers from the first century is
abundant, but *collegia* only appear during the next century.

individuals involved in the same – or a similar – trade. Nevertheless, this adjective is problematic. First, the relationships between membership in an association and practice of an occupation were complex and most of the time indirect. Secondly, as far as we know, professional *corpora* had the same activities as the other associations, whatever their Latin name – *collegia, corpora, sodalicia* ... Religious and convivial feasts, dedicated to protective deities, hold the first rank. Furthermore, association members made collective decisions about their common life and their organisation. They held deliberative assemblies, voted decrees, and elected magistrates. These activities took place in clubhouses that archaeologists often call *scholae*. Yet this term is also problematic, because ancient texts sometimes use it to refer to a room, and not to a whole building, and because not all the *scholae* attested were occupied by associations.[6] In any case, the decor of these meeting places resulted from a composition that the members wished to be as elegant as possible. Indeed, such layouts should reflect the occupants' social identity in the most favourable light. Statues, and the inscribed monuments which were often linked with them, were the master-pieces of these decorative assemblages. Many of them celebrated the imperial power in one way or another.

Relations between *corpora* and power resulted from the nature of these communities. They were private and voluntary associations, inasmuch as they gathered private persons (*privati*), who co-opted others freely. Nevertheless, the *corpora* had manifold relationships with public authorities. Firstly, at their foundation, they had to follow a legal procedure of authorisation, granted by the senate and also by local governments.[7] Secondly, the *corporati* tended to be recognised as a civic category.[8] They participated in civic life as official bodies, during festivals and public processions in particular, and their patrons often belonged to the local elite. In the great harbours and in Rome itself, they were also connected with representatives of the emperor. Thirdly, associations often defended the professional interests of their members, by direct contacts with the administration or through the support of protectors close to the imperial court.

As a result, Roman associations frequently expressed their loyalty towards authorities in general, and towards the emperor and his relatives in particular. This political expression had a major impact on the arrangement of their meeting places, in a mirror image of imperial ideology, since *privati* manifested what the imperial power

---

[6] Goffaux, 2011.   [7] Liu, 2005.   [8] Van Nijf, 1997; Tran, 2012a.

expected from its subjects.[9] From this point of view, the social rank of the *corporati* (and especially of the port boatmen) is an important parameter. Most of them belonged to the middling categories of Roman societies. Elites called them 'poor' (*pauperes*), but they were not needy (*egentes*). As a matter of fact, they were not truly poor. Membership in a *corpus* required the payment of an entry fee and then regular contributions. Furthermore, the *corporati* who wanted to assume prestigious positions had to act with generosity. The *lenuncularii* or *scapharii*, on whom we are going to focus, were specialised workers and not unskilled (and poorer) labourers. Even though slaves could join an association with the permission of their masters, there were only free men (including a lot of freedmen) in the professional *corpora* from Ostia. Most of the *lenuncularii* or *scapharii* possessed their own small boats (*lenunculi* or *scaphae*) and slaves who worked for them. Their social condition contributes to this key question: how did groups at different social levels use, react to, and even create imperial imagery and ideology?

The *lenuncularii* based in Roman harbours practised a 'small' trade. They unloaded maritime ships by transhipment or tugged them to the docks. With their workboats, they took on short-distance connections within port systems (such as the Ostia/Portus complex) and between seaports and river ports.[10] In principle, they should have belonged to a much lower social condition than the greatest merchants (*mercatores*), maritime ship-owners (*navicularii*) or even long-distance riverine transporters (*nautae*).[11] Nonetheless, 'small' crafts and trades could give rise to a few great fortunes. In fact, the leaders of *corpora* could reach a high social status, a much higher social status than ordinary members.[12] In Ostia, some of them joined the *ordo Augustalium*, a civic status-group composed of individuals designated by the city to organise annual ceremonies in honour of imperial power. They hoped that their sons could enter the local elite, especially when they were prevented from doing so themselves as freedmen. These rich and prestigious *corporati* played the first part when their communities expressed political feelings. As a matter of fact, such expressions and social climbing were strongly connected.[13]

---

[9] This indirect perception of imperial ideology is a topic that I share with Hellström, in this volume. Likewise, both of us have tried to emphasise the 'social agenda' of different groups that lay behind expressions of loyalty towards emperors.

[10] Meiggs, 1973: 294–8.   [11] On them, see Broekaert, 2013.   [12] Tran, 2006.

[13] In this volume, Hellström explores this connection at a higher social level, among local elites from *Africa Proconsularis*.

The *corpus traiectus Rusticeli* in Second-Century Ostia

As far as preserved evidence lets us know, an association of local boatmen from Ostia seems to have given priority in its activities to the expression of loyalty towards the Antonine dynasty. This *corpus traiectus Rusticeli* gathered *scapharii* or *lenuncularii* – these two words being synonyms – who shipped from a dock named after an individual called *Rusticelius*.[14] Almost all of the preserved inscriptions regarding this *corpus* pay tribute to the *domus Augusta*.[15] Seven of them are analysed below, and presented in full in the Appendix. They were discovered in different parts of the archaeological site of Ostia, because they were moved and/or reused from late antiquity onwards. Yet they form such a coherent series that they must come from the *corpus* meeting place.

On 19 September 145, M. Marius Primitivus gave two monuments dedicated to the adoptive sons of Antoninus Pius. The tribute paid to the future Lucius Verus is quite well preserved (see Appendix, 1). The other one, dedicated to Marcus Aurelius Caesar, formed a matching pair (2). The same donor appears with his father on another stone, on which two inscriptions have been engraved (3–4). A large part of the second text is missing. Only comparison with its twin suggests that it was probably a tribute to the future emperor Lucius Verus. Again, two tributes paid to the two designated successors of Antoninus Pius are set side by side. Images of the two Caesars would have been arranged in the same way, above the inscriptions.[16] Despite what L. Wickert considered in the *CIL*, this time the dedicant should be M. Marius [---] the father, rather than his son M. Marius Primitivus, because the dedicant is identified as *quinquennalis corporis*. Primitivus had probably reached too important a social rank to accept this internal honour. As a former *aedilis sacris Volkani*, he belonged to the colonial elite. Moreover, the presidency of a professional association corresponds much better with the social condition of his father, who was probably a wealthy freedman.[17]

Almost omnipresent in the epigraphy of the *corpus traiectus Rusticeli*, M. Marius Primitivus appears once again on a marble plaque engraved

---

[14] On the meaning of *traiectus* as 'dock', see Le Gall, 1953: 180–1.

[15] Engraved in 139, 140, or 145, *CIL* 14.247 might be a fragmentary *album* of this *corpus*. A *corporatus* named M. Marius [---] appears on it.

[16] I have tried to improve their restoration; the transcription is that proposed in Tran, 2012b: 333–4. Dimensions: 101 × 89 × 3–4 cm.

[17] There was a large majority of freedmen among the *seviri Augustales* from Ostia, and the citizens registered in the tribe *Palatina* were often of a servile descent.

twenty-one years after his first benefactions, on 15 December 166 (Appendix, 5). Inscribed in two columns, this text commemorates the gift of silver representations to the *corpus traiectus Rusticeli* by at least four different persons. During the second half of the second century, the *corpus traiectus Rusticeli* also received another *imago ex argento cum clipeo et Atlante* (6). The donor was a *curator* and thus a dignitary of the *corpus*. A last plaque, mentioning again the gift of an *imago ex argento cum clipeo et Atlante aereo*, has been discovered at the same place as the previous inscription, reused in a pavement (7). Its composition is so characteristic that the restoration of *traie[ct(us) Rustic(eli)]* (line 4) seems sure.

These seven inscriptions were displayed in the meeting place of the *corpus traiectus Rusticeli*, in the same way as decorative objects, and their textual content describes several imperial statuettes. Hence, almost twenty-five years ago, P. Herz studied the probable aspect of the *imagines cum clipeo et Atlante* quoted by inscriptions 5, 6, and 7.[18] The busts of the *domus Augusta* members would have been set on trays in the form of shields. Funerary or decorative art provides a very small sample of good parallels.[19] On a sarcophagus from Ostia, Atlas is kneeling down and carries a shield, on which the *lupa* is nursing Romulus and Remus (Fig. 9.1).[20] A sculpture preserved at the Villa Albani represents the titan bearing a shield.[21] The zodiac forms a circle on its edge and Jupiter sits on his throne at the centre. In the *corpus'* meeting place, Atlas bore these *imagines clipeatae* as if they were the celestial vault, so that the rulers of the empire appeared as the masters of the universe. In an ideological perspective, this discourse was not original at all; however, such a visual association between Atlas and the emperors was unusual.[22] Victory carrying a *clipeus* and balancing on a celestial sphere was a common symbol of the emperor's universal power. Yet – as far as we know – no other image of Atlas supporting imperial portraits is attested. So, the *lenuncularii traiectus Rusticeli* may have chosen a rare motif amongst imperial imagery, or even created a new one from a model unconnected with emperors.

The precious metal they employed (2.5 and 2 pounds of silver, mentioned by inscriptions 5 and 6 respectively) implies that these gifts corresponded to reasonably small statuettes.[23] Likewise, the layout and size of

---

[18] Herz, 1980–1.   [19] Schneider, 1997.

[20] Museo Archeologico Ostiense inv. 6. The epitaph of L. Caltilius Salutaris seems to be unpublished, though a picture is online on the EDCS database (no. 00294).

[21] Bol, 1994: 372–84, cat. 510.   [22] Fejfer, 2008: 129.

[23] Even though it is not an *imago clipeata*, the small bust of Lucius Verus from the treasure of Marengo indicates how the imperial statuettes possessed by *corpora* could look. See Bendinelli, 1937.

Figure 9.1 Sarcophagus with the *Lupa Capitolina*. Museo Archeologico Ostiense Inv. 102. Photograph © Archivio Fotografico del Parco Archeologico di Ostia Antica.

inscriptions 3 and 4 could fit with busts, rather than standing statues. The closed and relatively confined meeting places of the *corpora* could not host a lot of cumbersome monuments.[24] As a matter of fact, the size of the building where the *lenuncularii traiectus Rusticeli* met is completely unknown, but it might have been similar to the so-called *aula* and temple of the *corpus mensorum frumentariorum Ostiensium*.[25] The trapezoidal hall occupied by this Ostian association of grain measurers was 8.5 to 11.5 m wide and about 14 to 18 m long. Adjacent to it, their temple (probably dedicated to *Ceres Augusta*) was smaller (7.5 × 13.5 m).

Furthermore, when dates are preserved, the *dedicationes* of these sculptures reveal specific relations to imperial power. The first and second plaques were dedicated on 19 September, i.e. on Antoninus Pius' birthday. Likewise, Lucius Verus was born on 15 December, the date of dedication of inscription 5. The emperor's birthday gave the best occasion to offer a sacrifice to his Genius. Every feast of *dedicatio*, revealed by the mention of *divisiones sportularum*, had a religious and ritual dimension. In their relationship with the Antonine dynasty, the boatmen from the *traiectus Rusticeli* behaved as *cultores*, so that modern historians have often compared them with a religious association attested a few decades later, in 205: the *cultores Larum et imaginum dominorum nostrorum invictissimorum Augustorum praediorum Rusticelianorum*.[26]

---

[24] Bollmann, 1998: 138–45, emphasises that emperors and members of the *domus Augusta* held the first rank among honorific statues possessed by associations.

[25] Ostia Antica, *regio* I, *insula* XIX, 2–3. Bollmann, 1998: 291–5. In Ostia, too, the *collegium fabrum tignuariorum* gathered about 350 members in 198, who met in a 290 m² porticus (*ibid.*: 285).

[26] *CIL* 14.4570.

Another noticeable aspect of this dossier concerns the social identity of the benefactors. Two of the dedicants, [---]us Rufus and M. Marius [---] were magistrates of the *corpus traiectus Rusticeli*, as *curator* and *quinquennalis*. Regarding M. Marius Primitivus, nothing proves that he was a *corporatus*. The whole body of epigraphic evidence about Ostian *collegia* suggests that he could have remained close to his father's *corpus*, through his generosity, without being a *corporatus* himself. His office of *aedilis sacris Volkani* reflects his integration into the local elite, which would fit better with the rank of *patronus corporis*, rather than of ordinary member.[27] In any case, the *sevir Augustalis* M. Marius [---] and his son M. Marius Primitivus reveal a typical path of social-climbing families, moving from the servile population to the civic elite in two or three generations. Several cases are attested in Ostia.[28]

Like other families, the M. Marii benefited from mechanisms of social promotion linked with a specific relation to power. The rank of *sevir Augustalis* was a springboard for many freedmen enriched by harbour trades.[29] This civic honour was granted by decurional decree and consisted essentially in celebrating annual games dedicated to the *principes*.[30] Moreover, participation in local institutions, even through minor magistracies or priesthoods, was conceived as an involvement in the good government of the empire. As a result, candidates for social mobility expressed an ardent loyalty towards both local and imperial authority, and in particular towards the *principes*. Their demonstrations of loyalty belonged to a social habitus which implied subscribing to imperial ideology.[31] Because such individuals were numerous among the higher strata of *corpora*, they involved their communities – and the other social categories represented in them – in collective expressions of imperial loyalty. The *corpus traiectus Rusticeli* and the M. Marii were by no means an exception.

[27] The *aediles sacris Volcani faciundis* were young notables. They assisted the *pontifex Volcani*, a high priest of Ostia who exercised a general control over all public temples. See Meiggs, 1973: 173 and 178.

[28] Tran, 2006: 409–59.   [29] Mouritsen, 2011: 249–61.   [30] Van Haeperen, 2016.

[31] In the debate we had in Durham, especially between M. Hellström and me, I did not at all deny that homages to imperial power were instrumental; they served strategies of social climbing. I have, however, tried to highlight how social motivations and ideological expressions overlapped each other. In the end – I completely agree with A. Russell – we do not know whether Romans had fully internalised the ideology they propagated, or whether they were merely playing the role expected of them. Likewise, we cannot tell if their loyalty to emperors was heartfelt or not, which means that the second hypothesis is as uncertain as the first one.

The *corpus lenunculariorum traiectus Luculli* from Ostia

The *corpus lenunculariorum traiectus Luculli* was an association of boat-men similar to those belonging to the *corpus traiectus Rusticeli*, except that they sailed from a different dock. It may be that there was also a small portrait gallery of emperors in their meeting place.[32] But if this hypothesis is right, only the traces of two pieces, carved half a century apart, have been preserved (Appendix, 8–9). The two small moulded bases have the same shape. They measure a little less than 20 cm high, a little more than 20 cm wide and a dozen centimetres deep. They look like appropriate stands for statuettes or heads. Their formal similarity could have resulted from a coincidence, but their material aspect and their epigraphic content suggest that these small monuments come from the *corpus* headquarters.[33] During the Antonine era, the boatmen of the *traiectus Luculli* paid other tributes to the *domus Augusta* in their meeting place. The inscriptions were probably associated with figurative representations, whose nature is totally uncertain. Only fragments of white marble plaques are preserved.

Two *curatores* of the *corpus traiectus Luculli*, P. Octavius Nymphodotus and A. Egrilius Thallus, dedicated the first base to Marcus Aurelius (Appendix, 8), at an unknown moment of his principate (between 161 and 180). Both of them are also registered on an *album* of the *corporati qui pecuniam ad ampliandum templum contulerunt*.[34] The little base was dis-covered in 1969, during a dredging of the Tiber. The *corpus* itself engraved a second little moulded base to Gordian III, between 238 and 244 (9). Moreover, eight fragments of a white marble plaque were part of an inscription honouring L. Aelius Commodus, son of Antoninus Pius, i.e. the future Lucius Verus (10). Two former presidents, the *quinquennalicii* L. Naevius Saecularis and P. Sulpicius Hera, gave it to the *corpus*. They are also registered on an *album* of the *ordo corporatorum qui pecuniam ad ampliandum templum contulerunt*.[35] The second of the two men had

---

[32] Licordari, 1987. Our knowledge of the other Ostian *corpora* supports the hypothesis of a portrait gallery. The associations settled on the *campus* of the Magna Mater (*dendrophori*, *cannophori* and *hastiferi*) probably commissioned such a decorative programme, as a series of small bases dedicated to the Severan family suggests. See Bollmann, 1998: 309–23; Van Haeperen, 2018: 299–302. The *corporati* might also have carried such small busts in procession.

[33] Not all the tributes paid to emperors by Ostian *corpora* were installed in their regular meeting places. For example, the *navicularii codicarii* dedicated an inscription to Antoninus Pius, with the permission of the *praefectus annonae*. It was probably put in a public space of the harbour district (*CIL* 14.106).

[34] *CIL* 14.246.   [35] *CIL* 14.246; 5374.

a Greek cognomen and received the title of *Augustalis*. He therefore belonged to the same social environment, consisting of wealthy freedmen integrated into the city by the expression of loyalty to emperors, like M. Marius [---] and other dignitaries of the *corpus traiectus Luculli*.

The *corpus traiectus Luculli* used another marble plaque twice; this recycling implies that it was originally displayed in the association meeting place. The first side honoured Marcus Aurelius Caesar, after 146, since Antoninus Pius' son had received the tribunician power (Appendix, 11a). A. Egrilius Faustus, *quinquennalis* of the *corporati qui pecuniam ad ampliandum templum contulerunt* between 151 and 156, might have paid this tribute.[36] But, whether Licordari's restoration is right or not, the dedicant was certainly *sevir Augustalis* and president of the association formed by the individuals who had assumed this annual charge. Decades later, an homage to Commodus was engraved on the other face of the plaque (11b). The son of Marcus Aurelius acquired the *cognomen ex virtute* of *Germanicus Maximus* in 172, but we can be more precise: our inscription dates to the sixth, seventh, eighth, or ninth tribunician power of Commodus, that is to say from 181–5. The stone is so damaged that restorations are very difficult and uncertain. Nevertheless, its dedicant seems to share several common points with the previous one, from a social point of view.

In sum, in the headquarters of the *lenuncularii traiectus Luculli*, *imagines* of the emperors and their relatives were as omnipresent as in the seat of the *corpus traiectus Rusticeli*. Furthermore, the *lenuncularii traiectus Luculli* dedicated their meeting place, as a whole, to the *Numen* of the *domus Augusta*.[37] They did so after construction works of consolidation and embellishment, carried out with the permission of Ti. Julius Ferox, a *curator alvei Tiberis et riparum* in charge between 101 and 103. Finally, this meeting place should be identified as the *templum* that a group of *corporati* enlarged during the first decades of the second century. Indeed, it is certain that the *lenuncularii traiectus Luculli* are the *corporati qui pecuniam ad ampliandum templum contulerunt*, and vice versa.[38] Different

---

[36] *CIL* 14.246.

[37] *CIL* 14.5320: [N]*umini Domus Aug(ustae)*, | [co]*rpus lenunc(u)lariorum* | *traiectus Luculli pecunia sua* | *firmiori et cultiori opere* | *fecerunt,* | [per]*missu Ti(beri) Iuli Ferocis, curatoris aluei* | *Tiberis et riparum.*

[38] Tran, 2012b: 327–30. Besides the memberships of P. Octavius Nymphodotus, A. Egrilius Thallus, P. Sulpicius Hera, and L. Naevius Saecularis in both organisations, Cn. Sentius Felix was patron of the *corporati qui pecuniam ad ampliandum templum contulerunt* (*CIL* 14.5374), but his epitaph presents him as patron of the *corpus scapharior(um) et lenuncularior(um) traiect(us) Luculli* (*CIL* 14.409). This inscription gives an impressive and probably exhaustive list of patronages

elements converge and show that ceremonies in honour of the imperial power were major events, amongst the diverse religious feasts organised by *corpora*. The same picture emerges from inscriptions dealing with other workers of the Tiber.[39]

The *corpus piscatorum et urinatorum totius alvei Tiberis* and the Severans

The *corpus* of the Tiber fishermen and divers did not gather boatmen, properly speaking, but workers of other kinds who sailed on the river under administrative permission. They would have shared this status of authorised professionals with the *lenuncularii*, the *scapharii*, and the *navicularii codicarii*. Moreover, the *urinatores* were certainly in business with river transporters, since their occupation consisted of collecting goods fallen overboard.[40] Two honorific inscriptions reveal how important the celebration of Severan power was in the *corpus'* life. A manuscript dating from the second half of the sixteenth century preserves the memory of a base dedicated to Ti. Claudius Severus (Fig. 9.2; Appendix, 12). Its inscription mentioned two statues of Caracalla and Julia Domna given by this *quinquennalis* and *patronus*. All of these monuments were certainly situated in the regular meeting place of the *corpus piscatorum et urinatorum*. The expression *ex decreto ordinis corporis* – which means that a general assembly of the *corpus* voted this decree – might have referred to a decision not only to erect the base and the statues, but also to assign them a location in the association house.[41] This document highlights how the civic status of the most prestigious association members could impact the relations between the *corpora* and the imperial power.

---

assumed by Felix. Another Ostian *corpus*, gathering shipbuilders, occupied a *templum* as their common house: through its good preservation, it provides an illustrative example of a Roman association meeting place (Ostia Antica, *regio* III, *insula* II, 1–2).

[39] Gifts to a *collegium* commemorated by *AE* 1940.62 probably do not relate to the *corpus lenunculariorum traiectus Luculli*, but to the same social environment. Amongst benefactors, C. Nasennius Felix and P. Sextilius Agrippa are probably two *corporati qui pecuniam ad ampliandum templum contulerunt* (*CIL* 14.246). A third donor, Cn. Sergius Felix, may be the man who ceded a burial plot to M. Annius Marcion and his deceased wife: a *corporatus* registered on *CIL* 14.246, had the same name. *AE* 1940.62, is a marble plaque, which recalls several acts of generosity: in particular, the gifts of a statue of Marcus Aurelius Caesar (*Verissimus Caesar*), of a *statua acrolitha* of L. Aelius Commodus (the future Lucius Verus), of a bronze statue of Antoninus Pius and several silver portraits of the same rulers.

[40] *Dig.* XIV, 2, 4, 1.   [41] Cf. e.g. *CIL* 5.5287: *l(oco) d(ato) d(ecreto) colleg(ii)*.

Figure 9.2 Drawings of a statue base dedicated to Ti. Claudius Severus (*CIL* 6.1872) from the sixteenth-century *Iscrizioni antiche e monumenti di Roma*. Biblioteca Nazionale Centrale di Firenze. BNC, N.A. 618, c. 42r.

The *corpus* put the statues of Caracalla and Julia Domna amongst other sculptures. The base itself was decorated with relief sculpture that referred to the occupation of the *corporati* and, hence, proceeded from a professional pride. On the top part of the base were carved small boats (*scaphae*) sailing on the Tiber. On one side, Ti. Claudius Severus stood in a toga, with a *fascis* (symbolising his office of *lictor*) and a palm branch in his hand. The *corporati* thanked their protector and president (*patronus et quinquennalis III*) for his success in a negotiation with the administration. His diligence had allowed the fishermen and divers to obtain and then to conserve a navigational right (*navigatio scapharum*).[42] Severus' statue would have surmounted the base. The entire assemblage of texts and images honouring a benefactor of the *corpus* recalls two twin monuments carved during the third century: one completely preserved togate statue and a second small fragment with an inscription praising a protector for defending

---

[42] Tran, 2020.

the privileges of an association (*munimenta corporis*).[43] Carved at the feet of the *togatus*, a box (*scrinium*) contained legal documents in favour of the *corpus*. Since the fragment was discovered in the bed of the Tiber, it too might have belonged to an association that gathered river workers.

As a *lictor* and father of a Roman knight, Ti. Claudius Severus had the support required for defending the *corporati* and their rights. Indeed, such civic positions imply connections with representatives of the Roman state. So, Severus' social profile, the family promotion personified by his son, his ability to act like a perfect president, and his expression of a fervent loyalty towards imperial power converge. His personal behaviour, as much as his social success, encouraged all the *piscatores et urinatores* to make allegiance to the Severans. Their *corpus* paid tribute to Ti. Claudius Severus, and thus celebrated the installation of the statues of Caracalla and Julia Domna in its meeting place, on 17 August 206. It was not an ordinary sort of day, but corresponded to the Portunalia: the festival of Portunus, the protective god of the Tiber harbour. The fishermen and the divers must have celebrated it enthusiastically.[44] The inscription on the base also records that Severus gave money to give annual *sportulae* to the *corporati*. This birthday foundation – created at the same time – amounted indirectly to a regular renewal of a political allegiance, linked with the memory of Ti. Claudius Severus' generosity.

Another inscription, engraved a few years later, gives an idea of the praises that the *corpus piscatorum et urinatorum* could address to emperors on solemn occasions (Appendix, 13).[45] Given its singular style and content, it is worth reproducing here in full:

> [Pro salute et u]i[cto]ria! deo Imp(eratori) Caes(ari) M(arco)
>   Aurel[io diui]
> [Septimi Seueri f(ilio), O]ptimo Antonino Pio, sideribu[s in]
> [terram delapso, t]onitratori Aug(usto), orbis terrarum [pro-]
> [pagatori, domino] maximo. Prouidens imperi sui mai[esta-]   4
> [tem finesque eius] ampliauit, largam pac[e data]
> [auxit; coronauit la]urea dextra manu signum uictor[iae]

---

[43] Mommsen, 1891: 146–9. *CIL* 6.29814: *co|ns|tit||iones || corporis | munimenta*; Friggeri *et al.*, 2012: 485–6, n°VIII.8. *CIL* 6.29815: *c|o|[n|s]|t|i|t|u|t|i|o|n|es || corp(oris) munimenta*. See Tran, 2014: 143.

[44] They participated also in the *ludii piscatorii*, under the presidency of the urban *praetor*, on 7 June. See Tran, 2006: 317–18.

[45] *CIL* 6.1080 = 40638 (a. 211); Alföldy, 1996 (*AE* 1996.90).

[quae loco ueneratu]r curiae sacro urbis, ut in aeternum [illi]
[laus esset. Alia f]elicia tempora quatt<u>or in[se-]   8
[quantur ex hoc s]ancto die natiuitatis tuae! Ga[udi-]
[um omnium locis s]uscipias sanctis, manibusque suis o[mnes]
[exornent aras! L]anugin<e>i flores digna sunt uota! [Fecit]
[uerba numinis] sui: '"Nox Dea fit lux" Sic dic mea u[ota!']   12
[Corpus piscatorum] et urinatorum sua p(ecunia) p(osuit),
   primiceri[o . . .]
[hoc loco] urbis, qui Nymphas accipit omnes e[t est]
[sacerrimus corpo]ri toto octie(n)s denis circundatus annis
   grate m[erito].   16

For his welfare and victory! To the god emperor Caesar Marcus
Aurelius, son of the divine Septimius Severus, the best of all, Antoninus
Pius, fallen from the stars to earth, Thunderer Augustus, enlarger of the
world, the greatest master ever! By his foresight, he increased the
greatness of his empire and of its territory; he amassed bountiful glory
by giving peace. With his right hand he crowned with a laurel the statue
of Victory worshipped in the holy place of the urban Curia, so that it
received praise forever. May four other periods of happiness follow
(the one which went by) since the holy day of your birth![46] May you
receive the evidence of universal joy in the sanctuaries and may
everybody adorn the altars with their hands! Downy flowers are
appropriate votive offerings. Here are the words pronounced by his
divine will: '"The goddess Night becomes Light", these are the wishes
you have to pronounce for me.' The corpus of the fishermen and divers
erected (this monument) with its own money, gratefully and
deservedly, [---] being its president, in this place of the City, which
hosts all the Nymphs and has been – for the whole *corpus* – the most
sacred of all for eighty years.

Modern historians have insisted on the oddity of this inscription. Its
style is certainly extremely hyperbolic and flattering. It has seemed so
exceptional that some scholars have considered it a forgery made during
the Renaissance.[47] Yet G. Alföldy has shown that it was certainly an
authentic document. Because of its wordy emphasis, the praise of
Caracalla contrasts with the brevity of most honorific inscriptions. But it
is much less surprising, if we consider that it proceeds, directly or indirectly, from the rhetoric of imperial panegyric. Given the reference to

[46] I.e. 'may you live another hundred years!'
[47] Le Gall, 1953: 269 n.1; Martin, 1982: 405 n. 270.

imperial *nativitas*, such a speech may have been delivered on 4 April 211, in order to celebrate Caracalla's twenty-fifth birthday.[48] In sum, the overall tone gives an idea of the atmosphere surrounding association festivities in honour of emperors.

Unfortunately, this inscription was discovered outside of its original context, giving rise to much speculation. According to R. E. A. Palmer, the stone could come from a sanctuary of the Nymphs which was located in the *Horti Sallustiani*, between the Pincian and the Quirinal hills.[49] G. Alföldy disagreed with Palmer, declaring convincingly that it should belong near the Tiber, where the *piscatores* and *urinatores* who dedicated it worshipped.[50] Indeed, if the restorations of the last three lines are right, the *locus* mentioned must be the regular meeting place of the *corpus*, which would have been founded in 131. Hence, the statues of Caracalla and Julia Domna erected on 17 August 206 formed the decor of the festivities celebrated on 4 April 211.

The Same Model Attested in Provincial Harbours

In the other great harbours of the Roman west local boatmen and their *corpora* seem to have shared an environment very similar to the association structures attested in Rome and its pre-port. This is all the more noticeable in that it concerns professionals who were not in direct contact with each other. However, their expression of political loyalty and its materialisation in their meeting places were identical. So, for example, in 146, the *scapharii* settled in Seville (ancient Hispalis or Romula) dedicated two statue bases to Antoninus Pius and Marcus Aurelius Caesar (Appendix, 14–15).[51] Today, these white-marble pedestals are embedded in walls, but older descriptions refer to the small boats carved on their sides. Like the *piscatores* and *urinatores* from Rome, the *scapharii* settled in Hispalis associated political expression with affirmation of professional identity.[52]

---

[48] In fact, Caracalla was born on 4 April 188, but he seems to have antedated his birthday by two years, in order to increase his age difference with his brother Geta and to falsify his horoscope.

[49] Palmer, 1979: 1097–113. See *LTUR* 3, 349, s.v. *ad Nymphas*.   [50] *CIL* 6 s.n. 40638.

[51] On the associations' meeting places in Seville, see Goffaux, 2012: 216–18.

[52] Two other statues were set up in the association seat during the principate of Marcus Aurelius and Lucius Verus (161–9). They represented the Roman knight Sex. Julius Possessor, as *procurator* of the Baetis banks, and the military officer L. Castricius Honoratus, who would have been Possessor's technical assistant: *CIL* 2.1180 and 1183. Like the other one, these bases are

Finally, the *corpus lenunculariorum* from Arles possessed a set of statuary and epigraphic items, discovered only a few years ago in the river Rhône. It consists of an altar dedicated to the *Genius corporis* and a statue of Neptune (Fig. 9.3; Appendix, 16). For the moment, no representation of the Roman emperor is attested, but the plinth of the Neptune statue served as an epigraphic field for a dedication to the *Numina*

Figure 9.3 Statue of Neptune. Musée départemental Arles Antique-CG13 Inv. RHO.2007.05.1966. Photograph © R. Bénali.

embedded in a wall of Seville's cathedral. See Dardaine and Pavis d'Escurac, 1983; Le Roux, 1986; Remesal Rodriguez, 1991; Campbell, 2012: 260.

Auggg(ustorum). These three emperors were probably Septimius Severus, Caracalla, and Geta. In a more or less intense way, the *lenuncularii* from Arles used their association house as a place of political affirmation, where ordinary boatmen of the lower Rhône expressed their attachment to the reigning emperors. Was P. Petronius Asclepiades, the donor of the Neptune statue, one of them? It is uncertain, since the inscription mentions neither his membership in the *corpus* nor the titles that he could have received. As a result, it is possible that P. Petronius Asclepiades was a rich benefactor, who did not belong to the *corpus* but was in business with the boatmen. Given his Greek cognomen, he might have been a freedman, wealthy enough to offer a beautiful statue to his protégés. Given his plausible higher social status and because his behaviour encouraged the *corporati* to honour the emperors, he seems to have played the same role as the Ostian and Roman benefactors performed before.

A Few General Thoughts Based on Specific Cases

In sum, these documents emphasise how important monuments erected in honour of emperors in the headquarters of professional associations were, especially in the greatest harbours of the Roman west. Imperial *imagines* were a part of the decorative schemes of places where feasts and rituals celebrated the majesty of the *domus Augusta*. These objects fostered the politicisation of the lower classes, i.e. their involvement in Roman politics, because they spread ideological conceptions of the central power and, at the same time, expressed the adherence of *corporati* to the *imperium*. Of course, not all these monuments were – or were meant to be – seen by emperors or imperial representatives, but they helped *collegia* to earn a reputation for loyalty, which promoted their interests.[53] Is this all they were? To understand their functions fully, these monuments deserve to be considered from different angles as well. In a very concrete way, they consisted of decorative elements and, in one sense – if we may be a little bit provocative – nice pieces of furniture. At the least, they encourage us to imagine association houses where emperors, gods, patrons, rulers, and even work equipment were presented in iconography side by side, in the midst of tables, ceremonial seats, banquet beds, and candelabras. Likewise, texts engraved in honour of emperors and their relatives took their place

---

[53] This point echoes Hellström in this volume. By way of comparison, Marcus Aurelius knew (Fronto, *Ep. ad M. Caes.* 4.12.6) that modest painted portraits of him were present in a number of *tabernae* in Rome, even if he had not seen each of them.

amongst a great variety of inscriptions. The choice to isolate these documents from the others is partly arbitrary and thus may obscure some of their functions.

In the end, associations decorated their common houses because they were seeking social prestige. Whether they had political value or not, marble statues, silver statuettes or gracefully inscribed plaques pertained to a level of luxury that craftsmen had access to through associations. The opportunity to become involved in such an environment gave distinction, because it drew a line of demarcation between *corporati* and unskilled workers who were not admitted to *corpora*. Furthermore, professional associations competed with each other to have the most elegant seat and thereby to boost the prestige of a specific trade compared to the others. It is true that only the *corporati* and their guests could admire the entire arrangement of clubhouses. But, especially in Ostia, several meeting places opened onto the most important streets of the city: a beautiful facade and an open door could be sufficient to display luxury and to build a respectable reputation.

Of course, the taste for beautiful things cannot have removed any ideological content from objects intrinsically linked with imperial power. Both dimensions may have got the upper hand alternately, according to circumstances. *Corporati* would sometimes have met without paying much attention to the imperial imagery of their clubhouse, because it was completely integrated into their everyday environment. Yet, solemn events must have intensely reactivated the ideological effectiveness of these objects. The epigraphy and archaeology of associations' meeting places enable us to interpret them as stage sets. Yet we should go further and try to determine the performances the *corporati* enacted. These regularly assumed the shape of fervent ceremonies of allegiance to imperial power. They took place on carefully chosen days and sometimes periodically, in the frame of foundations. Moreover, these feasts involved the installation of new commemorative images and texts, which echoed the former ones. It is noteworthy that the preserved items often belonged to series or even to collections. Hence, Roman associations often based their demonstrations of loyalty to emperors on repetitive and cumulative practices.[54]

According to their inscriptions, *corporati* erected monuments in honour of emperors to translate feelings of loyalty towards power into action. For this purpose, they sometimes acted with great adulation. There is no reason

---

[54] On seriality and especially the visual impact of repetition, see also Hellström and Rowan in this volume.

to suspect they only pronounced empty words, and we should remember the ardent enthusiasm of the fishermen and divers from the Tiber celebrating Caracalla's birthday. It is even possible that these plebeians behaved in a less restrained way than the civic elite, concerned with their autonomy and conscious of their social superiority. Of course, we cannot know whether *corporati* fully internalised the feelings their dedications claim to express, but they may well have felt sincere gratitude to the emperors. At least, we cannot exclude it or minimise it on principle. Consistent expressions of loyalty formed part of a regular *habitus*, and decisions to erect honorific monuments were probably not only cynical ploys to achieve short-term goals.

However, *corporati* expressed deference towards imperial power for diverse reasons and with several goals in mind.[55] One part of their motivation was not political or ideological, but rather social. In fact, *corpora* aimed at appearing to be honourable communities, respected because of their official recognition and their integration into civic life. *Corporati* were recognised as members of a status-group, for example during civic processions or amongst the audience of public games. Underlining their behaviour as perfect subjects of the *princeps*, the decoration of their meeting places strengthened this quality. It made *corporati* proud, just as the antiquity of their communities did. For this reason, the fishermen and divers emphasised that their *corpus* had been occupying the same meeting place for eighty years. From this perspective, monuments dedicated to emperors could correspond to time markers. When they honoured Gordian III, the *corporati traiectus Rusticeli* would have regarded as such the tribute paid to Marcus Aurelius decades before. Homages paid to emperors belonged to self-sustaining traditions. Each generation followed the footsteps of the previous one and the longevity of these traditions brought social prestige too. In this way, the social interests of *corporati*, i.e. their quest for respectability, and the interests of imperial power, i.e. the population's adherence to its ideology, converged.

A few *corporati* contributed to this convergence decisively, by encouraging their peers to express loyalty towards imperial power. Association members shared a collective life, made up of friendship and community spirit. Yet very strong hierarchies also structured this common life.[56] Grand-sounding titles received by magistrates were not conventions lacking real social meaning. Indeed, associations were microcosms of Roman society and its popular

---

[55] This idea should be uncontroversial, even though a debate on the balance between different purposes is legitimate (see Hellström in this volume).

[56] Tran, 2006.

categories: they were, therefore, very fragmented. *Corpora* elites stood out because of their wealth and civic integration. Furthermore, professional associations helped them to control entire economic sectors. This study suggests that their control also encompassed the field of local and imperial politics. Civic distinctions, in particular the honour of *sevir Augustalis*, allowed the social promotion of association dignitaries and of their families. And those positions were intrinsically linked with an ostentatious allegiance to imperial power. So, the richest *corporati* made the poorer behave like them. The latter accepted the need to act in such a way collectively, because this behaviour determined the respectability that all the *corporati* looked for. In short, the wealthiest, who were usually engaged in following a path of social climbing, played a crucial role as intermediaries in the spread of imperial ideology. Therefore, the politicisation of the lower classes was not restricted to 'top-down' and 'bottom-up' phenomena. It was also based on the pivot position of a particular category of *corporati*, determined by their social aspirations.

EPIGRAPHIC APPENDIX

1. Homage to the Future Lucius Verus by M. Marius Primitivus

L(ucio) Aelio Aurelio Co[m]-
modo, Imp(eratoris) Caes(aris) T(iti) Ae[li]
Hadriani Antonini Au[g(usti)]
Pii p(atris) p(atriae) filio,   4
M(arcus) Marius M(arci) f(ilius) Pal(atina) Primit[iuus],
decur(ionum) dec(reto) aed(ilis) II sac(ris) V[olc(ani)]
fac(iundis), corpori traiect(us) Ru[stic(eli)]
s(ua) p(ecunia) d(onum) d(edit); ded(icata) XIII K(alendas)   8
   Oc[t(obres)],
Imp(eratore) Caes(are) Antonino II[II]
M(arco) Aurelio Caes(are) II c[o(n)s(ulibus)].[57]

To Lucius Aurelius Commodus, son of the emperor Caesar Titus Aelius
Hadrianus Antoninus Augustus Pius, father of the fatherland, Marcus
Marius Primitivus, son of Marcus, from the tribe Palatina, by decree of
the city councillors twice aedile in charge of the ceremonies of Vulcan,
gave (this monument) to the association of Rusticelius' dock at his own
expense. (Inscription) dedicated on the thirteenth day before the
Calends of October, under the fourth consulship of the emperor Caesar
Antoninus and the second consulship of Marcus Aurelius Caesar.

2. Homage to Marcus Aurelius Caesar by M. Marius Primitivus

[M(arcus) Mariu]s M(arci) f(ilius) Pal(atina) Prim[itiuus,
   decur(ionum) dec(reto) aed(ilis) II sa(cris) Volc(ani)]
[fa]c(iundis), corp(ori) traie(ctus) R[ustic(eli) s(ua) p(ecunia) d(ono)
   d(edit); ded(icata) XIII K(alendas) ---]
[Imp(eratore) Ca]esare Ant[onino ---]
[M(arco) Au]relio C[aesare ---].[58]   4

---

[57] *CIL* 14.4553 (34.5 × 39 × 6 cm).

[58] *AE* 1989.125 (Ost. inv. 7392); Royden, 1988, 242. Unfortunately, H. L. Royden published its
textual content in 1988 without a photograph, so no verification is yet possible.

Marcus Marius Primitivus, son of Marcus, from the tribe Palatina, by decree of the city councillors twice aedile in charge of the ceremonies of Vulcan, gave (this monument) to the association of Rusticelius' dock at his own expense. (Inscription) dedicated on the thirteenth day before the Calends of ---, under the --- consulship of the emperor Caesar Antoninus and the --- consulship of Marcus Aurelius Caesar.

3.   Homage to Marcus Aurelius Caesar by M. Marius [---]

M(arco) Aur[elio Caesari],	
Imp(eratoris) Ca[esaris T(iti) Aeli]	
Hadria[ni Antonini Aug(usti)]	
Pii [p(atris) p(atriae) filio],	4
M(arcus) Mar[ius ---],	
seuir A[ugustalis ---]	
corpori s[caphariorum]	
traiec[tus Rusticeli cum ? or nomine],	8
M(arc.) Ma[ri(.) M(arc.) f(ili.) Pal(atina)]	
Prim[itiu(.) fili(.)].[59]	

To Marcus Aurelius Caesar, son of the emperor Caesar Titus Aelius Hadrianus Antoninus Augustus Pius, father of the fatherland, Marcus Marius [---], *sevir Augustalis*, to the association of the boatmen of Rusticelius' dock, with (or on behalf of) his son Marcus Marius Primitivus, son of Marcus, from the tribe Palatina.

4.   Homage to the Future Lucius Verus

[---]us	
[--- c]orpori	
[--- scaph]ariorum	
[--- traiectus] Rusticeli ob	4
[honorem] q(uin)q(uennalitatis) s(ua) p(ecunia) p(osuit).[60]	

[---]us, to the association of the boatmen of Rusticelius' dock, erected (this monument) at his own expense, for the sake of the honour of *quinquennalis*.

---

[59] *CIL* 14.5328.   [60] *CIL* 14.5327.

5.   A Gift of *imagines* to the corpus traiectus Rusticeli

a)

> ---
> [---]++
> [--- Fel]ix et
> [---] Martinus
> [im]ag(ines) ex arg(ento) p(ondo) (duobus et uncia)   4
> [cum clipeo et Atl]ante aereu
> [corp(ori) t]raiectus
> [Rusti]celi d(ono) d(ederunt)
> [et ob ded(icationem)] diuiserunt   8
> [spor]tulas sing(ulis) (denarios) II
> ---

b)

> ---
> L(ucius) Faler[ius --- et]
> M(arcus) Mariu[s] M(arci) f(ilius) Prim[itiuus]
> corpor[i tr]aiect[us Rusticeli]
> imag[ines] s(upra) [s(criptas) d(ono) d(ederunt)]   4
> et ob d[e]d(icationem) diuise[runt sport(ulas) sing(ulis) (denarios)]
> II.
> Ded(icatae) XVIII [k(alendas) I]an(uarias), Pude[nte]
> [et Pollio]ne [co(n)s(ulibus).][61]   8

a)

[---] Felix and [---] Martinus gave images (made) of two pounds and a twelfth of silver, with a shield and an Atlas in bronze, to the association of Rusticelius' dock and, on the occasion of the dedication, they distributed two denarii to each (member) . . .

b)

Lucius Falerius [---] and Marcus Marius Primitivus, son of Marcus, gave to the association of Rusticelius' dock the *imagines* mentioned above, and, on the occasion of the dedication, they distributed two denarii to each (member). (Images) dedicated on the eighteenth day before the Calends of January, under the consulship of Pudens and Pollio.

---

[61] *CIL* 14.4554.

6. A Gift of an *imago* to the corpus traiectus Rusticeli

a)   ---

[--- Imp(eratoris) Caes(aris)]
[M(arci) Au]reli Antonin[i]
[Au]gusti
[---]us Rufus, curat(or)   4
[corp(ori) tr]aiect(us) Rustic(eli)
[imag(inem)] ex arg(ento) p(ondo) II cum
[clipeo e]t Atlante aer(eo) d(onum) d(edit)
[et ob de]d(icationem) diuisit uirit(im)   8
[sing(ulis)] (denarium) I; ded(icata) X k(alendas)
[--- co(n)s(ulibus)].

b)   ---

co[rp. ---]
---.62

... of the emperor Caesar Marcus Aurelius Antoninus Augustus, [---]us
Rufus, supervisor, gave an image (made) of two pounds of silver, with
a shield and an Atlas in bronze, to the association of Rusticelius' dock,
and, on the occasion of the dedication, he distributed a denarius to each
(member). (Image) dedicated on the tenth day before the Calends of [---]
under the consulship of ...

7. A Gift of an *imago* to the *corpus traiectus Rusticeli*

[---]Aug[ust. ---]
[--- V]aleriu[s ---]
[--- Qu]adratia[nus ---]
[co]rp(ori) traie[ct(us) Rustic(eli)]   4
[im]ag(inem) ex argento [p(ondo) --- cum]
[cl]ipeo et Atla[nte]
[aere]o d(ono) d(edit) et ob de[d(icationem)]
[di]uisit uirit(im) sin[g(ulis) (denarios) ---];   8
[de]d(icata) VIII id(us) Feb(ruarias), Ma[ximo]
[et] Orfi[to co(n)s(ulibus)].63

... Augustus ... Valerius ... Quadratianus ... gave an image (made) of
[---] pounds of silver, with a shield and an Atlas in bronze, to the

---

62 *CIL* 14.4556.   63 *CIL* 14.4555.

association of Rusticelius' dock, and, on the occasion of the dedication, he distributed [---] denarii to each (member). (Image) dedicated on the eighth day before the Ides of February, under the consulship of Maximus and Orfitus.

8. Homage to Marcus Aurelius

Imp(eratori) Aurelio
Antonino Aug(usto),
co(n)s(uli) III, P(ublius) Octauius
Nymphodotus et   4
A(ulus) Egrilius Thallus,
cura(tores) trei(ectus) Lucul(li) d(ono) d(ederunt).[64]

To the emperor Aurelius Antoninus Augustus, consul three times, Publius Octavius Nymphodotus and Aulus Egrilius Thallus, supervisors of Lucullus' dock, gave (this monument).

9. Homage to Gordian III

Imp(eratori) Caes(ari) M(arco) Antonio Gordiano
Pio Felici Aug(usto),
corp(us) tr(aiectus) Lucul(li).[65]   4

To the emperor Caesar Marcus Antonius Gordianus, Pius, Felix, Augustus, the association of Lucullus' dock.

10. Homage to the Future Lucius Verus

L(ucio) Aelio Commo[do],
[I]mp(eratoris) Antonini Aug(usti) [Pii p(atris)] p(atriae) fil(io),
[L(ucius)] Naeuius Saecular[is e]t
[P(ublius) Sul]picius Hera, Augusta[l(is)],   4
quin<quen>nalicius corporis
traiectus Luculli, sua p(ecunia) p(osuerunt).[66]

---

[64] *AE* 1987.193 (17 × 20 × 4–10 cm).

[65] *AE* 1987.194 (19 × 23 × 11.2–13.5 cm), discovered in 1951, in the so-called Basilica sul Decumano.

[66] *AE* 1987.197 (with a complement to *CIL* 14.5380) = 1989.128. The fragments come from several places in the Ostian remains; some of them have been reused.

To Lucius Aelius Commodus, son of the emperor Antoninus
Augustus, Pius, father of the fatherland, Lucius Naevius Saecularis
and Publius Sulpicius Hera, Augustalis, former presidents of the
association of Lucullus' dock, erected (this monument) at their own
expense.

11(a). Homage to Marcus Aurelius Caesar

M(arco) A[urelio]
C[aesari]
[---]
[---]+A[---]   4
[---]++ trib(unicia) p[ot(estate) ---]
[A(ulus) Egr]ilius Faustu[s ---]
[seuir] Aug(ustalis) idem q(uin)[q(uennalis) et q(uin)q(uennalis)
     corp(oris)]
[trai]ectus L[uculli ---]   8
[---] A(ul-) Egrili[---]
[---]iano [---]
[---] corp[---]
[lenu]ncul[ariorum]   12
[traiec]tus [Luculli].

To Marcus Aurelius Caesar ... holding the tribunician power ...
Aulus Egrilius Faustus, *sevir Augustalis*, likewise president (of the
seviri Augustales), and president of the association of Lucullus'
dock ... Aulus Egrilius ... [---]ianus ... the association of the
boatmen of Lucullus' dock.

11(b). Homage to Commodus

[M(arco) Aurelio Commodo]
[Anto]ni[no Aug(usto) Pio]
[fel(ici), G]erm(anico) m[ax(imo) ---]
[--- tri]b(unicia) pot(estate) VI[II ---]   4
M(arcus) An[---]
Ma[---]
[---]
[seuir August(alis) idem q(uin)]q(uennalis) et   8
[quinquenn(alis) co]rporis
[lenuncular(iorum) tr]aiectus
[Luculli].[67]

[67] *AE* 1987.176 = *CIL* 14.451 + inv. 6568.

To Marcus Aurelius Commodus Antoninus Augustus, Pius, Felix, great victor over the Germans . . . holding the tribunician power for the ninth time . . . Marcus An[---] Ma[---] . . . *sevir Augustalis*, likewise president (of the *seviri Augustales*), and president of the association of the boatmen of Lucullus' dock.

12. Homage to Ti. Claudius Severus

a)

Ti(berio) Claudio Esquil(ina) Seuero,	
decuriali lictori, patrono	
corporis piscatorum et	
urinator(um), q(uin)q(uennali) III eiusdem corporis,	4
ob merita eius:	
quod hic primus statuas duas una	
Antonini Aug(usti), domini n(ostri), aliam Iul(iae)	
Augustae, dominae nostr(ae), s(ua) p(ecunia) p(osuerit),	8
una cum Claudio Pontiano, filio	
suo, eq(uite) Rom(ano); et hoc amplius eidem	
corpori donauerit H̶S̶ X mil(ia) n(ummum),	
ut ex usuris eorum quodannis	12
natali suo, XVII K(alendas) Febr(uarias),	
sportulae uiritim diuidantur	
praesertim; cum nauigatio sca-	
pharum diligentia eius adquisita	16
et confirmata sit; ex decreto	
ordinis corporis piscatorum	
et urinatorum totius alu(ei) Tiber(is)	
quibus ex S(enatus) c(onsulto) coire licet; s(ua) p(ecunia)	20
p(osuerunt).	

b)

Dedic(ata) XVI K(alendas) Sept(embres), Nummio Albino et
   Fuluio Aemiliano co(n)s(ulibus).

c)

Praesentibus	
Iuuentio Corneliano et	
Iulio Felicissimo,	
patronis,	4
quinquennalib(us)	
Claudio Quintiano et	
Plutio Aquilino,	
curatorib(us)	8

Aelio Augustale et
Antonio Vitale et
Claudio Crispo.[68]

a)

To Tiberius Claudius Severus, from the tribe Esquilina, enrolled in
a *decuria* of *lictores*, patron of the association of the fishermen and
divers, president three times of the same association, because of his
merits: he was the first to erect at his own expense two statues, one
of Antoninus Augustus, our master, and the other of Julia Augusta,
our mistress, one with his son, the Roman knight Claudius
Pontianus; besides that, he gave 10,000 sestertii to the same
association, so that, with the interest, they might distribute
sportulae on his birthday, the seventeenth day before the Calends of
February, to each member present; the right to sail small boats was
granted and confirmed thanks to his carefulness. According to
a decree adopted by the order of the association of the fishermen
and divers of the whole Tiber channel, who are permitted to gather
by decree of senate; they erected (his monument) at their own
expense.

b)

(Statue) dedicated on the sixteenth day before the Calends of
September, under the consulship of Nummius Albinus and Fulvius
Aemilianus.

c)

Were present: the patrons Juventius Cornelianus and Julius
Felicissimus, the presidents Claudius Quintianus and Plutius
Aquilinus, the supervisors Aelius Augustalis, Antonius Vitalis and
Claudius Crispus.

13. Homage to Caracalla

[Pro salute et u]i[cto]ria! deo Imp(eratori) Caes(ari) M(arco)
      Aurel[io diui]
[Septimi Seueri f(ilio), O]ptimo Antonino Pio, sideribu[s in]
[terram delapso, t]onitratori Aug(usto), orbis terrarum [pro-]

---

[68] *CIL* 6.1872. See Tedeschi Grisanti and Solin, 2011, 289.

[pagatori, domino] maximo. Prouidens imperi sui mai[esta-]   4
[tem finesque eius] ampliauit, largam pac[e data]
[auxit; coronauit la]urea dextra manu signum uictor[iae]
[quae loco ueneratu]r curiae sacro urbis, ut in aeternum [illi]
[laus esset. Alia f]elicia tempora quatt<u>or in[se-]   8
[quantur ex hoc s]ancto die natiuitatis tuae! Ga[udi-]
[um omnium locis s]uscipias sanctis, manibusque suis o[mnes]
[exornent aras! L]anugin<e>i flores digna sunt uota! [Fecit]
[uerba numinis] sui: "'Nox Dea fit lux" Sic dic mea u[ota!']   12
[Corpus piscatorum] et urinatorum sua p(ecunia) p(osuit),
          primiceri[o . . .]
[hoc loco] urbis, qui Nymphas accipit omnes e[t est]
[sacerrimus corpo]ri toto octie(n)s denis circundatus annis
grate m[erito].[69]   16

For his welfare and victory! To the god emperor Caesar Marcus Aurelius, son
of the divine Septimius Severus, the best of all, Antoninus Pius, fallen from
the stars to earth, Thunderer Augustus, enlarger of the world, the greatest
master ever! By his foresight, he increased the greatness of his empire and of
its territory, he amassed bountiful glory by giving peace. With his right hand
he crowned with a laurel the statue of Victory worshipped in the holy place of
the urban Curia, so that it received praise forever. May four other periods of
happiness follow (the one which went by) since the holy day of your birth![70]
May you receive the evidence of universal joy in the sanctuaries and may
everybody adorn the altars with their hands! Downy flowers are appropriate
votive offerings. Here are the words pronounced by his divine will: "'The
goddess Night becomes Light", these are the wishes you have to pronounce
for me.' The corpus of the fishermen and divers erected (this monument)
with its own money, gratefully and deservedly, [---] being its president, in
this place of the City, which hosts all the Nymphs and has been – for the
whole *corpus* – the most sacred of all for eighty years.

---

[69] *CIL* 6.1080 = 40638 (a. 211); Alföldy, 1996 (*AE* 1996.90).
[70] I.e. 'may you live another hundred years!'

14. Homage to Antoninus Pius

Imp(eratori) Caes(ari) diui Hadriani f(ilio),
diui Traiani Parthici nepoti,
diui Neruae pronepoti,
T(ito) Aelio Hadriano Antonino   4
Aug(usto), pont(ifici) max(imo), trib(unicia) pot(estate) VIIII,
Imp(eratori) II, co(n)s(uli) IIII, p(atri) p(atriae),
scaphari qui Romulae
negotiantur   8
d(e) s(ua) p(ecunia) d(onum) d(ederunt).[71]

To the emperor Caesar Titus Aelius Hadrianus Antoninus
Augustus, son of the deified Hadrian, grandson of the deified
Trajan, victor over the Parthians, great-grandson of the deified
Nerva, high priest, holding the tribunician power for the ninth
time, hailed emperor twice, consul four times, father of the
fatherland, the boatmen who do business in Romula [i.e. Seville]
gave (this monument) at their own expense.

15. Homage to Marcus Aurelius Caesar

M(arco) Aurelio Vero
Caesari, Imp(eratoris) Caesaris Titi Aelii Ha-
driani Antoni-   4
ni Aug(usti) Pii, patris patriae filio,
co(n)s(uli) II
scaphari qui Romulae
negotiantur   8
d(e) s(ua) p(ecunia) d(onum) d(ederunt).[72]

To Marcus Aurelius Verus Caesar, son of the emperor Caesar Titus
Aelius Hadrianus Antoninus Augustus Pius, father of the
fatherland, consul twice, the boatmen who do business in Romula
gave (this monument) at their own expense.

---

[71] *CIL* 2.1168 (*CILA* 2.1, 8).   [72] *CIL* 2.1169 (*CILA* 2.1, 9).

16.   Dedication to the Numina Augustorum

Numinibus Auggg(ustorum) nnn(ostrorum),
honori corporis renunclariorum, P(ublius) Petronius Asclepiades donum dedit.[73]

To the divine powers of our three Augusti, in honour of the association
of the boatmen, Publius Petronius Asclepiades gave (this statue).

Bibliography

Agusta-Boularot, S. and E. Rosso (eds.) 2014. *Signa et tituli 2. Corpora et scholae:
lieux, pratiques et commémoration de la sociabilité en Gaule méridionale et
dans les régions voisines* (Nîmes: École antique de Nîmes).

Alföldy, G. 1996. '*Nox Dea fit lux!* Caracallas Geburtstag', in Bonamente, G. and
M. Mayer (eds.), *Historiae Augustae Colloquium Barcinonense* (Bari:
Edipuglia), 9–36.

Bendinelli, G. 1937. *Il tesoro di argentaria di Marengo* (Turin: V. Bona).

Bol, P. C. (ed.) 1994. *Forschungen zur Villa Albani: Katalog der Bildwerke. IV,
Bildwerke im Kaffeehaus* (Berlin: Mann).

Bollmann, B. 1998. *Römische Vereinshäuser: Untersuchungen zu den Scholae der
römischen Berufs-, Kult- und Augustalen-Kollegien in Italien* (Mainz: Philipp
von Zabern).

Broekaert, W. 2013. *Navicularii et negotiantes: A Prosopographical Study of Roman
Merchants and Shippers* (Rahden: Verlag Marie Leidorf).

Campbell, B. 2012. *Rivers and the Power of Ancient Rome: Studies in the History of
Greece and Rome* (Chapel Hill: University of North Carolina Press).

Christol, M. and N. Tran 2014. '*Tituli et signa collegiorum* en Gaule méridionale et
ailleurs: réflexions sur le décor des sièges de collèges à partir du cas arlésien',
in Agusta-Boularot, S. and E. Rosso (eds.), *Signa et tituli 2. Corpora et
scholae: lieux, pratiques et commémoration de la sociabilité en
Gaule méridionale et dans les régions voisines* (Nîmes: École antique de
Nîmes), 15–31.

Dardaine, S. and H. Pavis d'Escurac 1983. 'Le *Baetis* et son aménagement: l'apport
de l'épigraphie (*CIL*, II, 1180 et 1183)', *Ktema* 8: 307–15.

Fejfer, J. 2008. *Roman Portraits in Context* (Berlin; New York: De Gruyter).

Friggeri, R., M. G. Granino Cecere, and G. L. Gregori (eds.) 2012. *Terme di
Diocleziano: La collezione epigrafica* (Milan: Electa).

---

[73] *AE* 2009.822 and 823. See Christol and Tran, 2014.

Goffaux, B. 2011. '*Schola*: vocabulaire et architecture collégiale sous le Haut-Empire en Occident', *REA* 113: 47–67.

2012. 'À la recherche des édifices collégiaux hispaniques', in Dondin-Payre, M. and N. Tran (eds.), *Collegia: Le phénomène associatif dans l'Occident romain* (Bordeaux: Ausonius Éditions), 199–219.

Herz, P. 1980–1. 'Kaiserbilder aus Ostia', *BCAR* 87: 145–57.

Le Gall, J. 1953. *Le Tibre, fleuve de Rome dans l'Antiquité* (Paris: Presses universitaires de France).

Le Roux, P. 1986. 'L'huile de Bétique et le Prince: sur un itinéraire annonaire', *REA* 88: 247–71.

Licordari, A. 1987. 'I *lenuncularii traiectus Luculli* ad Ostia', *MGR* 12: 149–61.

Liu, J. 2005. 'Local governments and *collegia*: a new appraisal of the evidence', in Aubert, J.-J. and Z. Várhelyi (eds.), *A Tall Order: Writing the Social History of the Ancient World* (Munich: K. G. Saur), 279–310.

Martin, J.-P. 1982. *Providentia deorum: Recherches sur certains aspects religieux du pouvoir impérial romain* (Rome: École française de Rome).

Meiggs, R. 1973. *Roman Ostia* (Oxford: Clarendon Press).

Mommsen, T. 1891. '*Constitutiones corporis munimenta*', *ZRG* 12: 146–9 (= 1907. *Juristische Schriften*, Vol. 3 (Berlin, Weidmann), 286–9).

Mouritsen, H. 2011. *The Freedman in the Roman World* (Cambridge: Cambridge University Press).

Palmer, R. E. A. 1979. 'Severan ruler-cult and the moon in the city of Rome', in *ANRW* II.16.2, 1085–120.

Remesal Rodríguez, J. 1991. 'Sextus Iulius Possessor en la Bética', in *Alimenta: Estudios en homenaje al Dr Michel Ponsich (Gerión, Anejos 3)* (Madrid: Universidad Complutense), 282–95.

Rodríguez, O., N. Tran, and B. Soler (eds.) 2016. *Los espacios de reunión de las asociaciones romanas: Diálogos desde la arqueología y la historia, en homenaje a Bertrand Goffaux* (Seville: Editorial Universidad de Sevilla).

Rosso, E. 2013. '*Secundum dignitatem municipi*: les édifices collégiaux et leur programme figuratif, entre public et privé?', in Dardenay, A. and E. Rosso (eds.), *Dialogues entre sphère publique et sphère privée dans l'espace de la cité romaine* (Bordeaux: Ausonius Éditions), 67–122.

Royden, H. L. 1988. *The Magistrates of the Roman Professional Collegia in Italy from the First to the Third Century* A.D. (Pisa: Giardini Editori).

Schneider, R. M. 1997. 'Roma Aeterna – Aurea Roma: der Himmelsglobus als Zeitzeichen und Machtsymbol', in Assmann, J. and E. W. B. Hess-Lüttich (eds.), *Kult, Kalender und Geschichte: Semiotisierung von Zeit als kulturelle Konstruktion* (Tübingen: Gunter Narr Verlag), 103–33.

Tedeschi Grisanti, G. and H. Solin 2011. *Dis Manibus, pili, epitaffi et altre cose antiche di Giovannantonio Dosio* (Pisa: Edizioni ETS).

Tran, N. 2006. *Les membres des associations romaines: Le rang social des collegiati en Italie et en Gaule sous le Haut-Empire* (Rome: École française de Rome).

2012a. 'Associations privées et espace public: les emplois de *"publicus"* dans l'épigraphie des collèges de l'Occident romain', in Dondin-Payre, M. and N. Tran (eds.), *Collegia: Le phénomène associatif dans l'Occident romain* (Bordeaux: Ausonius Éditions), 63–80.

2012b. 'M. Sedatius Severianus et les corps de lénunculaires sous le principat d'Antonin le Pieux', *REA* 114: 323–44.

2014. 'C. Veturius Testius Amandus, les cinq corps de lénunculaires d'Ostie et la batellerie tibérine au début du IIIᵉ siècle', *MEFRA* 126: 131–45.

2020. 'Boatmen and their *corpora* in the great ports of the Roman west (second to third centuries AD)', in Arnaud, P. and S. Keay (eds.), *Roman Port Societies through the Evidence of Inscriptions* (Cambridge: Cambridge University Press), 85–106.

Van Haeperen, F. 2016. 'Origine et fonctions des *Augustales* (12 av. n.è.-37). Nouvelles hypothèses', *AC* 85: 127–55.

2018. 'Les dédicaces de *collegiati*: une marque de distinction?', *Cahiers du Centre Gustave-Glotz* 29: 295–309.

Van Nijf, O. M. 1997. *The Civic World of Professional Associations in the Roman East* (Amsterdam: J. C. Gieben).

10 | The Imperial Image in Media of Mechanical Reproduction

The Tokens of Rome

CLARE ROWAN

This contribution explores what the representation of the emperor on lead tokens can reveal about the dynamics of ideology formation.[1] A discussion of the ubiquity of the imperial portrait is followed by an introduction to the material; the chapter then turns to a series of case studies that demonstrate the permeable nature of the imperial portrait on small, portable objects that are produced in large volume.

In the correspondence between Marcus Aurelius and his Latin teacher Marcus Cornelius Fronto is a letter in which Fronto plays around (*ludere*) and acts a fool (*ineptire*), detailing his devotion to his pupil. The third of his admitted 'frivolities', before he turns back to more serious matters, is as follows:

> scis, ut in omnibus argentariis mensulis perguleis taberneis protecteis vestibulis fenestris usquequaque, ubique imagines vestrae sint volgo propositae, male illae quidem pictae pleraeque et crassa, lutea immo Minerva fictae scalptaeve; cum interim numquam tua imago tam dissimilis ad oculos meos in itinere accidit, ut non ex ore meo excusserit iactum osculei et savium.

> You know how at all the money-changers' tables, and in booths, shops, colonnades, entrance-courts, and windows, anywhere and anytime, there are your images on display to the crowds. They are quite badly painted, and many of them are sculpted and carved by heavy-handed (or more probably, talentless) artists. But even though I think your visage never looks more unlike you as I pass by, it still never fails to force a kiss from my mouth.[2]

---

[1] This contribution arises from the *Token Communities in the Ancient Mediterranean* project, which has received funding from the European Research Council (ERC) under the European Union's Horizon 2020 research and innovation programme under grant agreement No 678042. Citations from *BMCRLT* use the internal numbering system of the ancient lead tokens in the British Museum. A catalogue of these specimens is currently being prepared.
[2] Fronto, *Ep. ad M. Caes.* 4.12.4 (= 24.6 in Davenport and Manley, 2014). See Schneider, 2003: 61–2 for a discussion of this passage.

The ubiquity of imperial portraits of varying quality in the scene described by Fronto suggests that Rome was a city where the portrait of the emperor formed a backdrop to daily life. In spite of the unlikeness Fronto admits that he 'sees' Aurelius in the image and reacts accordingly, a response provoked by his affection and personal knowledge of the emperor.[3] But one imagines that not everyone reacted in the same way when they passed an imperial portrait, nor in an identical way every time – Fronto himself admits to occasionally being grumpy with Aurelius in the passage directly before that quoted here. The sheer number of imperial portraits in Rome provided innumerable viewing contexts, which, in turn, must have generated a wide variety of personal meanings and associations.

The image of the British queen might provide a parallel to think about the implications of Fronto's statement: the monarch's likeness is reproduced in newspapers, on coins, as waving dolls in storefronts, in graffiti, and on stamps, amongst innumerable other places. Many of these images may not bear a true likeness to the monarch, either because she has aged, or, as Fronto suggests, because the reproduction is in a sorry style.[4] The multiplicity of representations recalls the ideas expressed by Benjamin in his famous study *The Work of Art in the Age of Mechanical Reproduction*. In this essay Benjamin traced the changing nature of visual culture in the modern age. Art had previously been confined to a museum, church, or similarly 'appropriate' context; the technology of mass reproduction (e.g. photography, print) that arose during the industrial revolution meant that it came to be reproduced in a variety of media and displayed in a variety of contexts, which, in turn, changed the viewing experience.[5] The sudden ability to mechanically reproduce works of art in large volume and relatively cheaply meant that, for example, a marble sculpture once only seen within a museum might suddenly be photographed, printed, put on postcards and placed in multiple viewing contexts. This was a new phenomenon, but Benjamin acknowledged that the reproduction of artwork had also occurred in earlier periods, albeit on a smaller scale. Benjamin cited bronzes, terracottas, and coins as examples of this practice in antiquity; here we must note that amongst the images cited by Fronto are those on the

---

[3] The close personal relationship of Fronto with Marcus Aurelius is underlined in this passage by the allusion to the morning *salutatio* between patrons and clients, which, by this time, included a kiss from the client (Hurschmann, 2008). To be invited to the imperial *salutatio* was a sign of imperial favour; the passage thus also communicates Fronto's own prestigious position.

[4] For example, in Germany in 2015 the Queen was presented with a portrait of her younger self and was unable to recognise her father because of the style of the painting: www.theguardian.com/uk-news/2015/jun/24/queen-blue-horse-painting-german-state-visit.

[5] Benjamin, 1999: section 1.

money-changer's table. The effects of (mass) reproduction of images in antiquity, and how this contributed to the (co-)creation of imperial ideology, needs further scholarly attention.[6]

The mass of imperial portraits produced and reproduced within the Roman Empire must have resulted in individuals creating their own associations, as Pandey's contribution to this volume explores for Ovid. Indeed, the imperial portrait may have meant different things to different people, depending on their gender, class, region, age, and era.[7] Studies of modern-day leaders have demonstrated just such a diversity of associations. Buck-Morss, for example, has shown that during Barack Obama's 2008 presidential campaign the associations given to Obama and his image went well beyond the man himself or the control of his campaign team.[8] The famous 'Hope' poster, for example, was created independently by Shephard Fairey before it was adopted by Obama's campaign; the design is now a recognised visual topos reused in other contexts. Images live their own lives, and possess their own biographies. In particular, public, shared images that are open to reproduction have the power to shape a society and empower its users.[9] Once shared or made 'shareable', an image increases in power (since more people connect to it) and escapes the control of its maker, since the meaning of the image is extended by those who use or view it. The image of Obama came to embody the contradictory aspirations of different individuals (e.g. a US soldier in Afghanistan hoping for increased American military strength and an Afghan woman hoping for peace). Similarly, the moving, circulating imperial portrait must have led to multiple viewing contexts, meanings, and associations.[10]

I would argue that, to adopt the terminology of Buck-Morss, the imperial portrait was a 'shared' image. A shared image enters into collective consciousness, giving it a power to both reinforce and potentially disrupt social norms and conventions (as Ovid does in *Pont.* 2.8). An image that is restricted (e.g. locked in a museum storehouse or subject to restrictive copyright regulations), by contrast, cannot perform the same function since it is not widely recognisable, nor reproducible. The hidden and/or unintelligible images that referenced the praetorian guard explored by

---

[6] Die and hoard studies of Roman coinage have begun to think about the effects of mass reproduction in terms of imagery reception and communication (e.g. Noreña, 2011), but much of the discussion of reproductive media in antiquity has focused on aspects of production (the identification of dies and moulds, pattern books, techniques of production) rather than the impact of these types of objects.

[7] A concept also explored in Clarke, 2003.   [8] Buck-Morss, 2010.

[9] Mitchell, 2005; Buck-Morss, 2010.

[10] See Mwangi, 2002; Rowan, 2016a for this phenomenon on coinage.

Kelly in this volume might be seen as an example of a 'restricted' image; since these particular images were not widely recognised, the imagery was not reproduced in quantity. Although it is clear that in certain public or politically sensitive contexts the imperial image was tightly controlled – in the case of imperial cult (*neokoria*), for example, amongst client kings (as explored in Wilker's contribution), and within public/elite space (as discussed by Hellström) – on small, everyday, portable objects the imperial image was, quite literally, placed in the hands of the Roman people. These everyday images of the emperor, those that, at first sight, might not even look like the emperor, are representations that need further exploration in scholarship.[11]

The Tokens of Rome

During building works in Rome in the eighteenth and nineteenth centuries hundreds of lead monetiform objects came to light, particularly during works along the Tiber. One of the first publications of these objects was by Ficoroni, with a seminal catalogue later published by Rostovtzeff: *Tesserarum urbis Romae et suburbi plumbearum sylloge* (*TURS*).[12] Rostovtzeff consulted major museum holdings across Europe in compiling his work; despite the title of his catalogue, not all the pieces included came from Rome and its surrounds.[13] The analysis of tokens from different regions reveals regional variation in terms of material, manufacture, and design.[14] This contribution focuses specifically on the lead tokens that have a recorded find spot in Rome, specifically those accompanied in *TURS* by the phrase *in Tiberi reperta*, the tokens Rostovtzeff acquired in Rome and later donated to the Cabinet des Médailles in Paris (published in Rostovtzeff and Prou), and those from the Tiber published by Dressel and now in the Münzkabinett Berlin.[15]

---

[11] Though see Dahmen, 2001.

[12] Ficoroni, 1740; Rostovtzeff, 1903. An online version of these catalogues is underway and available at https://coins.warwick.ac.uk/token-types/.

[13] E.g. *TURS* 64 (from Hadrumetum), 509 (Aquileia), 863 (Frascati), 1193 (Nemi), 3119 (Smyrna); Rostovtzeff also cites Postolacca as a source for several entries, who published tokens from Athens.

[14] For example the tokens catalogued in Gülby and Kireç, 2008 display differences in fabric and design to those known from Roman Egypt, which are again different to those found in the Tiber, or from Athens.

[15] Rostovtzeff and Prou, 1900; Dressel, 1922.

These objects were labelled *tesserae*, a name that has persisted until the modern day despite the fact that it may be erroneous; these are not the *tesserae frumentariae* of our texts, for example, and one noun cannot hope to encapsulate the differing designs, shapes, and potential uses of these artefacts.[16] A variety of purposes for these objects have been proposed: in addition to the *tesserae* mentioned by texts in connection with distributions, they have variously been thought to have acted as tickets for events, transport tickets for river boats, money used in household and local community economies, substitute 'coins' to be given in festivals, gaming pieces, or counting tokens (*calculi*).[17] A bone token and several lead pieces have been found in excavations at Fregellae and are likely connected with the baths in the town, serving perhaps as entrance tickets, or as tokens to be exchanged for services once in the bathhouse.[18] The handful of known find locations from Rome suggest that tokens were distributed throughout the city: in addition to the banks of the Tiber, tokens and token moulds (made of palombino marble) have been found in the Roman forum near the portico of the Vestals, on the Esquiline, at Ostia, Hadrian's villa, and most recently in Neronian strata on the site of the *Curiae Veteres* on the Palatine.[19]

Rostovtzeff's catalogue focused on lead pieces cast from moulds (characteristic of tokens from Rome and Ostia), but ancient tokens were also made out of other materials – the tokens from Palmyra, for example, are mainly made from clay.[20] In Rome, tokens also existed in bronze, copper, or brass; these pieces were struck rather than cast and are generally of much higher quality (the infamous *spintriae*, a series which carried portraits of the Julio-Claudian imperial family, sexual scenes and other playful imagery, should be included amongst these).[21] A terracotta piece from Rome and now in the David Eugene Smith Collection at Columbia University with the head of Jupiter Ammon on one side and TIBI ME(?) | XXIII inscribed on the other side suggests that clay might also occasionally have been used for tokens in the capital.[22]

The lead tokens from the city of Rome carry a wide variety of designs. Many are images of deities or of a religious nature, with direct references to

---

[16] Virlouvet, 1988; 1995: 310–62.

[17] Rostovtzeff, 1905b; van Berchem, 1936; Thornton, 1980; Turcan, 1987: 51–65; Virlouvet, 1995: 362.

[18] Sironen, 1990; Pedroni, 1997.

[19] E.g. Rostovtzeff and Vaglieri, 1900: 256; Cesano, 1904: 208; Vaglieri, 1908: 332; 1912: 277; Bertoldi, 1997: 209; Stannard, 2015; Pardini *et al.*, 2016.

[20] Raja, 2015: 173.   [21] Buttrey, 1973; Küter, 2016.

[22] With thanks to Evan Jewell for bringing this piece and others to my attention. David Eugene Smith Collection of Mathematical Instruments (Box D6), Rare Book and Manuscript Library, Columbia University, no. 274. The final E at the end of the first line is uncertain.

the emperor (either through a portrait or an inscription) being less common.[23] The assortment of imagery and the distribution of tokens and token moulds throughout the city suggest that tokens served a variety of functions. If this hypothesis is correct, then this means that these objects must have been closely looked at: if small, leaden, circular objects could be used for distributions during a festival *or* during a banquet *or* for some other purpose, then it was only the image that communicated to users the object's validity.[24] Lead tokens, made cheaply from material that wears quickly, might have been single-use objects in many instances. But even a token made for a particular festival would have been closely examined, since, for example, the imagery would indicate for which specific day, product, or event the token was valid. In this sense, tokens offer both similarities and differences to Roman coinage. Coins were made from more durable materials, and were reused as the coin passed from user to user. Tokens may have been closely examined at a particular moment in time, while coinage was glanced at repeatedly over time.[25]

Rostovtzeff believed that the lead tokens were used by a variety of individuals and communities within Rome, but suggested the pieces carrying portraits of the emperor may have been created by the imperial government from Nero onwards in a cost-saving measure (cast lead being cheaper than struck brass or bronze).[26] In reality there is little difference between the quality and production techniques of the lead tokens Rostovtzeff thought 'imperial' and those he labelled as 'private'. Rather, we should view Roman lead tokens as objects produced not at the mint, but by a dispersed series of individuals and groups (including the imperial house), all utilising a similar production technique. The tokens made of bronze, copper, and orichalcum, the materials of money, may have been made at the mint or a specific workshop at the request of individuals or groups.[27]

---

[23] Direct references to the emperor also appear to be rare on tokens produced outside Rome. Gülby and Kireç, 2008: no. 203 from Ephesus may represent an imperial portrait, but, as discussed below, it can be difficult to identify these images with certainty. Turcan, 1987: no. 120, likely found in Lyon, shows a laureate bust (Caracalla?). Milne, 1971: no. 5416 (Egypt) and Dattari, 1901: no. 6437 (Egypt) also show an emperor. Antinous features on Egyptian tokens, but this may be because of his popularity as a god in the region. But these examples are a small amount within a much larger volume of material showing other designs.

[24] Other shapes (e.g. triangles, diamonds, squares) are known, but circular tokens are by far the most common.

[25] But the force of numismatic imagery is not lessened; see Mwangi, 2002 for a discussion.

[26] Rostovtzeff, 1905b: 27–30.

[27] Küter, 2016: 85 n. 6. The bronze tokens naming Gaius Mitreius, *magister iuventutis*, suggest that these higher-quality pieces were created by the same groups as lead pieces: a *magister* of the youth is also named on a lead piece, *TURS* 834.

Tokens invite a particular approach: these objects were designed for a specific purpose and a specific group, who would have understood the (frequently abbreviated) messages. This stands in contrast to other art reproduced on small objects, which were designed to appeal to a broader consumer base.[28] Indeed, handling lead tokens makes one realise just how much effort went into making particular messages clear on Roman coinage and other monuments. Many representations on Roman coins are labelled in the accompanying legend (e.g. a particular image is labelled as an *adlocutio* or *liberalitas* scene). This is not the case on lead tokens, and the targeted nature of their designs means that we can struggle to understand their significance, particularly in the case of the abbreviated Latin. Indeed, the abbreviation of both images and text that occurs on the tokens of Rome is, to my current knowledge, unparalleled in other media. These abbreviations may have been the result of the transfer of an image or text from one medium (e.g. a statue, relief, inscription) to these small lead objects (a process of remediation, discussed further below); acts of translation inevitably alter the message. But these abbreviations display a fluency and playfulness with Roman (visual) language that offers the potential for a deeper understanding of how Romans interacted with the mediascape around them.[29]

Coinage, Tokens, and Monuments in Motion

Many of the lead tokens in Rome are the size of the smallest Roman coin, the quadrans (*c.*14–18 mm), and some of their designs recall Roman quadrantes of the first century. Take for example Fig. 10.1, which shows a token found in the Tiber in Rome and a quadrans of 8 BCE. The token carries the name Q. Terentius Culleo, presumably the token's issuer.[30] The clasped hands echo the design of small change struck under Augustus, and the presentation

---

[28] Rostovtzeff, 1905b: 94–5.

[29] Clark, 2010 suggests that people can better understand abstract or surrogate situations when there is less detail in the representation (e.g. a schematic map drawn on paper as opposed to a detailed 3D model). This might offer a future avenue for the exploration of abbreviated or schematic images in the Roman world. Tokens in particular display a playfulness with money, something also identified in cryptocurrenices of the modern day, for which see Tooker, 2014: 29. A similar interaction and playfulness with broader Roman visual culture can be traced on Roman gems and glass pastes; see Maderna-Lauter, 1988.

[30] *TURS* 1323; Dressel, 1922: no. 4. See Gatti 1888: 439–40 for another of this type coming from the Tiber, along with 250 further tokens. Dressel (181) identifies this as the Q. Terentius Culleo who is listed as suffect consul in 40 in the consular *fasti* (Gallivan, 1979). Given that a large proportion of the tokens from the Tiber seem, on the basis of similarities to coin imagery, to date to the first half of the first century, the identification is certainly possible.

Figure 10.1 (left) Lead token. Q TERENTIVS CVLLEO around. / Clasped hands. *TURS* 1323, 17 mm, 12 h, 3.74 g, from the Tiber River in Rome. Formerly in the Dressel collection. Münzkabinett, Staatliche Museen zu Berlin, 18268503. Photographs: Bernhard Weisser, © Münzkabinett, Staatliche Museen zu Berlin. (right) Bronze quadrans. Clasped hands holding a caduceus, PVLCHER TAVRVS REGVLVS around. / III VIR A A A F F around s c. *RIC* I² Augustus 423, 17 mm, 6 h, 3.02 g. Image courtesy of the American Numismatic Society, 1975.114.4.

of Culleo's name on the other side also imitates coinage, running around the edge of the token in a circle. The quadrans shown here may not be the precise model (other Roman coins from later periods also show clasped hands), but the shape, size, and arrangement of the letters suggest that it is coinage that has formed the inspiration for this particular artefact. But the token does something that was no longer possible on coinage after Augustus: it carries the name of someone other than the emperor. (Moneyers' names, which frequently graced coinage of the Roman Republic, gradually disappeared from coinage under Augustus.) A very common token type found in the Tiber (with 205 reported examples) carries a *lituus* on one side and an hourglass-shaped altar on the other, images that also feature on Augustan quadrantes in the first half of the first century.[31] Other images that appear on both tokens from the Tiber and Roman quadrantes of the first century are an eagle with open wings, balanced scales, and a *modius* with corn-ears.[32]

It is entirely unsurprising that imperial coin imagery should be adapted in this way, since coinage, as a monument in motion, operated in a different way to other imperial monuments that were fixed in the landscape. Like modern media (Benjamin's photographs of artwork, for example), coins were a mass medium with an inherently unstable viewing context; one might encounter a coin image at the market, in a military camp, on a festival day, at home, or elsewhere. Moreover, the coin's image would be consistently juxtaposed against other images (e.g. other coins in circulation,

[31] *TURS* 1072; Dressel, 1922: no. 21. See *RIC* I² Augustus 421–5 for comparable images on Roman currency.
[32] *TURS* 301, 306, 383, 369 and *RIC* I² Augustus 227, Claudius 84, 85, 91.

or in an individual's purse), meaning that new associations would be continually generated.[33] The mobility of money meant that it was open to multiple meanings dependent on viewer and context, and, like Benjamin's work of art in the age of mechanical reproduction, this opened up 'ways of seeing' not possible with a monument fixed in a landscape, to which access routes were controlled.[34] We can trace this partly in texts: there are enough references to coins among ancient authors to demonstrate that the intended meaning of a coin was not necessarily the meaning ascribed to it by the user (at times to the detriment of the emperor concerned).[35] As mentioned above, images that are shared (not restricted) have the ability to escape the control of their makers and empower others, making the image more valuable as a communicative tool. It is thus not surprising that coin images should be readily adopted and remixed by the population of Rome.[36]

But as the image moved from coin to token, the meaning and associations of the image will have shifted, in the same way as meaning might change as a coin circulated. As mentioned above, images and words are abbreviated on tokens when compared to coins. One token from the Tiber carries the legend LAS on one side, and crossed cornucopiae, each topped with a human head, on the other (Fig. 10.2, left).[37] The design is similar to a sestertius struck under Tiberius (Fig. 10.2, right): scholars identify the two heads atop the cornucopiae on the coin type as the sons of Drusus the Younger, Tiberius Gemellus and Germanicus Julius Caesar. The type also appears under Antoninus Pius.[38] Imperial imagery, placed on an imperial monument in miniature (a coin), was then adapted and placed within a new context, now associated with the issuers of these tokens.

Although we are now comfortable discussing the social life of objects, we should consider that images too have a social life that goes beyond the media that carry them. The same image may exist on an arch, a coin, a token, as a descriptive piece of text, or in our mind as a mental image, and as it travels it

[33] Mwangi, 2002: 33–5.
[34] Clarke, 2003 similarly explores how monuments may have been read differently by different types of viewer.
[35] Krmnicek and Elkins, 2014. E.g. Suetonius' comment that Nero struck coinage of himself playing the lyre (Suet. *Ner.* 25.2) may have simply been Suetonius' (or someone else's) interpretation of an Apollo type – there is nothing to indicate this is Nero on the coinage itself (*RIC* I^2 Nero 73–82, 121–3, 205–11). Eusebius (*Vit. Const.* 15) records that Constantine portrayed himself on his coins with his eyes uplifted in prayer; the image, however, also recalls the uplifted eyes associated with posthumous representations of Alexander the Great, which may have been the intended reference.
[36] See also Dahmen, 2001: 274; Küter, 2016: 19.   [37] Dressel, 1922: no. 8.
[38] *RIC* III Antoninus Pius 185A–B, 857, 859, 961. With thanks to Charlotte Mann for pointing me to these types.

Figure 10.2 A lead token and a bronze sestertius: (left) Token. Two crossed cornucopiae, each topped with a young male head. / LAS. *TURS* 2418, 17 mm, 12 h, 2.97 g, from the Tiber River in Rome. Formerly in the Dressel collection. Münzkabinett, Staatliche Museen zu Berlin, 18268502. Photographs: B. Weisser, © Münzkabinett, Staatliche Museen zu Berlin. (right) Sestertius. Confronting heads of two boys on crossed cornucopiae (Tiberius Gemellus and Germanicus Julius Caesar?), with winged caduceus between them. / DRVSVS CAESAR TI AVG F DIVI AVG N PONT TR POT II around S C. *RIC* I^2 Tiberius 42, 34.5 mm, 6 h, 26.42 g. Image courtesy of the American Numismatic Society, 1957.172.1518.

gains new associations and creates new ways of seeing the world.[39] The extraordinary representation of Gemellus and Germanicus, once released on coinage, would have circulated as a monument in motion, glanced at in different contexts and alongside other monuments. The image was then adapted for representation in a different media, which in turn would have generated further associations. Once on a token, the image might then further act within this new context, shaping the event in which the token was used. On this particular piece, for example, the image may simply have communicated abundance, or the 'idea' of a coin, rather than carrying a strictly dynastic message. Imperial ideology was adapted, and the resultant creation perhaps no longer bore any connection to the imperial house. The meaning of LAS remains a mystery, but it may be an example of *tria nomina*; Roman graffiti, amphora stamps and other media often name individuals via their initials (e.g. LVP, CIP).[40] The abbreviation may have been meaningful only to the group using this particular artefact: the ability to 'understand' the token may have served to consolidate the feeling of 'belonging' to a particular community, in opposition to others for whom the meaning of the Latin was not clear.[41]

Given the similarities in shape and design between many tokens and Roman coinage, it has been suggested that some tokens might have functioned

[39] Kopytoff, 1986; Mitchell, 2005; Rowan, 2016a: 34–44.   [40] Benefiel, 2010: 73–4.

[41] This type of cryptic message is also known from Roman coinage, most famously with the issues of Carausius that carry the abbreviations RSR and INPCDA, which refer to specific lines of Virgil's works and were probably understood only by a literate inner elite (Bédoyère, 1998).

Figure 10.3 Lead token. Male bust right, OLYMPIANVS around. / EVCARPVS around H̶S̶ ∞. *TURS* 1460, 18 mm, 3.8 g. Image courtesy of the American Numismatic Society, 2002.42.3.

as small change, like the merchant tokens of more modern eras.[42] A handful of the tokens from Rome do make a direct reference to monetary amounts, including Fig. 10.3, which carries the legend OLYMPIANVS and a male portrait on one side, and the legend EVCARPVS around the amount of H̶S̶ ∞, or 1,000 sestertii.[43] More than 100 examples of tokens of this type emerged from the environs of the Tiber.[44] Once again the similarities to coinage are striking: the legend around the monetary amount is similar in design to the legend around s c on the sestertius shown in Fig. 10.2 (right), which was a common reverse design for Roman bronze coinage of the early imperial period. Instead of a bust of the emperor it is probably the bust of Olympianus that is shown; a legend encircles the portrait, similar to the obverse design of the majority of Roman imperial precious-metal currency.

It is unlikely that this small lead piece was in itself worth 1,000 sestertii. Rostovtzeff believed that many of the lead tokens must have functioned as money in small-scale economies, particularly within Roman household economies involving patrons and clients. This piece, then, might represent the fact that Olympianus and Eucarpus had created the equivalent of 1,000 sestertii to distribute amongst their own client circle, similar to the way an emperor might communicate his munificence with a *liberalitas* coin type.[45] Martial uses the word *plumbeus* (lead) to refer to the low value of *sportulae* (money or food given by patrons) in his work and Rostovtzeff suggested

[42] Rostovtzeff, 1905b: 104–9; Dressel, 1922: 182; Rostovtzeff, 1957: 182; Thornton, 1980: 338–9.

[43] *TURS* 1038 and 2680 may carry the denarius sign, X̶, although the symbol might also be read as a star. Rostovtzeff, 1905b: 99.

[44] Dressel, 1922: no. 5.   [45] Rostovtzeff, 1905b: 99.

this provided further evidence of lead tokens being used in this context.[46] It is difficult, however, to come to any firm conclusions on the basis of the satirist alone; other interpretations of his text have been proposed. Fig. 10.3 and tokens like it might also have been used for gambling or for some other purpose; there is simply not enough evidence available at the present time to come to a definitive conclusion. Indeed, given that some lead tokens carry legends that connect them to the Saturnalia (discussed below), a satiric context for this particular type cannot be ruled out.

Some tokens carry the portrait of the emperor and a legend naming him (discussed in the next section), but some simply carry a portrait. Given the style of many of these pieces, it is impossible to tell in many instances whether this is intended to be a representation of a member of the imperial family or a representation of the issuer of the token. One example is Fig. 10.4, a token carrying the portrait of a woman with a distinctly Flavian hairstyle. Rostovtzeff suggested this was the daughter of Titus, Julia Flavia, while Thornton, in an unpublished catalogue of tokens kept in the British Museum, suggested Domitia.[47] But it is just as likely that this is a representation of a private woman; imperial women formed a focal point for elite female

Figure 10.4 Lead token. Female bust right. / ıı. *TURS* 51, 20 mm, 3 h, 5.70 g. Object on study loan to the teaching collection, Department of Classics and Ancient History, The University of Warwick.

---

[46] Mart. 1.99.11–15 and 10.74.1–4; Rostovtzeff, 1905b: 110; Thornton, 1980: 349; with a more sceptical interpretation provided by Virlouvet, 1988: 123–4.

[47] There are no reported find spots for this token type, and to date the only examples known are two housed in the British Museum (Thornton, unpublished, *BMCRLT* nos. 878–9), and the specimen published here.

self-representation, and the legends on other tokens indicate that some might have been issued by women.[48] The very specific audience and context of these tokens meant that the image's meaning would presumably have been understood at the time, but it does create an ambiguity between the representations of individuals and representations of the emperor on everyday objects in Rome.

Tokens and the Creation of Imperial Ideology

Lead tokens also bore clearer representations of the imperial family, with Nero appearing with relative frequency.[49] Fig. 10.5 shows two examples of these tokens. On the first, the emperor's portrait is accompanied by the legend NERO CAESAR; on the other side is a representation of a soldier or the god Mars, with a palm branch behind.[50] Nero's portrait here brings to mind Fronto's comment about the varying quality of imperial images; but what Fronto suggests is that, no matter how poor the quality, the emperor might still be recognised. Examining the tokens that name Nero (and so we know the accompanying portrait is an intentional portrayal of the emperor), we find that several echo official imagery of the period, with types connecting him to Agrippina, to Roma, to Victory, and to Apollo playing the lyre.[51] Thus, these objects would have contributed, in the small circles in which they

Figure 10.5 (left) Lead token. Bare head of Nero left, NERO CAESAR around. / Mars or a soldier standing, holding spear in left hand and resting right hand on shield; large branch behind. *TURS* (Supplement) 3624 (cf. *TURS* 17, without branch), 18 mm, 12 h, 2.3 g. Photographs © Ashmolean Museum, University of Oxford. (right) Lead token. Laureate head of Nero right. / Charioteer (*auriga*) in a chariot with eight horses right. *TURS* 31, 18 mm, 12 h, 2.44 g. Photographs © Ashmolean Museum, University of Oxford.

---

[48] Fejfer, 2008: 331–72 on this phenomenon for sculpture. Examples include *TURS* 1131 (Apronia), 1207 (Domitia), 1240 (Hortensia), and 1248 (Julia).
[49] Thornton, 1980: 336.   [50] cf. Dressel, 1922: no. 2.
[51] *TURS* 14, 19, 25, 27 (no recorded find spots).

were used, to the overall ideology surrounding the emperor. For these types of tokens, which name only the emperor and no other individual, we cannot know whether the authority was the imperial house or other individuals. The imagery we see on these pieces is reminiscent of provincial coinage, another medium that can provide a useful framework for the interpretation of these objects. Provincial coinage carried local variations of imperial ideology, often reacting to or extending official images, and tokens indicate that the same process was taking place in the imperial capital.

Like provincial coinage, tokens also combined imperial portraiture with imagery not found on official money. One token from the Tiber juxtaposes Octavia on one side with Victory holding a wreath on the other, a connection not found on Roman coinage, which connects the goddess only with the emperor.[52] One type portrays Nero on one side and Claudia on the other, and another combines the head of Nero with a chariot of eight horses rather than the usual four (Fig. 10.5, right).[53] The rider appears to be carrying a whip, suggesting that what is represented is an eight-horse chariot race. The juxtaposition of a reference to an *octoiugus* and Nero brings to mind various comments from ancient authors about Nero's charioteering (he once fell while riding a chariot of ten horses).[54] The token is a material manifestation of this aspect of Nero's public image, although it is impossible to reconstruct whether the imagery was meant to be an ironic or critical commentary, or a more straightforward communication of imperial ideology.

Abbreviation of the imperial image is also found: one token (with no recorded find spot) places the letters N E on either side of the soldier/Mars seen in Fig. 10.5 (left), and then the letters C A E S above two clasped hands on the other.[55] The legend on both sides must be resolved as NERO CAESAR. Rostovtzeff suggests that a further token with the letters N C in a wreath might also refer to NERO CAESAR.[56] Abbreviations also exist for other imperial names, with several variations known for Titus and Domitian (e.g. Fig. 10.6).[57]

A series of tokens made from pewter, with very thin flans and carrying images of the Julio-Claudian dynasty, also demonstrate how tokens might adapt and extend the imperial image. A pewter token found in the river Garigliano, 80 miles south of Rome and 35 miles north of Naples, shows on

---

[52] *TURS* 33.   [53] *TURS* 31, 34 (no recorded find spots).

[54] Suet. *Ner.* 22.1–2, 24.2; Tac. *Ann.* 14.14; Cass. Dio 63.1.1, 63.6.2–3. Nero is also associated with chariot-racing on tokens of late antiquity (contorniates). See by way of example BM R.4857; BM R.4829; BM 1846,0910.270; BM 1844,0425.709; BM 1853,0512.242.

[55] *TURS* 18.

[56] *TURS* 22 (no recorded find spot). The other side of the token carries the legend ARM REG, which Rostovtzeff resolves as *Armenis Regis* (?).

[57] *TURS* 43–7 (no recorded find spots).

Figure 10.6 Lead token. IMP TCA = *Imp(erator) T(itus) Ca(esar)* / DOM CAE = *Dom(itianus) Cae(sar)*. *TURS* 46, 16 mm, 12 h, 1.59 g. Photographs © Ashmolean Museum, University of Oxford.

one side the bare head of Claudius and the legend TI CLAVDIVS CAES. On the other side is Venus standing left with her left hand resting on the head of a cupid, who holds a rudder, accompanied by the legend COLO VEN (another specimen of the same type is reported from the Liri).[58] The location of the find, the legend, and the image strongly a suggest a reference to the colony of Venusia, the 'City of Venus'.[59] This token was found alongside others showing Julia (daughter of Germanicus), Octavia (with Victory on the other side), and Nero.[60] Other artefacts from the river (small handled amphora, other tokens, small statuettes, curse tablets) are suggestive of a watery votive deposit. Another votive context is known from the sanctuary of Hercules at Alba Fucens. In the well within the sanctuary were found two lead tokens: one of the thin flan series showing Claudius on one side and Messalina on the other, and the other a lead token showing Nero on one side and Jupiter on the other, accompanied by the legend MAN FOR.[61] It is likely that the tokens became votive objects after fulfilling their original function. In selecting these items as an offering, the dedicants may have been influenced by the imagery on the

[58] Mitchiner, 1984: 107. The token is 21 mm, 3 g. Mitchiner's description of the token as showing Messalina and Britannicus is incorrect; for a better description and image see Clive Stannard's unpublished collection of cast lead tokens from the river Liri, 29.015.
[59] This particular subset of tokens is the topic for a forthcoming study by the author, on Italian tokens in the Julio-Claudian period.
[60] Mitchiner also suggests tokens are present showing Marcus Aurelius and Hadrian, but these specimens carry no legend, and the portraiture quality makes it difficult to be conclusive.
[61] Ceccaroni and Molinari, 2017. The token types are *TURS* 531 and Alba Fucens 1 (https://coins .warwick.ac.uk/token-types/id/albafucens1).

tokens and/or their materiality: these were lead 'coin-like' objects with little 'real world' value.[62]

It is thus clear that as the imperial image moved from one medium to another it attracted new meanings and was 'remixed', abbreviated, or extended. In this context it might be useful to borrow a term from media theory: remediation. The term was created to describe the process of translation of one medium into another: the text found on an *ostrakon*, for example, transferred into a book, and then into code to be saved onto a computer.[63] Media constantly comment on, reproduce and replace each other; indeed, media need other media to survive.[64] Moreover, acts of remediation (the reproduction of particular texts, images, topoi, etc.) solidify community and cultural memory, creating a shared and accepted 'history'.[65] In our case, the imagery carried on coinage (and perhaps else-where) was translated onto a token, whose design then simultaneously reinforces particular shared images even as they develop in meaning. We can take this concept further with the idea of premediation, which recog-nises that we see, remember, and record events according to culture; and culture is contained within media (books, sculpture, paintings, coins, etc.). Media not only solidify cultural memory and identity, but also shape our future experience and how this is recorded. This process has most clearly been explored for the wars of the twentieth century. British participants in World War I, for example, recorded their experiences according to class and culture: high-ranking officers often used the classical world as a framework to write about their experiences, while those from the middle class more commonly used Shakespeare.[66] As this contribution has begun to demonstrate, coinage may also have premediated and shaped experience in the Roman world.

Imperial Ideology, the Emperor, and Festivals

It is clear that one of the most pervasive imperial media in the Roman world, coinage, premediated experience and shaped its representation.

---

[62] Lead objects that imitate coinage are known from votive river contexts in Britain (e.g. Portable Antiquities Scheme BM-512402, BM-60DF84, SWYOR-7600E1). Sauer's analysis of the votive offerings at a spring in Bourbonne-les-Bains (France) indicates that very small-value coins (quadrantes) were frequently chosen as offerings, but it is clear that individuals consciously chose to offer coin pieces showing Augustus rather than Agrippa, so imagery also played a role in the selection process (Sauer, 2005: 20).

[63] Bolter and Grusin, 2000.   [64] Erll, 2007: 29–30.   [65] Erll, 2008; Rowan, 2020.

[66] Fussell, 1975; Erll, 2009.

Figure 10.7 Lead token. P GLITI GALLI around male head. / Rooster standing right holding a wreath and palm branch. *TURS* 1238, 19 mm, 12 h, 2.66 g. Photographs © Ashmolean Museum, University of Oxford.

Coinage was a key contributor to tokens' form and language of expression. A further example is Fig. 10.7, a lead token carrying the legend P GLITI GALLI around a male bust, presumably the representation of Gallus himself.[67] The other side of the token carries the image of a rooster (a pun on the name *Gallus*) carrying a wreath and palm branch, the traditional attributes of Victory.[68] Here, however, they are very clearly connected to Gallus and his *gens*. The wreath and palm branch were also connected to other victorious or joyful moments in Roman life: they are shown carried by victorious charioteers, for example, or in connection with festivals (Victory with a palm branch appears on the New Year's lamp discussed in Russell's contribution in this volume). Wreaths and palm branches also appear on lead tokens connected to the Saturnalia, which include the chant *io Sat[urnalia] io!*[69] Gallus' piece may also have been produced for the Saturnalia or some other festival; whatever the context, the occasion was represented on a token within a set visual language premediated by coinage. As a medium that circulated and pervaded daily life, coinage played a role in shaping people's experience; the process may have been unconscious, but was no less powerful for this. Banal objects like

[67] An additional image can be found at *TURS* Pl. IV, 33. Rostovtzeff, 1905b: 105 suggests this is the P. Glitius Gallus known from Tac. *Ann.* 15.56.71, who lived under Nero.
[68] The visual pun on Gallus' name ('canting type') has precedent on the coinage of the Roman Republic, where moneyers used coin types to advertise familial identity and history; e.g. the Torquati often placed a torque on coins when they were moneyers (e.g. *RRC* 411/1a–b).
[69] E.g. Rostovtzeff and Prou, 1900: no. 102 (from Rome); *TURS* 501–10.

coinage are powerful 'background media' to the everyday, acting upon us even if we are not aware of them.[70]

The Saturnalia, of course, turned social norms upside down temporarily, allowing satirical interaction with the emperor and other modes of power, if only to reinforce normative orders.[71] Thus some 'liberties' that might be taken with the imperial image appear to have been constrained by time; it is surely no accident that many of our surviving satirical works are set within the context of the Saturnalia. But the tokens representing the imperial family might have been created at any time; logic suggests that the government cannot have formally approved each and every use of the imperial portrait by each and every individual within the Roman Empire. Small objects like these tokens may not have necessarily needed imperial permission or attracted imperial notice, but they would nonetheless have formed part of the material experience of the Empire's inhabitants. They, and their creators, thus participated in the co-creation of the imperial image and imperial ideology.

Imperial portraits appear on tokens of *collegia*, *municipia*, and other organisations. Rostovtzeff suggested that the appearance of the imperial portrait in these contexts indicated that the associated festivals or groups were formed with the permission of the emperor, or that the emperor provided (partial) funding.[72] While this might be the case in some instances (the tokens themselves reveal nothing in this regard), the use of the imperial portrait across a variety of everyday media suggests that imperial permission or funding cannot have been the motivation in each case. Indeed, given that many *collegia* were created with the hope of increased social advancement or prestige, the imperial portrait may have been placed on the tokens of these associations because it was an image that connoted power and elite status, one that suggested a connection between the (relatively humble) community group and the very top of Roman society.[73] Fig. 10.8, for example, a token type found in the Tiber, carries a deified image of an emperor (Rostovtzeff believed it was Nerva) with the legend DI AVG, and the name of the association (*sodales consuales*) placed on the other side.

Rostovtzeff suggested this token, and others like it, may have been used in *collegia* distributions during imperial celebrations (e.g. the *dies imperii*); inscriptional evidence from Rome demonstrates that associations did distribute money, bread, and wine on such occasions.[74] Tokens carrying well wishes to the emperor (*feliciter*) may also have been created for similar

---

[70] Yarrow, 2013.   [71] Dolansky, 2011; Miller, 2012.   [72] Rostovtzeff, 1905b: 86.
[73] Perry, 2011: 508–11.   [74] Rostovtzeff, 1905b: 98; *CIL* 6.33885.

Figure 10.8 Lead token. Radiate head of an emperor, DI AVG on left. / SODAL CONSVA in two lines. *TURS* 879, 20 mm, 6 h, 2.42 g. Image courtesy of the American Numismatic Society, 1967.160.10.

contexts, although we have no evidence beyond the design of the tokens themselves to support this.[75] But if they were used on imperial festival days, or during festivities associated with the emperor, then we should pause to consider the implications: it is the organisations themselves who contributed to the creation of the material (and thus the experience) associated with this festival. Analogous evidence is a terracotta token from Palmyra that carries the name of the city in Greek and a female portrait that resembles an empress, perhaps Sabina (Marciana has also been suggested); given that many tokens in Palmyra are connected with banqueting, this object may have served as an invitation or ticket to a feast held by the city in Hadrian's honour when the emperor visited.[76]

The role festival objects had in contributing to the image of the emperor might also be seen on the tokens that carry the names of *curatores*. Rostovtzeff believed these referenced *curatores ludorum*, officials responsible for the games; however, *collegia* also had positions with this title.[77] What role, if any, these tokens played in festivals remains unknown, but the objects do join imperial imagery to the name of a *curator*. One example from the Tiber carries the legend CAECILIVS IVSTVS around the word CVR (again similar to the way that the legend moves around S C on Roman bronze coinage), while the other side of the token carries a shield decorated

---

[75] E.g. *TURS* 66 (no recorded find spot) with HAD AVG on one side of the token and P P F on the other, plausibly an abbreviation of *Hadriano Augusto patri patriae feliciter*. FEL also appears on bronze tokens with the portrait of Augustus; see Buttrey, 1973: 61 no. 5. On tokens and imperial acclamations see Burnett, 2016: 75–95.

[76] Salzmann, 1989.   [77] Rostovtzeff, 1905b: 49–51.

with a bust (of Caligula?) above an eagle with its wings spread.[78] Another token carries a laureate bust (Tiberius has been suggested) and the legend Q. CAECILIVS Q.F. OINOGENVS F around the word CVR.[79] Whether these objects were used as tickets, to organise distributions, or for some other purpose, we might plausibly connect them to particular events connected to the named *curatores*. The image of the emperor, then, would have formed a backdrop for the experience of the event, perhaps even unconsciously forming part of the individual or collective memory of a particular moment. This, in turn, would have shaped how the event was remembered.

Several tokens in museum collections or that have appeared on the market are pierced. Although some may have been altered more recently, it is safe to assume that some examples must have been pierced in antiquity, with the token then perhaps serving as a memento of a particular event.[80] The discovery of tokens in tombs also suggests that they might have transformed into souvenirs, a form of 'commemorative materiality'.[81] In a tomb from Mutina a copper *spintria* was found with traces of gold leaf on it, which makes the suggestion that these short-term, single-use objects might be converted into long-term objects of memory even more compelling.[82]

A Banal Image?

Fronto's comment to Marcus Aurelius suggests that the imperial image may have formed an (unconscious) backdrop to the everyday life of Rome's inhabitants, a 'banal' symbol much like a flag hanging limp in the corner of a post office building.[83] The imperial portrait, whether a good likeness or not, was likely present during numerous everyday occurrences inside and outside the home; in addition to coins, tokens, sculpture, and large monuments, we should also think about seals, weights, paintings, lamps, cakes, military equipment, and other everyday objects.[84] Not all of these images

---

[78] *TURS* 515, pl. IV 32.

[79] Rostovtzeff, 1905b: 48; Franke, 1984; Gregori, 1997: 165; Harris, 2000. Oinogenus was probably an equestrian.

[80] E.g. *BMCRLT* 524, a token with the image of Fortuna on one side and two facing busts on the other, which may, or may not, be imperial portraits.

[81] Munzi, 1997; Saunders, 2001: 479–80.

[82] Benassi *et al.*, 2003; Campana, 2009: 49. On *spintriae* see Buttrey, 1973 and Martini, 1999.

[83] Billig, 1995: 8, and 41 on the role of coinage.

[84] Dahmen, 2001. Examples include the Severan tondo, Harvard Art Museums 1949.82 (a weight with an imperial bust); Getty 83.AQ.377.206, 83.AQ.377.92 (lamps with a laureate portrait of Hadrian (?)); BM 1854,0717.53 (horse trappings from Xanten in Germany with an imperial bust

will have been high-quality likenesses, but nonetheless they were likely 'viewed' as the current ruler, as Fronto 'sees' Marcus Aurelius. It is from this perspective that we might begin to better understand activities like the reuse of a bust of Caracalla for a dedication to Constantine: perhaps many of the imperial images, like some of those we find on tokens, did not necessarily 'look like' the emperor, and perhaps they did not need to be a true likeness, at least in some contexts.[85]

A further example of the use of imperial portraits in the everyday can be found on another class of object commonly labelled as *tesserae*. These are the bone or ivory circular pieces with an image engraved in relief on one side and an incised inscription on the other, accompanied by an incised number in both Greek and Latin. These objects have been found throughout the Roman Empire, including Rome.[86] The discovery of fifteen such objects neatly stacked in a box in a child's tomb in Kerch (Crimea) means we now believe they are counters used to play a game whose rules have been lost to antiquity.[87] The pieces from Kerch are characteristic of the wider series, in that they displayed a variety of deities, Alexandrian suburbs, and Muses, all named in Greek on the other side. Amongst the fifteen was a piece showing a male bust. The other side of the counter names the bust as Augustus, CEBACTOC, and is accompanied by the number one (i and A). The imperial portrait on the other side bears only a vague resemblance to the official portraits of the first *princeps*. It appears, then, that amongst this elite child's playing counters was an image of Rome's first emperor; we should pause to think how the imperial image in this context sat alongside images of gods and Egyptian buildings, essentially to be used for play. Caesar, Tiberius, Nero, and empresses are also known on these playing pieces, at times represented almost in caricature.[88]

In certain contexts, however, portrait likeness did matter. Arrian writes in the *Periplus* that Hadrian's statue at Trapezus had some merit, but looked nothing like the 'original' and was of indifferent execution. Arrian goes on to request a statue from Hadrian 'worthy to be called yours', since the location was a good one for perpetuating the emperor's memory (he also requests new statues of Hermes and Apollo Philesius).[89] Arrian's last

---

of either Claudius or Nero). Boon, 1958 published a pastry cook's mould from Silchester with the representation of the Severan imperial family; see also Alföldi, 1938–41: 313–14, for the use of imperial imagery on Roman baked goods.

[85] Dahmen, 2001: 153, cat. 24, pl. 24.

[86] Graillot, 1896 on find spots in Rome and its environs. See also Capitoline Museums inv. AntCom 18584, 18586.

[87] Rostovtzeff, 1905a; Alföldi-Rosenbaum, 1976; 1980; Bianchi, 2015 (with further find contexts).

[88] Alföldi-Rosenbaum, 1984.   [89] Arr., *Peripl. M. Eux.* 1.2–3.

comment, on the quality of the location, provides a clue to interpreting the request. Highly visible images were controlled in a way that less conspicuous images were not (for example the imperial *imagines* of *corpora* discussed by Tran in this volume). It is thus frequently these very public images that were called into action or given ideological weight at specific moments. But many of the images carried on smaller objects, like those discussed in this contribution, escaped the *damnatio memoriae* and other pointed uses of imagery that took place on larger media.[90]

'The reproduced image increases in value by being shared.'[91] If we return to the idea of the 'shared' or empowering image, we may begin to explore how the image of the emperor shaped the cultural memories, identities, and experiences of different communities in the Roman world. The imperial image had its own life; it escaped the control of its maker. But this process only made the image more valuable: all who saw the emperor's visage may have had different associations dependent on time, experience, and place, but all recognised the image and could connect with it. The ability to communicate and connect to a disparate group of people through a single image is what gave the imperial portrait its value as a communicative, and community-building, tool. The very act of allowing wider use of the imperial likeness by multiple groups gave it power, as much as the image itself embodied the ultimate power of Roman society. As it lived its social life, the 'value' of the emperor's portrait in the minds of its users would only have increased as they too contributed to its reproduction.

Although this contribution has focused on the person of the emperor, tokens also engaged with imperial ideology beyond the emperor's portrait.[92] This, however, must remain an area for future study. Token images and contexts contributed to what ultimately must have been a perception of the emperor shaped by personal experience: location, time, and status would have determined how one understood the emperor and his family. To end with a provocation: adopting the idea of the *musée imaginaire* of the French theorist Malraux, might it be useful to think about an 'imperial image without walls', in which images moving in a social life

---

[90] For example, most coins of condemned emperors continued to circulate unaltered for years after the pertinent *damnatio memoriae*; even on provincial coinage, alterations or erasures of condemned emperors occur on relatively few specimens. Acts of *damnatio* are also rare on small personal objects like gems and cameos. See Calomino, 2016: 15–17.

[91] Buck-Morss, 2010: 58.

[92] E.g. through the representation of buildings. *TURS* 107–10 shows a triumphal arch (no recorded find spots).

were juxtaposed in the mind to create unique and differing understandings of the Roman emperors?

Conclusion: Reproduction and the Imperial Image

Scholars since Benjamin have identified the revolutionary effect of media of reproduction, and I would argue that it is no surprise that similar technology in the Roman world had similar effects. Coinage in particular was a technology of reproduction that formed a mass medium in motion that consciously or unconsciously shaped the daily experience of the empire's inhabitants. Coinage was also a medium that contributed to the memory of past events and shaped future representations: the similarities between tokens and coinage demonstrate this. Lead tokens, along with lamps, cakes, and other objects that were easily manufactured from cheap materials, contributed to a ubiquitous imperial image of the sort described by Fronto. The imperial image was 'shared', meaning that the emperor came to embody more associations than the Roman government ever intended. In this sense it might be better to talk of the 'imperial images' of a particular ruler. This type of perspective adds complexity to our traditional understanding of imperial ideology, but it is perhaps an approach more in keeping with how people experienced images and messages in the Roman Empire.

Alongside the large statues, triumphal arches, and other monuments that often attract scholarly attention, there was a world of images and ideology that did not require governmental approval or attract close government scrutiny. And this is important: I suggest that if the imperial image had been tightly controlled at all levels of society, then it would not have been as effective. A powerful image is one that all sectors of society might connect with, even if each person had a different idea of what the image 'meant'.[93] Allowing the inhabitants of the Roman Empire to be co-creators of imperial ideology meant that ultimately a more personalised, and thus more powerful, connection to the emperor was generated. The emperor was not simply the head of government, but an image that was connected to the very fabric of one's lived experience, even if the image of the ruler looked nothing like the man sitting on the throne.

---

[93] Rowan, 2016b.

Bibliography

Alföldi, A. 1938–41. 'Tonmodel und Reliefmedaillons aus den Donauländern', in *Laureae aquincenses, memoriae Valentini Kuzsinszky dicatae: Aquincumi babérágak, Kuzsinszky Bálint emlékének szenteli Budapest székesfőváros közönsége és a Pázmány-Egyetem Érem-és Régiségtani Intézete*. Dissertationes Pannonicae Series 2, 10 (Budapest: Institut für Münzkunde und Archaeologie der P. Pázmany-Universität), 312–41.

Alföldi-Rosenbaum, E. 1976. 'Alexandriaca: studies on Roman game counters III', *Chiron* 6: 205–39.

1980. 'Ruler portraits on Roman game counters from Alexandria (Studies on Roman game counters III)', in Stucky, R. A. and I. Jucker (eds.), *Eikones: Studien zum griechischen und römischen Bildnis* (Bern: Francke Verlag Bern), 29–39.

1984. 'Characters and caricatures on game counters from Alexandria', in Bonacasa, N. and A. Di Vita (eds.), *Alessandria e il mondo ellenistico-romano: Studi in onore di Achille Adriani* (Rome: 'L'Erma' di Bretschneider), 378–90.

Bédoyère, G. de la 1998. 'Caurausius and the marks RSR and INPCDA', *NC* 158: 79–88.

Benassi, F., N. Giordani, and C. Poggi 2003. 'Una tessera numerale con scena erotica da un contesto funerario di *Mutina*', *NAC* 32: 249–73.

Benefiel, R. R. 2010. 'Dialogues of ancient graffiti in the House of Maius Castricius in Pompeii', *AJA* 114: 59–101.

Benjamin, W. 1999. 'The work of art in the age of mechanical reproduction', in *Illuminations* (London: Pimlico), 211–44.

Bertoldi, M. E. 1997. *Antike Münzfunde aus der Stadt Rom (1870–1902): Il problema delle provenienze* (Berlin: Gebr. Mann Verlag).

Bianchi, C. 2015. '"Pedine alessandrine": testimoni illustri di un gioco ignoto', in Lambrugo, C., F. Slavazzi, and A. M. Fedeli, *I materiali della Collezione Archeologica 'Giulio Sambon' di Milano. 1. Tra alea e agòn: giochi di abilità e di azzardo* (Milan, Università degli Studi di Milano), 53–65.

Billig, M. 1995. *Banal Nationalism* (London: Sage Publications).

Bolter, J. D. and R. Grusin 2000. *Remediation: Understanding New Media* (Cambridge, MA: MIT Press).

Boon, G. C. 1958. 'A Roman pastrycook's mould from Silchester', *AntJ* 38: 237–40.

Buck-Morss, S. 2010. 'Obama and the image', in N. Curtis (ed.), *The Pictorial Turn* (London: Routledge), 49–68.

Burnett, A. 2016. 'Zela, acclamations, Caracalla – and Parthia?', *BICS* 59: 72–110.

Buttrey, T. 1973. 'The *spintriae* as a historical source', *NC* 13: 52–63.

Calomino, D. 2016. *Defacing the Past: Damnation and Desecration in Imperial Rome* (London: Spink).

Campana, A. 2009. 'Le spintriae: tessere romane con raffigurazioni erotiche', in *La donna romana: Immagini e vita quotidiana* (Cassino: Diana), 43–96.

Ceccaroni, E. and M. C. Molinari 2017. 'I reperti numismatici provenienti dai recenti scavi del santuario di Ercole di Alba Fucens' in Caccamo Caltabiano, M. (ed.), *XV International Numismatic Congress Taormina 2015: Proceedings* (Rome; Messina: International Numismatic Commission), 717–19.

Cesano, L. 1904. 'Matrici di tessere di piombo nei musei di Roma', *BCAR* 32: 203–14.

Clark, A. 2010. 'Material surrogacy and the supernatural: reflections on the role of artefacts in "off-line" cognition', in Malafouris, L. and C. Renfrew, *The Cognitive Life of Things: Recasting the Boundaries of the Mind* (Cambridge: McDonald Institute for Archaeological Research), 23–8.

Clarke, J. R. 2003. *Art in the Lives of Ordinary Romans* (Berkeley: University of California Press).

Dahmen, K. 2001. *Untersuchungen zu Form und Funktion kleinformatiger Porträts der römischen Kaiserzeit* (Münster: Scriptorium).

Dattari, G. 1901. *Numi Augg. Alexandrini: Catalogo della collezione G. Dattari* (Cairo: Arnaldo Forni Editore).

Davenport, C. and J. Manley 2014. *Fronto: Selected Letters* (London: Bloomsbury).

Dolansky, F. 2011. 'Celebrating the Saturnalia: religious ritual and Roman domestic life', in Rawson, B. (ed.), *A Companion to Families in the Greek and Roman Worlds* (Malden, MA: Blackwell), 487–503.

Dressel, H. 1922. 'Römische Bleimarken', *ZfN* 33: 178–83.

Erll, A. 2007. *Prämediation – Remediation: Repräsentation des indischen Aufstands in imperialen und post-kolonialen Medienkulturen (von 1857 bis zur Gegenwart)* (Trier: Wissenschaftlicher Verlag Trier).

2008. 'Literature, film, and the mediality of cultural memory', in Erll, A. and A. Nünning (eds.), *Media and Cultural Memory / Medien und kulturelle Erinnerung* (Berlin: De Gruyter), 389–98.

2009. 'Remembering across time, space, and cultures: premediation, remediation and the "Indian Mutiny"', in Erll, A. (ed.), *Mediation, Remediation, and the Dynamics of Cultural Memory* (Berlin: De Gruyter), 109–38.

Fejfer, J. 2008. *Roman Portraits in Context* (Berlin: De Gruyter).

Ficoroni, F. 1740. *I piombi antichi* (Rome: Girolamo Mainardi).

Franke, P. R. 1984. 'Q. Caecilius Q.F. Oinogenus F. Curator', *ZPE* 54: 125–6.

Fussell, P. 1975. *The Great War and Modern Memory* (Oxford: Oxford University Press).

Gallivan, P. A. 1979. 'The *fasti* for the reign of Gaius', *Antichthon* 13: 66–9.

Gatti, G. 1888. 'Oggetti scoperti nell'alveo del Tevere', *NSc*: 439–59.

Graillot, H. 1896. 'Une collection de tessères', *MEFRA* 16: 299–314.

Gregori, G. L. 1997. 'Alcune iscrizioni imperiali, senatorie ed equestri: nell'antiquarium comunale del Celio', *ZPE* 116: 161–75.

272   CLARE ROWAN

Gülby, O. and H. Kireç 2008. *Ephesian Lead Tesserae* (Selçuk: Selçuk Belediyesi).

Harris, W. V. 2000. 'A Julio-Claudian business family?', *ZPE* 13: 263–4.

Hurschmann, R. 2008. 'Salutatio', in Cancik, H. and H. Schneider (eds.), *Brill's New Pauly* (Leiden, Brill).

Kopytoff, I. 1986. 'The cultural biography of things: commoditization as process', in Appadurai, A. (ed.), *The Social Life of Things: Commodities in Cultural Perspective* (Cambridge: Cambridge University Press), 64–94.

Krmnicek, S. and N. Elkins 2014. 'Dinosaurs, cocks, and coins: an introduction to "Art in the Round"', in Krmnicek, S. and N. Elkins (eds.), *Art in the Round: New Approaches to Ancient Coin Iconography* (Tübingen: VML Verlag Marie Leidorf), 7–22.

Küter, A. 2016. '*Imitatio Alexandri* – the image of Drusus Minor on brass tokens of the Münzkabinett, Staatliche Museen zu Berlin', *JAC* 31: 85–122.

Maderna-Lauter, C. 1988. 'Glyptik', in Heilmeyer, W. D., E. La Rocca, and H. G. Martin (eds.) *Kaiser Augustus und die verlorene Republik* (Berlin: Kulturstadt Europas), 441–73.

Martini, R. 1999. 'Una tessera numerale bronzea con ritratto di Augustus in collezione privata. "Tessera triumphalium(?)": note per una discussione', *Annotazione Numismatiche Supplemento* 13: 12–15.

Miller, P. A. 2012. 'Imperial satire as Saturnalia', in Braund, S. and J. Osgood (eds.), *A Companion to Persius and Juvenal* (Malden, MA: Wiley-Blackwell), 314–33.

Milne, J. G. 1971. *Catalogue of Alexandrian Coins* (Oxford: Oxford University Press).

Mitchell, W. J. T. 2005. *What Do Pictures Want?* (Chicago: University of Chicago Press).

Mitchiner, M. 1984. 'Rome: imperial portrait tesserae from the city of Rome and imperial tax tokens from the province of Egypt', *NC* 144: 95–114.

Munzi, M. 1997. 'Quadranti anonimi e tessere monetali dalle tombe di Leptis Magna', *Annotazioni Numismatiche* 26: 589–93.

Mwangi, W. 2002. 'The lion, the native and the coffee plant: political imagery and the ambiguous art of currency design in colonial Kenya', *Geopolitics* 7: 31–62.

Noreña, C. 2011. 'Coins and communication', in Peachin, M. (ed.), *The Oxford Handbook of Social Relations in the Roman World* (Oxford: Oxford University Press), 248–68.

Pardini, G., M. Piacentini, A. C. Felici, M. L. Santarelli, and S. Santucci 2016. 'Matrici per tessere plumbee dalle pendici nord-orientali del Palatino: nota preliminare', in Ferrandes, A. F. and G. Pardini (eds.), *Le regole del gioco tracce archeologi racconti: Studi in onore di Clementina Panella* (Rome: Quasar), 649–67.

Pedroni, L. 1997. 'Tessere plumbee dalle terme di Fregellae', *BNum* 28–9: 203–10.

Perry, J. S. 2011. 'Organized societies: *collegia*', in Peachin, M. (ed.), *The Oxford Handbook of Social Relations in the Roman World* (Oxford: Oxford University Press), 499–513.

Raja, R. 2015. 'Staging "private" religion in Roman "public" Palmyra: the role of the religious dining tickets (banqueting *tesserae*)', in Ando, C. and J. Rüpke (eds.), *Public and Private in Ancient Mediterranean Law and Religion* (Berlin: De Gruyter), 165–86.

Rostovtzeff, M. 1903. *Tesserarum urbis romae et suburbi plumbearum sylloge* (St Petersburg: Commissionnaires de l'Académie impériale des sciences).

　　1905a. 'Interprétation des tessères en os avec figures, chiffres et légendes', *RA* 5: 110–24.

　　1905b. *Römische Bleitesserae: ein Beitrag zur Sozial- und Wirtschaftsgeschichte der römischen Kaiserzeit* (Leipzig: Dieterich'sche Verlagsbuchhandlung).

　　1957. *The Social and Economic History of the Roman Empire* (Oxford: Clarendon Press).

Rostovtzeff, M. and M. Prou 1900. *Catalogue des plombs de l'antiquité* (Paris: Chez C. Rollin et Feuardent).

Rostovtzeff, M. and D. Vaglieri 1900. 'Alveo del Tevere', *NSc*: 256–68.

Rowan, C. 2016a. 'Ambiguity, iconology and entangled objects on coinage of the Republican world', *JRS* 106: 21–57.

　　2016b. 'Imagining empire in the Roman Republic', in Haymann, F., W. Hollstein, and M. Jehne (eds.), *Neue Forschungen zur Münzprägung der römischen Republik* (Bonn: Habelt Verlag), 279–92.

　　2020. 'The remediation of cultural memory under Augustus', in Powell, A. (ed.), *Coinage of the Roman Revolution* (Swansea: The Classical Press of Wales), 175–92.

Salzmann, D. 1989. 'Sabina in Palmyra', in Cain, H.-U., H. Gabelmann, and D. Salzmann (eds.), *Festschrift für Nikolaus Himmelmann* (Mainz am Rhein: Philipp von Zabern), 361–8.

Sauer, E. 2005. *Coins, Cult and Cultural Identity: Augustan Coins, Hot Springs and the Early Roman Baths at Bourbonne-les-Bains* (Leicester: University of Leicester).

Saunders, N. J. 2001. 'Apprehending memory: material culture and war, 1919–1939', in Bourne, J., P. Liddle, and I. Whitehead (eds.), *The Great World War 1914–45* (London: Harper Collins), 476–88.

Schneider, R. M. 2003. 'Gegenbilder im römischen Kaiserporträt: die neuen Gesichter Neros und Vespasians' in Büschel, M. and P. Schmidt (eds.), *Das Porträt vor der Erfindung des Porträts* (Mainz am Rhein: Philipp von Zabern), 59–76.

Sironen, T. 1990. 'Una tessera privata del II secolo a.C. da Fregellae', *ZPE* 80: 116–20.

Stannard, C. 2015. 'Shipping tesserae from Ostia and Minturnae?', *NC* 175: 147–54.

Thornton, M. K. 1980. 'The Roman lead tesserae: observations on two historical problems', *Historia* 29: 335–55.

(unpublished). Roman lead tesserae in the British Museum.

Tooker, L. 2014. 'Conversation with ... Bill Maurer', *Exchanges: The Warwick Research Journal* 2: 20–34.

Turcan, R. 1987. *Nigra Moneta: Sceaux, jetons, tesseres, amulettes, plombs monétaires ou monétiformes, objects divers en plomb ou en étain d'époque romaine conservés au Musée des Beaux-Arts de Lyon* (Lyon: Diffusion de Boccard).

Vaglieri, D. 1908. 'XXIII. Ostia', *NSc*: 329–36.

    1912. 'Ostia', *NSc*: 273–80.

van Berchem, D. 1936. 'Tessères ou calculi? Essai d'interprétation des jetons romains en plomb', *RN* 39: 297–315.

Virlouvet, C. 1988. 'Plombs romains monétiformes et tessères frumentaires. A propos d'une confusion.', *RN* 30: 120–48.

    1995. *Tessera Frumentaria: Les procédures de distribution du blé à Rome à la fin de la République et au début de l'Empire* (Rome: École française de Rome).

Yarrow, L. 2013. 'Heracles, coinage and the west: three Hellenistic case-studies', in Prag, J. R. W. and J. Quinn (eds.), *The Hellenistic West: Rethinking the Ancient Mediterranean* (Cambridge: Cambridge University Press), 348–66.

11 | When Was an Imperial Image?

Some Reflections on Roman Art and Imagery

OLIVIER HEKSTER

Introduction

This is a volume about imperial imagery.[1] Inevitably, 'images' have been at the heart of several of the chapters. Yet, as we have seen, 'image' is a much-used but less-defined term. Does it have any coherence? Do 'imperial images' tell us anything about how a variety of reflections on the emperor were produced? Who, and how important, were the Roman 'spin doctors' in creating these 'images'? And how important were different multiple groups at different social levels? Which facets of representation (another value-laden term) does the imperial 'image' incorporate? What is 'image' and for whom? To what extent, also, are later notions of ancient images influenced and occasionally hijacked by contemporary needs? How influential are later readings? These are big questions that have been central to the various chapters of this volume, but without easy answers.

Discussions of Imperial Images 1: Propaganda

Many of these questions have also been at the heart of historical debate for decades. They have been central to research on imperial imagery over the past twenty years, if not much longer. The point of departure is often Paul Zanker's seminal 1987 *Augustus und die Macht der Bilder* (*The Power of Images in the Age of Augustus*), which gave an enormous stimulus to the inclusion of visual sources in our interpretations of the imperial period, and foregrounded the idea of a coherent programme of 'images' in

[1] I am very grateful to all participants of the inspiring workshops which are at the basis of this volume for their contributions and the discussions that have effectively formed this chapter. None of it would have been possible without Amy Russell and Monica Hellström, whose comments also massively improved my argument, as did the suggestions of Cambridge University Press's anonymous reviewers. Final thanks go to Thijs Goverde, who pointed me to Nelson Goodman twenty years ago. It has taken me all that time to see that he was right in the first place.

scholarship of the early 1990s onwards.[2] This move was an important shift away from looking at imperial imagery in terms of 'propaganda', often directly linked to comparisons between Roman emperors and totalitarian leaders of the 1930s.[3] Noticeably, Zanker tried to get away from the notion of an official propaganda apparatus in Augustan times, instead describing the creation of a coherent set of imperial images as 'the interplay of the image that the emperor himself projected and the honours bestowed on him more or less spontaneously'.[4] Yet his model did not deny imperial involvement in shaping the imperial image, formulated by Zanker as 'a case of aesthetics in the service of political ends'.[5]

Less often explicitly referred to (at least until its translation into English in 2004), but extremely influential, is Tonio Hölscher's 1987 *Römische Bildsprache als semantisches System* (*The Language of Images in Roman Art*), perhaps the best coherently argued approach to looking at Roman art in terms of communication. The core message of Hölscher's underlying thesis was that Roman art functioned as a 'semantic system', a language through which certain messages could be transmitted to the heterogenous – and often illiterate – population of an immense empire. Part of this thesis was the notion that references to specific styles of Greek art in a Roman context expressed specific values. Chosen styles were decided by function, and not necessarily by chronology.[6]

Underlying both Zanker's and Hölscher's work was the assumption that Roman images could be interpreted from the top down. Either the ruler or a small elite group of Romans 'understood' the language of images, and used this language to broadcast fairly well-delineated messages. This assumption was more explicitly formulated in Niels Hannestad's monumental 1986 *Roman Art and Imperial Policy*. For Hannestad, Roman images formed a political weapon through which 'good will towards the emperor among important groups of subjects' was generated.[7] Even if Hannestad's notion that almost all Roman 'imperial' art was a form of propaganda was heavily criticised, the idea of Roman images as a top-down-formulated form of communication has been predominant in much literature both before and after.

---

[2] Zanker, 1987, with clear influence of Simon, 1986.

[3] Especially influenced by Syme, 1939 and Alföldi, 1970, originally published in 1938–9. On the historical and historiographical context: Alföldy, 1972; Walter, 2003.

[4] Zanker, 1987: 3.   [5] Zanker, 1987: 54.

[6] Hölscher, 1987. Cf. Giuliani, 1986: 245: 'Die physiognomische Vielfätigkeit des Porträts ist ein deutliches Zeichen der Konkurrenzsituation, aus der heraus sie entstanden ist.'

[7] Hannestad, 1986: 343.

Debate in the decades following Hannestad, Hölscher, and Zanker has, mainly, focused on two of the central tenets of their work. Firstly, *how* and *why* was this top-down imagery transmitted? Many of these discussions have focused on the applicability of the term 'propaganda'. Secondly, who was communicating with whom? Which different groups of viewers can be recognised? Discussion here introduced 'viewers' and has increasingly looked at communication theory for inspiration.

The discussion of imperial images as a form of propaganda was particularly noticeable in the late 1990s and the first years of the twenty-first century.[8] In these years, discussion on whether Roman imperial images could be interpreted as propaganda was fierce. Directly following the publication of Zanker's *The Power of Images*, 'propaganda' as a term became disputed. The increased attention to visual sources on the part of ancient historians, however, which followed *The Power of Images*, also led to a number of scholars arguing in favour of 'propaganda' as a useful term to understand imperial Roman imagery.[9] Those trying to keep the term tended to focus on the crucial book *Propagandes* by Jacques Ellul (1962, translated in 1965 as *Propaganda: The Formation of Men's Attitudes*), especially Ellul's differentiation of 'propaganda' as divided into 'agitation propaganda' – aimed at changing attitudes – and 'integration propaganda' – aimed at reinforcing them. The latter, it was then argued, was applicable to the Roman world, even if the former was not. Those arguing against the term, on the other hand, tended to dismiss the term to avoid potentially misleading connotations; the term 'propaganda' had become so closely linked to the dictatorial regimes of the early twentieth century that it could no longer be used as a concept without making readers think of the Roman Empire as a proto-fascist state. For these authors, the very reason that the concept of 'propaganda' had appealed to Syme made it unacceptable now.[10]

More interesting, certainly for the purposes of this chapter, than discussions on the use of the terminology were discussions on the content of the concept. For in these discussions the question on what 'imperial images'

---

[8] As a rough indication, it is noticeable that a JSTOR search shows over 450 articles that have 'Rome' and 'propaganda' in the title for both the period 1995–2000 and 2000–5, whereas in the period 1985–90 the same search terms show a good 300 items, 1990–5 just over 400, and the period 2010–15 just above 200.

[9] Most prominently, perhaps, DeRose Evans, 1992. Equally, though outside of analysis of images as propaganda, one can see how late-antique panegyrics were regularly interpreted in propagandistic terms: e.g. Whitby, 1998.

[10] Ellul, 1965. In favour of using the term: Hochgeschwender, 2003; Enenkel and Pfeijffer, 2005. Arguing against: Eich, 2003; Lendon, 2006.

were came directly to the fore. In the scholarship, increasingly, one can trace a differentiation of what is deemed propagandistic based not on content but on the different media, and – importantly – the different agents creating the imagery in these media.[11] This foreshadows both the 'medial turn' in looking at source material and the notion of reciprocity in creating images, with different groups communicating different, sometimes even conflicting, preconceptions through images: what in this volume has become the 'social dynamics' of images.

For instance, the clearly propagandistic function of some imperial inscriptions was deemed clear. A prime example was the *Senatus Consultum de Cn. Pisone patre* (*SCPP*). This decree of the Senate reported an important story, which must have been new to a large part of its audience, putting forward explicit values in the telling. It presented the position and behaviour of the imperial family as crucial to the empire as a whole, and was deliberately disseminated.[12] Noticeably, the preferred 'image' of the imperial family was described in words, though the materiality of the inscription is emphasised through the way in which the edict needed to be transmitted. That imperial inscriptions *could* be propagandistic does of course not mean that all inscriptions *should* be seen as such. It has been recognised how different groups in the Roman Empire, such as the *ordines*, gladiators, or soldiers, seem to have used inscriptions for some sort of self-representation, without an expected reaction.[13]

Coins were another 'medium' often discussed in this context. The debate about whether and how images on coins were construed for propagandistic reasons was fierce.[14] Yet, again, for thinking about imperial images at a conceptual level, discussions about how image formation through coinage functioned was more interesting. There, emphasis has rightly been on how images on coins were part of a dialogue between the presentation and the expectation of power. Wolters, about a decade ago, rightly stressed the 'normality' of most coin types. Only images on coins that broke away from the norm would be publicly noticed.[15] Such 'new' images, it is fair to suppose, must have originated from the centre with a clear purpose to influence opinion – though that does not exclude dynamics in the creation of such images. Noticeably, 'abnormal' coins were minted especially in

---

[11] Still fundamental: Niquet, 2003; Wolters, 2003.   [12] Cooley, 1998: 208–10; Potter, 1999: 71.
[13] Niquet, 2003. Cf. Tran in this volume.
[14] See still Levick, 1999. Cf. Manders, 2012: 33–62 and Rowan, 2012: 4 on the possibilities of 'quantifying ideology' through coin messages.
[15] Wolters, 2003. Cf. already Wolters, 1999: 255–410.

periods of crisis. Thus, for instance, Galba's gold and silver coinage explicitly refers to his provincial support.[16]

Discussions of Imperial Images 2: Media and Messages

Discussions on how concepts linked to 'propaganda' could be employed in analysing Roman imperial imagery, rather than disputing the validity of the term itself for the Roman Empire, were of crucial influence on the debate on who was communicating with whom.[17] This, as stated above, was the second major debate that took place in the years following the publications of (amongst many others) Hannestad, Hölscher, and Zanker. In a way, the current volume, with its emphasis on the social dynamics of imagery, places itself in that debate. Again, a differentiation can be made between discussions dealing with definitions and formulations, and discussions about how to apply concepts to the ancient Roman society. The distinction here is not as stark as in the discussion surrounding propaganda, since there was no such clearly contested term in play.

To an extent, however, recent discussions concerning medialisation can be seen in a similar context to the discussion surrounding the use of 'propaganda'. At play is a principled methodological choice: do we need to look at the ancient world through the lens of modern (sociological) theory, or not? Notions of medialisation ultimately follow from Marshall McLuhan's famous dictum 'the medium is the message', which does not, in fact, argue that the medium *is* the message as such, but that medial constraints are so influential that the same apparent messages become different if formulated in different media.[18] In other words, in this view, technical constraints and limitations are of utmost importance in understanding cultural and ideological communication and changes. Different technical possibilities change what an image can do. New modes of transmitting information (like new artefacts) 'open a field to meaningfulness, whose options are, afterwards, constructed by social forces'.[19] Moreover, how a medium is understood also depends on how that medium has been used before. Everyone brings their prior conceptions to an image, which partly determines its perceived meaning.[20]

---

[16] Hekster, 2003: 26.
[17] Howgego, 1995: 71, sidestepping the term to deal with the 'undoubted political themes'.
[18] McLuhan, 1967, with the comments by Haesler and Dobré, 2016.
[19] Haesler and Dobré, 2016: 142.   [20] Hodge and Tripp, 1986: 17. Cf. Elsner, 1995: 159–72.

The transmission and reception of images, in such an analysis, become an integral part of the study of images. As W. J. T. Mitchell, one of the foremost scholars in the analysis of the so-called 'pictorial turn', has argued, in order to answer the question 'what is an image?', we must include the political and ideological strategies behind the construction of images, and the discourses surrounding images.[21] Recent applications of the concept of 'medialisation' in (classical) history, and especially discussions on whether or not to analyse ancient material through which images were transmitted (coins, historical reliefs, mosaics, etc.) as 'media', are part of the same debate.[22]

Discussion on whether the carriers of ancient images *can* be interpreted as media is important, but the application of methods and concepts from the field of image studies and communication theory is probably more fruitful. Hölscher's *Römische Bildsprache*, discussed above, with its emphasis on the semiotics of images, has been of great importance in this respect too. The creation and dissemination of images could be seen as a form of communication, with images as 'messages'. Consequently, it should be possible to recognise not only senders, but also receivers, and to discuss the process by which they communicated through images. One underlying question was for whom the Roman state monuments were intended: a discussion that in many ways was again opened by Tonio Hölscher and taken to a new level in the 1990s by Jaś Elsner.[23] Important was the recognition that there were various groups of viewers. Analyses started by looking at the many ways in which images were aimed at and could be understood by those different Roman viewers. It rapidly branched out into analyses of how different groups of viewers would understand images differently, with increasing attention paid to non-elite viewers.[24]

The importance of the differentiation of groups of viewers, both socially and spatially, has been systematically put to the fore by Jane Fejfer. She has emphasised the way imperial images were a sociohistorical phenomenon. The Roman Empire, after all, was extremely large and inhabited by a plurality of people. This multitude of groups, communities, individuals used imperial images as a way to position themselves in the world, specifying the relationship between dedicator, community, emperor, and empire.[25] These notions have been at the heart of various chapters within the current volume. Several of them have also taken a position in what seems to be the main current discussion about imperial images: the exact

[21] Mitchell, 2005.
[22] Frevert and Braungart, 2004; Kramer and Reitz, 2010; von den Hoff, 2011.
[23] Hölscher, 1984; Elsner, 1995.   [24] Clarke, 2003.   [25] Fejfer, 2008. Cf. Ando, 2000.

relation between sender and receiver in the creation of an image. More specifically, the question is whether there are such clear distinctions between sender and receiver, or whether there are reciprocal, or even parallel, processes taking place, with a range of imperial images as end result.[26]

There were, almost certainly, substantial differences between how different groups of viewers reacted to specific images. This has an impact on what we think that images were *meant* to communicate. Imperial images, it has been recognised, result as much from in-group reactions (what does the ruler want to hear?) as from out-group statements (what does the centre want the periphery to see and hear?). But it is not only about the differences between the message that emperors *want* to put forward and what those creating images *think* that needs to be said and shown. Expectations about what an emperor *should* want to show, and even be, were of great importance in how all sorts of images, at various levels, were constructed. One of the main themes of this volume, then, the aim to explore how ideologically charged images relating to imperial power were created, received, and reused, taking into account the contributions and interactions of multiple groups at all social levels, follows directly from this line of analysis.

Discussing viewers' perception of images also needs to include the complementary yet distinct relationship between images and texts. One way of doing this is by analysing the ancient texts that discuss how (elite) audiences experienced seeing specific images, describe expected connoisseurship, or formulate ancient methods of viewing.[27] A different way is looking at how text and image could interact within a single context – as in the case of the first-century wall-paintings in the 'House of Propertius' at Assisi, which are found alongside a series of Greek epigrams. They must have been meant to be 'viewed' in tandem, even if (or especially because) text and image create clear juxtapositions.[28] Both of these modes of analysis focus on elite perspectives, but image and text interacted for people with much lower levels of literacy on Roman coinage. Often, image and legend worked closely together, making the meaning of a specific coin type clearer, and often much less ambiguous.[29] Again, the communicative value of an image depended much on the context within which it was viewed and on the person viewing.[30]

---

[26] Noreña, 2001, which can be usefully contrasted to the argument set out by Witschel, 2004. On parallel images: Hekster, 2015.

[27] Elsner, 2007: 29–112.   [28] Squire, 2009: 239–96.   [29] Manders, 2012: 30.

[30] Dally *et al.*, 2014.

Past and Present of Imperial Images

This chapter has, so far, been mainly concerned with how the various contributions to this volume ultimately result from two larger historiographical debates in classical studies, about the transmission of ideology (*how* and *why* was imagery communicated?) and on agency (who was communicating with whom?). Yet, taking a more 'helicopter view' of the scholarship on Roman imperial imagery in the past decades, it may be possible to contextualise these two debates as well. Firstly, as has been noted before, it is striking how much of the rich literature on Roman imperial imagery that was written between the end of World War II and the end of the Cold War was, inevitably, a reflection on the times in which it was written, and strikingly politicised.[31] Contemporary politics influenced the academic debate. For those with personal experience of the regimes behind the Iron Curtain, imperial representation and imperial behaviour were central intellectual concerns.[32] The notion that imperial power was clothed in apparent modesty, through the important notion of a *civilis princeps* who put forward republican *virtutes*, fits surprisingly well into notions of western (Cold-War) diplomacy.[33] It might be worth reflecting on what the kaleidoscopic approach and refracting interpretation of imperial images in this volume betray of our current sociopolitical situation, though that is beyond the scope of the present chapter.

The two larger historiographical debates that have been central to this chapter were not, however, merely children of contemporary political concern. They also closely followed academic concerns that were discussed outside of the (art) historical discipline. Specifically, the introduction and development of two major concepts in the social sciences: the notions of 'framing' and 'agenda setting'. These concepts, which are by now familiar terms well beyond the academic sphere, stem from communication theory.

The term 'framing' originated in the 1970s, before the period that has been under discussion here.[34] Yet, it is striking (and as far as I know, has not been observed before) how the period in which the concept became increasingly current coincides with the time in which Roman imperial images were increasingly viewed in terms of their meaning within

---

[31] This observation was already put forward in Hekster, 2015: 29–30.
[32] Especially Rudich, 1993, 1997. Rudich, 2015: xiv explicitly refers to the author's 'youth in the Soviet Union'.
[33] Wallace-Hadrill, 1982.
[34] The two works most closely associated with the introduction of the concept are Bateson, 1972 and Goffman, 1974.

a communicative process. Framing, in short, is a way of selecting 'some aspects of a perceived reality and mak[ing] them more salient' by communication through text or image, so as to promote specific definitions, interpretations, moral evaluations, or solutions to perceived problems.[35] In the 1980s the term became *en vogue* in the social sciences, then in the humanities, and ultimately in society well beyond academia (with American politics a driving force in establishing household usage of the term).[36]

In the same period, though not quite at the same scale, the related concept of 'agenda setting' became increasingly common in both the social sciences and humanities.[37] Agenda setting, like framing, developed as a concept in the 1970s and experienced steady development in the following decades. The original notion was that 'media are influential in deciding what issues become major themes of public opinion', which was then further developed into a so-called 'second level of agenda setting', which hypothesises that 'the media also have an influence on how people make sense of a given theme'.[38] Discussions in classical studies about incorporating notions of 'propaganda' and 'mediatisation', and discussions about agency in ancient image-formation (top-down, bottom-up, reciprocal, or parallel), took place in the same period in which 'agenda setting' and 'framing' became buoyant in adjacent disciplines. It seems likely that these concepts influenced debate as much as contemporary politics did, and without explicit recognition (or even awareness) of their role. Political and academic contexts, in other words, have consistently influenced the study of Roman imperial images.

When Is Image?

In an influential 1978 essay, Nelson Goodman famously tried to change the art-historical question 'what is art?' into 'when is art?'.[39] He noted how an object may function as a work of art at one time but not another, and how the symbolic function of an object or event helps us decide when it could be perceived as art, and when not. A 'stone picked out of the driveway and

---

[35] Entman, 1993: 52.   [36] Lakoff, 1990.

[37] For an overview and analysis of the number of studies discussing agenda setting and framing from 1971 to 2005, see Weaver, 2007, esp. fig. 1. For the links between framing and agenda setting, see Scheufele, 2000.

[38] Original concept: McCombs and Shaw, 1972. On the definitions and developments: Takeshita, 2006: 275–6.

[39] Goodman, 1978: 57–70.

exhibited in a museum' is art (though not necessarily good art), whereas that self-same stone in the driveway is not.[40] In Goodman's words: 'How an object or event functions as a work explains how ... it may contribute to a vision of – and to the making of – a world.'[41]

Perhaps this is a useful way, too, of thinking of Roman imperial images. The question of whether an image should be seen as a form of propaganda, an expression of ideology, or a marker of specific group identity is probably not the most useful question. The discussions that were at the heart of this volume all related to the different contexts in which images were encountered. This includes both geographical and chronological contexts. Images, after all, continue to be seen and adapted as time continues. Their interpretations respond to and shape expectations.[42] Not only may different groups have different expectations of certain imperial images and interpret one image in very different ways; even a single individual may perceive an image differently in different contexts. An imperial image is always an image, but only in certain contexts will it have functioned as an *imperial* image. This axiom applies to how that image functioned in the Roman world, but equally to how modern scholars analyse such images.

None of this is to deny the importance of agency, though here, too, context plays an increasingly important role. Recent studies have emphasised the agency of artefacts themselves and the importance of so-called 'human–thing entanglement'. Things, it is argued, depend both on other things and on the humans that repair, replace, and transform them, whilst humans depend on those very things.[43] In the confrontation between humans and artefacts, the 'cultural biography' of an object plays an important role, with both the material from which an object is made and the style in which it is made being factors. For instance, the exceptional presence of artefacts from different times and places in Augustan Rome forced people who looked at or appropriated the images on these artefacts to think about their own culture. Creating an image in imperial Rome meant adopting a position towards the different pasts and different cultures that were visible in the city of Rome as never before.[44] Objects, and especially the context of these objects, in this view, play a major role in cultural transfer and the making of a worldview. Not only do small-scale interactions

---

[40] Goodman, 1978: 66.   [41] Goodman, 1978: 70.

[42] Recent trends to make explicit use of findings from cognitive and neurosciences are extremely useful in this context, and are clearly acknowledged by the authors involved in these studies, as opposed to the less direct influence of 'framing' and 'agenda setting' discussed above.

[43] Hodder, 2011.   [44] Rutledge, 2012: 221–86; Van Eck, Versluys, and ter Keurs, 2015.

between individuals constitute social dynamics, but also the interactions between individuals and objects, and even between the different objects.

All history, ultimately, is a reflection of its own time, and the study of historical images is no exception to that well-known statement. The notion of social dynamics that binds this volume together has inevitably influenced the authors of the chapters in the volume. Modern scholars are just as influenced by the different types of small-scale interactions in past and present that have created intellectual contexts as ancient viewers of imperial images were. The emphasis on the social dynamics of imagery in this volume is at some level a reaction to the increased fragmentation of groups in our own society, with different agents influencing each other at different moments in different constellations. Yet that does not diminish the methodological point that the different chapters in this volume make. They allow us to focus, more than before, on the question of *when* images function in which ways, and for how long. Perhaps the reason that 'image' is not often defined, is that we cannot say what an image is. We can only see how and when images function in certain ways.

Bibliography

Alföldi, A. 1970. *Die monarchische Repräsentation im römischen Kaiserreiche* (Darmstadt: Wissenschaftliche Buchgesellschaft).

Alföldy, G. 1972. 'Die Ablehnung der Diktatur durch Augustus', *Gymnasium* 79: 1–12.

Ando, C. 2000. *Imperial Ideology and Provincial Loyalty in the Roman Empire* (Berkeley: University of California Press).

Bateson, G. 1972. *Steps to an Ecology of Mind* (New York: Chandler).

Clarke, J. R. 2003. *Art in the Lives of Ordinary Romans: Visual Representation and Non-Elite Viewers in Italy, 100 B.C.–A.D. 315* (Berkeley: University of California Press).

Cooley, A. 1998. 'The moralizing message of the *Senatus Consultum De Cn. Pisone Patre*', *G&R* 45: 199–212.

Dally, O., T. Hölscher, S. Muth, and R. M. Schneider 2014. 'Einführung. Historien – Historie – Geschichte: wohin führen die Medien?', in Dally, O., T. Hölscher, S. Muth, and R. M. Schneider (eds.), *Medien der Geschichte – Antikes Griechenland und Rom* (Berlin; Boston: De Gruyter), 1–36.

DeRose Evans, J. 1992. *The Art of Persuasion: Political Propaganda from Aeneas to Brutus* (Ann Arbor: University of Michigan Press).

Eich, A. 2003. 'Die Idealtypen "Propaganda" und "Repräsentation" als heuristische Mittel bei der Bestimmung gesellschaftlicher Konvergenzen und

Divergenzen von Moderne und römischer Kaiserzeit', in Weber, G. and M. Zimmermann (eds.), *Propaganda, Selbstdarstellung und Repräsentation im römischen Kaiserreich des 1. Jhs. n. Chr.* (Stuttgart: Steiner), 41–84.

Ellul, J. 1965. *Propaganda: The Formation of Men's Attitudes* (New York: Vintage).

Elsner, J. 1995. *Art and the Roman Viewer: The Transformation of Art from the Pagan World to Christianity* (Cambridge: Cambridge University Press).

2007. *Roman Eyes: Visuality and Subjectivity in Art and Text* (Princeton: Princeton University Press).

Enenkel, K. A. E. and I. L. Pfeijffer 2005. 'Introduction', in Enenkel, K. A. E. and I. L. Pfeijffer (eds.), *The Manipulative Mode. Political Propaganda in Antiquity: A Collection of Case Studies* (Leiden; Boston: Brill), 1–12.

Entman, R. M. 1993. 'Framing: toward clarification of a fractured paradigm', *Journal of Communication* 43: 51–8.

Fejfer, J. 2008. *Roman Portraits in Context* (Berlin; New York: De Gruyter).

Frevert, U. and W. Braungart (eds.) 2004. *Sprachen des Politischen: Medien und Medialität in der Geschichte* (Göttingen: Vandenhoeck & Ruprecht).

Giuliani, L. 1986. *Bildnis und Botschaft: Hermeneutische Untersuchungen zur Bildniskunst der römischen Republik* (Frankfurt: Suhrkamp).

Goffman, E. 1974. *Frame Analysis: An Essay on the Organization of Experience* (Cambridge, MA: Harvard University Press).

Goodman, N. 1978. *Ways of Worldmaking* (Indianapolis: Hackett).

Haesler, A. and M. Dobré 2016. 'The medial turn in knowledge society', in Pomazan, V. (ed.), *Proceedings of the International Conference on Interdisciplinary Studies (ICIS 2016): Interdisciplinarity and Creativity in the Knowledge Society* (London: Intechopen), 141–7.

Hannestad, N. 1986. *Roman Art and Imperial Policy* (Aarhus: Aarhus University Press).

Hekster, O. 2003. 'Coins and messages: audience targeting on coins of different denominations?', in Erdkamp, P., O. Hekster, G. de Kleijn, S. T. A. M. Mols, and L. de Blois (eds.), *The Representation and Perception of Roman Imperial Power: Proceedings of the Third Workshop of the International Network Impact of Empire (Roman Empire, c.200 B.C.–A.D. 476), Netherlands Institute in Rome, March 20–23, 2002* (Amsterdam: J. C. Gieben), 20–35.

2015. *Emperors and Ancestors: Roman Rulers and the Constraints of Tradition* (Oxford: Oxford University Press).

Hochgeschwender, M. 2003. 'Die Erfindung der USA im Spiegel moderner Propagandatheorien', in Weber, G. and M. Zimmermann (eds.), *Propaganda, Selbstdarstellung und Repräsentation im römischen Kaiserreich des 1. Jhs. n. Chr.* (Stuttgart: Steiner), 103–24.

Hodder, I. 2011. 'Human–thing entanglement: towards an integrated archaeological perspective', *Journal of the Royal Anthropological Institute* 17: 154–77.

Hodge, B. and D. Tripp 1986. *Children and Television: A Semiotic Approach* (Stanford: Stanford University Press).

Hölscher, T. 1984. *Staatsdenkmal und Publikum: Vom Untergang der Republik bis zur Festigung des Kaisertums in Rom* (Konstanz: Universitätsverlag).

   1987. *Römische Bildsprache als semantisches System*. Abhandlungen der Heidelberger Akademie der Wissenschaften. Philosophisch-historische Klasse 1987, 2 (Heidelberg: Carl Winter).

Howgego, C. J. 1995. *Ancient History from Coins* (London: Routledge).

Kramer, N. and C. Reitz (eds.) 2010. *Tradition und Erneuerung: Mediale Strategien in der Zeit der Flavier* (Berlin; New York: De Gruyter).

Lakoff, G. 1990. *Don't Think of an Elephant: Know Your Values and Frame the Debate* (White River Junction, VT: Chelsea Green).

Lendon, J. E. 2006. 'The legitimacy of the Roman emperor: against Weberian legitimacy and imperial "strategies of legitimation"', in Kolb, A. (ed.), *Herrschaftsstrukturen und Herrschaftspraxis: Konzepte, Prinzipien und Strategien der Administration im römischen Kaiserreich* (Berlin: De Gruyter), 53–63.

Levick, B. 1999. 'Messages on the Roman coinage: types and inscriptions', in Paul, G. M. and M. Ierardi (eds.), *Roman Coins and Public Life under the Empire: E. Togo Salmon Papers II* (Ann Arbor: University of Michigan Press), 41–60.

Manders, E. 2012. *Coining Images of Power: Patterns in the Representation of Roman Emperors on Imperial Coinage, A.D. 193–284* (Leiden: Brill).

McCombs, M. E. and D. L. Shaw 1972. 'The agenda-setting function of mass media', *Public Opinion Quarterly* 36: 176–87.

McLuhan, M. 1967. *The Medium is the Message: An Inventory of Effects* (London: Bantam).

Mitchell, W. J. T. 2005. *What do Pictures Want? The Lives and Loves of Images* (Chicago: University of Chicago Press).

Niquet, H. 2003. 'Inschriften als Medium von "Propaganda" und Selbstdarstellung im 1. Jh. n. Chr.', in Weber, G. and M. Zimmermann (eds.), *Propaganda, Selbstdarstellung und Repräsentation im römischen Kaiserreich des 1. Jhs. n. Chr.* (Stuttgart: Steiner), 145–73.

Noreña, C. 2001. 'The communication of the emperor's virtues', *JRS* 91: 146–68.

Potter, D. S. 1999. 'Political theory in the Senatus Consultum Pisonianum', *AJPh* 120: 65–88.

Rowan, C. 2012. *Under Divine Auspices: Divine Ideology and the Visualisation of Imperial Power in the Severan Period* (Cambridge: Cambridge University Press).

Rudich, V. 1993. *Political Dissidence under Nero: The Price of Dissimulation* (London; New York: Routledge).

   1997. *Dissidence and Literature under Nero* (London; New York: Routledge).

   2015. *Religious Dissent in the Roman Empire: Violence in Judea at the Time of Nero* (London; New York: Routledge).

Rutledge, S. 2012. *Ancient Rome as a Museum: Power, Identity, and the Culture of Collecting* (Oxford: Oxford University Press).

Scheufele, D. 2000. 'Agenda setting, priming, and framing revisited: another look at cognitive effects of political communication', *Mass Communication and Society* 3: 297–316.

Simon, E. 1986. *Augustus: Kunst und Leben in Rom um die Zeitenwende* (Munich: Hirmer).

Squire, M. 2009. *Image and Text in Graeco-Roman Antiquity* (Cambridge; New York: Cambridge University Press).

Syme, R. 1939. *The Roman Revolution* (Oxford: Clarendon Press).

Takeshita, T. 2006. 'Current critical problems in agenda-setting research', *International Journal of Public Opinion Research* 18: 275–96.

Van Eck, C., M. J. Versluys, and P. ter Keurs 2015. 'The biography of cultures: style, objects and agency. Proposal for an interdisciplinary approach', *Les Cahiers de l'École du Louvre* 7: 2–22.

von den Hoff, R. 2011. 'Kaiserbildnisse als Kaisergeschichte(n): Prolegomena zu einem medialen Konzept römischer Herrscherporträts', in Winterling, A. (ed.), *Zwischen Strukturgeschichte und Biographie: Probleme und Perspektiven einer neuen Römischen Kaisergeschichte zur Zeit von Augustus bis Commodus* (Munich: Oldenbourg), 15–44.

Wallace-Hadrill, A. 1982. '*Civilis princeps*: between citizen and king', *JRS* 72: 32–48.

Walter, U. 2003. 'Passage in zwei Welten: "Die Römische Revolution" und die Sprache des Historikers', in Syme, R., C. Selzer, and U. Walter (eds.), *Die Römische Revolution. Machtkämpfe im antiken Rom: Grundlegend revidierte und erstmals vollständige Neuausgabe* (Stuttgart: Klett-Cotta), 735–47.

Weaver, D. H. 2007. 'Thoughts on agenda setting, framing, and priming', *Journal of Communication* 57: 142–7.

Whitby, M. 1998. *The Propaganda of Power: The Role of Panegyric in Late Antiquity* (Leiden; Boston: Brill).

Witschel, C. 2004. *Propaganda für den Princeps? Mechanismen der kaiserlichen Repräsentation im Imperium Romanum* (Munich: Habilitation).

Wolters, R. 1999. *Nummi Signati: Untersuchungen zur römischen Münzprägung und Geldwirtschaft* (Munich: Beck).

 2003. 'Die Geschwindigkeit der Zeit und die Gefahr der Bilder: Münzbilder und Münzpropaganda in der römischen Kaiserzeit', in Weber, G. and M. Zimmermann (eds.), *Propaganda, Selbstdarstellung und Repräsentation im römischen Kaiserreich des 1. Jhs. n. Chr.* (Stuttgart: Steiner), 175–204.

Zanker, P. 1987. *Augustus und die Macht der Bilder* (Munich: Beck).

Index

289